新 版
BASIC

ENGLISH GRAMMAR

Second Edition

Azar 英文文法系列（初級）

Betty Schrampfer Azar

敦煌書局
Prentice Hall Regents

Publisher: *Tina B. Carver*
Director of Production and Manufacturing: *Aliza Greenblatt*
Editorial Production/Design Manager: *Dominick Mosco*
Editorial/Production Supervision: *Janet Johnston*
Editorial Assistant: *Shelley Hartle*
Production Coordinator: *Ray Keating*
Cover Coordinator: *Merle Krumper*
Cover Production: *Molly Pike Riccardi*
Cover Design: *Joel Mitnick Design*
Interior Design: *Ros Herion Freese*
Illustrations: *Don Martinetti*

©1996 by Betty Schrampfer Azar

Published by PRENTICE HALL REGENTS
Prentice-Hall, Inc.
A Simon & Schuster Company
Upper Saddle River, New Jersey 07458

10 9 8 7 6 5 4 3 2 1

ISBN 0-13-368317-6
ISBN 0-13-368424-5 (Vol. A)
ISBN 0-13-368358-3 (Vol. B)

台灣版

著 作 人	Betty Schrampfer Azar
發 行 人	陳文良
翻 譯	陳麗芳
執行編輯	喻貴琪、吳青珠
文字編輯	張鳳凰
美術編輯	周姿廷
電腦排版	凱立國際印前印刷股份有限公司
發 行 所	敦煌書局股份有限公司
地 址	台北市中山北路二段103號
電 話	(02) 2537-1666（總機）
郵 撥	00141031
印 刷 所	盛利印刷有限公司
登 記 證	新聞局局版台業字0269號
版 次	1999年5月第一版
	2001年4月第一版三刷
定 價	310元

ISBN 957-606-336-1
有著作權・不准翻印

目録

第三章　現在式的表達（第二部份）

第四章　名詞和代名詞

第五章　過去式的表達

第六章　未來式的表達

第七章　能力的表達

第八章　名詞、代名詞和形容詞

新版序

　　《AZAR英文文法系列——初級》*Basic English Grammar*是專為ESL/EFL學生所設計的語言進修教材。它兼具了參考書和習作本的功能，能帶領學生認識英文的基本結構、意義和用法。透過廣泛而多樣的習題和互動式練習，學生可獲得充分的練習機會。雖然本書著眼於文法的介紹，但其同時也能促進所有語言技巧的增長。

　　新版大幅擴充內容範圍後，初學者更可從中習得基礎英文法的堅實精華。另外，書中增加了許多新的練習，並於每章之後提供綜合複習，以學生為中心作表達和互動練習。

感謝的話

對我而言，寫英文文法書是一項樂趣。在這個工作中，我得到許多優秀人才的協助：在討論會上做教學示範，並在新聞簡訊或國際性刊物上發表文章的熱心教師；探究第二語言技能之獲得方法的學者；清晰且有力地提出自己觀察心得的文法家；過去和現在曾撰寫其他 ESL/EFL 文法書的作家，他們提出有創意且紮實的方法，幫助學生了解及使用英文；給我珍貴的經驗分享的同事；以及知道如何塑造和推銷教學書籍的專業出版人士。我們彼此息息相關，相互倚賴。

最重要的，我要謝謝我的學生，他們坦然無隱地和我分享其學習經驗和需要，因而讓我瞭解了許多語言技能的獲得過程。

總而言之，我深深感激 ESL/EFL 環境中的所有教師、學者、作者、出版者和學生。

此外，我特別要感謝 Tina Carver, Janet Johnston 和 Shelley Hartle 的專業和友誼。也要感謝Barbara Matthies, Irene Juzkiw, Stacy Hagen, Nancy Price, Lawrence Cisar, Don Martinetti, Lizette Reyes, Stella Reilly, Marita Froimson, Joy Edwards, R.T. Steltz, Sue Van Etten, Ken Kortlever, Generessa Arielle 和Chelsea Azar 等人。同時也向我在1994年的亞洲之旅中，於韓國、日本和台灣所碰到的多位優秀教師和出版者致上謝意。

使用說明

適用程度

《Azar英文文法系列——初級》力求符合ESL／EFL班初級程度學生的需要。雖然教材前半部引介的文法和詞彙是針對低階或初級的學習者，但如果採取適當的步驟，本教材也可供中下程度的學生作爲快速複習及擴展文法能力之用。

本書《Azar英文文法系列——初級》*Basic English Grammar*是三冊系列教材中的第一冊。本系列的第二冊爲《Azar英文文法系列——基礎》*Fundamentals of English Grammar*，供中下或中級程度學生使用。第三冊爲《Azar英文文法系列——進階》*Understanding and Using English Grammar*，供中級至高級程度學生使用。

文法內容的編排

大體來說，每個單元都是由一組相關的中心文法結構和用法所組成。教材的編法是希望教師按編排的次序進行教學，前面各章的結構和詞彙則做爲後面各章內容的基礎。然而，如果所教的班級已是中下程度，而非初學者，教師可以適當調整教課內容的次序，以適合學生的需要及自己的教學目標。

文法的重點以圖表方式呈現，並搭配有例句和解釋；例句的意義力求一目了然，解釋儘可能簡單，並將術語減到最少。儘管如此，學生一開始仍有可能不了解圖表中的某些部分。按照編者的構想，圖表在課堂上可作爲學習的起跳板；教師可以根據當時的課堂情形講解自己編造的例句，並將這些例句與教材中的例句連繫起來，作爲進行文法練習的準備。有時還可以直接作用法練習，一邊練習，一邊講解文法的形式和意義，然後再回到圖表，以便進行歸納。

文法圖表對不同的學生有不同的作用。有的學生點滴不漏地背誦圖表；有的則很少留意或根本不知留意，這一點視他們的學習方法而定。有的學生先從圖表獲得初步的知識後才敢大膽應用；而有的在作用法練習的時候就能大膽地運用各種知識，僅偶而參考圖表。無論如何，圖表不一定要成爲課外作業來「背誦」。圖表只是學習的起點，以及往後的參考材料而已。

詞彙

本書將詞彙量的增加視爲增強文法使用能力的要素，詞彙的引用都是經過按步就班循序編排的。有時候，教師必須在作練習時多花些時間講解新詞彙，之後課堂上的教學就會容易一些，學生在家裡也就不必花大量時間在查閱字典上。有的練習是經過特別設計的，以幫助學生在演練結構用法的同時加強認識新字。本書中許多插圖是爲了方便詞彙的教與學。

練習

　　練習的目的，是要促使學生盡快運用所學的文法結構來談論自己─包括自己從事的活動、思想以及周圍的環境。總之，本書任何單元內的練習，一開始是集中在形式和意義的熟練運用上，而後再著重獨立地運用和綜合各種語言技巧的練習。

　　除了口頭練習，大多數練習需要先課外準備，然後在課堂內進行。通常教師可以講解圖表中文法的重點，在課堂上叫學生做練習的前三、四題，然後指定其餘的題目作爲下堂課上課前的準備作業。學生在家裡事先預習，比起他們在課堂上毫無準備地做練習，往往受益會更多。如果學生已經在家裡預習好，課堂上講解的時間就會減少，也可以引起更有效率的討論。

「書寫練習」：爲學生課後作業，交給老師批改用。

「口頭練習，闔上課本」：則有不同的使用方法及目的，分述如下：

(a) 做這些練習時應鼓勵學生闔上課本。如果學生對某個練習感到太困難，或是覺得無從著手，可以先看看課本，而後闔上。

(b) 在練習開始時，可以先舉一、二個例子來說明句型。可以口頭補充說明例子，亦可將關鍵詞寫在黑板，幫助學生集中注意力於主要結構上，作爲他們答題時的參考。

(c) 做某些練習時，偶爾可以指定一名學生充當教師，由這位學生來主導練習，給其他學生提示並判斷回答是否妥當，而教師則退到教室的一角。並非所有的練習都適合由學生充當「教師」，但有許多的練習是可以這麼做的。教師可以事先爲第二天的練習指定一位學生做「教師」，並在課外與他或她一起做好準備。通常由學生來指導口頭練習所花的時間會兩倍於教師指導練習的時間；但如果時間允許，這對「學生教師」來說會是一次難得的經驗，同時也會使全班感到興趣盎然。

(d) 另外一種進行方式是將學生分組或配對練習，並由其中一位學生翻開課本指導練習。

(e) 許多練習，特別是學生相互發問的練習，其目的是要引導學生進行自動自發的討論。這些練習大都附有一組範例（針對主要句型）和不同的主題，供課堂上自由使用。這種練習可以鼓勵學生把自己的口頭回答加以延伸，擴展爲一些有趣的回答，而把文法重點暫時擱在一邊。語言自然的相互交流比形式的準確更爲重要。學生在輕鬆自在的課堂氣氛中，與同學或教師自然的用英語做簡短交談時，出現少量錯誤是被允許的，也是意料中的事。

(f) 經常的複習非常重要，而這個部份就是十分快速方便的複習方式。在一堂課開始時或結束前，可以挪出五分鐘或十分鐘複習前面幾課的（口頭練習，闔上課本）。學生除了從結構用法的加強和詞彙中受益外，還會因爲自己更加流暢的回答而信心大增。如果時間允許，還可以指定一位「學生教師」指導同學做複習練習。

(g)（口頭練習，闔上課本）中的標記（.....），是表示要教師說出一位學生的名字；有時候時間和地點會同時放在括號內，表示要提出一個與班上學生有關的用語。教師可以刪去練習中無關的項目，而適用於當時的課堂環境以及學生個別的情況。

(h) 標有（口頭練習）字樣的練習，學生可翻閱課本做練習，但毋須書寫或課前準備。

　　希望本教材能帶給教師和學生們許多愉快、充實的上課時光。

BETTY S. AZAR

Langley, Washington

第一章
BE 動詞和 HAVE 的用法

■ **練習 1**：認識同學和教師的名字。將他們的名字填入下列空格中。

1-1 名詞 + IS + 名詞：單數

名詞 ＋ IS ＋ 名詞 (a) **Canada is** a **country.**	「單數」指的就是「一個，不是兩個或多個」。 (a) 句中： *Canada* = 單數名詞 　　　　　　*is* = 單數動詞 　　　　　　*country* = 單數名詞
(b) Mexico is **a c**ountry.	*a* 經常置於單數名詞前面 (b) 句中：*a* 置於單數名詞 *country* 的前面。*a* 稱爲「冠詞」。
(c) **A** cat is **an a**nimal.	*a* 和 *an* 意思相同。兩個都是冠詞。 *a* 用在以子音開頭的字前面：如 *b, c, d, f, g, h, j, k* 等。 例如：*a bed, a cat, a dog, a friend, a girl* 　*an* 用在以 *a, e, i* 和 *o*★ 開頭的字前面。 例如：*an animal, an ear, an island, an office*

★*an* 有時也用在以 *u* 開頭的字前面。請參閱表 4-7
a, e, i, o 和 *u* 等字母稱爲「母音」
其他的字母皆稱爲「子音」。

■ **練習 2**：用冠詞 a 或 an 完成下列各句。

1. _____ horse is _____ animal.

2. English is _____ language.

3. Chicago is _____ city.

4. Korea is _____ country.

5. Europe is _____ continent.

6. _____ dictionary is _____ book.

7. _____ hotel is _____ building.

8. _____ bear is _____ animal.

9. _____ bee is _____ insect.

10. _____ ant is _____ insect.

animal	*continent*	*insect*
city	*country*	*language*

1. Arabic is _____ *a language* _____ .

2. Rome is _____ *a city* _____ .

3. A cat is _____ *an animal* _____ .

4. Asia is _____ .

5. Tokyo is _____ a city _____ .

6. Spanish is _____ .

7. Mexico is _____ a city _____ .

8. London is _____ a city _____ .

9. A bee is _____ .

10. South America is _____ .

11. A dog is _____ .

12. China is _____ .

13. Russian is _____ .

14. A cow is _____ .

15. A fly is _____ .

■ **練習 4 ― 口語練習**：用自己的話完成下列句子。盡量多想幾種可能的答案。

1. . . . is a language.
   → *English is a language.*
   → *Spanish is a language.*
   → *Arabic is a language.*
   → *Etc.*

2. . . . is a country.

3. . . . is a city.

4. . . . is a continent.

5. . . . is an animal.

6. . . . is an insect.

(a) 名詞 + ARE + 名詞 **Cats** **are** **animals.**	「複數」表示「二個，三個，或更多」。 *Cats* = 複數名詞 *are* = 複數動詞 *animals* = 複數名詞
(b) 單數： *a cat, an animal.* 複數： *cats, animals*	名詞的複數要加 **-s**. *a* 和 *an* 只能用於單數名詞。
(c) 單數： *a city, a country.* 複數： *cities, countries*	有些 *-y* 結尾的字有特殊的複數型態：即省略 *-y*，加上 *-ies*。★
(d) 名詞 and 名詞 + ARE + 名詞 (d) **Canada and China are countries.** (e) **Dogs and Cats are animals.**	兩個名詞以 *and* 相連時，*be* 動詞要用 *are*。 (d) 句中：*Canada* 是單數名詞。*China* 也是單數名詞。它們以 *and* 相連時就成了複數，也就是「不只一個」。

★有關 *-y* 結尾的字，後面加 *-s* / *-es* 的情形，請參閱表 2-6

■ **練習 5**：將下列單數的句子改成複數的句子。

單數 複數

1. An ant is an insect. → *Ants are insects.*

2. A computer is a machine. → _____

3. A dictionary is a book. → _____

4. A chicken is a bird. → _____

5. A rose is a flower. → _____

6. A carrot is a vegetable. → _____

7. A rabbit is an animal. → _____

■ **練習 6**：用 is 或 are 以及一個框內的名詞完成下列句子。請使用名詞正確的單數型態（a 或 an 或複數型態。）

```
  animal        country       language
  city          insect        machine
  continent
```

1. A dog _____*is an animal*_____.

2. Dogs _____*are animals*_____.

3. Spanish _____.

4. Spanish and Chinese _____.

5. Asia _____.

6. Asia and Africa _____.

7. Thailand and Viet Nam _____.

8. Thailand _____.

9. Butterflies _____.

10. A butterfly _____.

11. An automobile _____.

12. Automobiles _____.

13. London _____.

14. London and Baghdad _____.

■ **練習 7 — 口語練習**：練習用自己的話完整說出下列句子。

例：. . . a country.
答：(Brazil is) a country.

1. . . . a country.	6. . . . cities.	11. . . . countries in Asia.
2. . . . countries.	7. . . . animals.	12. . . . a city in Europe.
3. . . . languages.	8. . . . an insect.	13. . . . a plant.
4. . . . a language.	9. . . . a peninsula.	14. . . . a vegetable.
5. . . . a city.	10. . . . streets in this city.	15. . . . a season.

例：Cows
答：Cows are animals.

1. English
2. England
3. Butterflies
4. Chickens
5. Europe
6. Roses
7. A carrot
8. Russian and Arabic
9. Spring
10. Japan and Venezuela
11. A computer
12. A bear
13. Bees
14. An ant
15. Winter and summer
16. September and October
17. A dictionary
18. Typewriters
19. A Honda
20. (*names of cars, cities, countries, continents, animals, insects*)

1-3 代名詞 + BE 動詞 + 名詞

單數			複數			
代名詞 +	BE 動詞 +	名詞	代名詞 +	BE 動詞+名詞		*I* *you* *she* *he* *it* *we* *they* } = 代名詞
(a) *I*	*am*	a student.	(f) *We*	*are*	students.	
(b) *You*	*are*	a student	(g) *You*	*are*	students.	
(c) *She*	*is*	a student	(h) *They*	*are*	students.	
(d) *He*	*is*	a student				*am* *is* *are* } = *be* 動詞
(e) *It*	*is*	a country.				

	代名詞意指名詞
(i) *Rita* is in my class. ***She*** is a student.	(i) 句中：*she*（女）= Rita
(j) *Tom* is in my class. ***He*** is a student.	(j) 句中：*he*（男）= Tom
(k) *Rita* and *Tom* are in my class. ***They*** are students.	(k) 句中：*they* = Rita and Tom

■ **練習 9**：使用動詞 am, is 或 are 並搭配名詞 a student 或 students 來完成下列各句。

1. We _____*are students*_____.

2. I _____.

3. Rita goes to school. She _____.

4. Rita and Tom go to school. They _____.

5. You *(one person)* _____.

6. You *(two persons)* _____.

■ **練習10 — 口語練習（闔上書本）**：用 be 動詞＋a student / students 的型態完成下列各句，並用手指出主詞。

例：　(Yoko)（教師說出一位學生的名字。）
答：　Yoko is a student.（並用手指著Yoko回答。）

1.　(. . .)	6.　(. . .)
2.　(. . .) and (. . .)	7.　(. . .) and (. . .)
3.　I	8.　They
4.　(. . .) and I	9.　You
5.　We	10.　(. . .) and (. . .) and (. . .)

除了做以上的練習外，另外再加一個句子，說明前面的主詞人物來自哪個國家。

11.　(*Yoko*)
　　→　*Yoko is a student. She is from Japan.*

12.　(*Luis*) and (*Pablo*)
　　→　*Luis and Pablo are students. They are from South America.*

13.　(. . .)

14.　(. . .) and (. . .)

15.　Etc.

1-4　BE 動詞的縮寫

	代名詞　＋　BE　→　縮寫			說話時，人們經常將兩個字連起來說。縮寫(contraction)＝兩個字合在一起寫。
AM	I　＋　am　→　***I'm***		（a）***I'm*** a student.	
IS	she　＋　is　→　***she's*** he　＋　is　→　***he's*** it　＋　is　→　***it's***		（b）***She's*** a student. （c）***He's*** a student. （d）***It's*** a city.	主詞代名詞＋be 動詞的縮寫形式經常會用在說話和寫作當中。
ARE	you　＋　are　→　***you're*** we　＋　are　→　***we're*** they　＋　are　→　***they're***		（e）***You're*** a student. 　　***You're*** students. （f）***We're*** students.	標點符號：縮寫中的符號（'）稱爲縮寫號 (apostrophe)。

注意：縮寫號要寫在線的上方，不可置於線上。

正：　_I'm a student._

誤：　_I,m a student._

1. *Sara* is a student. _____*She's*_____ in my class.

2. *Jim* is a student. _____ in my class.

3. I have *one brother*. _____ twenty years old.

4. I have *two sisters*. _____ students.

5. I have *a dictionary*. _____ on my desk.

6. I like *my classmates*. _____ friendly.

7. I have *three books*. _____ on my desk.

8. *My brother* is twenty-six years old. _____ married.

9. *My sister* is twenty-one years old. _____ single.

10. *Yoko and Ali* are students. _____ in my class.

11. I like *my books*. _____ interesting.

12. I like *grammar*. _____ easy.

13. *Kate and I* live in an apartment. _____ roommates.

14. We live in *an apartment*. _____ on Pine Street.

15. *I* go to school. _____ a student.

16. I know *you*. _____ in my English class.

1-5　BE 動詞的否定式

(a) Tom $\begin{bmatrix} \textbf{\textit{is not}} \\ \textbf{\textit{isn't}} \end{bmatrix}$ a teacher. He is a student.	*not* 使句子成為否定句。 *not* 可和 *is* 及 *are* 縮寫： 縮寫：　*is* + *not* = *isn't* 縮寫：　*are* + *not* = *aren't*
(b) Tom and Ann $\begin{bmatrix} \textbf{\textit{are not}} \\ \textbf{\textit{aren't}} \end{bmatrix}$ teachers.	
(c) I **am not** a teacher.	此處 *am* 和 *not* 不縮寫。

■ **練習 12**：根據事實完成下列各句。

1. Korea ___*isn't*___ a city. It ___*'s a country*___.

2. Horses _____ insects. They _____.

3. Asia _____ a country. It _____.

4. Bees and ants _____ animals. They _____.

5. Arabic _____ a country. It _____.

6. I _____ a professional photographer. I _____.

Ms. Black

Jim

Mr. Rice

Mike

Ann

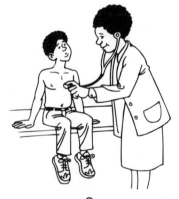

Sue

7. Ann _____ a gardener. She _____.

8. Mike _____ a gardener. He _____ an artist.

9. Jim _____ a bus driver. He _____.

10. Sue _____ a photographer. She _____.

11. Mr. Rice _____ a police officer. He isn't _____.

12. Ms. Black isn't _____. She _____.

1-6 BE 動詞 + 形容詞

	名詞	+	BE 動詞	+	形容詞
(a)	A ball		is		***round***.
(b)	Balls		are		***round***.
(c)	Mary		is		***intelligent***.
(d)	Mary and Tom		are		***intelligent***.

	代名詞	+	BE 動詞	+	形容詞
(e)	I		am		***hungry***.
(f)	She		is		***young***.
(g)	They		are		***happy***.

round
intelligent
hungry } = 形容詞
young
happy

形容詞經常會出現在 *be* 動詞 (*am, is, are*) 後面，用來描述或說明句首的名詞或代名詞。★

★句首的名詞或代名詞稱為「主詞」。請參閱表 4-1。

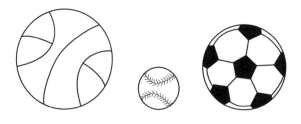

■ **練習 11**：完成下列各圖。

學生A： 畫出 happy, sad 和 angry 的表情。然後把畫拿給學生 B 看。

學生B： 說出學生 A 畫中的情緒。
例如： *She is angry. He is sad. They are happy.*

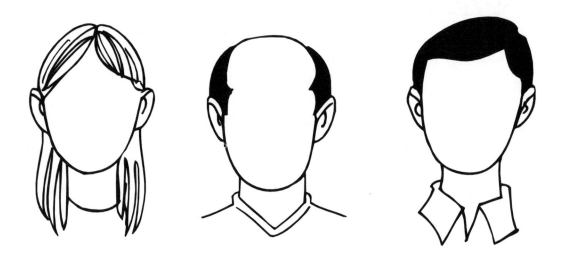

beautiful	*expensive*	*open*
clean	*fast*	*poor*
cold	✔ *happy*	*short*
dangerous	*noisy*	*sour*
easy	*old*	*tall*

1. I'm not sad. I *'m happy* _____.

2. Ice isn't hot. It _____.

3. Mr. Thomas isn't rich. He _____.

4. My hair isn't long. It _____.

5. My clothes aren't dirty. They _____.

6. Flowers aren't ugly. They _____.

7. Cars aren't cheap. They _____.

8. Airplanes aren't slow. They _____.

9. Grammar isn't difficult. It _____.

10. My sister isn't short. She _____.

11. My grandparents aren't young. They _____.

12. The dormitory isn't quiet. It _____.

13. The door isn't closed. It _____.

14. Guns aren't safe. They _____.

15. Lemons aren't sweet. They _____.

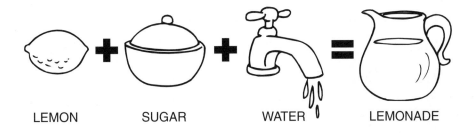

LEMON   SUGAR   WATER   LEMONADE

■ **練習15 — 口語練習（閤上書本）：**用形容詞描述教室內的物品。

> 例： round, square, flat
>
> 問學生A： （教師先在黑板上寫下：round, square, flat，然後拿起或指著某樣圓形的物品。）
> Tell me about this ring that I'm holding. Use one of the words on the board.
>
> 學生A答： It's round.
>
> 問學生B： Tell me about this coin.
>
> 學生B答： It's round. It's flat.

1. round (a ring, a coin, a circle drawn on the board)
2. square (a box, a desk, a figure drawn on the board)
3. flat (a coin, a desktop)
4. full (a pocket, a hand)
5. empty (a pocket, a hand)
6. wet (a street on a rainy day, a licked finger)
7. dry (indoors on a rainy day, an unlicked finger)
8. dirty (a hand or a piece of paper rubbed on the floor)
9. clean (a hand or a piece of paper not rubbed on the floor)
10. long (a string, a strip of paper, someone's hair)
11. short (a string, a strip of paper, someone's hair)
12. heavy (a desk, a pile of books)
13. light (a piece of paper, a pen)
14. loud (a knock on a door or desk top, one's speaking voice)
15. soft (a knock on a door or desk top, one's speaking voice)
16. quiet (no sound at all in the classroom)

■ **練習 16：**用 is 或 are 搭配一個框內的形容詞造句。每個形容詞只使用一次。

beautiful	✔ *hot*	*sour*
cold	*important*	*square*
dry	*large/big*	*sweet*
flat	*round*	*wet*
funny	*small/little*	

1. Fire ____*is hot*_____.

2. Ice and snow _____.

3. A box _____.

4. Balls and oranges _____.

5. Sugar _____.

12 ■ 第一章

6. An elephant _____,

   but a mouse _____.

7. A rain forest _____,

   but a desert _____.

8. A lemon _____.

9. A joke _____.

10. Good health _____.

11. Flowers _____.

12. A coin _____ small, round, and _____.

■ **練習 17**：用 is, isn't, are 或 aren't 完成下列各句。

1. A ball _____ *isn't* _____ square.

2. Balls _____ *are* _____ round.

3. A mouse _____ big.

4. Lemons _____ yellow.

   Ripe bananas _____ yellow too.

5. A lemon _____ sweet. It _____ sour.

6. A diamond _____ cheap.

7. Diamonds _____ expensive.

8. Apples _____ expensive.

9. The earth _____ flat. It _____ round.

10. My pen _____ heavy. It _____ light.

11. This room _____ dark. It _____ light.

12. English grammar _____ hard. It _____ easy.

13. This exercise _____ difficult. It _____ easy.

14. My classmates _____ friendly.

15. A turtle _____ slow.

16. Airplanes _____ slow.

    They _____ fast.

17. The floor in the classroom _____ clean.

    It _____ dirty.

18. The weather _____ cold today.

19. The sun _____ bright today.

20. Ice cream and candy _____ sour. They _____ sweet.

21. My shoes _____ comfortable.

22. My desk _____ comfortable.

23. Flowers _____ ugly. They _____ beautiful.

24. Traffic at rush hour _____ noisy. It _____ quiet.

■ **練習18 — 口語練習：**你符合下列這些字所描述的情況嗎？

例：Hungry?

答：I'm hungry. 或：I'm not hungry.

1. hungry?	11. angry?
2. thirsty?	12. nervous?
3. sleepy?	13. friendly?
4. tired?	14. lazy?
5. old?	15. hardworking?
6. young?	16. famous?
7. happy?	17. sick?
8. homesick?	18. healthy?
9. married?	19. friendly?
10. single?	20. shy?

1. big?
2. small?
3. old?
4. modern?
5. clean?
6. dirty?
7. friendly?
8. unfriendly?
9. safe?
10. dangerous?

■ 練習 20 — 口語練習：（闔上書本）：用 is / isn't 或 are / aren't 造句。

例：A ball \ round
答：A ball is round.
例：Balls \ square
答：Balls aren't square.

1. A box \ square
2. A box \ round
3. The earth \ flat
4. The earth \ round
5. Bananas \ red
6. Bananas \ yellow
7. Diamonds \ expensive
8. Diamonds \ cheap
9. Apples \ expensive
10. Air \ free
11. Cars \ free
12. A pen \ heavy
13. A pen \ light
14. Flowers \ ugly
15. A rose \ beautiful
16. A turtle \ fast
17. A turtle \ slow
18. Airplanes \ slow
19. Airplanes \ fast
20. English grammar \ difficult
21. English grammar \ easy
22. This exercise \ hard
23. The weather \ hot today
24. The weather \ cold today
25. Lemons \ sweet
26. Ice cream and candy \ sour
27. Traffic \ noisy
28. City streets \ quiet
29. Education \ important
30. Good food \ important
31. Good food and exercise \ important
32. The students in this class \ very intelligent

■ 練習 21 — 口語練習：（闔上書本）：說出符合所給之形容詞性質的物品。

例： round
教師：Name something that is round.
學生：(A ball, an orange, the world, my head, etc.) is round.

1. hot
2. square
3. sweet
4. sour
5. large
6. flat
7. little
8. important
9. cold
10. funny
11. beautiful
12. expensive
13. cheap
14. free
15. delicious

(a) Maria is **here**. (b) Bob was **at the library**.	(a)句中：*here* = 地點 (b)句中：*at the library* = 地點 地點用語經常跟在 *be* 動詞後面。
(c) Maria is $\begin{cases} \textit{here.} \\ \textit{there.} \\ \textit{downstairs.} \\ \textit{upstairs.} \\ \textit{inside.} \\ \textit{outside.} \\ \textit{downtown.} \end{cases}$	地點用語可能只是一個字，如 (c) 中的例子。
(d) Bob was $\begin{array}{ll} \text{介系詞} & \text{名詞} \\ \textit{at} & \textit{the library.} \\ \textit{on} & \textit{the bus.} \\ \textit{in} & \textit{his room.} \\ \textit{at} & \textit{work.} \\ \textit{next to} & \textit{Maria.} \end{array}$	地點用語也可能是介系詞片語，如 (d) 的情形。 介系詞 + 名詞就稱為「介系詞片語」。 *At the library* = 介系詞片語。

常用的介系詞

above	*between*	*next to*
at	*from*	*on*
behind	*in*	*under*

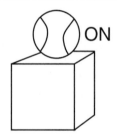
ON

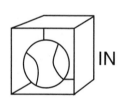
IN

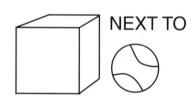
NEXT TO

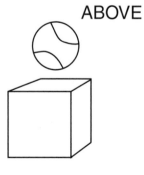
ABOVE

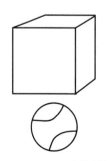

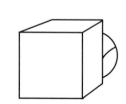
BEHIND

UNDER

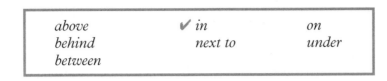

above	✔ in	on
behind	next to	under
between		

1.

The cat is _____*in*_____ the desk.

2.

The cat is _____ the desk.

3.

The cat is _____ the desk.

4.

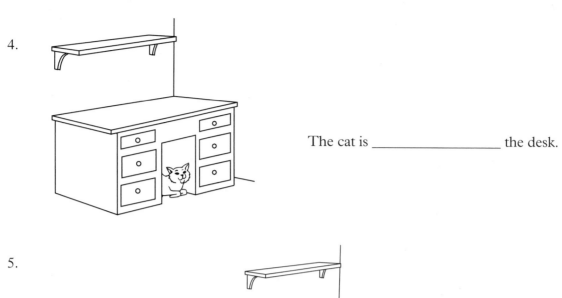

The cat is _____ the desk.

5.

The cat is _____ two desks.

6.

The cat is _____ the desk.

7.

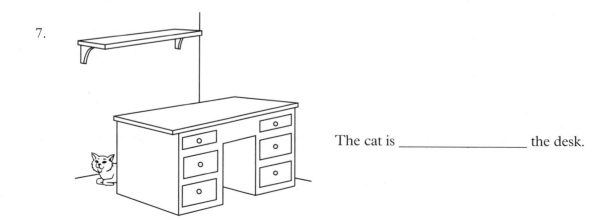

The cat is _____ the desk.

1. Mike is in his apartment.
   → *in* = 介系詞
   → *in his apartment* = 介系詞片語

2. Mr. Lee is at the airport.

3. Ali is from Egypt.

4. My book is on my desk.

5. Bob's pen is in his pocket.

6. The post office is on First Street.

7. The post office is next to the bank.

8. My feet are under my desktop.

9. My nose is between my cheeks.

10. My apartment is on the third floor. It is above Mr. Kwan's apartment.

■ **練習 24** ─ 口語練習（闔上書本）：練習使用表示地點的介系詞。

例： under
教師： Put your hand under your chair. Where is your hand?
學生： My hand is under my chair. / It's under my chair.

1. *on*   Put your pen on your book. Where is your pen?
2. *in*   Put your pen in your book. Where's your pen?
3. *under*   Put your pen under your book. Where's your pen?
4. *next to* Put your pen next to your book. Where's your pen?
5. *on*   Put your hand on your ear.   Where's your hand?
6. *next to* Put your hand next to your ear. Where's your hand?
7. *above*   Put your hand above your head. Where's your hand?
8. *next to* Stand next to (. . .). Where are you?
9. *between* Stand between (. . .) and (. . .). Where are you?
10. *between* Put your pen between two books. Where's your pen?
11. *behind* Put your hand behind your head. Where's your hand?
12. 照指示做： Put your pen   in your hand.
                     . . . on your arm.
                     . . . behind your neck.
                     . . . between your hands.
                     . . . under your book.
                     . . . next to your book.
                     . . . above your book.

(a)	主詞	+ BE 動詞 +	名詞	句首的名詞或代名詞稱爲「主詞」。
	I	am	*a student.*	
(b)	主詞	+ BE 動詞 +	形容詞	*be* 動詞是一種「動詞」。英文幾乎所有的句子都有一個主詞和一個動詞。
	He	is	*intelligent.*	
(c)	主詞	+ BE 動詞 +	位置用語	以主詞 + *be* 動詞爲首的句子，後面通常有三種結束的方式：
	We	are	*in class.*	• 加一名詞，如 (a) 句的情形 • 加一形容詞，如 (b) 句的情形 • 加一地點，如 (c) 句的情形

■ **練習 25**：寫出下列各句中所用的 be 動詞形態（am, is 或 are），再寫出接在 be 動詞後的文法結構。

	BE 動詞	+	承接詞
1. We're students. →	*are*	+	名詞
2. Anna is in Rome. →	*is*	+	地點
3. I'm hungry. →	*am*	+	形容詞
4. Dogs are animals. →	_____	+	_____
5. Jack is at home. →	_____	+	_____
6. He's sick. →	_____	+	_____
7. They're artists. →	_____	+	_____
8. I'm in class. →	_____	+	_____
9. Gina is upstairs. →	_____	+	_____
10. My pockets are empty. →	_____	+	_____

1. Grammar is easy.
   ("Grammar's easy.")

2. Rita is a student.

3. My book is on the table.

4. My books are on the table.

5. The weather is cold today.

6. My brother is twenty-one years old.

7. The window is open.

8. The windows are open.

9. My money is in my wallet.

10. Mr. Smith is a teacher.

11. Tom is at home now.

12. The sun is bright today.

13. My roommate is from Chicago.

14. My roommates are from Chicago.

15. My sister is a student in high school.

1-9 BE 動詞在 YES / NO 問句中的用法

疑問句	敘述句	疑問句中，*be* 動詞置於主詞前面。
BE 動詞 + 主詞 (a) *Is* **she** a student? (b) *Are* **they** at home?	主詞 + BE 動詞 **She** *is* a student. **They** *are* at home.	標點符號：疑問句後面要加問號 (?)。 敘述句結尾用句點 (.)。

回答問題時，通常只用簡答 (*short answer*)，有時也會用完整的回答 (*long answer*)。注意以下的簡答：
肯定回答 *yes* 之後，*be* 動詞不可與作為主詞的代名詞縮寫。★
否定回答 *no* 之後，有兩種縮寫形式，意義相同。

疑問句	簡答 + （完整回答）	
(c) *Is she* a student?	→ Yes, ***she is.***★	*(She's a student.)*
	→ No, ***she's not.***	*(She's not a student.)* 或：
	→ No, ***she isn't.***	*(She isn't a student.)*
(d) *Are they* at home?	→ Yes, ***they are.***★	*(They're at home.)*
	→ No, ***they're not.***	*(They're not at home.)* 或：
	→ No, ***they aren't.***	*(They aren't at home.)*

★ 誤：*Yes, she's.*
  誤：*Yes, they're.*

1. A: _____*Are you tired?*_____

   B: _____*No, I'm not.*_____ (I'm not tired.)

2. A: _____*Is Anna in your class?*_____

   B: _____*Yes, she is.*_____ (Anna is in my class.)

3. A: _____

   B: _____ (I'm not homesick.)

4. A: _____

   B: _____ (Bob is homesick.)

5. A: _____

   B: _____ (Sue isn't here today.)

6. A: _____

   B: _____ (The students in this class are intelligent.)

7. A: _____

   B: _____ (The chairs in this room aren't comfortable.)

8. A: _____

   B: _____ (I'm not married.)

9. A: _____

   B: _____ (Tom and I are roommates.)

10. A: _____

    B: _____ (A butterfly is not a bird.)

學生A：書本打開。用 Are you...? 句型向同學發問。
學生B：書本閤上。回答學生A的問題。

例： hungry

學生A：(Yoko), are you hungry?
學生B：Yes, I am. 或：No, I'm not.

1. hungry
2. sleepy
3. thirsty
4. married
5. single
6. tired
7. homesick
8. lazy
9. cold
10. comfortable
11. a student
12. a teacher
13. a famous actor
14. in the middle of the room

角色互換

15. in the back of the room
16. in the front of the room
17. in class
18. in bed
19. at the library
20. at home
21. in (name of this city)
22. in (name of another city)
23. in Canada
24. in the United States
25. from the United States
26. from (name of country)
27. a student at (name of school)

■ 練習 29 — 口語練習（閤上書本）：學生互相作問答練習。

學生A： 書本打開。用 be 動詞 + 主詞的句型向同學發問。
學生B：書本閤上。回答學生 A 的問題。

例： a ball \ round

學生A：(. . .), is a ball round?
學生B：Yes, it is.

例： a ball \ square

學生A：(. . .), is a ball square?
學生B：No, it isn't. 或： No, it's not.

角色互換

1. a mouse \ big
2. sugar \ sweet
3. lemons \ sweet
4. ice cream and candy \ sour
5. the world \ flat
6. the world \ round
7. your desk \ comfortable
8. your shoes \ comfortable
9. your eyes \ brown
10. the sun \ bright today
11. the weather \ cold today

12. your pen \ heavy
13. apples \ expensive
14. diamonds \ cheap
15. English grammar \ easy
16. the floor in this room \ clean
17. butterflies \ beautiful
18. turtles \ intelligent
19. your dictionary \ under your desk
20. your books \ on your desk
21. your desk \ in the middle of the room
22. your pen \ in your pocket

疑問句	簡答 + （完整回答）
BE 動詞 + 主詞	
（a）***Is*** ***the book*** on the table?	→ Yes, ***it is.*** *(The book is on the table.)*
（b）***Are*** ***the books*** on the table?	→ Yes, ***they are.*** *(The books are on the table.)*
WHERE + BE 動詞 + 主詞	
（c）***Where*** ***is*** ***the book?***	→ ***On the table.*** *(The book is on the table.)*
（d）***Where*** ***are*** ***the books?***	→ ***On the table.*** *(The books are on the table.)*

WHERE 用來問地點。在問句中，要置於句首，在 BE 動詞前面。

■ **練習 30：**根據提示造問句。

1. A: ___*Is Kate at home?*___
   B: Yes, she is. (Kate is at home.)

2. A: ___*Where is Kate?*___
   B: At home. (Kate is at home.)

3. A: _____
   B: Yes, it is. (Cairo is in Egypt.)

4. A: _____
   B: In Egypt. (Cairo is in Egypt.)

5. A: _____
   B: Yes, they are. (The students are in class today.)

6. A: _____
   B: In class. (The students are in class today.)

7. A: _____
   B: On Main Street. (The post office is on Main Street.)

8. A: _____
   B: Yes, it is. (The train station is on Grand Avenue.)

9. A: _____
   B: Over there. (The bus stop is over there.)

10. A: _____
    B: At the zoo. (Sue and Ken are at the zoo today.)

■ **練習 31 — 口語練習（闔上書本）**：用 where 向同學提出問題。

例： your pen
學生A： Where is your pen?
學生B： （自由作答）

1. your grammar book
2. your dictionary
3. your money
4. your books
5. (. . .)

6. (. . .) and (. . .)
7. your sunglasses
8. your pen
9. your apartment

10. your parents
11. the post office
12. *(the names of places in this city: a store, landmark, restaurant, etc.)*

■ **練習 32 — 口語練習**：學生用 where 疑問句互相問答，回答的學生要用手指出地圖上的位置。

例： Washington, D.C.
學生A： Where's Washington, D.C.?
學生B： （指著地圖）It's here.

提示：

1. New York City
2. Los Angeles
3. Montreal
4. Miami
5. Toronto
6. Washington, D. C.
7. the Great Lakes
8. the Rocky Mountains
9. the Mississippi River
10. Mexico City

Washington, D.C.

1-11 HAVE 和 HAS 的用法

單數	複數	
(a) **I** **have** a pen.	(f) **We** **have** pens.	*I*
(b) **You** **have** a pen.	(g) **You** **have** pens.	*you*
(c) **She** **has** a pen.	(h) **They** **have** pens.	*we* + **have**
(d) **He** **has** a pen.		*they*
(e) **It** **has** blue ink.		
		she
		he + **has**
		it

■ **練習 33**：用 have 和 has 完成下列各句。

1. We _____*have*_____ grammar books.

2. I _____ a dictionary.

3. Kate _____ a blue pen. She _____ a blue notebook too.

4. You _____ a pen in your pocket.

5. Bob _____ a notebook on his desk.

6. Anna and Bob _____ notebooks. They _____ pens too.

7. Samir is a student in our class. He _____ a red grammar book.

8. I _____ a grammar book. It _____ a red cover.

9. You and I are students. We _____ books on our desks.

10. Mike _____ a wallet in his pocket. Sara _____ a wallet in her purse.

11. Nadia isn't in class today because she _____ the flu.

12. Mr. and Mrs. Johnson _____ two daughters.

單數		複數		主格型態		所有格型態
				I	→	*my*
(a) **I** have a book.		(e) **We** have books.		*you*	→	*your*
My book is red.		*Our* books are red.		*she*	→	*her*
				he	→	*his*
(b) **You** have a book.		(f) **You** have books.		*we*	→	*our*
Your book is red.		*Your* books are red.		*they*	→	*their*

(c) **She** has a book.	(g) **They** have books.
Her book is red.	*Their* books are red.

I *possess* a book. = I *have* a book. = It is *my* book.

(d) **He** has a book.
His book is red.

My, our, her, his, our 和 *their* 稱爲所有格形容詞 (*possessive adjectives*)，置於名詞前面。

■ **練習 34**：用 my, your, his, her, our 或 their 完成下列各句。

1. I have a pen. _____My_____ pen is blue.

2. You have a pen. _____ pen is black.

3. Kate has a pen. _____ pen is green.

4. Jim has a pen. _____ pen is yellow.

5. Sara and I have pens. _____ pens are gray.

6. Sara and you have pens. _____ pens are red.

7. Sam and Kate have pens. _____ pens are orange.

8. I have a sister. _____ sister is twenty-one years old.

9. Ann has a car. _____ car is a Ford.

10. You have a pen. _____ pen is a ballpoint.

11. Jim and you have mustaches. _____ mustaches are dark.

12. Ann and Alex have a baby. _____ baby is eight months old.

13. Alice and I have notebooks. _____ notebooks are green.

14. Ann has a brother. _____ brother is in high school.

15. Ken has a coat. _____ coat is brown.

16. We have a dog. _____ dog is gray and white.

1. I _____*have*_____ a book. _____*My*_____ book is interesting.

2. Bob _____ a bookbag. _____ bookbag is green.

3. You _____ a raincoat. _____ raincoat is brown.

4. Kate _____ a raincoat. _____ raincoat is red.

5. Ann and Jim are married. They _____ a baby. _____ baby is six months old.

6. Ken and Sue _____ a daughter. _____ daughter is ten years old.

7. John and I _____ a son. _____ son is seven years old.

8. I _____ a brother. _____ brother is sixteen.

9. We _____ grammar books. _____ grammar books are red.

10. Tom and you _____ bookbags. _____ bookbags are green.

11. Ann _____ a dictionary. _____ dictionary is red.

12. Mike _____ a car. _____ car is blue.

■ 練習 36：用 my, your, her, his, our 或 their 完成下列各句。

1. Rita is wearing a blouse. _____ blouse is light blue.

2. Tom is wearing a shirt. _____ shirt is yellow and brown.

3. I am wearing jeans. _____ jeans are blue.

4. Bob and Tom are wearing boots. _____ boots are brown.

5. Sue and you are wearing dresses. _____ dresses are red.

6. Ann and I are wearing sweaters. _____ sweaters are green.

7. You are wearing shoes. _____ shoes are dark brown.

8. Sue is wearing a skirt. _____ skirt is black.

9. John is wearing a belt. _____ belt is white.

10. Sue and Ann are wearing slacks. _____ slacks are dark gray.

11. Tom is wearing slacks. _____ slacks are dark blue.

12. I am wearing earrings. _____ earrings are gold.

字 彙 表

顏色	衣物	飾物
black	belt	bracelet
blue, dark blue, light blue	blouse	earrings
blue green	boots	necklace
brown, dark brown, light brown	coat	ring
gray, dark gray, light gray	dress	watch/wristwatch
green, dark green, light green	gloves	
orange	hat	
pink	jacket	
purple	jeans	
red	pants	
tan, beige	sandals	
white	shirt	
yellow	shoes	
gold	skirt	
silver	slacks	
	suit	
	sweater	
	tie, necktie	
	T-shirt	

■ **練習 37 — 口語練習（闔上書本）**：用所有形容詞 + 名詞 + is / are + 顏色的句型，描述在教室中看到的衣物、飾品及其顏色。

例：

教師： Look at Ali. Tell me about his shirt. What color is his shirt?
學生： His shirt is blue.

教師： Look at Rosa. What is this?
學生： A sweater.
教師： Tell me about her sweater. What color is it?
學生： Her sweater is red.

教師： Look at me. What am I touching?
學生： Your shoes.
教師： Tell me about the color.
學生： Your shoes are brown.

1-13 THIS 和 THAT 的用法

(a) I have a book in my hand. ***This book*** is red.	*this* book = 距自己較近的書
(b) I see a book on your desk. ***That book*** is blue.	*that* book = 距自己較遠的書
(c) ***This*** is my book.	
(d) ***That*** is your book.	
(e) ***That's*** her book.	縮寫：*that is = that's*

THAT BOOK

■ 練習 38 — 口語練習（闔上書本）：使用 this 和 that，觸摸並指出教室內的物品。

例：book
答：This is my book. That is your book.

1. book
2. pen
3. notebook
4. purse
5. dictionary
6. bookbag
7. coat
8. hat
9. pencil
10. pencil sharpener
11. watch
12. nose

■ 練習 39 — 口語練習（闔上書本）：使用 this 和 that，觸摸並指出教室內的物品。

例：red \ yellow
答：This (book) is red. That (shirt) is yellow.

1. red \ blue
2. red \ green
3. red \ yellow
4. blue \ black
5. white \ black
6. orange \ green
7. red \ pink
8. dark blue \ light blue
9. black \ gray
10. gold \ silver
11. dark brown \ tan
12. purple \ red

1-14 THESE 和 THOSE 的用法

	單數		複數
（a）My books are on my desk. ***These*** are my books.	*this*	→	*these*
（b）Your books are on your desk. ***Those*** are your books.	*that*	→	*those*

■ **練習 40**：用括弧內的字完成下列各句。

1. *(This, These)* _____***These***_____ books belong to me. *(That, Those)*

   _____***That***_____ book belongs to Kate.

2. *(This, These)* _____ coat is black. *(That, Those)* _____

   coats are tan.

3. *(This, These)* _____ earrings are gold. *(That, Those)* _____

   earrings are silver.

4. *(This, These)* _____ pencil belongs to Alex. *(That, Those)*

   _____ pencil belongs to Alice.

5. *(This, These)* _____ sunglasses belong to me. *(That, Those)*

   _____ sunglasses belong to you.

6. *(This, These)* _____ exercise is easy. *(That, Those)* _____

   exercises are hard.

7. Students are sitting at *(this, these)* _____ desks, but *(that, those)*

   _____ desks are empty.

8. *(This, These)* _____ book is on my desk. *(That, Those)*

   _____ books are on your desk.

■ **練習 41 — 口語練習（闔上書本）**：使用 these 和 those，觸摸並指出教室內的物品。

例：books
答：These are my books. Those are your books.

1. books	5. jeans
2. pens	6. things
3. shoes	7. glasses/sunglasses
4. earrings	8. notebooks

例：book
答：This is my book. That is your book.
例：books
答：These are my books. Those are your books.

1. book
2. books
3. dictionary
4. pens
5. pen
6. coats
7. shoes
8. wallet
9. purse
10. glasses

1-15 WHAT 和 WHO + BE 動詞的問句

(a) **What is** this (thing)? → It's a pen. (b) **Who is** that (man)? → That's Mr. Lee. (c) **What are** those (things)? → They're pens. (d) **Who are** they? → They're Mr. and Mrs. Lee.	*what* 用來問和事、物有關的問題。 *who* 用來問和人有關的問題。 注意：在 *what* 和 *who* 的疑問句中 • *is* 後面接單數。 • *are* 後面接複數。
(e) **What's** this? (f) **Who's** that man?	縮寫：*who is = who's* *what is = what's*

■ **練習 43**：用 what 或 who 以及 is 或 are 完成下列問句。

1. A: ____*Who is*_____ that woman?
   B: She's my sister. Her name is Sonya.

2. A: _____ those things?
   B: They're ballpoint pens.

3. A: _____ that?
   B: That's Ms. Walenski.

4. A: _____ this?
   B: That's my new notebook.

5. A: Look at those people over there. _____ they?
   B: I'm not sure, but I think they're new students from Thailand.

6. A: _____ your name?
   B: Anita.

7. A: _____ your grammar teacher?
   B: Mr. Cook.

8. A: _____ your favorite teachers?
   B: Mr. Cook and Ms. Rosenberg.

9. A: _____ a rabbit?
   B: It's a small furry animal with big ears.

10. A: _____ bats?
    B: They're animals that can fly. They're not birds.

■ **練習 44 — 口語練習**：說出教室內的物品和人。請學生依指示向同學發問。

例： What's this?
學生A： What's this? (指著文法書)
學生B： It's your grammar book.
例： Who's that?
學生A： Who's that? (指著一位同學)
學生B： That's Ivan.

1. What's this?
2. What's that?
3. Who's this?
4. Who's that?
5. What are those?
6. What are these?

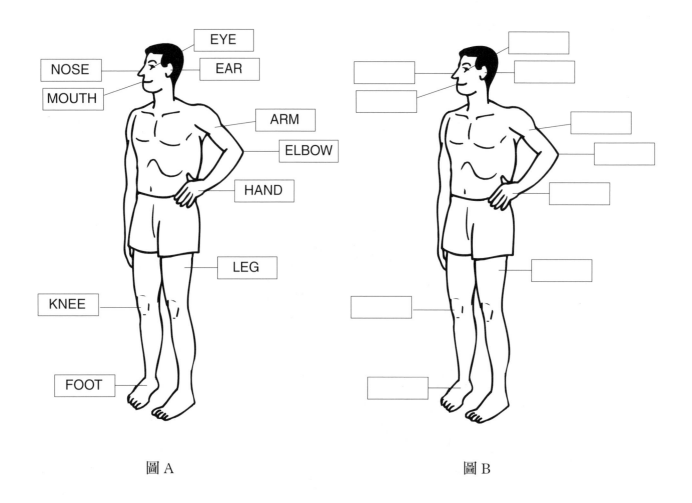

圖 A   圖 B

■ **練習 46 — 口語練習（閤上書本）**：練習使用 this, that, these 和 those。

例： hand

教師：What is this?（老師指著自己的手）
學生：That is your hand.

或

教師：What is that?（老師指著學生的手）
學生：This is my hand.

1. nose   6. knee
2. eyes   7. foot
3. arm   8. shoulder
4. elbow   9. fingers
5. legs   10. ears

■ **練習 47**— 口語練習：用 What's this? What's that? What are these? What are those? 向同學提出和
下圖有關的問題。

例：
學生A：What's this?（指著樹）
學生B：That's a tree.
學生A：What are those?（指著馬）
學生B：Those are horses.
依此類推。

：學生各自畫一幅圖，並用 What's this? What's that? What are these? 等問題來互相問答。

圖的提示：

1. this classroom
2. some of the people in this classroom
3. your family
4. your room / apartment / house
5. a scene at a zoo
6. an outdoor scene

■ **練習 49 — 複習**：找出名詞、形容詞、代名詞、所有格形容詞、和介系詞片語並畫線。

第一部份：找出名詞和形容詞。

    名詞   形容詞
1. <u>Balls</u> are <u>round</u>.

2. Flowers are beautiful.

3. Birds have wings.

4. Bats aren't birds.

5. Bats aren't blind.

第二部份：找出代名詞和所有格形容詞。

        代名詞   所有格形容詞
6. Bats have wings, but <u>they</u> aren't birds. Bats use <u>their</u> wings to fly.

7. I have a grammar book. It's red. My dictionary is red too.

8. My book is red, and your book is red too.

9. An egg isn't square. It's oval.

10. Tina has three sons. She is at home today. They are at school. Her sons are good

    students.

第三部份：找出介系詞片語。

介系詞片語

11. Libya is <u>in Africa</u>.

12. Po is from Beijing.

13. My books are on my desk.

14. I'm at school.

15. My middle finger is between my index finger and my ring finger.

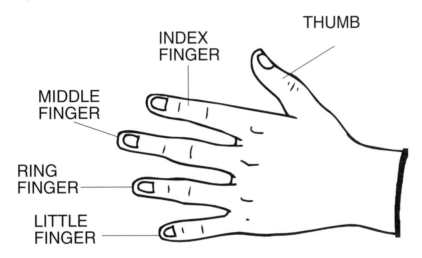

■ **練習 50 — 複習**：訂正句子中的錯誤。

1. We ~~is~~ ^{are} students.

2. I no hungry.

3. I am student.　He is teacher.

4. Yoko not here.　She at school.

5. I'm from Mexico.　Where you are from?

6. Roberto he is a student in your class?

7. Those pictures are beautifuls.

8. This is you dictionary.　It not my dictionary.

9. Mr. Lee have a brown coat.

10. They aren't here today.

11. This books are expensive.

12. Cuba is a island.

13. Florida and Korea is peninsula.

■ **練習 51 — 複習**：選擇正確答案完成句子。

例：Those ____ _B_ ____ expensive.
             A. book is   B. books are   C. books is

1. Ann _____ a grammar book.
             A. have   B. is   C. has

2. This floor _____.
             A. dirty is   B. dirty   C. is dirty

3. _____ yellow.
             A. A banana are   B. A banana is   C. Bananas is

4. *Bob:* _____ is your apartment?
   Ann: It's on Forest Street.
             A. What   B. Where   C. Who

5. Mike is _____ engineer.
             A. a   B. an   C. on

6. Give this to Ann. It is _____ dictionary.
             A. she   B. an   C. her

7. *Yoko:* _____ these?
   Gina: My art books. I'm taking an art history course this semester.
             A. What is   B. Who are   C. What are

8. *Tom:* Are you hungry?

   Sue: Yes, _____.
             A. I'm   B. I'm not   C. I am

9. _____ books are really expensive.
             A. Those   B. They   C. This

10. *Tina:* _____ that?
    Jim: That's Paul Carter.
        A. Who's   B. What's   C. Where's

11. That is _____.
        A. a mistakes   B. mistakes   C. a mistake

12. *Paul:* _____ in your class?
    Eric: No.
        A. Mr. Kim   B. Is Mr. Kim   C. Mr. Kim is he

■ **練習 52 — 複習**：用 am, is 或 are 完成句子。必要時可加入 not。

1. Lemons _____ vegetables.

2. A lemon _____ a kind of fruit.

3. I _____ from the United States.

4. We _____ human beings.

5. Eggs _____ oval.

6. Chickens _____ birds, but bats _____ birds.

7. Salt _____ sweet. Sugar _____ sweet.

8. Soccer _____ a sport.

9. Soccer and basketball _____ sports.

10. Africa _____ a country. It _____ a continent.

■ **練習 53 — 複習**：完成下列句子。

1. A: _____*Are*_____ you a student at this school?

   B: Yes, _____.

   A: Where _____ you from?

   B: I _____ Korea.

2. A: Where _____ your book?

   B: Yoko _____ it.

   A: Where _____ your notebooks?

   B: Ali and Roberto _____ my notebooks.

3. A: _____ this?

   B: It _____ picture of my family.

   A: _____ this?

   B: That's _____ father.

   A: _____ they?
   B: My brother and sister.

4. A: Are you a _____?

   B: No, _____ not. I'm a _____.

5. A: Are _____ expensive?

   B: Yes, _____.

   A: Is _____ expensive?

   B: No, _____.

6. A: What's _____?
   B: I don't know. Ask someone else.

   A: What's _____?

   B: It's _____.

7. A: _____ an animal?
   B: Yes.

   A: _____ animals?
   B: Yes.

   A: _____ an insect?
   B: No, it's not. It's an animal too.

8. A: _____ countries in Asia?
   B: Yes, they are.

   A: _____ a country in South America?
   B: Yes, it is.

   A: _____ a country in Africa?

   B: No, it's not. It's a country in _____.

9. A: Where _____?

   B: He's _____.

   A: Where _____?

   B: They're _____.

10. A: _____ a turtle?
    B: Just a minute. Let me look in my dictionary. Okay. A turtle is a reptile.

    A: _____ a reptile?

    B: _____ an animal that has cold blood.

    A: _____ snakes reptiles too?

    B: Yes. _____ reptiles too.

■ 練習 54 — 複習：兩人一組練習。

學生A：書本打開，提供指示。
學生B：書本閤上，畫出學生 A 指示的圖。

1. Draw a ball on a box.
2. Draw a ball above a box.
3. Draw a ball next to a box.
4. Draw a ball under a box.
5. Draw a ball in a box.
6. Draw a banana between two apples.
7. Draw a square above a circle.
8. Draw a flower. Draw a tree next to the flower. Draw a bird above the tree. Draw a turtle under the flower.

角色互換

9. Draw a circle next to a triangle.
10. Draw a circle in a triangle.
11. Draw a circle above a triangle.
12. Draw a triangle between two circles.
13. Draw a circle under a triangle.
14. Draw an apple on a banana. Draw an apple above a banana.
15. Draw a tree. Draw a person next to the tree. Draw the sun above the tree.
16. Draw a cloud. Draw a bird under the cloud. Draw a bird above the cloud. Draw a bird in the cloud.

學生A： 用以下的介系詞提供指示。
學生B： 做出學生 A 指示的動作。

例： in
學生A： Put your pen in your pocket.
學生B： （學生 B 將筆放入口袋中。）

角色互換

1. in	8. in
2. on	9. between
3. above	10. behind
4. under	11. above
5. between	12. on
6. next to	13. next to
7. behind	14. under

■ 練習 56 — 複習：替 Carlos 完成下面這篇作文。

(1) My name ____is____ Carlos. ____I am OR I'm____ from Mexico.

(2) _____ a student. _____ twenty years old.

(3) My family lives in Mexico City. _____ father _____ a

(4) businessman. _____ fifty-one years old. _____ mother

(5) _____ a housewife. _____ forty-nine years old.

(6) I _____ two sisters and one brother. The names of my sisters

(7) _____ Rosa and Patricia. Rosa _____ a teacher.

(8) _____ twenty-eight years old. Patricia _____ a student.

(9) _____ eighteen years old. The name of _____ brother

(10) _____ Pedro. _____ an engineer. He is married. He

(11) _____ two children.

(12) I live in a dormitory. _____ a tall building. _____ on

(13) Pine Street. My address _____ 3225 Pine St. I live with my roommate.

(14) _____ name is Bob. _____ from Chicago.

(15) _____ nineteen years old.

(16) I like my classes. _____ interesting. I like _____

(17) classmates. _____ friendly.

My name _____. I _____ from _____. _____ a student.

_____ years old.

My family lives in _____. _____ father _____ years old. _____

mother _____ years old.

I have _____ sister(s) and _____ brother(s). The name(s) of my sister(s)

_____. _____ is a/an _____. _____ years old. *(Write about each sister.)*

The name(s) of my brother(s) _____. _____ is a _____. _____ years

old. *(Write about each brother.)*

I live in *(a dormitory, a house, an apartment)* _____. My address _____. I

live with _____. _____ name(s) _____.

I like _____ classes. _____ are _____ and _____. I like _____

classmates. They _____.

第二章
現在式的表達（第一部分）

2-1　現在簡單式的型態與基本意義

	單數	複數	注意：she, he, it（第三人稱單數）後面的動詞字尾要加 -s：talks。
第一人稱	**I** *talk*	**we** *talk*	
第二人稱	**you** *talk*	**you** *talk*	
第三人稱	**she** *talks*	**they** *talk*	
	he *talks*		
	it *rains*		

（a）I *eat* breakfast **every morning**. （b）Ann *speaks* English **every day**. （c）We *sleep* **every night**. （d）They *go* to the beach **every weekend**.	現在簡單式表示習慣。(a)句中：吃早餐是一種習慣，一個慣常的活動。*every morning = Monday morning, Tuesday morning, Wednesday morning, Thursday morning, Friday morning, Saturday morning, Sunday morning* 星期一至星期天每天的早晨。

習慣

我每天早上的習慣

(a) eat breakfast

1. *The alarm clock rings.*

(b) go to class

2. ___*I turn off the alarm clock.*___

(c) put on my clothes

3. _____

(d) drink a cup of coffee/tea

4. _____

(e) shave

5. _____

(f) put on my make-up

6. _____

(g) take a shower/bath

7. _____

(h) get up

8. _____

(i) pick up my books

9. _____

(j) walk to the bathroom

10. _____

(k) watch TV

11. _____

(l) look in the mirror

12. _____

✔ (m) turn off the alarm clock

13. _____

(n) go to the kitchen/the cafeteria

14. _____

(o) brush/comb my hair

15. _____

(p) say good-bye to my roommate/
wife/husband

16. _____

17. _____

(q) brush my teeth

18. _____

(r) do exercises

19. _____

(s) wash my face

20. _____

(t) stretch, yawn, and rub my eyes

21. _____

(u) *other habits*

22. _____

2-2 頻率副詞的用法：ALWAYS, USUALLY, OFTEN, SOMETIMES, SELDOM, RARELY, NEVER

always 100%	*usually* 99%–90%	*often* 90%–75%	*sometimes* 75%–25%	*seldom* 25%–10%	*rarely* 10%–1%	*never* 0%

主詞 + 頻率副詞 + 現在簡單式動詞	*always, usually, often, sometimes, seldom, rarely* 和 *never* 稱為「頻率副詞」，置於主詞和現在簡單式動詞之間。★
(a) **Bob** *always* **comes** to class. (b) **Mary** *usually* **comes** to class. (c) **We** *often* **watch** TV at night. (d) **I** *sometimes* **drink** tea with dinner. (e) **They** *seldom* **go** to the movies. (f) **Anna** *rarely* **makes** a mistake. (g) **I** *never* **eat** paper.	主詞 + $\begin{cases} always \\ usually \\ often \\ sometimes \\ seldom \\ rarely \\ never \end{cases}$ + 動詞

★頻率副詞有時也置於句首或句尾。例如：***Sometimes*** I get up at seven. I ***sometimes*** get up at seven. I get up at seven ***sometimes***. 另外，頻率副詞與 *be* 動詞連用的情況，請參閱表 2-3。

	Sun.	Mon.	Tues.	Wed.	Thurs.	Fri.	Sat.
Ann **always** drinks tea with lunch.	☕	☕	☕	☕	☕	☕	☕
Bob **usually** drinks tea with lunch.		☕	☕	☕	☕	☕	☕
Maria **often** drinks tea with lunch.			☕	☕	☕	☕	☕
Gary **sometimes** drinks tea with lunch.					☕	☕	☕
Ali **seldom** drinks tea with lunch.						☕	☕
Georgia **rarely** drinks tea with lunch.							☕
Joy never **drinks** tea with lunch.							

■ **練習 2 — 口語練習**：找出句中的主詞和動詞，然後將頻率副詞填入句中。

1. *always*   I eat breakfast. → *I always eat breakfast.*
2. *usually*   I get up at 7:00.
3. *often*   I drink two cups of coffee in the morning.
4. *never*   I eat carrots for breakfast.
5. *seldom*   I watch TV in the morning.
6. *sometimes*   I have tea with dinner.
7. *usually*   Bob eats lunch at the cafeteria.
8. *rarely*   Ann drinks tea.

9.	*always*	I do my homework.
10.	*often*	We listen to music after dinner.
11.	*never*	John and Sue watch TV in the afternoon.
12.	*always*	The students speak English in the classroom.

■ **練習 3 — 口語練習**：用 always, usually, often, sometimes, seldom, rarely 和 never 敘述你每天下午五點以後的活動（習慣）。

1. eat dinner	15. study
2. eat dinner at six o'clock	16. study English grammar
3. eat dinner at eight o'clock	17. drink milk
4. watch TV	18. play with my children
5. listen to music	19. kiss my husband / wife
6. go to a movie	20. have a snack
7. go shopping	21. go to bed
8. go dancing	22. go to bed at eleven o'clock
9. go swimming	23. go to bed after midnight
10. spend time with my friends	24. go to bed early
11. talk on the phone	25. go to bed late
12. speak English	26. turn off the lights
13. write a letter	27. dream
14. read a newspaper	28. dream in English

2-3 頻率副詞和 BE 動詞的連用

主詞　+　BE　+　頻率副詞	
動詞	
Tom + *is* + { *always* / *usually* / *often* / *sometimes* / *seldom* / *rarely* / *never* } + late for class.	頻率副詞置於 *be* 動詞之後。
主詞　+　頻率副詞　+　其他的	
現在式動詞	
Tom + { *always* / *usually* / *often* / *sometimes* / *seldom* / *rarely* / *never* } + *comes* late.	除了 *be* 動詞以外，頻率副詞置於所有的現在簡單式動詞之前。

    1. *always*   *always*
                         Ann is ^ on time for class.

    2. *always*   *always*
                         Ann ^ comes to class on time.

    3. *often*   Sue is late for class.

    4. *often*   Sue comes to class late.

    5. *never*   Ron is happy.

    6. *never*   Ron smiles.

    7. *usually*   Bob is at home in the evening.

    8. *usually*   Bob stays at home in the evening.

    9. *seldom*   Tom studies at the library in the evening.

   10. *seldom*   Tom is at the library in the evening.

   11. *rarely*   I eat breakfast.

   12. *often*   I take the bus to school.

   13. *usually*   The weather is hot in July.

   14. *never*   Sue drinks coffee.

   15. *sometimes* She drinks tea.

■ **練習 5 — 書寫練習**：敘述你典型的一天，從早上起床到就寢。用以下的詞語來描述活動的先後次序：
then, next, at...o'clock, after that, later。

例： I usually get up at seven-thirty. I shave, brush my teeth, and take a shower. Then I put on my clothes and go to the student cafeteria for breakfast. After that I go back to my room. I sometimes watch the news on TV. At 8:15 I leave the dormitory. I go to class. My class begins at 8:30. I'm in class from 8:30 to 11:30. After that I eat lunch. I usually have a sandwich and a cup of tea for lunch. （繼續寫到一天的活動結束。）

有聲子音	無聲子音	有些子音是「有聲子音」，須用喉頭發音。例如 /b/ 這個音就要用喉頭發音。(a) 中的尾音是有聲子音。
(a) /b/　rub 　 /d/　ride 　 /v/　drive	(b) /p/　sleep 　 /t/　write 　 /f/　laugh	有些子音是「無聲子音」，就不須用喉頭發音，只要透過唇和齒將氣推出。例如 /p/ 的發音就是透過嘴唇推氣發音。(b) 中的尾音是無聲子音。
(c) rubs　=　*rub*/**z**/ 　 rides　=　*ride*/**z**/ 　 drives　=　*drive*/**z**/	(d) sleeps　=　*sleep*/**s**/ 　 writes　=　*write*/**s**/ 　 laughs　=　*laugh*/**s**/	有聲子音後面的 -s 要唸成 /**z**/ 的音，如 (c) 中的情形。 無聲子音後面的 -s 要唸成 /**s**/ 的音，如 (d) 中的情形。

I can feel my voice box. It vibrates.

■ **練習 6**：下列句子中的動詞尾音是有聲子音。字尾的 -s 要唸成 /z/。大聲唸出這些句子。

1. Cindy rides the bus to school.
　　　　ride/z/

2. Jack usually drives his car to school.
　　　　　　　drive/z/

3. Rain falls.
　　　fall/z/

4. Sally often dreams about her boyfriend.
　　　　　　dream/z/

5. Sometimes Jim runs to class.
　　　　　　　run/z/

6. Tina wears blue jeans every day.
　　　　wear/z/

7. Ann always sees Mr. Lee at the market.
　　　　　　see/z/

找出下列句子的動詞。先唸動詞，然後再大聲唸出整個句子。

8. The teacher often stands in the front of the room.

9. George lives in the dormitory.

10. Jean rarely smiles.

11. Sam always comes to class on time.

12. It rains a lot in Seattle.

13. Jack always remembers his wife's birthday.

14. It snows in New York City in the winter.

■ **練習 7**：下列句子中的動詞尾音是無聲子音。字尾的 -s 要唸成 /s/。大聲唸出這些句子。

1. Mike sleeps for eight hours every night.
     sleep/s/
2. Our teacher always helps us.
                    help/s/
3. Jack writes a letter to his girlfriend every day.
     write/s/
4. Sara never laughs.
            laugh/s/
5. Sue usually drinks a cup of coffee in the morning.
             drink/s/
6. Kate walks to school every day.
     walk/s/

找出下列句子的動詞。先唸動詞，然後再大聲唸出整個句子。

7. My child often claps her hands.

8. Olga always bites her pencil in class.

9. Maria usually gets up at seven-thirty.

10. Yoko asks a lot of questions in class.

11. Ahmed always talks in class.

12. Sue coughs because she smokes.

cough cough

2-5 動詞字尾加 -es 的拼法與發音

		拼法	發音	
-sh	(a) push	→	*pushes*	*push*/əz/	動詞字尾： *-sh, -ch, -ss, -x*
-ch	(b) teach	→	*teaches*	*teach*/əz/	拼法： 後面加 *-es*
-ss	(c) kiss	→	*kisses*	*kiss*/əz/	發音： /əz/
-x	(d) fix	→	*fixes*	*fix*/əz/	

■ **練習 8** ：用提示的動詞完成下列各句。

1. *brush*   Anita _____ *brushes* _____ her hair every morning.

2. *teach*   Alex _____ English.

3. *fix*   A mechanic _____ cars.

4. *drink*   Sonya _____ tea every afternoon.

5. *watch*   Joon–Kee often _____ television at night.

6. *kiss*   Peter always _____ his children goodnight.

7. *wear*   Tina usually _____ jeans to class.

8. *wash*   Eric seldom _____ dishes.

9. *walk*   Jessica _____ her dog twice each day.

10. *stretch,*   When Don gets up in the morning, he _____
     yawn   and _____ .

2-6 在動詞字尾是 -y 的字後面加 -s / -es

(a)	**cry**	→	**cries**	動詞字尾： 子音 + *-y*
	try	→	**tries**	拼法： 把 *y* 改成 *i*，然後加 **-es**
(b)	**pay**	→	**pays**	動詞字尾： 母音 + *-y*
	enjoy	→	**enjoys**	拼法： 加 **-s**

1. *pay, always*　　Boris _____*always pays*_____ his bills on time.

2. *cry, seldom*　　Our baby _____ at night.

3. *study*　　　　Paul _____ at the library every day.

4. *stay, usually*　　Jean _____ home at night.

5. *fly*　　　　　Kunio is a pilot. He _____ a plane.

6. *carry, always*　　Carol _____ her books to class.

7. *pray*　　　　Jack _____ every day.

8. *buy, seldom*　　Ann _____ new clothes.

9. *worry*　　　　Tina is a good student, but she _____

　　　　　　　 about her grades.

10. *enjoy*　　　　Don _____ good food.

2-7　不規則的單數動詞：HAS, DOES, GOES

（a） I **have** a book. （b） He **has** a book.	she he it }	+ **has** /hæz/
（c） I **do** my work. （d） She **does** her work.	she he it }	+ **does** /dəz/
（e） They **go** to school. （f） She **goes** to school.	she he it }	+ **goes** /goz/

have, do 和 *go* 用於第三人稱單數時，有不規則的形式：

have	→	*has*
do	→	*does*
go	→	*goes*

■ **練習 10**：用提示的動詞完成下列各句。

1. *do*　　　Pierre always _____*does*_____ his homework.

2. *do*　　　We always _____*do*_____ our homework.

3. *have*　　Yoko and Kunio _____ their books.

4. *have*　　Ali _____ a car.

5. *go*　　　Bill _____ to school every day.

6. *go*　　　My friends often _____ to the beach.

7. *do*　　　Anna seldom _____ her homework.

8. *do*　　　We _____ exercises in class every day.

9. *go, go*　Roberto _____ downtown every weekend. He and his wife

　　　　　_____ shopping.

10. *have*　　Jessica _____ a snack every night around ten.

拼法	發音	
(a) rub → *rubs* ride → *rides* smile → *smiles* dream → *dreams* run → *runs* wear → *wears* drive → *drives* see → *sees* snow → *snows*	rub/z/ ride/z/ smile/z/ dream/z/ run/z/ wear/z/ drive/z/ see/z/ snow/z/	第三人稱單數的現在簡單式動詞，通常字尾只加 *-s*，如 (a) 和 (b)。 (a) 組中：動詞字尾是有聲子音，**-s**發音為 /**z**/。
(b) drink → *drinks* sleep → *sleeps* write → *writes* laugh → *laughs*	drink/s/ sleep/s/ write/s/ laugh/s/	(b) 組中：動詞字尾是無聲子音，**-s**發音為 /**s**/。
(c) push → *pushes* teach → *teaches* kiss → *kisses* fix → *fixes*	push/əz/ teach/əz/ kiss/əz/ fix/əz/	動詞字尾： -sh, -ch, -ss, -x 拼法： 加 -es 發音： /**əz**/
(d) cry → *cries* study → *studies*	cry/z/ study/z/	動詞字尾： 子音 + -y 拼法： 把 y 改成 i，然後加 **-es**
(e) pay → *pays* buy → *buys*	pay/z/ buy/z/	動詞字尾： 母音 + -y 拼法： 加 **-s**
(f) have → **has** go → **goes** do → **does**	/hæz/ /gowz/ /dəz/	*have, go* 和 *do* 的第三人稱單數為不規則變化。

■ **練習 11** — 口語練習（閤上書本）：用提示的動詞說出每日的活動。

例：
教　師：eat
學生A：I eat breakfast every morning.
教　師：What does (...) do every morning?
學生B：He/She eats breakfast.

教　師：eat
學生A：I always eat dinner at the student cafeteria.
教　師：What does (...) always do?
學生B：He/She always eats dinner at the student cafeteria.

1. eat	6. study	11. listen to
2. go	7. get up	12. wash
3. drink	8. watch	13. put on
4. brush	9. speak	14. carry
5. have	10. do	15. kiss

■ **練習 12 — 口語練習（闔上書本）：** 將自己早上的習慣說給同學聽。（可以參照你列在練習 1 的內容。）然後由同學將你早上的日常習慣寫成摘要。

提示：
學生A：告訴學生 B 十五項你每天早上所做的事。
學生B：邊聽學生 A 敘述，邊做筆記。（稍後用這些筆記寫一段摘要，描述學生 A 早上的日常習慣。）

然後角色互換。
學生B：告訴學生 A 十五項你每天早上所做的事。
學生A：邊聽學生 B 敘述，邊做筆記。

當你們敘述完後，都要各別寫一篇描述對方早上日常活動的摘要。要特別注意動詞字尾的 -s / -es。

■ **練習 13：** 將括弧內的字改成現在簡單式以完成下列各句。請特別注意單、複數、拼法，和字尾 -s / -es 的發音。

1. The students *(ask, often)* _____ *often ask* _____ questions in class.

2. Pablo *(study, usually)* _____ at the library every evening.

3. Olga *(bite)* _____ her fingernails when she is nervous.

4. Don *(cash)* _____ a check at the bank once a week.

5. Sometimes I *(worry)* _____ about my grades at school.

   Sonya *(worry, never)* _____ about her grades.

   She *(study)* _____ hard.

6. Ms. Jones and Mr. Anderson *(teach)* _____ at the local high

   school. Ms. Jones *(teach)* _____ math.

7. Birds *(fly)* _____. They *(have)* _____ wings.

8. A bird *(fly)* _____. It *(have)* _____ wings.

9. Jason *(do, always)* _____ his homework. He

   (go, never) _____ to bed until his homework is finished.

10. Mr. Cook *(say, always)* _____ hello to his neighbor in the morning.

11. Ms. Chu *(pay, always)* _____ attention in class.

She *(answer)* _____ questions. She *(listen)*

_____ to the teacher. She *(ask)* _____ questions.

12. Sam *(enjoy)* _____ cooking. He *(try, often)* _____

to make new recipes. He *(like)* _____ to have company for dinner.

He *(invite)* _____ me to dinner once a month. When I arrive, I *(go)*

_____ to the kitchen and *(watch)* _____ him

cook. He *(have, usually)* _____ three or four

pots on the stove. He *(watch)* _____ the pots carefully. He *(make)*

_____ a big mess in the kitchen when he cooks. After dinner, he

(wash, always) _____ all the dishes and *(clean)*

_____ the kitchen. I *(cook, never)* _____.

It *(be)* _____ too much trouble. But my friend Sam *(love)*

_____ to cook.

(a)	**I**	***do not***	drink coffee.	否定句：	*I*	
	We	***do not***	drink coffee.		*we*	+ *do not* + 主要動詞
	You	***do not***	drink coffee.		*you*	
	They	***do not***	drink coffee.		*they*	
(b)	**She**	***does not***	drink coffee.		*she*	
	He	***does not***	drink coffee.		*he*	+ *does not* + 主要動詞
	It	***does not***	drink coffee.		*it*	

	do 和 *does* 稱為助動詞 *(helping verbs)*。
	注意 (b) 中：第三人稱單數的主要動詞字尾不加 -s；字尾的 -s 變為 *does* 的一部分。 誤： *She does not drinks coffee.*
(c) I ***don't*** drink tea. They ***don't*** have a car. (d) He ***doesn't*** drink tea. Mary ***doesn't*** have a car.	縮寫形式： *do not* = *don't* 　　　　　 *does not* = *doesn't* 口語中經常用縮寫形式。 書寫中也常用縮寫形式。

■ **練習 14**：用提示的字造否定句。

1. *like, not*　Ingrid _____*doesn't like*_____ tea.

2. *like, not*　I ____*don't like*____ tea.

3. *know, not*　Mary and Jim are strangers. Mary _____ Jim.

4. *need, not*　It's a nice day today. You _____ your umbrella.

5. *snow, not*　It _____ in Bangkok in the winter.

6. *speak, not*　I _____ French.

7. *be, not*　I _____ hungry.

8. *live, not*　Butterflies _____ long.

9. *have, not*　A butterfly _____ a long life.

10. *be, not*　A butterfly _____ large.

11. *be, not*　Butterflies _____ large.

12. *have, not*　We _____ class every day.

13. *have, not*   This city _____ nice weather in the summer.

14. *be, not*   It _____ cold today.

15. *rain, not*   It _____ every day.

■ **練習 15**：用括弧內的字，以現在簡單式完成下列各句。

1. Alex *(like)* _____*likes*_____ tea, but he *(like, not)* _____*doesn't like*_____ coffee.

2. Sara *(know)* _____ Ali, but she *(know, not)* _____
   _____ Hiroshi.

3. Pablo and Maria *(want)* _____ to stay home tonight. They *(want, not)*
   _____ to go to a movie.

4. Robert *(be, not)* _____ hungry. He *(want, not)* _____
   _____ a sandwich.

5. Mr. Smith *(drink, not)* _____ coffee, but Mr. Jones
   (drink) _____ twelve cups every day.

6. I *(be, not)* _____ rich. I *(have, not)* _____
   a lot of money.

7. This pen *(belong, not)* _____ to me. It *(belong)*
   _____ to Pierre.

8. My friends *(live, not)* _____ in the dorm. They *(have)*
   _____ an apartment.

9. It *(be)* _____ a nice day today. It *(be, not)* _____ cold. You
   (need, not) _____ your coat.

10. Today *(be)* _____ a holiday. We *(have, not)* _____
    class today.

carry	go	smoke
do	shave	speak
drink	make	
eat	put on	

1. Bob _____ *doesn't go* _____ to school every day.

2. My roommates are from Japan. They _____ Spanish.

3. Fred has a beard. He _____ in the morning.

4. Sue has a briefcase. She _____ a bookbag to class.

5. We _____ to class on Sunday.

6. Sally takes care of her health. She _____ cigarettes.

7. Jane and Alex always have lunch at home. They _____ at the cafeteria.

8. Sometimes I _____ my homework in the evening. I watch TV instead.

9. Jack is a careful writer. He _____ mistakes in spelling when he writes.

10. My sister likes tea, but she _____ coffee.

11. I'm lazy. I _____ exercises in the morning.

12. Sometimes Ann _____ her shoes when she goes outside. She likes to walk barefoot in the grass.

口語練習（闔上書本）：將句子改爲否定句。

教　師：eat breakfast every day
學生A：I don't eat breakfast every day.
教　師：Tell me about (Student A).
學生B：She / He doesn't eat breakfast every day.

1. walk to school every day
2. shave every day
3. read a newspaper every day
4. go shopping every day
5. study grammar every day
6. watch TV every day
7. write a letter every day
8. go dancing every day
9. drink coffee every day
10. eat lunch every day
11. listen to music every day
12. come to class every day

■ **練習 18 —** 口語練習：用提示的字說出符合事實的句子。

1. Grass \ be blue. → *Grass isn't blue.*
2. Grass \ be green. → *Grass is green.*
3. Dogs \ have tails. → *Dogs have tails.*
4. People★ \ have tails. → *People don't have tails.*
5. A restaurant \ sell shoes.
6. A restaurant \ serve food.
7. People \ wear clothes.
8. Animals \ wear clothes.
9. A child \ need love, food, care, and toys.
10. A child \ need a driver's license.
11. Refrigerators \ be hot inside.
12. Refrigerators \ be cold inside.
13. Electricity \ be visible.
14. Light \ be visible.
15. Fresh vegetables \ be good for you.
16. Junk food★★ \ be good for you.
17. Cats \ have whiskers.
18. Birds \ have whiskers.
19. An architect \ design buildings.
20. Doctors \ design buildings.
21. Doctors \ take care of sick people.
22. A bus \ carry people from one place to another.
23. The weather \ be very hot today.
24. It \ be very cold today.
25. Glass \ break.
26. Rubber \ be flexible.
27. Rubber \ break.
28. English \ be an easy language to learn.
29. People in this city \ be friendly.
30. It \ rain a lot in this city.
31. Apples \ have seeds.
32. Scientists \ have all the answers to the mysteries of the universe.

★ *People* 是個複數名詞，須用複數動詞。
★★ 垃圾食品 *(Junk food)* 是指含有大量脂肪或糖份，但營養價值低的食物。

DO / DOES + 主詞　+　　主要動詞	現在簡單式的問句型態
(a) **Do**　　　**you**　　　**like**　　coffee?	*Do I* *Do you* *Do we*　　+主要動詞（原形） *Do they*
(b) **Does**　　**Bob**　　**like**　　coffee?	*Does she* *Does he*　　+主要動詞（原形） *Does it*
	注意 (b) 中：疑問句中的主要動詞字尾不加 *-s*。 字尾的 *-s* 變爲 *does* 的一部份。 誤：　*Does Bob likes coffee?*
(c) **Are you** a student? (d) 誤：　*Do you be a student?*	主要動詞是 *be* 動詞形式時，不須用 *do*。 有關 *be* 動詞在問句中的型態，請參閱表 1-9。

疑問句	簡答 + （完整回答）	現在簡單式的 *yes / no* 問句可用 *do,*
(e) *Do* you *like* tea?　→	Yes, I **do**.　(I *like* tea.) No, I **don't**.　(I *don't like* tea.)	*don't, does, doesn't* 作簡答。
(f) *Does* Bob *like* tea?　→	Yes, he **does**.　(He *likes* tea.) No, he **doesn't**.　(He *doesn't like* tea.)	

■ **練習 19**：用括弧內的提示造疑問句並做簡答。

1. A: ___Do you like tea?___

    B: ___Yes, I do.___ (I like tea.)

2. A: ___Do you like coffee?___

    B: ___No, I don't.___ (I don't like coffee.)

3. A: _____

    B: _____ (I don't speak Japanese.)

4. A: _____

    B: _____ (Ann speaks French.)

5. A: _____

    B: _____ (Ann and Tom don't speak Arabic.)

6. A: _____

    B: _____ (I do exercises every morning.)

7. A: _____

    B: _____ (I don't have a Spanish-English dictionary.)

8. A: _____

    B: _____ (Sue has a cold.)

9. A: _____

    B: _____ (The teacher comes to class every day.)

10. A: _____

    B: _____ (Jim and Sue don't do their homework every day.)

11. A: _____

    B: _____ (It rains a lot in April.)

12. A: _____

    B: _____ (My parents live in Baghdad.)

■ **練習 20 ─ 口語練習（闔上書本）**：練習發問和回答問題。

教師： walk to school every day
學生A： Do you walk to school every day?
學生B： Yes, I do.　或：No, I don't.
學生A： Does *(Student B)* walk to school every day?
學生C： Yes, he / she does.　或：No, he / she doesn't.

1. walk to school every day
2. watch TV every day
3. eat breakfast every day
4. speak English every day
5. come to class every day
6. get up at seven o'clock every day
7. talk on the phone every day
8. go to the bank every day

9. wear blue jeans every day
10. have a car
11. have a bicycle
12. like ice cream
13. like *(name of city)*
14. live in *(name of a hotel)*
15. live in an apartment
16. go shopping every day

■ **練習 21**：用班上同學的名字造疑問句，並作簡答。

1. A: ____*Does (Carlos) speak English?*_____

    B: ____*Yes, he does.*____ (He speaks English.)

2. A: _____Does (Yoko) speak Spanish?_____

   B: _____No, she doesn't._____ (She doesn't speak Spanish.)

3. A: _____Is (Ali) in class today?_____

   B: _____No, he isn't._____ (He isn't in class today.)

4. A: _____

   B: _____ (He comes to class every day.)

5. A: _____

   B: _____ (They're in class today.)

6. A: _____

   B: _____ (She sits in the same seat every day.)

7. A: _____

   B: _____ (He has a mustache.)

8. A: _____

   B: _____ (She doesn't have a bicycle.)

9. A: _____

   B: _____ (He's wearing blue jeans today.)

10. A: _____

    B: _____ (He wears blue jeans every day.)

11. A: _____

    B: _____ (They aren't from Indonesia.)

12: A: _____

    B: _____ (They don't have dictionaries on their desks.)

13. A: _____

    B: _____ (She's writing in her book right now.)

14. A: _____

    B: _____ (She studies hard.)

15. A: _____

    B: _____ (They speak English.)

(WHERE) + DO / DOES+ 主詞 + 主要動詞					簡答
(a)	**Do**	they	**live**	in Tokyo? →	**Yes**, they do. / **No**, they don't.
(b) **Where**	**do**	they	**live?**	→	**In Tokyo.**
(c)	**Does**	Gina	**live**	in Rome? →	**Yes**, she does. / **No**, she doesn't.
(d) **Where**	**does**	Gina	**live?**	→	**In Rome.**

注意：(a) 句和 (c) 句稱爲是非問句 (yes / no question)，這種問句可以用 yes 或 no 回答。(b) 句和 (d) 句稱爲訊息問句 (information question)，回答中要提供訊息。where 用來詢問有關地方的訊息。

注意：例句中yes / no question 和 information question 的型態是相同的：
DO / DOES + 主詞 + 主要動詞

■ **練習 22**：造疑問句。

1. A: _____*Does Jean eat lunch at the cafeteria every day?*_____
   B: Yes, she does. (Jean eats lunch at the cafeteria every day.)

2. A: _____*Where does Jean eat lunch every day?*_____
   B: At the cafeteria. (Jean eats lunch at the cafeteria every day.)

3. A: _____
   B: At the post office. (Peter works at the post office.)

4. A: _____
   B: Yes, he does. (Peter works at the post office.)

5. A: _____
   B: Yes, I do. (I live in an apartment.)

6. A: _____
   B: In an apartment. (I live in an apartment.)

7. A: _____
   B: At a restaurant. (Bill eats dinner at a restaurant every day.)

8. A: _____
   B: In the front row. (I sit in the front row during class.)

9. A: _____
   B: At the University of Wisconsin. (Jessica goes to school at the University of Wisconsin.)

10. A: _____
    B: On my desk. (My book is on my desk.)

11. A: _____

    B: To class. (I go to class every morning.)

12. A: _____

    B: In class. (The students are in class right now.)

13. A: _____

    B: In Australia. (Kangaroos live in Australia.)

■ **練習 23 — 口語練習（闔上書本）：**用 where 向同學發問。

    例：   live

    學生A： Where do you live?

    學生B： （自由作答）

1. live	9. go after class
2. eat lunch every day	10. eat dinner
3. sit during class	11. be *(name of a student in this room)*
4. study at night	12. be *(names of two students)*
5. go to school	13. be *(name of a country or city)*
6. buy school supplies	14. be *(names of two countries or cities)*
7. buy your groceries	15. be *(something a student owns)*
8. go on weekends	16. be *(some things a student owns)*

2-12 現在簡單式：用 WHEN 和 WHAT TIME 造訊息問句

疑問詞	+	DOES / DO+ 主詞	+	主要動詞			簡答
(a) **When**	do	you	go	to class?	→		*At nine o'clock.*
(b) **What time**	do	you	go	to class?	→		*At nine o'clock.*
(c) **When**	does	Anna	eat	dinner?	→		*At six P.M.*
(d) **What time**	does	Anna	eat	dinner?	→		*At six P.M.*
(e) What time *do you **usually*** go to class?			疑問句中頻率副詞 *usually* 要緊接在主詞之後。 疑問詞 + DOES / DO + 主詞 + USUALLY + 主要動詞				

■ **練習 24**：造疑問句。

1. A: _____*When / What time do you eat breakfast?*_____
   B: At 7:30 (I eat breakfast at 7:30 in the morning.)

2. A: _____*When / What time do you usually eat breakfast?*_____
   B: At 7:00. (Alex usually eats breakfast at 7:00.)

    3. A: _____
   B: At 6:45. (I get up at 6:45.)

4. A: _____
   B: At 6:30. (Maria usually gets up at 6:30.)

    5. A: _____
   B: At 8:15. (The movie starts at 8:15.)

6. A: _____
   B: Around 11:00. (I usually go to bed around 11:00.)

    7. A: _____
   B: At half-past twelve. (I usually eat lunch at half-past twelve.)

8. A: _____
   B: At 5:30. (The restaurant opens at 5:30.)

    9. A: _____
   B: At 9:05. (The train leaves at 9:05.)

10. A: _____
   B: Between 6:30 and 8:00. (I usually eat dinner between 6:30 and 8:00.)

11. A: _____

    B: At 10:00 P.M. (The library closes at 10:00 P.M. on Saturday.)

12. A: _____

    B: At a quarter past eight. (My classes begin at a quarter past eight.)

■ **練習 25 — 口語練習（闔上書本）：**用 when 和 what time 向同學發問。

例： eat breakfast

學生A： When / What time do you eat breakfast?

學生B： （自由作答）

1. get up
2. usually get up
3. eat breakfast
4. leave home in the morning
5. usually get to class
6. eat lunch
7. go back home
8. get home
9. have dinner
10. usually study in the evening
11. go to bed

2-13 摘要：以 BE 動詞和 DO 造訊息問句

疑問詞	+ BE 動詞	+ 主詞		完整回答
(a) Where	*is*	Thailand?	→	Thailand *is* in Southeast Asia.
(b) Where	*are*	your books?	→	My books *are* on my desk.
(c) When	*is*	the concert?	→	The concert *is* on April 3rd.
(d) What	*is*	your name?	→	My name *is* Yoko.
(e) What time	*is*	it?	→	It *is* ten-thirty.

疑問詞	+ DO	+ 主詞	+ 主要動詞		完整回答
(f) Where	*do*	you	*live?*	→	I *live* in Los Angeles.
(g) What time	*does*	the plane	*arrive?*	→	The plane *arrives* at six-fifteen.
(h) What	*do*	monkeys	*eat?*	→	Monkeys *eat* fruit, plants, and insects.
(k) When	*does*	Bob	*study?*	→	Bob *studies* in the evenings.

注意：問句中的 be 動詞是主要且唯一的動詞時，主詞置於 be 動詞之後。現在簡單式中用的是 be 動詞以外的動詞時，主詞置於 do / does 和主要動詞之間。

■ **練習 26**：用 is, are, does 或 do 完成下列對話中的問句。

對話一

(1) A: What time _____ the movie start?

(2) B: Seven-fifteen. _____ you want to go with us?

(3) A: Yes. What time _____ it now?

(4) B: Almost seven o'clock. _____ you ready to leave?
    A: Yes, let's go.

對話二

(5) A: Where _____ my keys to the car?

(6) B: I don't know. Where _____ you usually keep them?
    A: In my purse. But they're not there.
    B: Are you sure?

(7) A: Yes. _____ you see them?

(8) B: No. _____ they in one of your pockets?
    A: I don't think so.

(9) B: _____ your husband have them?
    A: No. He has his own set of car keys.
    B: Well, I hope you find them.
    A: Thanks.

對話三

(10) A: _____ you go to school?
     B: Yes.

(11) A: _____ your brother go to school too?
     B: No. He quit school last semester. He has a job now.

(12) A: _____ it a good job?

B: Not really.

(13) A: Where _____ he work?

B: At a restaurant. He washes dishes.

(14) A: _____ he live with you?

B: No, he lives with my parents.

(15) A: _____ your parents unhappy that he quit school?

B: They're very unhappy about it.

(16) A: _____ they want him to return to school?

B: Of course. They don't want him to be a dishwasher for the rest of his life. They have many dreams for him and his future.

■ **練習 27**：用適當問句完成以下對話。

1. A: ___*What time does the concert begin?*___
   B: At eight. (The concert begins at eight.)

2. A: ___*Is San Francisco foggy in the winter?*___
   B: Yes, it is. (San Francisco is foggy in the winter.)

3. A: _____
   B: In May. (The weather starts to get hot in May.)

4. A: _____
   B: Yes. (I dream in color.)

5. A: _____
   B: Yes. (Igor comes from Russia.)

6. A: _____
   B: Russia. (Olga comes from Russia.)

7. A: _____
   B: Yes, he is. (Ivan is from Russia.)

8. A: _____
   B: In Moscow. (Red Square is in Moscow.)

9. A: _____
   B: Yes. (Birds sleep.)

   A: _____
   B: In trees and bushes or in their nests. (They sleep in trees and bushes or in their nests.)

藍鯨（Blue whale）

10. A: _____
    B: The blue whale. (The biggest animal on earth is the blue whale.)

11. A: _____
    B: No, they aren't. (Whales aren't fish.)

    A: _____
    B: Yes, they are. (They are mammals.)

    A: _____
    B: Yes, they do. (They breathe air.)

12. A: _____
    B: No, it isn't. (A seahorse isn't a mammal.)

13. A: _____
    B: A very small fish that looks a little like a horse.
       (A seahorse is a very small fish that looks
       a little like a horse.)

海馬（Seahorse）

14. A: _____
    B: Yes. (A starfish has a mouth.)

    A: _____
    B: In the middle of its underside. (It is in the middle of its underside.)

    A: _____
    B: Clams, oysters, and shrimp. (A starfish eats clams, oysters, and shrimp.)

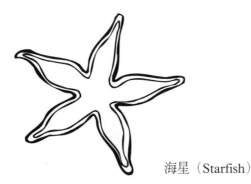

海星（Starfish）

1. A: Do _____?
   B: No, I don't.

2. A: Where are _____?
   B: I don't know.

3. A: What time does _____?

   B: _____

4. A: When do _____?

   B: _____

5. A: Is _____?

   B: _____

6. A: What is _____?

   B: _____

7. A: Are _____?

   B: _____

8. A: What are _____?

   B: _____

9. A: What do _____?

   B: _____

10. A: What does _____?

    B: _____

■ **練習 29 — 口語練習／書寫練習**：詢問某人（朋友、室友、同學等）的日常行程。然後將詢問所得資料寫成一篇作文。

問題提示：

What do you do every morning?
What do you do every afternoon?
What do you do every evening?

What time do you . . . ?
When do you . . . ?
Where do you . . . ?

2-14 用 IT 談論時間

疑問句	回答	
(a) What day is it?	*It's* Monday.	英文中，人們用 *it* 表示（談論）時間。
(b) What month is it?	*It's* September.	
(c) What year is it?	*It's* _____.	有關星期、月份和數詞的說法，見書後附錄 2 和附錄 3。
(d) What's the date today?	*It's* September 15th.	
	It's the 15th of September.	有關時間的說法，見附錄 4。
(e) What time is it?	*It's* 9:00.★	
	It's nine.	
	It's nine o'clock.	
	It's nine (o'clock) A.M.	

★美式英文在時和分之間使用冒號：9:00A.M.。 英式英文則用一個點：9.00A.M.。

■ **練習 30**：用 what 造疑問句。

1. A: ___*What day is it?*___
   B: It's Tuesday.

2. A: _____
   B: It's March 14th.

3. A: _____
   B: Ten-thirty.

4. A: _____
   B: March.

5. A: _____
   B: It's six-fifteen.

6. A: _____
   B: The 1st of April.

7. A: _____
   B: Wednesday.

8. A: _____
   B: July 3rd.

9. A: _____
   B: It's 6:05.

10. A: _____
    B: It's 10:55.

2-15 表示時間的介系詞

at	(a) We have class **at** one o'clock. (b) I have an appointment with the doctor **at** 3:00. (c) We sleep **at** night.	*at* + 某一特定的時間 *at* + *night*（晚上）
in	(d) My birthday is **in** October. (e) I was born **in** 1960. (f) We have class **in** the morning. (g) Bob has class **in** the afternoon. (h) I study **in** the evening.	*in* + 特定的月份 *in* + 特定的年份 *in* + *the morning*（早上） *in* + *the afternoon*（下午） *in* + *the evening*（傍晚以後時間）
on	(i) I have class **on** Monday. (j) I was born **on** October 31, 1975.	*on* + 星期中的某一天 *on* + 特定的日期
from ... to	(k) We have class **from** 1:00 **to** 2:00.	*from*（某一特定時間） *to*（某一特定時間）

■ **練習 31**：用時間介詞完成下列句子。

1. We have class _____*at*_____ ten o'clock.

2. We have class _____ ten _____ eleven.

3. I have class _____ the morning.

4. I work _____ the afternoon.

5. I study _____ the evening.

6. I sleep _____ night.

7. I was born _____ May.

8. I was born _____ 1979.

9. I was born _____ May 25.

10. I was born _____ May 25, 1979.

11. The post office isn't open _____ Sunday.

12. The post office is open _____ 8:00 A.M. _____ 5:00 P.M. Monday.

13. The post office closes _____ 5:00 P.M.

■ **練習 32**：用時間介詞完成下列句子。

1. Jane has an appointment with the dentist _____ ten-thirty.

2. We go to class _____ the morning.

3. The bank is open _____ Friday, but it isn't open _____ Saturday.

4. My birthday is _____ February.

5. I was born _____ February 14, 1973.

6. I watch television _____ the evening.

7. I go to bed _____ night.

8. The bank is open _____ 9:00 A.M. _____ 4:00 P.M.

9. I was in high school _____ 1988.

10. Our classes begin _____ January 10.

11. I study at the library _____ the afternoon.

12. We have a vacation _____ August.

2-16 用 IT 談論天氣

(a) *It's* sunny today. (b) *It's* hot and humid today. (c) *It's* a nice day today.	英文中，人們通常用 *it* 談論天氣。
(d) *What's the weather like* in Istanbul in January? (e) *How's the weather* in Moscow in the summer?	詢問天氣時，人們通常會說：*What's the weather like?* 或 *How's the weather?*

■ **練習 33 — 口語練習**：今天天氣如何？用以下的字談論今天的天氣。

例： hot
答： It's hot today.　或：It isn't / It's not hot today.

1. hot	7. cloudy	13. gloomy
2. warm	8. partly cloudy	14. humid
3. cool	9. clear	15. muggy
4. chilly	10. nice	16. stormy
5. cold	11. windy	17. freezing
6. sunny	12. foggy	18. below freezing

■ **練習 34 — 口語練習**：將華氏溫度改成攝氏溫度，並填上適當的形容詞。

┌─────────────────────────────────────┐
│   38° C   0° C   │
│   24° C   -18°C   │
│ ✔ 10° C   │
└─────────────────────────────────────┘

FARENHEIT	CELSIUS	DESCRIPTION
1. 50°F	_10°C_	_cool, chilly_
2. 32°F	_____	_____
3. 100°F	_____	_____
4. 75°F	_____	_____
5. 0°F	_____	_____

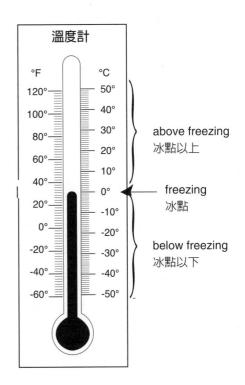

溫度計

above freezing
冰點以上

freezing
冰點

below freezing
冰點以下

■ **練習 35**：以下是將一溫度系統轉為另一溫度系統時，快速獲得近似度數的方法。★

┌──┐
│ • 攝氏轉為華氏：將攝氏度數乘以二再加 30。   │
│   │
│   例：   12°C x 2 = 24 + 30 = 54°F. （精確度數： 12°C = 53.6°F.） │
│   20°C x 2 = 40 + 30 = 70°F. （精確度數： 20°C = 68°F.）   │
│   35°C x 2 = 70 + 30 = 100°F. （精確度數： 35°C = 95°F.）   │
│   │
│ • 華氏轉為攝氏：將華氏度數減 30 後再除以二。   │
│   │
│   例：   60°F - 30 = 30 ÷ 2 = 15°C. （精確度數： 60°F = 15.6°C.） │
│   80°F - 30 = 50 ÷ 2 = 25°C. （精確度數： 80°F = 26.7°C.） │
│   90°F - 30 = 60 ÷ 2 = 30°C. （精確度數： 90°F = 32.2°C.） │
└──┘

將以下溫度分別由攝氏轉為華氏，以及由華氏轉為攝氏。算出近似度數。

1. 22°C → _22°C = 約為 74°F (22°C x 2 = 44 + 30 = 74°F)_
2. 2°C   6. 45°F
3. 30°C   7. 70°F
4. 10°C   8. 58°F
5. 16°C   9. 100°F

───────────
★要算出精確度數，請用以下公式：攝氏度數 =5 / 9 (°F-32)或
　　　　　　　　　　　　　　　華氏度數 =9 / 5 (℃) + 32。

ABDUL AND PABLO

S (lives = live + /z/)

(1) My friend Abdul live▲ in an apartment near school.   (2) He walk to school almost every day.   (3) Sometimes he catch a bus, especially if it's cold and rainy outside.   (4) Abdul share the apartment with Pablo.   (5) Pablo come from Venezuela. (6) Abdul and Pablo go to the same school.   (7) They take English classes.   (8) Abdul speak Arabic as his first language, and Pablo speak Spanish.   (9) They communicate in English.   (10) Sometimes Abdul try to teach Pablo to speak a little Arabic, and Pablo give Abdul Spanish lessons.   (11) They laugh a lot during the Arabic and Spanish lessons.   (12) Abdul enjoy having Pablo as his roommate, but he miss his family back in Saudi Arabia.

SNAKES

(13) Snakes eat all sorts of things.   (14) Eggs are a favorite food of many snakes. (15) When a snake eat an egg, the snake first curl around the egg. (16) It don't want the egg to roll away.   (17) Then the snake open its mouth and move the egg into its throat. (18) It squeeze the egg with muscles in its neck.   (19) The egg break and go into the snake's stomach.   (20) Then the snake spit out the eggshell. (21) Snakes love to eat eggs.

■ 練習 37 — 複習：用括弧內的字完成下列句子。使用現在簡單式的動詞。

1. *(Anita, go)* _____Does Anita go_____ to her uncle's house every day?

2. *(monkeys, eat)* _____ insects?

3. A: I usually *(remember, not)* _____ my dreams.

   (you, remember) _____ your dreams?

B: Sometimes. I often *(write)* _____ my dreams down as soon as I wake up. I *(like)* _____ to think about my dreams. I *(try)* _____ to understand them.

4. I *(understand, not)* _____ my brother. He *(have, not)* _____ a job or a place to live. He *(sleep)* _____ at his friends' apartments. He *(take, not)* _____ _____care of himself. I *(worry)* _____ about him all the time.

5. Ocean waves *(be)* _____ interesting. In an ocean wave, water *(move)* _____ up and down, but the water *(move, not)* _____ _____ forward. This movement *(be)* _____ the same as the movement you can see in a rope. If you shake one end of a rope, waves *(run)* _____ along the rope, but the rope *(move, not)* _____ _____ forward. The water in an ocean wave *(move)* _____ forward only when a wave *(reach)* _____ land. Then an ocean wave *(carry)* _____ sand and other things forward when it *(hit)* _____ a sandy beach.

6. A: *(you, study)* _____ a lot?

B: I *(study)* _____ at least three hours every night. My roommate *(study)* _____ at least five hours. She's very serious about her education. How about you? *(you, spend)* _____ a lot of time studying?

A: No, I don't. I (spend) _____ as little time as possible. I

(like, not) _____ to study.

B: Then why (you, be) _____ a student?

A: My parents (want) _____ me to go to school. I (want, not)

_____ to be here.

B: In that case, I (think) _____ that you should drop out of school

and find a job until you figure out what you want to do with your life.

7. I (have) _____ two roommates. One of them, Sam, is always neat

and clean. He (wash) _____ his clothes once a week. (you, know)

_____ Matt, my other roommate? He (be) _____

the opposite of Sam. For example, Matt (change, not) _____ the

sheets on his bed. He (keep) _____ the same sheets week after

week. He (wash, never) _____ his clothes.

He (wear) _____ the same dirty jeans every day. Sam's side of the

room (be, always) _____ neat, and Matt's side

(be, always) _____ a mess. As my mother

(say, always) _____ , it (take) _____ all kinds of

people to make a world.

1. A: _____
   B: No, I don't.

2. A: _____
   B: Yes, I am.

3. A: _____
   B: In an apartment.

4. A: _____
   B: Six-thirty.

5. A: _____
   B: Monday.

6. A: _____
   B: At home.

7. A: _____
   B: No, he doesn't.

8. A: _____
   B: No, she isn't.

9. A: _____
   B: South of the United States.

10. A: _____
    B: Yes, it is.

11. A: _____
    B: Yes, they do.

12. A: _____
    B: In Southeast Asia.

13. A: _____
    B: Hot in the summer.

14. A: _____
    B: September.

15. A: _____
    B: Yes, I do.

lives

1. Yoko ~~live~~ in Japan.

2. Ann comes usually to class on time.

3. Peter watch TV every evening.

4. Anita carry a briefcase to work every day.

5. She enjoy her job.

6. I no know Joe.

7. Mike don't like milk. He never drink it.

8. Tina doesn't speaks Chinese. She speakes Spanish.

9. Do you are a student?

10. Does your roommate sleeps with the window open?

11. A: Do you like strong coffee?

    B: Yes, I like.

12. Where your parents live?

13. What time is your English class begins?

14. Olga isn't need a car. She have a bicycle.

15. Do Pablo does his homework every day?

■ 練習 40 — 複習：選擇正確答案，完成下列句子。

1. Alex _____ know French.
   A. isn't   B. doesn't   C. don't

2. _____ Alex speak Russian?
   A. Is   B. Does   C. Do

3. _____ Alex from Canada?
   A. Is   B. Does   C. Do

4. When _____ you usually study?
   A. are   B. does   C. do

5. Anita _____ a job.
   A. no have   B. no has   C. doesn't have

6. Omar _____ his new car every Saturday.
   A. wash   B. washs   C. washes

7. Where does Tina _____ to school?
   A. go   B. goes   C. to go

8. Fumiko _____ English at this school.
   A. study   B. studies   C. studys

9. Fumiko and Omar _____ students at this school.
   A. is   B. are   C. be

10. They _____ speak the same language.
    A. aren't   B. doesn't   C. don't

■ 練習 41 — 複習：自由發揮，完成下列對話。

1. A: Do you _____?

   B: Yes, I do. How about you? Do you _____?

   A: _____.

2. A: _____ don't _____.
   B: I know.

3. A: _____ doesn't _____.

   B: Really? Does _____?
   A: I don't know.

4. A: Where is _____?
   B: At home.

   A: Where does _____?
   B: On Fifth Avenue.

5. A: _____?
   B: Yes, I do.

   A: _____?
   B: No, he doesn't.

   A: _____?
   B: Yes, I am.

   A: _____?
   B: No, he isn't.

6. A: Do you like _____?

   B: Yes, of course I _____. Everybody _____.

7. A: What _____ snakes?

   B: They _____ long, thin animals. They _____ have legs.

   A: _____ snakes reptiles?

   B: Yes, they _____.

   A: _____ snakes eat eggs?

   B: Yes, they _____.

8. A: _____ you usually _____ in the morning?

   B: _____.

   A: When _____?

   B: _____.

■ **練習 42 — 複習：**兩人一組，依下列步驟練習。

1. 學生A：說出五項學生 B 的身體特徵（例如，描述頭髮顏色、眼睛顏色、直髮或捲髮、眼鏡等）。
   學生B：對學生 A 的描述表示同意或不同意。

   例：
   學生A： You have dark hair.
   學生B： （點頭表示同意）
   學生A： You have black eyes.
   學生B： No, I have brown eyes.
   學生A： You have dark brown eyes.
   學生B： Okay. That's right.
   學生A： You wear glasses.
   學生B： Yes.
   依此類推，然後角色互換，換學生 B 描述學生 A 的外貌。

2. 學生A：問學生 B 五個有關其所擁有和沒有的物品（例如，車子、電腦、寵物、小孩等）。
   學生B：回答問題。

   例：
   學生A： Do you have a car?
   學生B： No.
   學生A： Do you have a computer.
   學生B： Yes, but it's not here. It's in my country.
   依此類推，然後角色互換。

3. 學生A：問學生 B 五個有關其喜好的問題（例如，食物和飲料的種類、音樂、電影、書籍等）。
   學生B：回答問題。

   例：
   學生A： Do you like pizza?
   學生B： Yes.
   學生A： Do you like the music of（歌手或合唱團名）?
   學生B： No, I don't.
   依此類推，然後角色互換。

4. 寫一篇描述他人的文章。內容包括其身體特徵、喜好及擁有或沒有什麼。

■ **練習 43 — 複習**：詢問同學家鄉的資料，並根據資料寫一份記錄。詢問有關下列的問題：家鄉的名稱，
位置，人口數，天氣以及某一月份的平均氣溫等。

例：
學生A： What's your hometown?
學生B： Athens.
學生A： Where is it located?
學生B： In southwestern Greece on the Aegean Sea.
學生A： What's the population of Athens?
學生B： 3,507,000.
學生A： What's the weather like in Athens in May?
學生B： It's mild. Sometimes it's a little rainy.
學生A： What's the average temperature in May?
學生B： The average temperature is around 8° Celsius.

同學家鄉資料的記錄表

人名	Sypros			
家鄉	Athens			
位置	SW Greece on Aegean Sea			
人口	almost 4 million			
氣候	mild in May (around 8°C, in the mid-forties Fahrenheit)			

第三章
現在式的表達（第二部份）

3-1 BE 動詞 + ING：現在進行式

am	+	*-ing*	(a) I *am sitting* in class right now.
is	+	*-ing*	(b) Rita *is sitting* in class right now.
are	+	*-ing*	(c) You *are sitting* in class right now.

(a) 句中：說這句話時，我在課堂上；我正坐著，不是站著。「坐著」這個動作正在發生的同時我說出這句話。

am, is, are = 助動詞
sitting = 主動詞

am, is, are + *-ing* = 現在進行式

■ **練習 1 — 口語練習（闔上書本）**：用 am / is / are + wearing 練習現在進行式的用法

第一部份：你和同學今天的穿著為何？依實狀回答問題。

例：
教師：Rosa, what are you wearing today?
學生：I'm wearing a white blouse and a blue skirt.
教師：What is Jin Won wearing?
學生：He's wearing blue jeans and a sweat shirt.
教師：What color is his sweat shirt?
學生：It's gray with red letters.
教師：What else is Jin Won wearing?
學生：He's wearing sneakers, white socks, and a wristwatch. Etc.

第二部份：先說出某一特定衣著或飾物，要學生辨識並說出穿戴此衣物的人。

例： a (blue) shirt
答： Marco is wearing a blue shirt.

例： (blue) shirts
答： Marco and Abdul are wearing blue shirts.

提示：

1. (gold) earrings
2. blue jeans
3. a blouse

4. a (red) blouse
5. (gray) slacks
6. (brown) boots

7. a (black) belt
8. a necklace
9. running shoes

■ 練習 2 — 口語練習：說出以下這些動物正在做什麼？

例： Smile.
教　師：(Student A), please smile. What are you doing?
學生A：I'm smiling.
教　師：(Student A) and (Student B), please smile. (Student A), what are you and (Student B) doing?
學生A：We're smiling.
教　師：(Student C), what are (Student A and Student B) doing?
學生C：They're smiling.
教　師：(Student A), please smile. (Student B), what is (Student A) doing?
學生B：He / She is smiling.

1. Stand in the middle of the room.
2. Sit in the middle of the room.
3. Stand in the back of the room.
4. Smile.
5. Stand between (. . .) and (. . .).
6. Touch the floor.
7. Touch the ceiling.
8. Touch your toes.
9. Open / Close the door / window.
10. Close / Open the door / window.
11. Shake hands with (. . .).
12. Smile at (. . .).
13. Stand up and turn around in a circle.
14. Hold your book above your head.
15. Hold up your right hand.
16. Hold up your left hand.
17. Touch your right ear with your left hand.
18. Stand up.
19. Sit down.
20. Clap your hands.

■ **練習 4 — 口語練習（闔上書本）：** 描述教師和同學正在做什麼，以練習現在進行式。（表演者應持續動作，直至口語描述結束。）

例： drink
教師： （教師作喝水狀） What am I doing?
學生： You're drinking.

例： drive
教　師：(Student A), drive. Pretend to drive.
學生A：（學生作駕駛狀）
教　師：What are you doing?
學生A：I'm driving.
教　師：What is (. . .) doing?
學生B：He / She's driving.

1. eat
2. read
3. sleep
4. write
5. walk
6. run
7. fly
8. smile
9. laugh
10. cry
11. dance
12. wave
13. push
14. pull
15. clap
16. kick
17. count
18. stand in back of (. . .)
19. touch (. . .)
20. shake hands with (. . .)
21. sit on the floor

3-2 動詞字尾加 -ING 的拼法

	動詞字尾 → -ING 型態		
規則 1：	一個子音字母★ + -e	→	去 -e，加 -ing
	sm*ile*	→	sm*iling*
	wr*ite*	→	wr*iting*
規則 2：	一個母音字母★ + 一個子音字母	→	重複子音字母，加 -ing★★
	s*it*	→	s*itting*
	r*un*	→	r*unning*
規則 3：	兩個母音字母 + 一個子音字母	→	加 -ing；不要重複子音字母
	r*ead*	→	r*eading*
	r*ain*	→	r*aining*
規則 4：	兩個子音字母	→	加 -ing；不要重複子音字母
	st*and*	→	st*anding*
	pu*sh*	→	pu*shing*

★ 母音字母 = a, e, i, o, u.
　子音字母 = b, c, d, f, g, h, j, k, l, m, n, p, q, r, s, t, v, w, x, y, z.
★★ 規則 2 的例外：w, x 和 y 字母不必重複。
snow → *snowing*　　*fix* → *fixing*　　*say* → *saying*

■ **練習 5**：寫出下列動詞的 -ing 型態。

1. stand ___standing___
2. smile _____
3. run _____
4. rain _____
5. sleep _____
6. stop _____
7. write _____
8. eat _____
9. count _____
10. wear ___wearing___

11. ride _____
12. cut _____
13. dance _____
14. put _____
15. sneeze _____
16. plan _____
17. snow _____
18. fix _____
19. say _____
20. cry _____

1. dream _____   6. hit _____

2. come _____   7. hurt _____

3. look _____   8. clap _____

4. take _____   9. keep _____

5. bite _____   10. camp _____

11. shine _____   16. pay _____

12. win _____   17. study _____

13. join _____   18. get _____

14. sign _____   19. wait _____

15. fly _____   20. write _____

■ **練習 7 — 口語練習**：練習用現在進行式描述動作。

學生A： 根據指示做出動作。維持該動作直至學生 B 完成描述。
學生B： 用現在進行式描述學生 A 的動作。

例： erase the board
學生A：（學生 A 持續擦黑板的動作。）
學生B：（…）他／她正在擦黑板。

1. erase the board   10. bite your finger
2. draw a picture on the board   11. hit your desk
3. sneeze   12. drop your pen
4. cough   13. tear a piece of paper
5. wave at your friends   14. break a piece of chalk
6. sign your name on the board   15. fall down
7. clap your hands   16. sing, hum, or whistle
8. walk around the room   17. sleep
9. count your fingers   18. snore

| 19. chew gum | 21. hold your grammar book between your feet |
| 20. *(two students)* throw and catch *(something in the room)* | 22. carry your book on the top of your head to the front of the room |

■ **練習 8 — 口語練習（闔上書本）**：練習 -ing 的拼法。教師表演動作，學生將動作描寫下來。

例： wave
教師： （作揮手狀並問：what am I doing?）
學生書寫： *waving*

1. smile
2. cry
3. laugh
4. sit
5. stand
6. sleep
7. clap
8. write
9. eat
10. run
11. sing
12. read
13. drink
14. sneeze
15. fly
16. cut (a piece of paper)

3-3 現在進行式：疑問句

疑問句				簡答 + （完整回答）
(a)	BE 動詞 + 主詞 + -ING			
	Is Mary *sleeping*			→ Yes, *she is*. (She's sleeping.) → No, *she's not*. (She's not sleeping.) → No, *she isn't*. (She isn't sleeping.)
(b)	*Are* you *watching* TV?			→ Yes, *I am*. (I'm watching TV.) → No, *I'm not*. (I'm not watching TV.)
	疑問詞 + BE 動詞 + 主詞 + -ING			
(a) *Where*	*is*	Mary	*sleeping*?	→ *On the sofa.* (She's sleeping on the sofa.)
(b) *Why*	*are*	you	*watching* TV?	→ *Because I like this program.* (I'm watching TV because I like this program.)

■ **練習 9**：根據提示造疑問句，並回答問題。

1. A: What ___*are you writing?*___
   B: A letter. (I'm writing a letter.)

2. A: ___*Is Ali reading a book?*___
   B: No, ___*he isn't/he's not.*___ (Ali isn't reading a book.)

3. A: _____

   B: Yes, _____ (Anna is eating lunch.)

4. A: Where _____
   B: At the Red Bird Cafe.   (She's eating lunch at the Red Bird Cafe.)

5. A: _____

   B: No, _____ (Mike isn't drinking a cup of coffee.)

6. A: What _____
   B: A cup of tea.   (He's drinking a cup of tea.)

7. A: _____

   B: No, _____. (The girls aren't playing in the street.)

8. A: Where _____
   B: In the park.   (They're playing in the park.)

9. A: Why _____
   B: Because they don't have school today.   (They're playing in the park because they don't have school today.)

10. A: Hi, kids. _____

   B: No, _____. (We aren't drawing pictures with our
      crayons.)

   A: Oh? Then what _____

   B: Maps to our secret place in the woods. (We're drawing maps to our secret place
      in the woods.)

   A: Why _____
      Because we have a buried treasure at our secret place in the woods. (We're
      drawing maps because we have a buried treasure at our secret place in the
      woods.)

■ **練習 10 — 口語練習（闔上書本）**：用現在進行式練習 yes / no 問句。教師先發給學生紙張，上面
　　　　　　　　　　　　　　　　　寫有 86 頁練習 4 之指示。

   學生A： 依自己紙上的指示表演。
   學生B： 用現在進行式問學生 A 或另一位同學一個 yes / no 問句。

   例： 　　drive （寫於紙上）
   學生A： （學生 A 作駕駛狀。）
   學生B： Are you driving?
   學生A： Yes, I am.
   或
   學生B： (Student C), is (Student A) driving?
   學生C： Yes, he / she is.

■ **練習 11**：用 where, why 和 what 造疑問句。

   1. A: _____*What are you writing?*_____
      B: A letter. (I'm writing a letter.)

   2. A: _____
      B: Because I'm happy. (I'm smiling because I'm happy.)

3. A: _____
   B: My grammar book. (I'm reading my grammar book.)

4. A: _____
   B: Because we're doing an exercise. (I'm reading my grammar book because we're doing an exercise.)

5. A: _____
   B: In the back of the room. (Roberto is sitting in the back of the room.)

6. A: _____
   B: Downtown. (I'm going downtown.)

7. A: _____
   B: Because I need to buy some shoes. (I'm going downtown because I need to buy some shoes.)

8. A: _____
   B: Blue jeans and a sweatshirt. (Akihiko is wearing blue jeans and a sweatshirt today.)

3-4 現在簡單式和現在進行式的比較

直述句： （a）I **sit** in class *every day*. （b）I **am sitting** in class *right now*. （c）The teacher **writes** on the board *every day*. （d）The teacher **is writing** on the board *right now*.	• 現在簡單式用來表達習慣或平常的活動，如 (a), (c) 和 (e)。 • 現在進行式用來表達說話者說話當時正在發生的動作，如 (b), (d) 和 (f)。
疑問句： （e）**Do** you **sit** in class every day? （f）**Are** you **sitting** in class right now? （g）**Does** the teacher **write** on the board every day? （h）**Is** the teacher **writing** on the board right now?	• 現在簡單式的疑問句中，用 *do* 和 *does* 作爲助動詞。 • 現在進行式的疑問句中，用 *am, is* 和 *are* 作爲助動詞。
否定句： （i）I **don't sit** in class every day. （j）I**'m not sitting** in class right now. （k）The teacher **doesn't write** on the board every day. （l）The teacher **isn't writing** on the board right now.	• 現在簡單式的否定句中，用 *do* 和 *does* 作爲助動詞。 • 現在進行式的否定句中，用 *am, is* 和 *are* 作爲助動詞。

1. I *(walk)* _____walk_____ to school every day. I *(take, not)*

    _____don't take_____ the bus.

2. I *(read)* _____ the newspaper every day. I *(read, not)*

    _____ my grammar book every day.

3. A: What *(you, read)* _____ right now?

    B: I *(read)* _____ my grammar book.

4. Robert *(cook)* _____ his own dinner every evening.

5. Right now Robert is in his kitchen. He *(cook)* _____ rice and beans for dinner.

6. Robert is a vegetarian. He *(eat, not)* _____ meat.

7. *(you, cook)* _____ your own dinner every day?

8. A: *(you, want)* _____ your coat?
    B: Yes.

    A: *(be, this)* _____ your coat?

    B: No, my coat *(hang)* _____ in the closet.

9. A: *(Tom, have)* _____ a black hat?
    B: Yes.

    A: *(he, wear)* _____ it every day?
    B: No.

    A: *(he, wear)* _____ it right now?

    B: I *(know, not)* _____. Why do you care about Tom's hat?

    A: I found a hat in my apartment. Someone left it there. I *(think)*

    _____ that it belongs to Tom.

10. Ahmed *(talk)* _____ to his classmates every day in class. Right now he

    (talk) _____ to Yoko.

11. Yoko and Ahmed *(sit)* _____ next to each other in class every day, so they

    often *(help)* _____ each other with their grammar exercises. Right now

    Yoko *(help)* _____ Ahmed with an exercise on present verb tenses.

12. It *(rain)* _____ a lot in this city, but it *(rain, not)*

_____ right now.   The sun *(shine)*

_____. *(it, rain)* _____ a lot
in your hometown?

13. A: Hello?
    B: Hello. This is Mike. Is Tony there?
    A: Yes, but he can't come to the phone right now. He *(eat)*

    _____ dinner. Can he call you back in about ten minutes?
    B: Sure. Thanks. Bye.
    A: Bye.

14. Tony's family *(eat)* _____ dinner at the same time every day. During

dinner time, Tony's mother *(let, not)* _____ the children talk
on the phone.

15. A: What are you doing? *(you, work)* _____ on
    your English paper?

    B: No, I *(study, not)* _____. I *(write)*

    _____ a letter to my sister.

    A: *(you, write)* _____ to her often?

    B: I *(write, not)* _____ a lot of letters to anyone.

    A: *(she, write)* _____ to you often?

    B: Yes. I *(get)* _____ a letter from her about once a week. *(you, write)*

    _____ a lot of letters?

    A: Yes. I *(like)* _____ to write letters.

16. Olga Burns is a pilot for an airline company in Alaska. She *(fly)* _____

almost every day. Today she *(fly)* _____ from Juno to Anchorage.

17. A: Where *(the teacher, stand, usually)* _____
    every day?

    B: She usually *(stand)* _____ in the front of the room every day.

    A: Where *(she, stand)* _____ today?

    B: She *(stand)* _____ in the middle of the room.

18. A: Excuse me. *(you, wait)* _____ for the downtown bus?

B: Yes, I *(be)* _____. Can I help you?

A: Yes. What time *(the bus, stop)* _____ here?
B: Ten thirty-five.

19. A: *(animals, dream)* _____?

B: I don't know. I suppose so. Animals *(be, not)* _____ very different from human beings in lots of ways.

A: Look at my dog. She *(sleep)* _____. Her eyes *(be)*

_____ closed. At the same time, she *(yip)* _____

and *(move)* _____ her head and her front legs. I *(be)*

_____ sure that she

(dream) _____

right now. I'm sure that

animals *(dream)*

_____.

YIP, ZZZ, YIP, ZZZ, YIP, YIP, ZZZ, YIP.

3-5　非動作動詞不用於現在進行式

(a) I'm hungry *right now*. *I want* an apple. （誤：*I am wanting an apple.*）	有些動詞不可使用於現在進行式。它們稱爲非動作動詞（*nonaction verbs*）。(a) 句中：*want* 是一個非動作動詞。*want* 表示身體或情緒上的需要，而不是一個動作。(b) 句中：*hear* 也是非動作動詞。*hear* 表示一種感官的經驗，而不是一個動作。
(b) I *hear* a siren. *Do* you *hear* it too? （誤：*I'm hearing a siren. Are you hearing it too?*）	

非動作動詞

want	*hear*	*understand*
need	*see*	*know*
like	*smell*	*believe*
love	*taste*	*think*（意指 *believe*）★
hate		

★*think* 有時可用於進行式。請參閱討論 *think about* 和 *think that* 的表 3-10。

1. Alice is in her room right now. She *(read)* _____*is reading*_____ a book.

   She *(like)* _____*likes*_____ the book.

2. It *(snow)* _____ right now. It's beautiful! I *(like)*

   _____ this weather.

3. I *(know)* _____ Jessica Jones. She's in my class.

4. The teacher *(talk)* _____ to us right now. I *(understand)*

   _____ everything she's saying.

5. Don is at a restaurant right now. He *(eat)* _____ dinner. He

   (like) _____ the food. It *(taste)* _____ good.

6. (Sniff-sniff). I *(smell)* _____ gas. *(you, smell)*

   _____ it too?

7. Jason *(tell)* _____ us a story right now. I *(believe)*

   _____ his story. I *(think)* _____ that his story is true.

8. Ugh! That cigar *(smell)* _____ terrible.

9. Look at the picture. Jane *(sit)* _____ in a

   chair. A cat *(sit)* _____ on her lap.

   Jane *(hate)* _____ the cat.

10. Look at the picture. Mr. Allen *(hold)*

    _____ a cat. He *(love)*

    _____ the cat. The cat *(lick)*

    _____ Mr. Allen's face.

3-6 SEE, LOOK AT, WATCH, HEAR 和 LISTEN TO 的用法

SEE, LOOK AT 和 WATCH (a) I **see** many things in this room.	(a) 句中：看見 *see* = 非動作動詞。眼睛睜開就看得見。看見是一種生理的反應，而非有計畫的動作。
(b) I'**m looking at** the clock. I want to know the time.	(b) 句中：注視 *look at* = 動作動詞。注視是一種有計畫或故意的動作，是爲了某種理由才注視。
(c) Bob **is watching** TV.	(c) 句中：觀看 *watch* = 動作動詞。*watch* 是長時間的動作，*look at* 是短時間的動作。
HEAR 和 LISTEN TO (d) I'm in my apartment. I'm trying to study. I **hear** music from the next apartment. The music is loud.	(d) 句中：聽見 *hear* = 非動作動詞。聽見是非計畫的動作，它表示一種生理的反應。
(e) I'm in my apartment. I'm studying. I have a tape recorder. I'**m listening to** music. I like to listen to music when I study.	(e) 句中：傾聽 *listen (to)* = 動作動詞。是爲了某一目的才傾聽。

■ **練習 14 — 口語練習**：回答下列問題。

1. What do you see in this room?
   Now look at something. What are you looking at?

2. Turn to page 85 of this book. What do you see?
   Now look at one thing on that page. What are you looking at?

3. Look at the floor. What do you see?

4. Look at the chalkboard. What do you see?

5. What programs do you like to watch on TV?

6. What sports do you like to watch?

7. What animals do you like to watch when you go to the zoo?

8. What do you hear right now?

9. What do you hear when you walk down the street?

10. What do you hear at night in the place where you live?

11. What do you listen to when you go to a concert?

12. What do you listen to when you go to a language laboratory?

3-7 NEED 和 WANT + 名詞或不定詞

		動詞 + 名詞	need 比 want 強烈。need 表示需求非常強烈。
(a)	We	*need* *food*.	
(b)	I	*want* *a sandwich*.	need 和 want 後面加名詞或不定詞。
		動詞 + 不定詞	
(c)	We	*need* *to eat*.	不定詞 = to + 原形動詞。★
(d)	I	*want* *to eat* a sandwich.	

★原形動詞 = 字尾不加 -s, -ed 或 -ing 的動詞。
　原形動詞的例子：*come, help, answer, write*
　不定詞的例子：*to come, to help, to answer, to write*

■ **練習 15**：用框內的字以不定詞 to + 動詞的型態完成下列句子。

buy	*do*	*listen to*	*play*	*walk*
call	*get*	*marry*	*take*	*wash*
cash	*go*	*pay*	*talk to*	*watch*

1. Anna is sleepy. She wants _____*to go*_____ to bed.

2. I want _____ downtown today because I need

   _____ a new coat.

3. Mike wants _____ TV. There's a good program on Channel 5.

4. Do you want _____ soccer with us at the park this afternoon?

5. I need _____ Jennifer on the phone.

6. I want _____ to the bank because I need _____ a check.

7. James doesn't want _____ his homework tonight.

8. My clothes are dirty. I need _____ them.

9. John loves Mary. He wants _____ her.

10. David's desk is full of overdue bills. He needs _____ his bills.

11. It's a nice day. I don't want _____ the bus home today. I want

    _____ home instead.

12. Do you want _____ some music on the radio?

13. Helen needs _____ an English course.

14. Where do you want _____ for lunch?

1. A: *(go \ you \ want)* _____Do you want to go_____ downtown this afternoon?

   B: Yes, I do. *(I \ buy \ need)* _____I need to buy_____ a winter coat.

2. A: Where *(you \ go \ want)* _____ for dinner tonight?
   B: Rossini's Restaurant.

3. A: What time *(be \ need \ you)* _____ at the airport?
   B: Around six. My plane leaves at seven.

4. A: *(want not \ Jean \ go)* _____ to the baseball game.
   B: Why not?
   A: Because *(she \ need \ study)* _____ for a test.

5. A: I'm getting tired. *(take \ I \ want)* _____ a break for a few minutes.
   B: Okay. Let's take a break. We can finish the work later.

6. A: *(go back \ Peter \ want)* _____ to his apartment.
   B: Why?
   A: Because *(he \ want \ change)* _____ his clothes before he goes to the party.

7. A: *(come \ we \ need not)* _____ to class on Friday.
   B: Why not?
   A: It's a holiday.

8. A: Where *(you \ go \ want)* _____ for your vacation?
   B: *(I \ want \ visit)* _____ Niagara Falls, New York City, and Washington, D.C.

9. A: May I see your dictionary? *(I \ look up \ need)* _____ a word.
   B: Of course. Here it is.
   A: Thanks.

10. A: *(come \ want \ you)* _____ with us to the park?
    B: Sure. Thanks. *(I \ get \ need)* _____ some exercise.

3-8 WOULD LIKE 的用法

(a)	I'm thirsty. I **want** a glass of water.	(a) 和 (b) 意思相同，但 *would like* 較 *want* 有禮貌。*I would like* 是表達 *I want* 較得體的方式。
(b)	I'm thirsty. I **would like** a glass of water.	
(c)	**I would like** **You would like** **She would like** **He would like** **We would like** **They would like** } a glass of water.	注意 (c) 中： *would* 字尾不加 -s。 *like* 字尾也不加 -s。
(d)	縮寫形式 **I'd** = **I would** **you'd** = **you would** **she'd** = **she would** **he'd** = **he would** **we'd** = **we would** **they'd** = **they would**	口語中，*would* 通常縮寫成 *'d*。 書寫中，也時常會使用 *would* 和代名詞的縮寫。
(e)	WOULD LIKE + 不定詞 I **would like** **to eat** a sandwich.	注意 (e) 中：*would like* 之後可接不定詞。
(f)	WOULD + 主詞 + LIKE **Would** you **like** some tea?	疑問句中，*would* 要置於主詞之前。
(g)	Yes, I **would**. (I would like some tea.)	簡答 *would like* 的疑問句時，可單獨使用 *would* 一字。

■ **練習 17 ─ 口語練習**：用 would like 改寫下列各句，並且討論口語中 would 縮寫的用法。★

1. Tony wants a cup of coffee.
   → *Tony would like a cup of coffee.*
2. He wants some sugar in his coffee.
3. Ahmed and Anita want some coffee, too.
4. They want some sugar in their coffee, too.
5. A: Do you want a cup of coffee?
   B: Yes, I do. Thank you.
6. I want to thank you for your kindness and hospitality.
7. My friends want to thank you, too.
8. A: Does Robert want to ride with us?
   B: Yes, he does.

───────────

★日常說話中，*would* 幾乎總是和代名詞縮寫在一起。*I'd like to go* 和 *I like to go* 之間的差別有時很難聽得出來。此外，*would* 在說話中也經常和名詞縮寫在一起（但書寫中則否）。*My friends'd like to come with us* 和 *My friends like to come with us* 之間是有差別的，但有時候很難聽得出其差別。

1. Who's hungry right now? (. . .), are you hungry? What would you like?
2. Who's thirsty? (. . .), are you thirsty? What would you like?
3. Who's sleepy? What would you like to do?
4. What would you like to do this weekend?
5. What would you like to do after class today?
6. What would you like to have for dinner tonight?
7. What countries would you like to visit?
8. What cities would you like to visit in *(the United States, Canada, etc.)*?
9. What languages would you like to learn?
10. You listened to your classmates. What would they like to do? Do you remember what they said?
11. Pretend that you are a host at a party at your home and your classmates are your guests. Ask them what they would like.
12. Think of something fun to do tonight or this weekend. Using *would you like,* invite a classmate to join you.

3-9　WOULD LIKE 和 LIKE 的比較

(a)　I ***would like to go*** to the zoo. (b)　I ***like to go*** to the zoo.	(a) 句中：*I would like to go to the zoo.* 表示我想去動物園 "*I want to go to the zoo.*"。 (b) 句中：*I like to go to the zoo.* 表示我喜歡動物園 "*I enjoy the zoo.*" *would like* 表示我現在或未來想做某事。 *like* 表示我始終、通常或經常喜歡某事物。

■ 練習 19 — 口語練習：回答下列問題。

1. Do you like to go to the zoo?
2. Would you like to go to the zoo with me this afternoon?
3. Do you like apples?
4. Would you like an apple right now?
5. Do you like dogs?
6. Would you like to have a dog as a pet?
7. What do you like to do when you have free time?
8. What do you need to do this evening?
9. What would you like to do this evening?
10. What would you like to do in class tomorrow?

■ 練習 20：用自己的話完成下列句子。

1. I need to _____ every day.

2. I want to _____ today.

3. I like to _____ every day.

4. I would like to _____ today.

5. I don't like to _____ every day.

6. I don't want to _____ today.

7. Do you like to _____?

8. Would you like to _____?

9. I need to _____ and

   _____ today.

10. _____ would you like to _____ this evening?

3-10 THINK ABOUT 和 THINK THAT 的用法

		THINK + ABOUT + 名詞	(a) 句中:我心裡每天都想到家人。
(a)	I	*think* *about* *my family* every day.	(b) 句中:我的頭腦正忙碌著。現在我腦中正想著文法。
(b)	I *am* *thinking* *about* *grammar* right now.		

		THINK + THAT + 敘述句	(c) 句中:依我之見,*Sue* 是懶惰的。我認為 *Sue* 很懶惰。
(c)	I	*think* *that* *Sue is lazy.*	表達自己的想法時,用 *think that*。
(d)	Sue	*thinks* *that* *I am lazy.*	*think about* 常用於現在進行式。
(e)	I	*think* *that* *the weather is nice.*	*think that* 則幾乎不曾用於現在進行式。 誤:*I am thinking that Sue is lazy.*

(f) I *think that* Mike is a nice person. (g) I *think* Mike is a nice person.	(f) 句和 (g) 句意義相同。 說話時經常會省略 *think* 後面的 *that*。

■ **練習 21**:用 I think (that) 表達自己的意見。

1. English grammar is easy / hard / fun / interesting.

   I think (that) English grammar is . . .

2. People in this city are friendly / unfriendly / kind / cold.

   _____

3. The food at *(name of a place)* is delicious / terrible / good / excellent / awful.

   _____

4. Baseball is interesting / boring / confusing / etc.

   _____

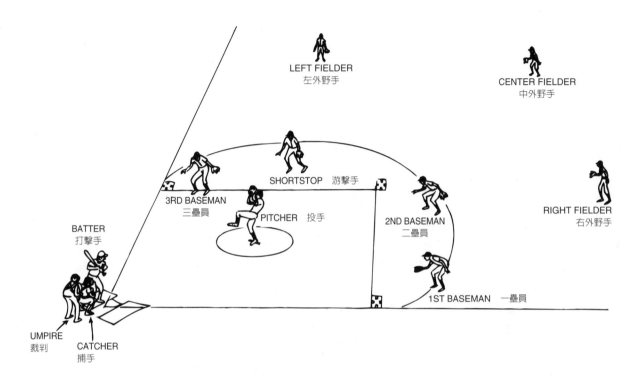

■ **練習 22**：完成下列句子。

1. I think that the weather today is _____

2. I think my classmates are _____

3. Right now I'm thinking about _____

4. In my opinion, English grammar is _____

5. In my opinion, soccer is _____

6. I think that my parents are _____

7. I think this school _____

8. I think about _____

9. I think that _____

10. In my opinion, _____

■ **練習 23 — 口語練習**：針對以下主題陳述自己意見。

　　例： books
　　答： I think that *War and Peace* is an excellent novel.
　　　　In my opinion, *War and Peace* is an excellent novel.

　　1. this city　　　　　　　4. movies
　　2. your English classes　5. food
　　3. music　　　　　　　　6. a current local, national, or international news story

■ **練習 24 — 複習**：用括弧內的字完成下列句子。使用現在簡單式或過去進行式；必要時，用不定詞。

the baby	= Bobby
the daughter	= Ellen
the son	= Paul
the mother	= Mrs. Smith
the father	= Mr. Smith
the cat	= Pussycat
the bird	= Tweetie
the mouse	= Mickey

(1)　　　　The Smiths are at home. It is evening. Paul *(sit)* _____ on

(2)　the sofa. He *(read)* _____ a newspaper. Ellen *(sit)*

(3)　_____ at the desk. She *(study)* _____.

(4)　While she is studying, she *(listen to)* _____ music on her

(5)　radio. Paul *(hear)* _____ the music, but he *(listen to, not)* _____

(6)　_____ it right now. He *(concentrate)* _____

(7)　on the weather report in the newspaper. He *(think about)* _____

(8)　_____ the weather report.

(9)　　　　Ellen *(study)* _____ her chemistry text. She *(like)*

(10)　_____ chemistry. She *(think)* _____ that chemistry is easy.

(11) She (think about) _____ chemical formulas. She

(12) (understand) _____ the formulas. She (like) _____

(13) her chemistry course, but she (like, not) _____ her history course.

(14)   Mrs. Smith is in the kitchen. She (cook) _____ dinner.

(15) She (cut) _____ up vegetables for a salad. Steam (rise)

(16) _____ from the pot on the stove. Mrs. Smith (like, not)

(17) _____ to cook, but she (know) _____ that her family

(18) has to eat good food. While she (make) _____ dinner, Mrs. Smith

(19) (think about) _____ a vacation on the beach. Sometimes

(20) Mrs. Smith (get) _____ tired of cooking all the time, but she (love)

(21) _____ her family very much and (want) _____ to take care

(22) of their health. Her husband (know, not) _____ how to cook.

(23)   Mr. Smith (stand) _____ near the front door. He (take, off)

(24) _____ his coat. Under his coat, he (wear) _____

(25) _____ a suit. Mr. Smith is happy to be home. He (think about)

(26) _____ dinner. After dinner, he (want)

(27) _____ (watch) _____ television. He (need)

(28) _____ (go) _____ to bed early tonight because he has a busy

(29) day at work tomorrow.

(30)   In the corner of the living room, a mouse (eat) _____ a piece

(31) of cheese. The mouse thinks that the cheese (taste) _____ good.

(32) Pussycat (see, not) _____ the mouse. She (smell, not)

(33) _____ the mouse. Pussycat (sleep) _____ .

(34) She (dream about) _____ a mouse.

(35)   Bobby is in the middle of the living room. He (play) _____

(36) with a toy train. He (see, not) _____ the mouse because he

(37) (look at) _____ his toy train. The bird, Tweetie, (sing)

(38) _____ . Bobby (listen to, not) _____

(39) _____ the bird. Bobby is busy with his toy train. But Mrs.

(40) Smith can hear the bird. She *(like)* _____ *(listen to)*

(41) _____ Tweetie sing.

3-11 THERE + BE 動詞

THERE + BE 動詞 + 主詞 + 地方
（a）***There***   ***is***   ***a bird***   in the tree.
 	
（b）***There***   ***are***   ***four birds***   in the tree.
	There + be 動詞，用來表示某物存在於某一特定地點。
	注意：主詞置於 *be* 動詞之後：
	    there + is + 單數名詞
	    there + are + 複數名詞

（c）***There's*** a bird in the tree.
 	
（d）***There're*** four birds in the tree.
	縮寫形式：
	    there + is = there's
	    there + are = there're

■ **練習 25**：用 is 或 are 完成下列句子。

1. There _____*is*_____ a grammar book on Ahmed's desk.

2. There _____*are*_____ many grammar books in this room.

3. There _____ two pens on Pierre's desk.

4. There _____ a pen on my desk.

5. There _____ thirty-one days in July.

6. There _____ only one student from Singapore in our class.

7. There _____ three students from Argentina.

8. There _____ ten sentences in this exercise.

9. There _____ a wonderful restaurant on 33rd Avenue.

10. There _____ many problems in the world today.

■ **練習 26 — 口語練習**：用 there is 或 there are 造句。並將指定的片語（詞組）用在句中。

1. a book \ on my desk
   → *There is (There's) a book on my desk.*

2. on Ali's desk \ some books
   → *There are (There're) some books on Ali's desk.*

3. on the wall \ a map

4. some pictures \ on the wall

5. in this room \ three windows

6. fifteen students \ in this room

7. in the refrigerator \ some milk

8. a bus stop \ at the corner of Main Street and 2nd Avenue

9. in Canada \ ten provinces

10. on television tonight \ a good program

■ **練習 27 — 口語練習**：每人在教室的桌子上放一，兩樣東西（例如：硬幣、幾根火柴、筆、字典），然後再以 there is 和 there are 描述桌上物品。

例：
學生A：There are three dictionaries on the table.
學生B：There are some keys on the table.
學生C：There is a pencil sharpener on the table.

■ **練習 28 — 口語練習／書寫練習**：用 there is 和 there are 描述你的教室。

例：I would like to describe this room. There are three windows.
There is a green chalkboard. Etc.

3-12 THERE + BE 動詞：YES / NO 疑問句

疑問句	簡答
BE + THERE + 主詞	
(a) **Is** **there** **any milk** in the refrigerator? →	*Yes, **there is**.* → *No, **there isn't**.*
(b) **Are** **there** **any eggs** in the refrigerator? →	*Yes, **there are**.* → *No, **there aren't**.*

■ 練習 29 — 口語練習：用 Is there...? 或 Are there...? 句型以及下列名詞，詢問同學有關圖中冰箱內物品的問題。

例：
學生A： Is there any milk in the refrigerator?
學生B： Yes, there is.

例：
學生A： Are there any onions in the refrigerator?
學生B： No, there aren't.

1. milk
2. onions
3. cheese
4. butter
5. eggs
6. bread
7. apples
8. potatoes
9. orange juice
10. strawberries
11. oranges
12. fruit
13. meat
14. roses
15. flour

■ 練習 30 — 口語練習：用 there + be 動詞做問答練習。

學生A： 用 Is there...? 或 Are there...? 問同學有關這個城市的問題（課本打開）。
學生B： 回答問題（課本闔上）

例：
學生A： Is there a zoo in （城市名）?
學生B： Yes, there is. 或： No, there isn't. 或： I don't know.

1. a zoo
2. an airport
3. an aquarium
4. any lakes
5. a train station
6. a subway
7. any good restaurants
8. a good (Vietnamese) restaurant
9. a botanical garden
10. any swimming pools
11. an art museum
12. a good public transportation system

■ 練習 31 — 口語練習：用自己的話完成下列句子。

例： There . . . in this building.
答： There are five floors in this building.
There are many classrooms in this building.
There is an elevator in this building. Etc.

1. There . . . in this building.

2. There . . . in this city.

3. There . . . in my country.

4. There . . . in the world.

5. There . . . in the universe.

■ **練習 32 — 口語練習**：用 there is / there are 和一個地方詞語（例如：印度、第一街等），做問答練習。

例： any wild monkeys
學生A：Are there any wild monkeys in New York City?
學生B：No. There aren't any wild monkeys in New York City, but there are monkeys at the Bronx Zoo.

1. any elephants	6. any skyscrapers
2. any high mountains	7. any famous landmarks
3. a movie theater	8. any students from Indonesia
4. a bookstore	9. any red grammar books
5. any apartments for rent	10. an elevator

3-13 THERE + BE 動詞：用 HOW MANY 造疑問句

疑問句	簡答 +（完整回答）
HOW MANY+ 主詞　+　ARE　+ THERE + 地方 (a) ***How many***　***chapters***　***are***　***there***　in this book? → (b) ***How many***　***provinces*** ***are***　***there***　in Canada?　→	Twelve. (There are twelve chapters in this book.) Ten. (There are ten provinces in Canada.)

■ **練習 33 — 口語練習（閣上書本）**：用 how many 向同學提出問題。

例： days in a week
學生A：How many days are there in a week?
學生B：Seven. 或： There are seven days in a week.

1. pages in this book	6. countries in North America
2. chapters in this book	7. continents in the world
3. letters in the English alphabet	8. windows in this room
4. states in the United States	9. floors in this building
5. provinces in Canada	10. people in this room

■ **練習 34 — 口語練習**：兩人一組，互相用 how many 詢問及回答有關教室的問題。

例： desks
學生A：How many desks are there in this room?
學生B：Thirty-two. 或：There are thirty-two desks in this room.
學生A：That's right. 或：No, I count thirty-three desks.

1. windows	4. teachers	7. grammar books
2. doors	5. women	8. dictionaries
3. students	6. men	9. etc.

例：
學生A： Are there any dogs in the picture?
學生B： No, there aren't any dogs in the picture.
學生A： Where are the boots?
學生B： The boots are next to the picnic bench.
學生A： How many trees are there?
學生B： There's only one tree.

■ 練習 36 — 複習：用自己的話完成下列各句。

1. I need . . . because . . . .
2. I want . . . because . . . .
3. I would like . . . .
4. Would you like . . . ?
5. Do you like . . . ?
6. There is . . . .
7. There are . . . .
8. I'm listening to . . . , but I also hear . . . .
9. I'm looking at . . . , but I also see . . . .
10. I'm thinking about . . . .
11. I think that . . . .
12. In my opinion, ...
13. How many . . . are there . . . ?
14. Is there . . . ?

3-14 表示地方的介系詞

(a) My book is **on** my desk.	(a) 句中： on = 介系詞 　　　　my desk = 介系詞的受詞 　　　　on my desk = 介系詞片語
(b) Tom lives **in** the United States. 　　 He lives **in** New York City. (c) He lives **on** Hill Street. (d) He lives **at** 4472 Hill Street.	居處的表示法： in + 國家和城市 　　　　　　　　 on + 街、大道、路等 　　　　　　　　 at + 住址 （in 和 at 的詳細資料，請參閱表 7-17 ）

一些表示位置的介系詞★

above	far (away) from	inside
around	in	near
at	in back of	next to
behind	in the back of	on
below	in front of	on top of
beside	in the front of	outside

★表示地方的介系詞也稱爲地方介詞 (prepositions of place)。

The book is **beside** the cup.
The book is **next to** the cup.
The book is **near** the cup.

The book is **between** two cups.

In picture C, the book is **far away from** the cup.

The cup is **on** the book.
The cup is **on top of** the book.

The cup is **under** the book.

The cup is **above** the book.

A hand is **around** the cup.

H.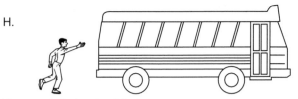

The man is **in back of** the bus.
The man is **behind** the bus.

I.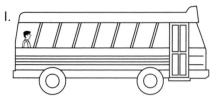

The man is **in the back of** the bus.

J.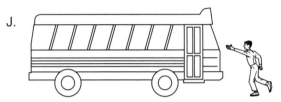

The man is **in front of** the bus.
In H and J, the man is **outside** the bus.

K.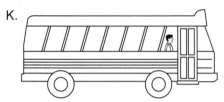

The man is **in the front of** the bus.
In I and K, the man is **inside** the bus.

L.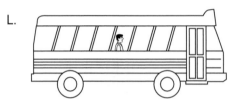

The man is **in the middle of** the bus.

■ **練習 37**：用地方介詞完成句子。答案可能不只一個。

1. The apple is ___*on, on top of*___ the plate.

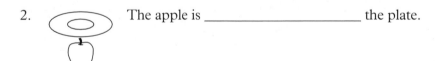

2. The apple is _____ the plate.

3. The apple is _____ the plate.

4. The apple is _____ the glass.

5.

The apple isn't near the glass. It is _____ the glass.

6.  The apple is _____ the glass.

7. 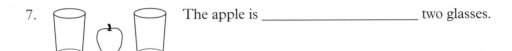 The apple is _____ two glasses.

8.  A hand is _____ the glass.

9.

The dog isn't inside the car. The dog is _____ the car.

10.

The dog is in _____ of the car.

11.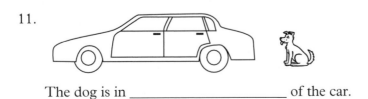

The dog is in _____ of the car.

12.

The dog is in _____ of the car.

13.

The dog is in _____ of the car.

■ **練習 38 — 口語練習**：兩人一組，選用教室內的物品（書、筆、橡皮擦、杯子、你的手等），示範下列介系詞的意義。

例：

學生A：Can you show me the meaning of "under"?

學生B：Yes. The pen is under the book. Now it's your turn to demonstrate the meaning of "under."

學生A：Okay. My hand is under this table.

1. under	7. in the middle of	13. in back of
2. above	8. around	14. in front of
3. next to	9. near	15. in the back of
4. between	10. far (away) from	16. in the front of
5. inside	11. behind	
6. on top of	12. below	

■ **練習 39**：用 in, on 或 at 完成下列句子。

1. Pablo lives _____ Canada.

2. He lives _____ Toronto.

3. He lives _____ Lake Street.

4. He lives _____ 5541 Lake Street _____ Toronto, Canada.

完成下列各句。

5. I live _____. *(name of country)*

6. I live _____. *(name of city)*

7. I live _____. *(name of street)*

8. I live _____. *(address)*

■ **練習 40 ─ 複習**：以下是有關 John 和 Mary 的一些圖片。

MARY   JOHN

A. 字彙表

eat dinner	*a bowl*	*meat*
hold a knife and a fork	*a bowl of salad*	*a piece of meat*
have a steak for dinner	*a candle*	*a plate*
burn	*a cup*	*a restaurant*
	a cup of coffee	*a saucer*
	a fork	*a spoon*
	a glass	*a steak*
	a glass of water	*a table*
	a knife	*a waiter*
	a vase of flowers	

B. 回答問題。

1. What is Mary doing?
2. What do you see on the table?
3. What is Mary holding in her right hand? in her left hand?
4. What is in the bowl?
5. What is on the plate?
6. What is in the cup?
7. What is burning?
8. Is Mary eating breakfast?
9. Is Mary at home? Where is she?
10. What is she cutting?

C. 完成下列句子。

11. Mary is sitting _____ a table.

12. There is a candle _____ the table.

13. There is coffee _____ the cup.

14. Mary _____ holding a knife _____ her right hand.

15. She's _____ a restaurant.

16. She _____ at home.

17. She _____ eating breakfast.

A. 字彙表

> study at the library   the circulation desk
> read a book   a librarian
> take notes   a shelf（單數）
>   shelves （複數）★

B. 回答問題。

1. What is John doing?
2. What do you see in the picture?
3. Is John at home? Where is he?
4. Is John reading a newspaper?
5. Where is the librarian standing?
6. Is John right-handed or left-handed?

C. 完成下列句子。

7. John is studying _____ the library.

8. He is sitting _____ a table.

9. He is sitting _____ a chair.

10. His legs are _____ the table.

11. There are books _____ the shelves.

12. John is writing _____ a piece of paper.

13. He's taking notes _____ a piece of paper.

14. He _____ reading a newspaper.

15. The librarian _____ standing _____ the circulation desk.

16. Another student is sitting _____ John.

★有關名詞的不規則複數形式，請參閱表 4-5。

A. 字彙表

write a check★	*a bank*	*name and address*
sign a check	*cash*	*first name/given name*
sign her name	*a check*	*middle initial*
	the date	*last name/family name/surname*

B. 回答問題。

1. What is Mary doing?
2. What is Mary's address?
3. What is Mary's full name?
4. What is Mary's middle initial?
5. What is Mary's last name?

6. How much money does Mary want?
7. What is in the upper left corner of the check?
8. What is in the lower left corner of the check?
9. What is the name of the bank?

C. 完成下列句子。

10. Mary is writing a _____.

11. She is signing _____ name.

12. The name _____ the bank is First National Bank.

13. Mary lives _____ 3471 Tree Street.

14. Mary lives _____ Chicago, Illinois.

15. Mary's name and address is _____ the upper left corner _____ the check.

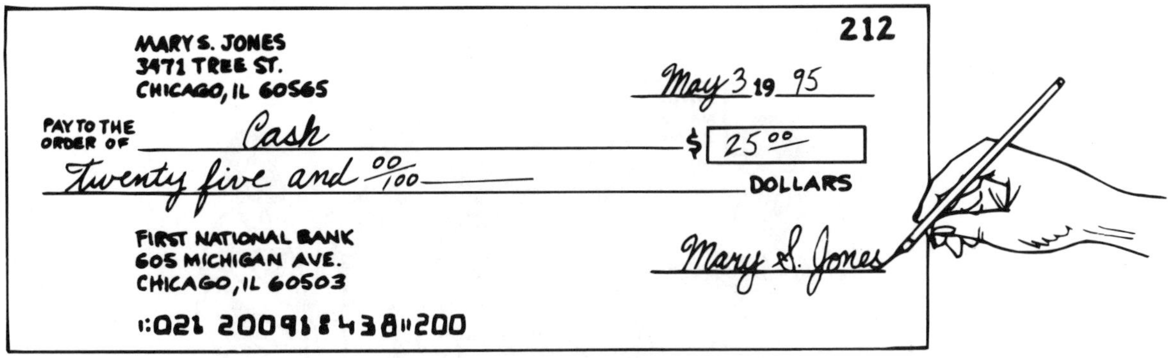

```
                                                      212
    MARY S. JONES
    3471 TREE ST.
    CHICAGO, IL 60565          May 3 19 95

PAY TO THE
ORDER OF        Cash                          $ 25 00
Twenty five and 00/100                          DOLLARS

    FIRST NATIONAL BANK
    605 MICHIGAN AVE.                    Mary S. Jones
    CHICAGO, IL 60503

    �semicolon021 200918438 200
```

★*Check* 是美式英文的拼法，英式英文拼作 *cheque*。兩者發音相同。

A. 字彙表

cash a check	*a bank teller*	*a man*（單數）
stand in line	*a counter*	*men*（複數）★
	a line	*a woman*（單數）
		women（複數）★
		people（複數）★

B. 回答問題。

1. What is Mary doing?
2. Is Mary at a store? Where is she?
3. What do you see in the picture?
4. Who is standing behind Mary, a man or a woman?
5. Who is standing at the end of the line, a man or a woman?

6. How many men are there in the picture?
7. How many women are there in the picture?
8. How may people are there in the picture?
9. How many people are standing in line?

C. 完成下列句子。

10. Mary is _____ a bank.

11. Four people _____ standing in line.

12. Mary is standing _____ the counter.

13. The bank teller is standing _____ the counter.

14. A woman _____ standing _____ Mary.

15. Mary _____ standing _____ the end _____ the line.

16. A man _____ standing _____ the end _____ the line.

17. A businessman _____ standing _____ the woman with the big hat and the young man in jeans.

★有關名詞的不規則複數形式，請參閱表 4-5。

A. 字彙表

cook	*a kitchen*	*bread*
cook dinner	*a list/a grocery list*	*coffee*
make dinner	*a pot*	*an egg*
taste (food)	*a refrigerator*	*butter*
	a stove	*milk*
	a pepper shaker	*pepper*
	a salt shaker	*salt*

B. 回答問題。

1. What is John doing?
2. What do you see in the picture?
3. Where is John?
4. Is John tasting his dinner?
5. Is John a good cook?

6. Where is the refrigerator?
7. What is on the refrigerator?
8. Is the food on the stove hot or cold?
9. Is the food in the refrigerator hot or cold?

C. 完成下列句子。

10. John is making dinner. He's _____ the kitchen.

11. There is a pot _____ the stove.

12. The stove is _____ the refrigerator.

13. There is a grocery list _____ the refrigerator door.

14. A salt shaker and a pepper shaker are _____ the stove.

15. There is hot food _____ top _____ the stove.

16. There is cold food _____ the refrigerator.

A. 字彙表

watch TV / television	*a cat*	*a living room*
sit on a sofa	*a dog*	*a rug*
sing	*a fish*	*a singer*
sleep	*a fishbowl*	*a sofa*
swim	*a floor*	*a TV set / a television set*
	a lamp	

B. 回答問題。

1. What are John and Mary doing?
2. What do you see in the picture?
3. Are Mary and John in a kitchen? Where are they?
4. Where is the lamp?
5. Where is the rug?
6. Where is the dog?
7. Where is the cat?
8. Is the cat walking? What is the cat doing?
9. What is the dog doing?
10. What is on top of the TV set?
11. Is the fish watching TV?
12. What is on the TV screen? What are John and Mary watching?

C. 完成下列句子。

13. John and Mary _____ watching TV.

14. They _____ sitting _____ a sofa.

15. They _____ sleeping.

16. There is a rug _____ the floor.

17. A dog _____ sleeping _____ the rug.

18. A cat _____ sleeping _____ the sofa.

A. 字彙表

talk to (someone)	*an arrow*	*a piece of paper*
talk on the phone	*a calendar*	*a telephone book*
talk to each other	*a heart*	*a wall*
smile	*a phone/a telephone*	
draw a picture	*a picture*	
	a picture of a mountain	

B. 回答問題。

1. What are John and Mary doing?
2. What do you see in the picture?
3. Is John happy? Is Mary happy?
   Are John and Mary smiling?
4. Are they sad?
5. Who is standing? Who is sitting?
6. Is John in his bedroom?
   Where is John?
7. What is Mary drawing?
8. What is on Mary's table?
9. What is on the wall next to the refrigerator?
10. Where is the clock?
11. What time is it?
12. What is on the wall above the table?

C. 完成下列句子。

13. John and Mary _____ talking _____ the phone.

14. John _____ talking _____ Mary. Mary _____ talking

    _____ John. They _____ talking to _____ other.

15. John is _____ the kitchen. He's standing _____ the refrigerator.

16. There is a calendar _____ the wall next to the refrigerator.

17. Mary _____ sitting _____ a table. She's _____ a picture.

18. There is a telephone book _____ the table.

19. There is picture _____ a mountain _____ the table.

A. 字彙表

sleep	*a bed*
dream	*a dream*
dream about (someone / something)	*a head*
	a pillow

B. 回答問題。

1. What is Mary doing?
2. What is John doing?
3. What are Mary and John doing?
4. What do you see in the picture?
5. Is Mary in her bedroom?
6. Is John in class? Where is he?
7. Is John standing or lying down?
8. Is Mary dreaming?
9. Are Mary and John dreaming about each other?
10. Are John and Mary in love?

C. 完成下列句子。

11. John and Mary _____ sleeping. They are _____ bed.

12. John _____ dreaming _____ Mary. Mary _____ dreaming _____ John. They _____ dreaming _____ each other.

13. Mary's head is _____ a pillow.

14. John and Mary _____ in the living room.

15. They _____ asleep. They _____ awake.

16. John and Mary love each other. They are _____ love.

1. I *(sit)* _____ *am sitting* _____ in class right now. I *(sit, always)*

   _____ *always sit* _____ in the same seat every day.

2. Ali *(speak)* _____ Arabic, but right now he *(speak)*

   _____ English.

3. Right now we *(do)* _____ an exercise in class. We *(do)*

   _____ exercises in class every day.

4. I'm in class now. I *(look)* _____ at my classmates. Kim

   (write) _____ in his book. Francisco *(look)*

   _____ out the window. Yoko *(bite)* _____

   her pencil. Abdullah *(smile)* _____. Maria *(sleep)*

   _____. Jung-Po *(chew)* _____ gum.

5. The person on the bench in the picture below is Barbara. She's an accountant. She

   (work) _____ for the government. She *(have)* _____

   an hour for lunch every day. She *(eat, often)* _____ lunch in

   the park. She *(bring, usually)* _____ a sandwich and

   some fruit with her to the park. She *(sit, usually)* _____

   on a bench, but sometimes she *(sit)* _____ on the grass. While she's at the

   park, she *(watch)* _____ people and animals. She *(watch)*

_____ joggers and squirrels. She *(relax)* _____ when she eats at the park.

6. Right now I *(look)* _____ at a picture of Barbara. She *(be, not)* _____ at home in the picture. She *(be)* _____ at the park. She *(sit)* _____ on a bench. She *(eat)* _____ her lunch. Some joggers *(run)* _____ _____ on a patch through the park. A squirrel *(sit)* _____ on the ground in front of Barbara. The squirrel *(eat)* _____ a nut. Barbara *(watch)* _____ _____ the squirrel. She *(watch, always)* _____ _____ squirrels when she eats lunch in the park. Some ducks *(swim)* _____ in the pond in the picture, and some birds *(fly)* _____ in the sky. A police officer *(ride)* _____ a horse. He *(ride)* _____ a horse through the park every day. Near Barbara, a family *(have)* _____ a picnic. They *(go)* _____ on a picnic every week.

■ **練習 42 ─ 口語練習**：帶一、兩張自己國家或任何有趣的圖片到課堂上。請同學描述這些圖片。

■ **練習 43 ─ 書寫練習**：選擇一張同學帶到課堂上的圖片，並寫一篇作文描述之。

■ **練習 44 ─ 複習**：選擇正確答案完成句子。

1. Jack lives _____ China.
   A. in   B. at   C. on

2. Anita and Pablo _____ TV right now.
   A. watch   B. watching   C. are watching

3. "_____ you writing a letter to your parents?"
   "No. I'm studying."
   A. Do   B. Are   C. Don't

4. I _____ like to write letters.
   A. no   B. am not   C. don't

5. "Jack has six telephones in his apartment."

"I _____ you. No one needs six telephones in one apartment."
    A. am not believing   B. believe   C. don't believe

6. When I want to know the time, I _____ a clock.
    A. see   B. watch   C. look at

7. I need _____ a new notebook.
    A. buy   B. to buy   C. buying

8. "_____ a cup of tea?"
"Yes, thank you."
    A. Would you like   B. Do you like   C. Like you

9. "Do you know Fatima?"

"Yes, I do. I _____ she is a very nice person."
    A. am thinking   B. thinking   C. think

10. There _____ twenty-two desks in this room.
    A. be   B. is   C. are

11. Pilots sit _____ an airplane.
    A. in front of   B. in the front of   C. front of

12. I live _____ 6601 Fourth Avenue.
    A. in   B. on   C. at

■ 練習 45 — 複習：更正錯誤。

1. It's rainning today. I am needing my umbrella.

2. Do you want go downtown with me?

3. There's many problems in big cities today.

4. I like New York City. I am thinking that it is a wonderful city.

5. Does Abdul be sleeping right now?

6. Why you are going downtown today?

7. I'm listening you.

8. Are you hearing a noise outside the window?

9. I'd like see a movie tonight.

10. Kunio at a restaurant right now. He usually eat at home, but today he eatting dinner at a restaurant.

11. I am liking flowers. They are smelling good.

12. Mr. Rice woulds likes to have a cup of tea.

13. How many students there are in your class?

14. Alex is siting at his desk. He writting a letter.

15. Yoko and Ivan are study grammar right now. They want learn English.

16. Where do they are sitting today?

第四章
名詞和代名詞

■ **練習 1**：說出屬於以下各種類的物品，並將其列成一張表。將你列的表和同學列的表作比較。此練習中，你所用的字稱為名詞 (nouns)。

1. Name clothing you see in this room. *(shirt)*
2. Name kinds of fruit. *(apple)*
3. Name things you drink. *(coffee)*
4. Name parts of the body. *(head)*
5. Name kinds of animals. *(horse)*
6. Name cities in the United States and Canada. *(New York, Montreal . . .)*
   NOTE: The names of cities begin with capital letters.
7. Name languages. *(English)* NOTE: The names of languages begin with capital letters.
8. Name school subjects. *(history)*

4-1　名詞：主詞和受詞

(a) 名詞 **Birds** | fly. 　主詞　　動詞 (b) 名詞　　　　　　名詞 **John** | is holding | a **pen**. 　主詞　　　動詞　　　受詞	名詞可作句子的主詞，也可作動詞的受詞。★ (a) 句中：Birds 是一個名詞，是句子的主詞。 (b) 句中：pen 是一個名詞，前面有冠詞 a； 　　a pen 是動詞 is holding 的受詞。
(c) 名詞　　　　　　　名詞 **Birds** | fly | in | the **sky**. 　主詞　動詞　介詞　介詞的受詞 (c) 名詞　　　　　　名詞　　　　　名詞 **John** | is holding | a **pen** | in | his **hand**. 　主詞　　　動詞　　　受詞　介詞　介詞的受詞	名詞可作介詞的受詞用。 (c) 句中：in 是介詞 (prep.)。名詞 sky（前有冠詞 the）是介詞 in 的受詞。 常用的介詞有：*about, across, at, between, by, for, from, in, of, on, to, with*。

★有些動詞後面可接受詞，這種動詞稱為及物動詞（*transitive verbs* 縮寫成 v. t.）。有些動詞不可接受詞，這種動詞稱為不及物動詞（*intransitive verbs* 縮寫成 v. i.）。

■ **練習 2**：依第 1、2 句的方式描述下列各句的文法結構。找出名詞，並指明該名詞的作用是以下哪一種：

- 句子的主詞？
- 動詞的受詞？
- 介詞的受詞？

1. Marie studies chemistry.

Marie	studies	chemistry	(none)	(none)
主詞	動詞	動詞的受詞	介詞	介詞的受詞

→　*Marie* = 名詞→句子的主詞
chemistry = 名詞→動詞 *studies* 的受詞

2. The children are playing in the park.

The children	are playing	(none)	in	the park
主詞	動詞	動詞的受詞	介詞	介詞的受詞

→　*children* = 名詞→句子的主詞
park = 名詞→介詞 *in* 的受詞

3. Children like candy.

主詞	動詞	動詞的受詞	介詞	介詞的受詞

4. The teacher is erasing the board with her hand.

主詞	動詞	動詞的受詞	介詞	介詞的受詞

5. Mike lives in Africa.

主詞	動詞	動詞的受詞	介詞	介詞的受詞

6. The sun is shining.

主詞	動詞	動詞的受詞	介詞	介詞的受詞

7. Robert is reading a book about butterflies.

主詞	動詞	動詞的受詞	介詞	介詞的受詞

8. Tom and Ann live with their parents.

主詞	動詞	動詞的受詞	介詞	介詞的受詞

9. Monkeys eat fruit and insects.

| 主詞 | 動詞 | 動詞的受詞 | 介詞 | 介詞的受詞 |

10. Mary and Bob help Sue with her homework.

| 主詞 | 動詞 | 動詞的受詞 | 介詞 | 介詞的受詞 |

11. Ships sail across the ocean.

| 主詞 | 動詞 | 動詞的受詞 | 介詞 | 介詞的受詞 |

12. Water contains hydrogen and oxygen.

| 主詞 | 動詞 | 動詞的受詞 | 介詞 | 介詞的受詞 |

4-2 形容詞 + 名詞

(a) I don't like **cold** weather. 　　　　　　　（形容詞）+（名詞）	形容詞形容名詞：*cold weather, hot weather, nice weather, bad weather*。
(b) Alex is a **happy** child. 　　　　　　（形容詞）+（名詞）	形容詞置於名詞之前。
(c) The **hungry** boy has a **fresh** apple. 　　　（形容詞）+（名詞）　　（形容詞）+（名詞）	
(d) The *weather*　is　　　**cold**. 　　　（名詞）+（*be* 動詞）+（形容詞）	提醒：形容詞可置於 *be* 動詞之後；此時形容詞用來描述句子的主詞。（見表 1-6）

常用形容詞

beautiful–ugly	*good–bad*	*angry*	*important*	**Nationalities-國籍**
big–little	*happy–sad*	*bright*	*intelligent*	*American*
big–small	*large–small*	*busy*	*interesting*	*Canadian*
cheap–expensive	*long–short*	*delicious*	*kind*	*Chinese*
clean–dirty	*noisy–quiet*	*famous*	*lazy*	*Egyptian*
cold–hot	*old–new*	*favorite*	*nervous*	*Indonesian*
dangerous–safe	*old–young*	*free*	*nice*	*Italian*
dry–wet	*poor–rich*	*fresh*	*ripe*	*Japanese*
easy–hard	*sour–sweet*	*honest*	*serious*	*Korean*
easy–difficult	*strong–weak*	*hungry*	*wonderful*	*Malaysian*
				Mexican
				Saudi Arabian

■ **練習 3**：找出下列句子的形容詞和名詞。

1. Jim has an expensive bicycle.
   → *Jim* = 名詞；*expensive* = 形容詞；*bicycle* = 名詞

2. My sister has a beautiful house.

3. We often eat at an Italian restaurant.

4. Maria sings her favorite songs in the shower.

5. Olga likes American hamburgers.

6. You like sour apples, but I like sweet fruit.

7. Political leaders make important decisions.

8. Heavy traffic creates noisy streets.

9. Poverty causes serious problems in the world.

10. Young people have interesting ideas about modern music.

■ **練習 4**：在句中填入適當的形容詞。（請至少想出三種可能的形容詞來完成句子。）

1. I don't like *cold / hot / wet / rainy / bad / etc.* weather.

2. Do you like _____ food?

3. I admire _____ people.

4. _____ people make me angry.

5. Pollution is a / an _____ problem in the modern world.

6. I had a / an _____ experience yesterday.

■ **練習 5**：找出句中所有的名詞，且指出該名詞的作用是以下哪一種：
   • 句子的主詞？
   • 動詞的受詞？
   • 介詞的受詞？

1. Bob and his wife like coffee with their breakfast.
   Bob = 名詞→句子的主詞
   wife = 名詞→句子的主詞
   coffee = 名詞→動詞 like 的受詞
   breakfast = 名詞→介詞 with 的受詞

2. Jack doesn't have a radio in his car.

3. Monkeys and apes have thumbs.

4. Scientists don't agree on the origin of the earth.

5. Does Janet work in a large office?

6. Egypt has hot summers and mild winters.

7. Many Vietnamese farmers live in small villages near their fields.

8. Large cities face many serious problems.

9. These problems include poverty, pollution, and crime.

10. An hour consists of sixty minutes. Does a day consist of 1440 minutes?

4-3 代名詞：主格和受格

代名詞主格	代名詞受格	主格 – 受格
(a) *I* speak English.	(b) Bob knows *me*.	*I* – *me*
(c) *You* speak English.	(d) Bob knows *you*.	*you* – *you*
(e) *She* speaks English.	(f) Bob knows *her*.	*she* – *her*
(g) *He* speaks English.	(h) Bob knows *him*.	*he* – *him*
(i) *It* starts at 8:00.	(j) Bob knows *it*.	*it* – *it*
(k) *We* speak English.	(l) Bob talks to *us*.	*we* – *us*
(m) *You* speak English.	(n) Bob talks to *you*.	*you* – *you*
(o) *They* speak English.	(p) Bob talks to *them*.	*they* – *them*

(q) I know **Tony**. **He** is a friendly person. (r) I like **Tony**. I know **him** well.	代名詞和名詞意義相同。(q) 句中：he 和 Tony 同義。文法上，代名詞即用來指稱或替代名詞。代名詞 he 和 him 都是指 Tony。
(s) I have **a red book**. **It** is on my desk.	有時代名詞指的是一個名詞片語 (noun phrase)。(s) 句中：it 指 a red book 這整個片語。

■ **練習 6**：用代名詞（I, me, he, him 等）完成下列句子。

1. Rita has a book. _____She_____ bought _____it_____ last week.

2. I know the new students, but Tony doesn't know _____ yet.

3. I wrote a letter, but I can't send _____ because I don't have a stamp.

4. Tom is in Canada. _____ is studying at a university.

5. Bill lives in my dorm. I eat breakfast with _____ every morning.

6. Ann is my neighbor. I talk to _____ every day. _____

   and _____ have interesting conversations together.

7. I have two pictures on my bedroom wall. I like _____.

   _____ are beautiful.

8. Ann and I have a dinner invitation. Mr. and Mrs. Brown want _____
   to come to dinner at their house.

9. Judy has a new car. _____ is a Toyota.

10. My husband and I have a new car. _____ got _____ last
    month.

■ **練習 7**：用代名詞完成下列句子。

1. A: Do you know Kate and Jim?

   B: Yes, _____I_____ do. I live near _____them_____.

2. A: Is the chemical formula for water H_3O?

   B: No, _____ isn't. _____ is H_2O.

3. A: Would Judy and you like to come to the movie with us?

   B: Yes, _____ would. Judy and _____ would enjoy

   going to the movie with _____.

4. A: Do Mr. and Mrs. Kelly live in the city?

   B: No, _____ don't. _____ live in the suburbs. I

   visited _____ last month.

5. A: Do you know how to spell "Mississippi"?

   B: Sure! I can spell _____. _____ is easy to spell.

6. A: Is Paul Cook in your class?

   B: Yes, _____ is. I sit next to _____.

7. A: Yoko and I are going to go downtown this afternoon. Do you want to come with

      _____?

   B: I don't think so, but thanks anyway. Chris and _____ are going to

      go to the library. _____ need to study for our test.

8. A: Do you and Jack want to join me for dinner tonight at a Chinese restaurant?

   B: Jack and _____ usually eat at home. _____ need to
      save our money.

   A: _____ is not an expensive restaurant, and the food is really good.

   B: Okay. Can you meet Jack and _____ there around six?
   A: Great! See you then.

9. A: Do George and Mike come over to your house often?

   B: Yes, _____ do. I invite _____ to my house often.
      We like to play cards together.
   A: Who usually wins your card games?

   B: Mike. _____ is a really good card player. We can't beat _____.

10. A: Hi, Ann. How do you like your new apartment?

    B: _____ is very nice.
    A: Do you have a roommate?

    B: Yes. Maria Hall is my roommate. Do you know _____?

        _____ is from Miami.

    A: No, I don't know _____. Do you get along with _____?

    B: Yes, _____ enjoy living together. You must visit

        _____ sometime. Maybe _____ can come over for
        dinner sometime soon.
    A: Thanks. I'd like that.

4-4 名詞：單數和複數

單數	複數		
(a) **one pen** **one apple** **one cup** **one elephant**	**two pens** **three apples** **four cups** **five elephants**	大部份名詞的複數：名詞字尾加 *-s*	
(b) **baby** **city**	**babies** **cities**	名詞字尾： 複數形式：	子音字母 + *-y* 將 *y* 改成 *i*，加 *-es*
(c) **boy** **key**	**boys** **keys**	名詞字尾： 複數形式：	母音字母 + *-y* 字尾加 *-s*
(d) **wife** **thief**	**wives** **thieves**	名詞字尾： 複數形式：	*-fe* 或 *-f* 將 *f* 改成 *v*，加 *-es*
(e) **dish** **match** **class** **box**	**dishes** **matches** **classes** **boxes**	名詞字尾： 複數形式： 發音：	*-sh, -ch, -ss, -x* 加 *-es* /əz/
(f) **tomato** **potato** **zoo** **radio**	**tomatoes** **potatoes** **zoos** **radios**	名詞字尾： 複數形式： 名詞字尾： 複數形式：	子音字母 + *-o* 加 *-es* 母音字母 + *-o* 加 *-s*

■ **練習 8：**用框內名詞的複數形式完成句子。每個名詞限用一次。

框 A：

> baby   cowboy   lady
> ✔ boy   dictionary   party
> city   key   tray
> country

1. Mr. and Mrs. Parker have one daughter and two sons. They have one girl and two

   _____*boys*_____.

2. The students in my class come from many _____.

3. Women give birth to _____.

4. My money and my _____ are in my pocket.

5. I know the names of many _____ in the United States and Canada.

6. I like to go to _____ because I like to meet and talk to people.

7. People carry their food on _____ at a cafeteria.

8. We always use our _____ when we write compositions.

9. Good evening, _____ and gentlemen.

10. _____ ride horses.

框 B:

knife	*life*	*wife*
leaf	*thief*	

11. Please put the _____, forks, and spoons on the table.

12. Sue and Ann are married. They are _____. They have husbands.

13. We all have some problems in our _____.

14. Police officers catch _____.

15. It is fall. The _____ are falling from the trees.

框 C:

bush	*match*	*tax*
class	*potato*	*tomato*
dish	*sandwich*	*zoo*
glass	*sex*	

16. Bob drinks eight _____ of water every day.

17. There are two _____: male and female.

18. Please put the _____ and the silverware on the table.

19. All citizens pay money to the government every year. They pay their

_____.

20. I can see trees and _____ outside the window.

21. I want to light the candles. I need some _____.

22. When I make a salad, I use lettuce and _____.

23. Sometimes Sue has a hamburger and French-fried _____ for dinner.

24. Some animals live all of their lives in _____.

25. Mehmet is a student. He likes his

_____.

26. We often eat _____ for lunch.

A 組：有聲子音與有聲母音後的 -s 發音為 /z/。

1. taxicabs	7. years
2. beds	8. lives
3. dogs	9. trees
4. balls	10. cities
5. rooms	11. boys
6. coins	12. days

B 組：無聲子音後的 -s 發音為 /s/。

13. books	16. groups
14. desks	17. cats
15. cups	18. students

C 組：字尾的 -s / -es 發音為 /əz/ 的情形。

- 在尾音 "s" 的後面：
  - 19. classes
  - 20. glasses
  - 21. horses
  - 22. places
  - 23. sentences
  - 24. faces
  - 25. offices
  - 26. pieces
  - 27. boxes
  - 28. sexes

- 在尾音 "z" 的後面：
  - 29. sizes
  - 30. exercises
  - 31. roses
  - 32. noises

- 在尾音 "sh" 的後面：
  - 33. dishes
  - 34. bushes

- 在尾音 "ch" 的後面：
  - 35. matches
  - 36. sandwiches

- 在尾音 "ge / dge" 的後面：
  - 37. pages
  - 38. ages
  - 39. oranges
  - 40. bridges
  - 41. edges

★詳細情形，請參閱表 2-8。

1. There are twenty desks in the room.

2. Oranges are usually sweet.

3. Roses are beautiful flowers. Rose bushes are beautiful.

4. The weather is terrible. It's raining cats and dogs.

5. We are reading sentences aloud.

6. I like to visit new places.

7. We do exercises in class.

8. I need two pieces of paper.

9. Don wants three sandwiches for lunch.

10. At the zoo you can see tigers, monkeys,

    birds, elephants, bears, and snakes.

11. Department stores sell many sizes of clothes.

12. The students are carrying books and bookbags.

13. The teachers have their offices in this building.

14. Engineers build bridges.

15. People have two ears, two eyes, two arms, two hands,

    two legs, and two feet.

16. Square tables and rectangular tables have four edges.

17. My dictionary has 350 pages.

18. I like apples, bananas, strawberries,

    and peaches.

19. There are three colleges in this city.

20. My apartment has cockroaches in the kitchen.

單數	複數	例句：
(a) *child*	***children***	Mr. Smith has one *child*. Mr. Cook has two ***children***.
(b) *foot*	***feet***	I have a right *foot* and a left *foot*. I have two ***feet***.
(c) *man*	***men***	I see a *man* on the street. I see two ***men*** on the street.
(d) *mouse*	***mice***	My cat sees a *mouse*. Cats like to catch ***mice***.
(e) *tooth*	***teeth***	My *tooth* hurts. My ***teeth*** are white.
(f) *woman*	***women***	There's one *woman* in our class. There are ten ***women*** in your class.
(g) *fish*	***fish***	Bob has an aquarium. He has one *fish*. Sue has an aquarium. She has seven ***fish***.
(h) （無）★	***people***	There are fifteen ***people*** in this room. （注意：*people* 字尾不加 *-s*。）

★*people* 是複數名詞，沒有單數形式。

■ **練習 11 —口語練習（閤上書本）**：將下列各題改成 two ＋ 名詞的複數形式。

例：　one child
答：　two children

1. one child	7. one fish	13. one sentence	19. one girl
2. one woman	8. one page	14. one man	20. one exercise
3. one tooth	9. one place	15. one orange	21. one tooth
4. one foot	10. one banana	16. one foot	22. one woman
5. one man	11. one child	17. one knife	23. one boy and
6. one mouse	12. one desk	18. one sex	one woman

■ **練習 12**：本練習是個名詞遊戲。請盡可能在各欄空格內填入以空格前面的字母為首的名詞，而且必須符合該欄指定的類別。填完一欄後，計算該欄的名詞總數即為得分。

欄1 自然界的事物	欄2 飲食類	欄3 動物昆蟲類	欄4 （某商店）販賣的商品
A _air_	A	A	A
B _bushes_	B	B	B
C	C	C	C
D	D	D	D
E _earth_	E	E	E
F _fish_	F	F	F
G _grass_	G	G	G
H	H	H	H
I _ice_	I	I	I
J	J	J	J
K	K	K	K
L _leaves_	L	L	L
M	M	M	M
N	N	N	N
O _oceans_	O	O	O
P _plants_	P	P	P
Q	Q	Q	Q
R _rain_	R	R	R
S _stars_	S	S	S
T _trees_	T	T	T
U	U	U	U
V	V	V	V
W _water_	W	W	W
X	X	X	X
Y	Y	Y	Y
Z	Z	Z	Z
分數：___13___	分數：_____	分數：_____	分數：_____

	單數	複數	可數名詞
可數名詞	*a book* *one book*	*books* *two books* *some books* *a lot of books* *many books* *a few books*	單數： *a* + 名詞 *one* + 名詞　　複數： 名詞 + *-s*
不可數名詞	*money* *some money* *a lot of money* *much money* *a little money*	（無）	不可數名詞 單數： 前面不加 *a*。 前面不加 *one*。　　複數： 不可數名詞沒有複數型態。

常用不可數名詞

advice	*mail*	*bread*	*pepper*
furniture	*money*	*cheese*	*rice*
help	*music*	*coffee*	*salt*
homework	*peace*	*food*	*soup*
information	*traffic*	*fruit*	*sugar*
jewelry	*weather*	*meat*	*tea*
luck	*work*	*milk*	*water*

■ **練習 13**：請注意句中斜體字的部分，將其中的名詞以畫線的方式標示出來，並判斷其爲可數 (count) 或不可數 (noncount)。

1. (COUNT)　NONCOUNT　He sits on *a chair*.

2. COUNT　(NONCOUNT)　He sits on *furniture*.

3. COUNT　NONCOUNT　She has *a coin*.

4. COUNT　NONCOUNT　She has *some money*.

5. COUNT　NONCOUNT　She has *some letters*.

6. COUNT　NONCOUNT　She has *some mail*.

7. COUNT　NONCOUNT　The street is full of *traffic*.

8. COUNT　NONCOUNT　There are *a lot of cars* in the street.

9. COUNT　NONCOUNT　I know *a fact* about bees.

10. COUNT　NONCOUNT　I have *some information* about bees.

11. COUNT　NONCOUNT　The teacher gives us *homework*.

12. COUNT	NONCOUNT	We have *an assignment*.
13. COUNT	NONCOUNT	I like *music*.
14. COUNT	NONCOUNT	Would you like *some coffee?*
15. COUNT	NONCOUNT	Our school has *a library*.
16. COUNT	NONCOUNT	People want *peace* in the world.
17. COUNT	NONCOUNT	I need *some advice*.
18. COUNT	NONCOUNT	Tom has *a good job*.
19. COUNT	NONCOUNT	He likes *his work*.
20. COUNT	NONCOUNT	Would you like *some water* with your food?
21. COUNT	NONCOUNT	Maria wears *a lot of jewelry*.
22. COUNT	NONCOUNT	She wears *earrings, rings, necklaces,* and *bracelets*.

■ **練習 14 — 口語練習：**說出教室內的物品來完成下列各句。注意名詞單、複數的應用。

1. I see a _____. I see a _____.

   I see a _____ and a _____.

2. I see two _____.

3. I see three / four / five / six / etc. _____.

4. I see some _____.

5. I see a lot of _____.

6. I see many _____.

4-7 AN 和 A 的用法比較

(a) **A** dog is **an a**nimal.	a 和 an 置於單數可數名詞前面。 (a) 句中：dog 和 animal 是單數可數名詞。
(b) I work in **an o**ffice. (c) Mr. Lee is **an o**ld man.	an 置於以母音 a, e, i 和 o 為首的字前面：an apartment, an elephant, an idea, an ocean。 (c) 句中：請注意，因為形容詞 old 的字首是母音，且後面的名詞 man 是單數可數名詞，所以使用 an。
(d) I have **an** uncle. 比較： (e) He works at **a** university.	字首是 u，且發音為母音的字前面要用 an：an uncle, an ugly picture。 字首是 u，且發音為 /ju/ 的字前面要用 a：a university, a usual event。
(f) I need **an** hour to finish my work. 比較： (g) I live in **a** house. He lives in **a** hotel.	字首是 h，但 h 不發音，開頭的發音反而變成母音的字，前面要用 an：an hour, an honor。 字首是 h，且 h 有發音的字，前面要用 a。

■ **練習 15**：用 a 或 an 完成下列各句。

1. Bob is eating _____ apple.

2. Tom is eating _____ banana.

3. Alice works in _____ office.

4. I have _____ idea.

5. I have _____ good idea.

6. Sue is talking to _____ man.

7. Sue is talking to _____ old man.

8. I need to see _____ doctor.

9. Cuba is _____ island.

10. Mary is reading _____ article in the newspaper.

11. Bill is _____ uncle. He has _____ niece and two nephews.

12. _____ hour has sixty minutes.

13. _____ horse has hooves.

14. Miss Anderson has _____ job.

15. She has _____ unusual job.

16. _____ university is _____ educational institution.

■ 練習 16：用 a 和 an 完成下列各句。

1. Carol is _____ nurse.

2. I live in _____ apartment building.

3. I live in _____ noisy apartment building.

4. Jake has _____ honest face.

5. Does Mark own _____ horse?

6. A fly is _____ insect.

7. Sonya's English class lasts _____ hour.

8. I had _____ interesting experience.

9. My father has _____ office downtown. It's _____ insurance office.

10. Gary and Joel are having _____ argument in the cafeteria. It is _____ unpleasant situation.

11. Are you _____ responsible person?

12. _____ angry woman is complaining to the store's manager.

13. _____ healthy person gets regular exercise.

14. Janet is _____ honorable person.

15. My uncle Jake has never said _____ unkind word. He is _____ very special man.

4-8 A / AN 和 SOME 的用法比較

(a) I have **a** pen. (b) I have **some** pens.	*a / an* 置於單數可數名詞前面。 (a)句中：*pen* 是個單數可數名詞。 *some* 置於複數可數名詞前面。 (b)句中：*pens* 是個複數可數名詞。
(c) I have **some** rice.	*some* 可置於不可數名詞前面。★ (c)句中：*rice* 是不可數名詞。

★切記：不可數名詞沒有複數型態。不可數名詞在文法上是單數的。

1. Bob has _____ *a* _____ book on his desk. → *book* = 單數可數名詞

2. Bob has _____ *some* _____ books on his desk. → *books* = 複數可數名詞

3. I see _____ desk in this room.

4. I see _____ desks in this room.

5. Are _____ students standing in the front of the room?

6. Is _____ student standing in the middle of the room?

7. I'm hungry. I would like _____ apple.

8. The children are hungry. They would like _____ apples.

9. _____ children are playing in the street.

10. _____ child is playing in the street.

11. We are doing _____ exercise in class.

12. We are doing _____ exercises in class.

■ **練習 18**：在下列各句的名詞前填入 a, an 或 some，並分析該名詞是單數可數名詞或是不可數名詞。

1. I need _____ *some* _____ money. → *money* = 不可數名詞

2. I need _____ *a* _____ dollar. → *dollar* = 單數可數名詞

3. Alice has _____ mail in her mailbox.

4. Alice has _____ letter in her mailbox.

5. I'm hungry. I would like _____ fruit.

6. I would like _____ apple.

7. Jane is hungry. She would like _____ food.

8. She would like _____ sandwich.

9. I'm thirsty. I'd like _____ water.

10. I'd like _____ glass of water.

11. Ann would like _____ milk.

12. I need _____ sugar for my coffee. Please hand me the sugar. Thanks.

13. I want to make _____ sandwich.

14. I need _____ bread and _____ cheese.

15. I'd like to have _____ soup with my sandwich.

■ **練習 19**：使用 a / an 或 some。

1. Sonya is wearing _____ *some* _____ silver jewelry. She's wearing

   _____ *a* _____ necklace and _____ *some* _____ earrings.

2. We have _____ table, _____ sofa, and

   _____ chairs in our living room.

3. We have _____ furniture in our living room.

4. Sue has a CD player. She is listening to _____ music.

5. I'm busy. I have _____ homework to do.

6. Jane is very busy. She has _____ work to do.

7. Jane has _____ job. She is _____ teacher.

8. I'm hungry. I would like _____ orange.

9. The children are hungry. They would like _____ oranges. They

   would like _____ fruit.

10. I need _____ information about the bus schedule.

11. I'm confused. I need _____ advice.

12. I'm looking out the window. I see _____ cars, _____

    bus, and _____ trucks on the street. I see _____ traffic.

13. Bob is having _____ beans, _____ meat, and

    _____ bowl of soup for dinner.

■ **練習 20**：用提示的字完成下列各句。在可數名詞後面加 -s（或寫出不規則之複數型態）。不可數名詞後面不要加 -s。

1. *money*   I need some _____ *money* _____.

2. *desk*   I see some _____ *desks* _____ in this room.

3. *man*   Some _____ *men* _____ are working in the street.

4. *music*   I want to listen to some _____.

5. *flower*   Don wants to buy some _____ for his girlfriend.

6. *information*   I need some _____.

7. *jewelry*   Fred wants to buy some _____.

8. *furniture*   We need to buy some _____.

9. *chair*   We need to buy some _____.

10. *child*   Some _____ are playing in the park.

11. *homework*   I can't go to the movie because I have some _____ to do.

12. *advice*   Could you please give me some _____?

13. *suggestion*   I have some _____ for you.

14. *help*   I need some _____ with my homework.

15 *tea*   I'm thirsty. I would like some _____.

16. *food*   I'm hungry. I would like some _____.

17. *sandwich*   We're hungry. We want to make some _____.

18. *animal*   I see some _____ in the picture.

19. *banana*   The monkeys are hungry. They would like some _____.

名詞和代名詞 ■ **147**

20. *fruit*   I'm hungry.   I would like some _____.

21. *weather*   We're having some hot _____ right now.

22. *picture*   I have some _____ of my family in my wallet.

23. *rice, bean*   I usually have some _____ and

                           _____ for dinner.

■ **練習 21**：請試著將下列句子中斜體字的名詞改爲複數，並將 a 改爲 some。必要時，可將句子作其他的改變。

1. There is *a chair* in this room. 複數 → *There are some chairs in this room.*

2. There is *some furniture* in this room. 複數 → （無）

3. I have *a coin* in my pocket.

4. I have *some money* in my wallet.

5. There is *some mail* in my mailbox.

6. There is *a letter* in my mailbox.

7. There's *a lot of traffic* on Main Street.

8. There's *a car* on Main Street.

9. Our teacher assigns *a lot of homework*.

10. I like rock *music*.

11. Hong Kong has hot *weather*.

12. I need *some information* and *some advice* from you.

13. There's *a dictionary* on the shelf.

14. I'd like to put *some cheese* on my *bread*.

15. I hope you do well on your exam. Good *luck!*

例：book	例：books	例：money
答：a book	答：some books	答：some money

1. desk
2. desks
3. animal
4. animals
5. chair
6. chairs
7. furniture
8. child
9. children
10. music
11. homework
12. flower
13. information

14. apple
15. man
16. old man
17. men
18. bananas
19. banana
20. fruit
21. island
22. jewelry
23. university
24. uncle
25. rice
26. boys

27. window
28. horse
29. hour
30. dishes
31. women
32. oranges
33. orange
34. place
35. places
36. water
37. mail
38. letter
39. letters

40. bread
41. office
42. food
43. table
44. cheese
45. matches
46. adjective
47. advice
48. house
49. people
50. potatoes
51. potato
52. sugar

■ 練習 23：將句中必須改成複數的名詞挑出來並改正。

1. Toronto and Bangkok are big ~~city.~~ → *cities*

2. I need some information. → （不須修改）

3. Horse are large animals.

4. I like to listen to music when I study.

5. I have two small child.

6. I like to tell them story.

7. There are sixty minute in an hour.

8. Korea and Japan are country in Asia.

9. Children like to play with toy.

10. Our teacher gives us a lot of homework.

11. My bookcase has three shelf.

12. There are five woman and seven man in this class.

13. Bangkok has a lot of hot weather.

14. Are you hungry? Could I get you some food?

15. Taiwan and Cuba are island.

16. I drink eight glass of water every day.

17. Tomato are red when they are ripe.

18. There is a lot of traffic at five o'clock.

19. Before dinner, I put dish, spoon, fork, knife, and napkin on the table.

20. I have many friend. I don't have many enemy.

4-9 不可數名詞的計量方式

（a）I'd like **some** water. （b）I'd like **a glass of** water. （c）I'd like **a cup of** coffee. （d）I'd like **a piece of** fruit.	不可數名詞利用計量單位來表示某一定量，例如： *a glass of,* *a cup of, a piece of*。 （a）句中：*some water* = 不明確的數量。 （b）句中：*a glass of water* = 明確的數量。

常用的計量單位

a bag of rice	*a bunch of bananas*	*a jar of pickles*
a bar of soap	*a can of corn★*	*a loaf of bread*
a bottle of beer	*a carton of milk*	*a piece of cheese*
a bowl of cereal	*a glass of water*	*a sheet of paper*
a box of candy	*a head of lettuce*	*a tube of toothpaste*

★英式英文的用法是： *a tin of corn*。

bag   bar   bottle   box

can   carton   jar   tube   bunch

■ **練習 24**：用 a piece of, a cup of, a glass of, 或 a bowl of 完成下列各句。想像你又餓又渴，你會想要什麼？

1. ___*a cup of / a glass of*___ tea

2. _____ bread

3. _____ water

4. _____ coffee

5. _____ cheese

6. _____ soup

7. _____ meat

8. _____ wine

9. _____ fruit

10. _____ rice

■ **練習 25**：填入名詞以完成下列各句。

1. At the store, I bought a carton of ___*orange juice / milk / etc.*___

2. I also bought a tube of _____ and two bars of

   _____.

3. I got a can of _____ and a jar of _____.

4. I also got a loaf of _____ and a box of _____.

5. I wanted to get a head of _____, but none of it looked fresh.

6. I got a couple of bottles of _____ and a jar of _____.

■ **練習 26 — 口語練習（闔上書本）**：用 I would like 以及 a / an 或 some 完成下列句子。

例： coffee
答： I would like some coffee. 或：I would like a cup of coffee.

例： new pen
答： I'd like a new pen.

1. coffee	9. apple	17. sandwich	25. new shirt/blouse
2. money	10. oranges	18. meat	26. new shoes
3. dollar	11. water	19. roast beef	27. tea
4. paper	12. new pencil	20. soup	28. cheese
5. new book	13. information	21. salt	29. rice
6. new books	14. help	22. sugar	30. bread
7. fruit	15. advice	23. fish	31. chicken
8. banana	16. food	24. new car	32. new furniture

1. I don't have a lot of money. → *I don't have much money.*

2. Tom has a lot of problems.

3. I want to visit a lot of cities in the United States and Canada.

4. I don't put a lot of sugar in my coffee.

5. I have a lot of questions to ask you.

6. Sue and John have a small apartment. They don't have a lot of furniture.

7. You can see a lot of people at the zoo on Sunday.

8. Dick doesn't get a lot of mail because he doesn't write a lot of letters.

9. Chicago has a lot of skyscrapers. Montreal has a lot of tall buildings too.

10. Mary is lazy. She doesn't do a lot of work.

11. I don't drink a lot of coffee.

12. Don is a friendly person. He has a lot of friends.

13. Do you usually buy a lot of fruit at the market?

14. Does Don drink a lot of coffee?

15. Do you write a lot of letters?

■ **練習 28**：用 many 或 much 完成下列問句。

1. How _____*much*_____ money do you have in your wallet?

2. How _____*many*_____ roommates do you have?

3. How _____ languages do you speak?

4. How _____ homework does your teacher usually assign?

5. How _____ tea do you drink in a day?

6. How _____ sugar do you put in your tea?

7. How _____ sentences are there in this exercise?

8. How _____ water is there in an Olympic-size swimming pool?

_____

★*much* 通常只用於否定句和疑問句，很少用於敘述句。

例： students in this room
疑問句：How many students are there in this room?

例： coffee in that pot
疑問句：How much coffee is there in that pot?

1. restaurants in this city
2. desks in this room
3. furniture in this room
4. letters in your mailbox today
5. mail in your mailbox today
6. cheese in the refrigerator
7. bridges in this city
8. traffic on the street right now
9. cars on the street
10. people in this room

■ 練習 **30**：將下列各句中的 some 改成 a few 或 a little。可數名詞用 a few，不可數名詞用 a little。
（參見表 4-6）

1. I need some paper. → *I need a little paper.*

2. I usually add some salt to my food.

3. I have some questions to ask you.

4. Bob needs some help. He has some problems. He needs some advice.

5. I need to buy some clothes.

6. I have some homework to do tonight.

7. I usually get some mail every day.

8. I usually get some letters every day.

9. When I'm hungry in the evening, I usually eat some cheese.

10. We usually do some oral exercises in class every day.

bush	*foot*	*information*	*page*
child	*fruit*	*knife*	*paper*
city	*furniture*	✔ *match*	*piece*
country	*help*	*money*	*sex*
edge	*homework*	*monkey*	*traffic*

1. I want to light a candle. I need some _____*matches*_____.

2. I have a lot of _____ in my wallet. I'm rich.

3. There are two _____ : male and female.

4. I would like to visit many _____ in the United States. I'd like to visit Chicago, Los Angeles, Dallas, Miami, and some others.

5. There are some _____ , forks, and spoons on the table.

6. I want to take the bus downtown, but I don't know the bus schedule. I need some

   _____ about the bus schedule.

7. I want to write a letter. I have a pen, but I need some _____.

8. There are three _____ in North America: Canada, the United States, and Mexico.

9. There are a lot of trees and _____ in the park.

10. Bob is studying. He has a lot of _____ to do.

11. I like to go to the zoo. I like to watch animals. I like to watch elephants, tigers, and

    _____.

12. There is a lot of _____ on the street during rush hour.

13. My dictionary has 437 _____.

14. This puzzle has 200 _____.

15. Barbara has four suitcases. She can't carry all of them. She needs some _____.

16. Susie and Bobby are seven years old. They aren't adults. They're _____.

17. A piece of paper has four _____.

18. We need a new bed, a new sofa, and some new chairs. We need some new _____.

19. People wear shoes on their _____.

20. I like apples, oranges, and bananas. I eat a lot of _____.

■ **練習 32**：將框內的字填入句中。必要時，請用複數形式。

advice	*glass*	*potato*	*tray*
centimeter	*horse*	*sentence*	*valley*
dish	*inch*	*size*	*weather*
fish	*leaf*	*strawberry*	*woman*
foot	*man*	*thief*	*work*

1. _____ fall from the trees in autumn.

2. Sometimes I have a steak, a salad, and French-fried _____ for dinner.

3. When the temperature is around 35°C (77°F), I'm comfortable. But I don't like very hot _____.

4. Cowboys ride _____.

5. Plates and bowls are called _____.

6. Married _____ are called wives.

7. _____ steal things: money, jewelry, cars, etc.

8. _____ are small, red, sweet, and delicious.

9. People carry their food on _____ at a cafeteria.

10. I'm not busy today. I don't have much _____ to do.

11. Sweaters in a store often have four _____ : small, medium, large, and extra large.

12. I have a problem. I need your help. I need some _____ from you.

13. Some _____ have mustaches.

14. Mountains are high, and _____ are low.

15. Ann has five _____ in her aquarium.

16. In some countries, people use cups for their tea. In other countries, they usually use

_____ for their tea.

17. There are 1200 _____ in a meter.

18. There are 12 _____ in a foot.★

19. There are 3 _____ in a yard.★

20. There are twenty-five _____ in this exercise.

4-10 THE 的用法

(a) A: Where's David? B: He's in **the** *kitchen*.	說者與聽者所想的是同一個人或物時，會用 *the*。*the* 表示某一特定的名詞。 (a)句中：A 和 B 所想的是同一個廚房。
(b) A: I have two pieces of fruit for us, an an apple and a banana. Which do you want? B: I'd like **the** *apple*, thank you.	(b)句中：當 B 說 *the apple* 時，A 和 B 兩人想的是同一個蘋果。

(c) A: It's a nice summer day today.
    The *sky* is blue. **The** *sun* is hot.
    B: Yes, I really like summer.
	(c)句中：A 和 B 想的是同一個天空（天空只有一個），和同一個太陽（太陽也只有一個）。

(d) Mike has **a** *pen* and **a** *pencil*.
    The *pen* is blue.
    The *pencil* is yellow.
 	
(e) Mike has **some** *pens* and *pencils*.
    The *pens* are blue.
    The *pencils* are yellow.
	the 後面可以加：
	   • 單數可數名詞，如 (d)。
	   • 複數可數名詞，如 (e)。
	   • 不可數名詞，如 (f)。
	換句話說，*the* 可以和三種名詞的任何一種合用。

(f) Mike has **some** *rice* and **some** *cheese*.
    The *rice* is white.
    The *cheese* is yellow.
	注意例句中：說者第二次提到某一個名詞時，會使用 *the*。因為第二次提到該名詞時，說者和聽者想的就是同一物品了。
	   第一次提： I have **a** *pen*.
	   第二次提： **The** *pen* is blue.

————————
★1英吋 (*inch*) =2.54公分 (*centimeters*)。1英呎 (*foot*) = 30.48公分 (*centimeters*)。1碼 (*yard*) =0.91公尺 (*meters*)。

1. I have _____*a*_____ notebook and _____ grammar book. _____ notebook is brown. _____ grammar book is red.

2. Right now Pablo is sitting in class. He's sitting between _____ woman and
   _____ man. _____ woman is Graciela. _____ man is Mustafa.

3. Susan is wearing _____ ring and _____ necklace. _____ ring is
   on her left hand.

4. Tony and Sara are waiting for their plane to depart. Tony is reading _____
   magazine. Sara is reading _____ newspaper. When Sara finishes _____
   newspaper and Tony finishes _____ magazine, they will trade.

5. In the picture below, there are four figures: _____ circle, _____ triangle,
   _____ square, and _____ rectangle. _____ circle is next to
   _____ triangle. _____ square is between _____ triangle and
   _____ rectangle.

circle	triangle	square	rectangle

6. Linda and Anne live in _____ apartment in _____ old building. They
   like _____ apartment because it is big. _____ building is very old. It
   was built more than one hundred years ago.

7. I gave my friend _____ card and _____ flower for her birthday.
   _____ card wished her "Happy Birthday." She liked both _____ card
   and _____ flower.

8. We stayed at _____ hotel in New York. _____ hotel was very expensive.

■ **練習 34**：用 the 和 a / an 完成下列句子。

(1)　A: Look at the picture on this page of your grammar book. What do you see?

(2)　B: I see _____ chair, _____ desk, _____ window, _____ plant.

(3)　A: Where is _____ chair?

(4)　B: _____ chair is under _____ window.

(5)　A: Where is _____ plant?

(6)　B: _____ plant is beside _____ chair.

(7)　A: Do you see any people?

(8)　B: Yes. I see _____ man and _____ woman. _____ man is standing. _____ woman is sitting down.

(9)　A: Do you see any animals?

(10)　B: Yes. I see _____ dog, _____ cat, and _____ bird in _____ cage.

(11)　A: What is _____ dog doing?

(12)　B: It's sleeping.

(13)　A: How about _____ cat?

(14)　B: _____ cat is watching _____ bird.

1. A: I need to go shopping. I need to buy _____ coat.

   B: I'll go with you. I need to get _____ umbrella.

2. A: Hi! Come in!

   B: Hi! _____ weather is terrible today! It's cold and wet outside.
   A: Well, it's warm in here.
   B: What should I do with my coat and umbrella?

   A: You can put _____ coat in that closet. I'll take _____ umbrella and

   put it in _____ kitchen where it can dry.

3. My cousin Jane has _____ good job. She works in _____ office. She

   uses _____ computer.

4. A: How much longer do you need to use _____ computer?
   B: Why?
   A: I need to use it too.
   B: Just five more minutes, then you can have it.

5. A: I need _____ stamp for this letter. Do you have one?
   B: Yes. Here.
   A: Thanks.

6. A: Would you like _____ egg for breakfast?

   B: No thanks. I'll just have _____ glass of juice and some toast.

7. A: Do you see my pen? I can't find it.

   B: There it is. It's on _____ floor.
   A: Oh. I see it. Thanks.

8. A: Be sure to look at _____ moon tonight.
   B: Why?

   A: _____ moon is full now, and it's beautiful.

9. A: Can I call you tonight?

   B: No. I don't have _____ telephone in my apartment yet. I just moved in
      yesterday.

10. A: Could you answer _____ telephone? Thanks.
    B: Hello?

(a) Ø *Apples* are good for you. (b) Ø *Students* use Ø *pens* and Ø *pencils*. (c) I like to listen to Ø *music*. (d) Ø *Rice* is good for you.	無冠詞 (符號是 Ø) 用於表示通稱的情形: • 複數可數名詞,如 (a) 和 (b) • 不可數名詞,如 (c) 和 (d)。
(e) Tom and Ann ate some fruit. **The** *apples* were very good, but **the** *bananas* were too ripe. (f) We went to a concert last night. **The** *music* was very good.	比較:(a) 句中,*apples* 一字是通稱,指的是所有的蘋果, 故不須用冠詞。 (e) 句中,*apples* 一字指的是特定的蘋果,所以前面 要加 *the*。它指的是 Tom 和 Ann 吃掉的蘋果。 比較:(c) 句中,*music* 是通稱。 (f) 句中,*the music* 則指特定音樂。

■ **練習 36**:用 the 或 (無冠詞 Ø) 完成下列句子。

1. _____Ø_____ sugar is sweet.

2. Could you please pass me _____*the*_____ sugar?

3. Oranges are orange, and _____ bananas are yellow.

4. There was some fruit on the table. I didn't eat _____ bananas because they were soft and brown.

5. Everybody needs _____ food to live.

6. We ate at a good restaurant last night. _____ food was excellent.

7. _____ salt tastes salty, and _____ pepper tastes hot.

8. Could you please pass me _____ salt? Thanks. And could I have _____ pepper too?

9. _____ coffee is brown.

10. Steven made some coffee and some tea. _____ coffee was very good. I didn't taste _____ tea.

11. I like _____ fruit. I also like _____ vegetables.

12. There was some food on the table. The children ate _____ fruit, but they didn't want _____ vegetables.

13. _____ pages in this book are full of grammar exercises.

14. _____ books consist of _____ pages.

4-12 SOME 和 ANY 的用法

肯定句：	(a) Alice has **some money**.	肯定句用 *some*。
否定句：	(b) Alice doesn't have **any money**.	否定句用 *any*。
疑問句：	(c) Does Alice have **any money**? (d) Does Alice have **some money**?	疑問句可用 *some* 或 *any*。
(e) I don't have **any money**. （不可數名詞） (f) I don't have **any matches**. （複數可數名詞）		*any* 可與不可數名詞及複數可數名詞連用。

■ **練習 37**：用 some 或 any 完成下列句子。

1. Sue has _____*some*_____ money.

2. I don't have _____*any*_____ money.

3. Do you have _____*some/any*_____ money?

4. Do you need _____ help?

5. No, thank you. I don't need _____ help.

6. Ken needs _____ help.

7. Anita usually doesn't get _____ mail.

8. We don't have _____ fruit in the apartment. We don't have _____ apples, _____ bananas, or _____ oranges.

9. The house is empty. There aren't _____ people in the house.

10. I need _____ paper. Do you have _____ paper?

11. Heidi can't write a letter because she doesn't have _____ paper.

12. Steve is getting along fine. He doesn't have _____ problems.

13. I need to go to the grocery store. I need to buy _____ food. Do you need to buy _____ groceries?

14. I'm not busy tonight. I don't have _____ homework to do.

15. I don't have _____ money in my purse.

16. There are _____ beautiful flowers in my garden this year.

例：　desks
學生A：Do you see any desks in this room?
學生B：Yes, I do. I see some desks / a lot of desks / twenty desks.

例：　monkeys
學生A：Do you see any monkeys in this room?
學生B：No, I don't. I don't see any monkeys.

1. books	6. food	11. hats	16. red sweaters
2. flowers	7. curtains	12. signs on the wall	17. dogs or cats
3. dictionaries	8. paper	13. bicycles	18. bookshelves
4. birds	9. bookbags	14. erasers	19. women
5. furniture	10. children	15. pillows	20. light bulbs

■ **練習 39**：在下列各句中填入 any 或 a。不可數名詞和複數可數名詞用 any。單數可數名詞用 a。

1. I don't have _____*any*_____ money.

2. I don't have _____*a*_____ pen.

3. I don't have _____*any*_____ brothers or sisters.

4. We don't need to buy _____ new furniture.

5. Mr. and Mrs. Kelly don't have _____ children.

6. I can't make _____ coffee. There isn't _____ coffee in the house.

7. Ann doesn't want _____ cup of coffee.

8. I don't like this room because there aren't _____ windows.

9. Amanda is very unhappy because she doesn't have _____ friends.

10. I don't need _____ help. I can finish my homework by myself.

11. I don't have _____ comfortable chair in my dormitory room.

12. I'm getting along fine. I don't have _____ problems.

13. Joe doesn't have _____ car, so he has to take the bus to school.

14. I don't have _____ homework to do tonight.

15. I don't need _____ new clothes.★

16. I don't need _____ new suit.

_____
★*clothes* 是複數名詞，因此 *clothes* 一字沒有單數型態。

4-13 不定代名詞：SOMETHING, SOMEONE, ANYTHING, ANYONE

肯定句：	(a) Mary bought **something** at the store. (b) Jim talked to **someone** after class.	肯定句中用 *something* 或 *someone*。
否定句：	(c) Mary didn't buy **anything** at the store. (d) Jim didn't talk to **anyone** after class.	否定句中用 *anything* 或 *anyone*。
疑問句：	(e) Did Mary buy **something** at the store? 　　Did Mary buy **anything** at the store? (f) Did Jim talk to **someone** after class? 　　Did Jim talk to **anyone** after class?	疑問句中可用 *something / someone* 或 *anything / anyone*。

■ **練習 40**：用 something, someone, anything, 或 anyone 完成下列句子。★

1. I have _____ *something* _____ in my pocket.

2. Do you have _____ in your pocket?

3. Ken doesn't have _____ in his pocket.

4. I bought _____ when I went shopping yesterday.

5. Rosa didn't buy _____ when she went shopping.

6. Did you buy _____ when you went shopping?

7. My roommate is speaking to _____ on the phone.

8. Yuko didn't tell _____ her secret.

9. I talked to _____ at the phone company about my bill.

10. Did you talk to _____ about your problem?

11. Kim gave me _____ for my birthday.

12. Paul didn't give me _____ for my birthday.

13. Did Paul give you _____ for your birthday?

14. My brother is sitting at his desk. He's writing a letter to _____.

15. The hall is empty. I don't see _____.

_____

★*someone* 和 *somebody* 同義；*anyone* 和 *anybody* 同義。你也可以在以上練習中，使用 *somebody* 和 *anybody*。

16. A: Listen. Do you hear a noise?

    B: No, I don't. I don't hear _____.

17. A: Did you talk to Jim on the phone last night?

    B: No. I didn't talk to _____.

18. A: Where's your bicycle?

    B: _____ stole it.

19. A: Does _____ have a some change? I need to use the pay phone.
    B: Here.
    A: Thanks. I'll pay you back later.

20. A: What did you do last weekend?

    B: I didn't do _____. I stayed home.

4-14　不定代名詞：NOTHING 和 NO ONE

（a）I *didn't say anything*. （b）I *said nothing*.	(a) 句和 (b) 句意思相同。 動詞爲否定時用 *anything*。 動詞爲肯定時用 *nothing*。★
（c）Bob *didn't see anyone* at the park. （d）Bob *saw no one* at the park.	(c) 句和 (d) 句意思相同。 動詞爲否定時用 *anyone*。 動詞爲肯定時用 *no one*。★

★誤：　*I didn't say nothing.*
　誤：　*Bob didn't see no one at the park.*

■ **練習 41**：用 anything, nothing, anyone 或 no one 完成下列句子。

1. Jim doesn't know _____ about butterflies.

2. Jim knows _____ about butterflies.

3. Jean didn't tell _____ about her problem.

4. Jean told _____ about her problem.

5. There's _____ in my pocket. It's empty.

6. There isn't _____ in my pocket.

7. Liz went to a shoe store, but she didn't buy _____.

8. Liz bought _____ at the shoe store.

9. I got _____ in the mail today. My mailbox was empty.

10. George sat quietly in the corner. He didn't speak to _____.

11. The office is closed from 12:00 to 1:00. _____ is there during the lunch hour.

12. I know _____ about nuclear physics.

13. _____ was at home last night. Both my roommate and I were out.

14. Joan has a new apartment. She doesn't know _____ in her apartment building yet.

15. A: Do you know _____ about Iowa?

    B: Iowa? I know _____ about Iowa.
    A: It's an agricultural state that is located between the Mississippi and Missouri rivers.

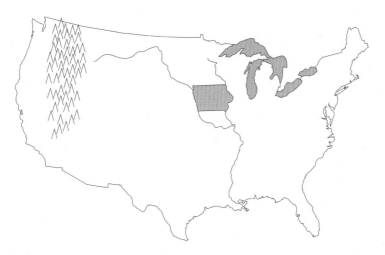

■ **練習 42 — 複習**：描述各句的文法結構。

1. Mr. Cook is living in a hotel.

Mr. Cook	is living	(none)	in	a hotel
主詞	動詞	受詞	介詞	介詞的受詞

2. Anita carries her books in her bookbag.

主詞	動詞	受詞	介詞	介詞的受詞

3. Snow falls.

| 主詞 | 動詞 | 受詞 | 介詞 | 介詞的受詞 |

4. Monkeys sleep in trees.

| 主詞 | 動詞 | 受詞 | 介詞 | 介詞的受詞 |

5. The teacher is writing words on the chalkboard.

| 主詞 | 動詞 | 受詞 | 介詞 | 介詞的受詞 |

6. I like apples.

| 主詞 | 動詞 | 受詞 | 介詞 | 介詞的受詞 |

■ **練習 43 — 複習**：完整的句子有主詞和動詞；不完整的句子是沒有主詞和動詞的一組字。以下各題內的字組如果是完整的句子，就將第一個字母改成大寫，並在句尾加上標點符號（句號或問號）。假如是不完整的句子，則寫上 Inc. 表示不完整 "Incomplete"。

1. monkeys like bananas → *Mmonkeys like bananas.*

2. in my garden → *Inc.*

3. do you like sour apples → *Ddo you like sour apples?*

4. rain falls

5. teaches English

6. this class ends at two o'clock

7. do the students go to class on Saturdays

8. in the classroom

9. my mother works in an office

10. my father to foreign countries on business every month

11. in Spain this month

12. does your brother have a job

13. does not work

14. where do you work

15. my brother lives in an apartment

16. has a roommate

17. the apartment has two bedrooms

18. a small kitchen and a big living room

19. on the third floor

20. pays the rent on the first day of every month

■ **練習 44 — 複習**：選擇正確答案完成句子。

1. My sister and I live together. Our parents call _____*A*_____ on the telephone often.
   A. us   B. them   C. we   D. they

2. Tom has a broken leg. I visit _____ in the hospital every day.
   A. he   B. him   C. them   D. it

3. Sue and I are good friends. _____ spend a lot of time together.
   A. They   B. You   C. We   D. She

4. Our children enjoy the zoo. We take _____ to the zoo often.
   A. it   B. they   C. them   D. him

5. Mary drives an old car. She takes good care of _____.
   A. her   B. them   C. it   D. him

6. Jack and _____ don't know Mr. Bush.
   A. I   B. me   C. us   D. them

7. Ms. Gray is a lawyer in Chicago. Do you know _____?
   A. them   B. it   C. him   D. her

8. Ahmed lives near Yoko and _____.
   A. I   B. me   C. him   D. her

9. My sister and a friend are visiting me. _____ are visiting here for two days.
   A. She   B. They   C. We   D. Them

10. Do _____ have the correct time?
   A. you   B. them   C. him   D. her

1. Omar a car has. → *Omar has a car.*

2. Our teacher gives tests difficult.

3. I need an advice from you.

4. Alex helps Mike and I.

5. I like rock musics. I listen to them every day.

6. Babys cry.

7. Mike and Tom in an apartment live.

8. There are seven woman in this class.

9. I don't like hot weathers.

10. I usually have a egg for breakfast.

11. There are nineteen peoples in my class.

12. Sun rises every morning.

13. Olga and Ivan has three childrens.

14. The students in this class do a lot of homeworks every day.

15. How many language do you know?

16. I don't have many money.

17. There is twenty classroom in this building.

18. I don't know nothing about ancient history.

■ **練習 46 — 複習**：兩人一組，假裝明天你們將一起遷入新公寓。你們會需要什麼？互相提問題，並討論你們的需要。

接著以書寫的方式，列出二十至三十樣你們需要的物品，並寫明<u>數量</u>（two, some, a lot of, a little 等等）。用 We need... 的句型完成句子。

例： We need . . .
　　1. a sofa.
　　2. two beds.
　　3. a can opener.
　　4. some spaghetti.
　　5. a little fruit.
　　6. some bookcases. etc.

■ **練習 47 — 複習**：用 I see... 的句型列出圖中所有的物品，並盡量寫出數量（例如：three spoons）或計量單位（例如：a box of candy）。單數可數名詞用 a （例如：a fly）。

例： I see three spoons, a box of candy, a fly, etc.

■ **練習 48 — 複習**：兩人一組，就下一頁圖片中的人和物做問答練習。

例：
學生A： How many boys are there in the picture?
學生B： There are three boys in the picture.
學生A： Are there any flowers?
學生B： No, there aren't any flowers in the picture.
學生A： Are you sure?
學生B： Well, hmmm. I don't see any flowers.
學生A： Oh?

第五章
過去式的表達

5-1　BE 動詞的用法：過去式

現在式	過去式
(a) I **am** in class **today**. (c) Alice **is** at the library **today**. (e) My friends **are** at home **today**.	(b) I **was** in class **yesterday**. (d) Alice **was** at the library **yesterday**. (f) My friends **were** at home **yesterday**.

BE 動詞的過去簡單式		
單數 **I was** **you were**（一個人） **she was** **he was** **it was**	複數 **we were** **you were**（不只一人） **they were**	*I* *she* *he* ⎫ *+ was* *it* *we* *you* ⎫ *+ were* *they*

■ 練習 1 — 口語練習：將下列句子改成過去式。

1. Bob is in class today. → *He was in class yesterday too.*

2. I'm in class today. → *I was in class yesterday too.*

3. Mary is at the library today.

4. We're in class today.

5. You're busy today.

6. I'm happy today.

7. The classroom is hot today.

8. Ann is in her office today.

9. Tom is in his office today.

10. Ann and Tom are in their offices today.

例： I'm in class.
答： I'm in class **today**. I was in class **yesterday too**.
例： (. . .) is in class.
答： (. . .) is in class **today**. She / He was in class **yesterday too**.

1. We're in class.
2. I'm in class.
3. (. . .) is in class
4. (. . .) and (. . .) are in class.
5. (. . .) is here.
6. (. . .) is absent.
7. I'm tired.
8. (. . .) and (. . .) are (in the front row).
9. The door is open/closed.
10. It's hot/cold.

5-2 BE 動詞的過去式：否定句

	否定式的縮寫：	was + not = wasn't
(a) I **was not** in class yesterday.		were + not = weren't
(b) I **wasn't** in class yesterday.		

(c) They **were not** at home last night.	*I* *she* *he* *it* ⎫ + *wasn't* *we* *you* *they* ⎫ + *weren't*
(d) They **weren't** at home last night.	

■ **練習 3**：用 wasn't 或 weren't 以及表示過去時間的語詞完成下列句子。

現在		過去
today	→	*yesterday*
this morning	→	*yesterday morning*
this afternoon	→	*yesterday afternoon*
tonight	→	*last night*
this week	→	*last week*

1. Ken is here today, but _____*he wasn't here yesterday.*_____

2. I'm at home tonight, but _____*I wasn't at home last night.*_____

3. Olga is busy today, but _____

4. We're in class this morning, but _____

5. Tom is at the library tonight, but _____

6. It's cold this week, but _____

7. Alex and Rita are at work this afternoon, but _____

8. Mr. and Mrs. Jones are at home tonight, but _____

9. You're in class today, but _____

10. Dr. Ruckman is in her office this afternoon, but _____

5-3 BE 動詞的過去式：疑問句

YES / NO 問句	簡答 ＋（完整回答）
（a）***Were you*** in class yesterday? （*be* 動詞）＋（主詞）	→ ***Yes, I was.*** (I was in class yesterday.) → ***No, I wasn't.*** (I wasn't in class yesterday.)
（b）***Was Carlos*** at home last night? （*be* 動詞）＋（主詞）	→ ***Yes, he was.*** (He was at home last night.) → ***No, he wasn't.*** (He wasn't at home last night.)
訊息疑問句	簡答 ＋（完整回答）
（c）***Where were you*** yesterday? *Where* ＋（*be* 動詞）＋（主詞）	→ ***In class.*** (I was in class yesterday.)
（d）***Where was Jennifer*** last night? *Where* ＋（*be* 動詞）＋ （主詞）	→ ***At home.*** (She was at home last night.)

■ **練習 4**：造疑問句並作簡答。

1. *(you \ at home \ last night)*

    A: ___*Were you at home last night?*___

    B: No, ___*I wasn't.*___

2. *(Mr. Yamamoto \ absent from class \ yesterday)*

    A: _____

    B: Yes, _____

3. *(Alex and Sue \ at home \ last night)*

    A: _____

    B: Yes, _____

4. *(you \ nervous \ the first day of class)*

    A: _____

    B: No, _____

5. (Ahmed \ at the library \ last night)

A: _____

B: Yes, _____

6. (Mr. Shin \ in class \ yesterday)

A: _____

B: No, _____

A: Where _____
B: At home.

7. (you and your wife \ in Canada \ last year)

A: _____

B: No, _____

A: Where _____
B: In Ireland.

■ **練習 5**：造疑問句並作簡答。

1. (you \ in class \ yesterday)

A: _____*Were you in class yesterday?*_____

B: Yes, _____*I was.*_____

2. (Anita \ in class \ today)

A: _____*Is Anita in class today?*_____

B: No, _____*she isn't.*_____ She's absent.

3. (you \ tired \ last night)

A: _____

B: Yes, _____. I went to bed early.

4. (you \ hungry \ right now)

A: _____

B: No, _____, but I'm thirsty.

5. *(the weather \ hot in New York City \ last summer)*

A: _____

B: Yes, _____. It was very hot.

6. *(the weather \ cold in Alaska \ in the winter)*

A: _____

B: Yes, _____. It's very cold.

7. *(Yoko and Mohammed \ here \ yesterday afternoon)*

A: _____

B: Yes, _____

8. *(the students in this class \ intelligent)*

A: _____

B: Of course _____! They are very intelligent!

9. *(Mr. Tok \ absent \ today)*

A: _____

B: Yes, _____

A: Where _____

B: _____

10. *(Tony and Benito \ at the party \ last night)*

A: _____

B: No, _____

A: Where _____

B: _____

11. *(Mr. and Mrs. Rice \ in town \ this week)*

A: _____

B: No, _____. They're out of town.

A: Oh? Where _____

B: _____

12. *(Anna \ out of town \ last week)*

A: _____

B: Yes, _____

A: Where _____

B: _____

■ **練習 6 — 口語練習（閤上書本）**：兩人一組做問答練習。假如學生 B 答 yes，該練習問題就此結束；假如學生 B 答 no，學生 A 應接著再以 where 發問。

例：　　in class \ now
學生A：（ . . .), are you in class now?　（學生 A 打開書本。）
學生B：Yes, I am.　（學生 B 閤上書本。）

例：　　at the library \ last night
學生A：（ . . .), were you at the library last night?
學生B：No, I wasn't.
學生A：Where were you?
學生B：I was (at home / in my room / at a party, etc.)

1. at home \ now
2. at home \ yesterday morning
3. at home \ last night
4. in class \ two days ago
5. in（本市某處）\ now
6. in（本市）\ last year
7. （你的老師）\ in class \ yesterday
8. （某兩位同學） here \ yesterday

角色互換。學生 B 向學生 A 提出問題。

9. in（本國）\ two weeks ago
10. in（本國）\ two years ago
11. in（某市）\ now
12. at（本市某座公園）\ yesterday afternoon
13. at（本市某出名地方）\ this morning★
14. at（學生愛去的地方）\ last night
15. （教師名）\ at home \ last night
16. （某兩位學生）\（某建築物）\ yesterday afternoon

★學生 B：假如你是在早上問此問題，就用現在式動詞。假如發問時，已是下午或晚間，則用過去式動詞。

5-4 過去簡單式：動詞字尾加 -ED

現在簡單式：	（a）I **walk** to school **every day**.	動詞 + -ed = 過去簡單式
過去簡單式：	（b）I **walked** to school **yesterday**.	
		I
現在簡單式：	（c）Ann **walks** to school **every day**.	you
過去簡單式：	（d）Ann **walked** to school **yesterday**.	she
		he ⎫
		it ⎬ + walked（動詞 + -ed）
		we ⎭
		they

■ **練習 7**：用框內的字，以現在簡單式或過去簡單式完成下列句子。

ask	✔ rain	wait
cook	shave	walk
dream	smile	watch
erase	stay	work

1. It often _____ *rains* _____ in the morning. It _____ *rained* _____
   yesterday.

2. I _____ to school every morning. I _____ to
   school yesterday morning.

3. Sue often _____ questions. She _____ a
   question in class yesterday.

4. I _____ a movie on television last night. I usually

   _____ TV in the evening because I want to improve my English.

5. Mike _____ his own dinner yesterday evening. He

   _____ his own dinner every evening.

6. I usually _____ home at night because I have to study. I

   _____ home last night.

7. I have a job at the library. I _____ at the library every evening. I

   _____ there yesterday evening.

8. When I am asleep, I often _____. I _____
   about my family last night.★

_____

★*dream* 的過去式可寫成 *dreamed* 或 *dreamt*。

9. Linda usually _____ for the bus at a bus stop in front of her

    apartment building. She _____ for the bus there yesterday morning.

10. The teacher _____ some words from the board a couple of minutes ago. He used his hand instead of an eraser.

11. Our teacher is a warm, friendly person. She often _____ when she is talking to us.

12. Rick doesn't have a beard anymore. He _____ five days ago.

    Now he _____ every morning.

5-5 表示過去時間的語詞：YESTERDAY, LAST 和 AGO

注意：
(a)中：*yesterday* 可和 *morning, afternoon* 與 *evening* 合用。
(b)中：*last* 可和 *night*，一段長時間（*week, month, year*），季節（*spring, summer,* 等），以及一週的七天合用。
(c)中：*ago* 指「以前」，置於某一段特定時間之後（例如：*two minutes + ago, five years + ago*）。

YESTERDAY	LAST	AGO

(a) Bob was here . . .
    yesterday.
    yesterday morning.
    yesterday afternoon.
    yesterday evening.
	(b) Sue was here . . .
	    last night.
	    last week.
	    lat month.
	    last year.
	
	    last spring.
	    last summer.
	    last fall.
	    last winter.
	
	    last Monday.
	    last Tuesday.
	    last Wednesday.
		(c) Tom was here . . .
		    five minutes ago.
		    two hours ago.
		    three days ago.
		    a (one) week ago.
		    six months ago.
		    a (one) year ago.

1. I dreamed about you _____*last*_____ night.

2. I was downtown _____ morning.

3. Two students were absent _____ Friday.

4. Ann wasn't at home _____ night.

5. Ann wasn't at home _____ evening.

6. Carmen was out of town _____ week.

7. I visited my aunt and uncle _____ fall.

8. Roberto walked home _____ afternoon.

9. My sister arrived in Miami _____ Sunday.

10. We watched TV _____ night.

11. Ali played with his children _____ evening.

12. Yoko arrived in Los Angeles _____ summer.

13. I visited my relatives in San Francisco _____ month.

14. My wife and I moved into a new house _____ year.

15. Mrs. Porter washed the kitchen floor _____ morning.

■ **練習 9**：用時間 + ago 完成下列句子。

1. I'm in class now, but I was at home ___*ten minutes ago/two hours ago/etc.*___

2. I'm in class today, but I was absent from class _____

3. I'm in this country now, but I was in my country _____

4. I was in *(name of a city)* _____

5. I was in elementary school _____

6. I arrived in this city _____

7. There is a nice park in this city. I was at the park _____

8. We finished EXERCISE 2 _____

9. I was home in bed _____

10. It rained in this city _____

動詞字尾加 -ed 有三種發音： /t/, /d/, 和 /əd/。

動詞字尾	動詞原型		動詞過去式		發音	
無聲子音★	(a)	*help*	*helped*	→	*help*/t/	• 動詞字尾如爲無聲子音，後面的 *-ed* 唸成 /t/，如 (a)。
		laugh	*laughed*	→	*laugh*/t/	
		guess	*guessed*	→	*guess*/t/★★	
有聲子音★	(b)	*rub*	*rubbed*	→	*rub*/d/	• 動詞字尾如爲有聲子音，後面的 *-ed* 唸成 /d/，如 (b)。
		live	*lived*	→	*liv*/d/	
		seem	*seemed*	→	*seem*/d/	
字尾是 -d 或 -t	(c)	*need*	*needed*	→	*need*/əd/	• 動詞字尾如爲字母 *d* 或 *t*，後面的 *-ed* 唸成 /əd/，如 (c)。
		want	*wanted*	→	*want*/əd/	

★　有關無聲子音和有聲子音的詳細資料，請參閱表 2-4。
★★　*guessed* 和 *guest* 兩字發音相同。

■ **練習 10**：大聲唸出框中的字，然後用它們完成下列句子。

A 組：無聲子音後的 *-ed* 唸成 /t/：

1. walked	✔ 5. watched	9. kissed	13. laughed
2. worked	6. touched	10. erased	14. coughed
3. cooked	7. washed	11. helped	
4. asked	8. finished	12. stopped	

15. I _____*watched*_____ TV last night.

16. Anna _____ to class yesterday instead of taking the bus.

17. I _____ the dirty dishes after dinner last night.

18. Jim _____ the board with an eraser.

19. Robert loves his daughter. He _____ her on the forehead.

20. The joke was funny. We _____ at the funny story.

21. The rain _____ a few minutes ago. The sky is clear now.

22. I worked for three hours last night. I _____ my homework about nine o'clock.

23. Steve _____ my shoulder with his hand to get my attention.

24. Mr. Wilson _____ in his garden yesterday morning.

25. Judy _____ because she was sick. She had the flu.

26. Don is a good cook. He _____ some delicious food last night.

27. Linda _____ a question in class yesterday.

28. I had a problem with my homework. The teacher _____ me before class.

B 組：有聲子音後面的 -ed 唸成 /d/ :

1. rained	5. smiled	9. remembered
2. signed	6. killed	10. played
3. shaved	7. sneezed	11. enjoyed
4. arrived	8. closed	12. snowed

13. It's winter. The ground is white because it _____ yesterday.

14. Anita _____ in this city three weeks ago. She

_____ at the airport on September 3rd.★

15. The girls and boys _____ baseball after school yesterday.

16. When Ali got a new credit card, he _____ his name in ink on the back of the card.

17. Rick used to have a beard, but now he doesn't. He _____ this morning.

18. The students' test papers were very good. The teacher, Mr. Jackson, was very

pleased. He _____ when he returned the test papers.

19. I _____ the party last night. It was fun. I had a good time.

20. The window was open. Mr. Chan _____ it because it was cold outside.

21. The streets were wet this morning because it _____ last night.

22. "Achoo!" When Judy _____, Ken said, "Bless you." Oscar said, "Gesundheit!"

★注意 *arrive* 後面的介詞用法：
  I arrive *in* + 國家或城市。
  I arrive *at* + 某一特定地方（建築物、機場、房子、公寓、聚會等）。
  arrive 後面可接 *in* 或 *at*，但不可接 *to*。
  誤：*She arrived to the United States.*
  誤：*She arrived to the airport.*

23. I have my books with me. I didn't forget them today. I

_____ to bring them to class.

24. Mrs. Lane was going crazy because there was a fly
in the room. The fly was buzzing all around

the room. Finally, she _____
it with a rolled up newspaper.

C 組：字尾 /t/ 和 /d/ 字母後面的 -ed 唸成 /əd/：

1. waited	5. invited
2. wanted	6. needed
3. counted	7. added
4. visited	8. folded

9. The children _____ some candy after dinner.

10. Mr. Miller _____ to stay in the hospital for two weeks after he had
an operation.

11. I _____ the number of students in the room.

12. Mr. and Mrs. Johnson _____ us to come to their house last
Sunday.

13. Last Sunday we _____ the Johnsons.

14. I _____ the letter before I put it in the envelope.

15. Kim _____ for the bus at the corner of 5th Avenue and Main
Street.

16. The boy _____ the numbers on
the chalkboard in arithmetic class yesterday.

例： walk to the front of the room
學生A：（學生 A 走到教室前面）。
教　師：What did (. . .) do?
學生B：She/He walked to the front of the room.
教　師：What did you do?
學生A：I walked to the front of the room.

1. smile	11. wash your hands （做出動作）
2. laugh	12. touch the floor
3. cough	13. point at the door
4. sneeze	14. fold a piece of paper
5. shave （做出動作）	15. count your fingers
6. erase the board	16. push （教室內某物品）
7. sign your name	17. pull （教室內某物品）
8. open the door	18. yawn
9. close the door	19. pick up your pen
10. ask a question	20. add two and two on the board

5-7 動詞加 -ED 的拼法

	動詞字尾	→	-ED 的形式
規則 1：	動詞字尾：一個子音字母 + -e smile erase	→	加 -d smiled erased
規則 2：	一個母音字母 + 一個子音字母* stop rub	→	重複子音字母，加 -ed stopped rubbed
規則 3：	兩個母音字母 + 一個子音字母 rain need	→	加 -ed：不重複子音字母 rained needed
規則 4：	兩個子音字母 count help	→	加 -ed：不重複子音字母 counted helped
規則 5：	子音字母 + -y study carry	→	將 -y 改成 -i, 加 -ed studied carried
規則 6：	母音字母 + -y play	→	加 -ed：不必將 -y 改成 -i played

*例外：x 不重複（fix + -ed = fixed）。w 不重複 (snow + -ed = snowed)。
注意：以一個母音字母加一個子音字母結尾的雙音節動詞（例如：visit, open），請參閱表 5-8。

		-ED	**-ING**
1.	count	_counted_	_counting_
2.	stop		
3.	smile		
4.	rain		
5.	help		
6.	dream		
7.	clap		
8.	erase		
9.	rub		
10.	yawn		
11.	study		
12.	stay		
13.	worry		
14.	enjoy		

■ 練習 **13**：用框內動詞的正確形式完成句子。

carry	✔ finish	stay
clap	learn	stop
cry	rub	taste
enjoy	smile	wait
fail		

1. I _____finished_____ my homework at nine last night.

2. We _____ some new vocabulary yesterday.

3. I _____ the soup before dinner last night. It was delicious.

4. Linda _____ for the bus at the corner yesterday.

5. The bus _____ at the corner. It was on time.

_____

★ *-ing* 形式的拼法請參閱表 5-8。

6. We _____ the play at the theater last night. It was very good.

7. At the theater last night, the audience _____ when the play was over.

8. Ann _____ her suitcases to the bus station yesterday. They weren't heavy.

9. The baby _____ her eyes because she was sleepy.

10. I _____ home and watched a sad movie on TV last night. I _____ at the end of the movie.

11. Mike _____ his examination last week. His grade was "F."

12. Jane _____ at the children. She was happy to see them.

■ 練習 14：寫出下列動詞的正確 -ed 形式，以及該 -ed 形式的正確發音：/t/, /d/, /əd/.

		-ED 形式			發音
1.	wait	waited	wait	+	/əd/
2.	spell	spelled	spell	+	/d/
3.	kiss	kissed	kiss	+	/t/
4.	plan	_____	plan	+	_____
5.	join	_____	join	+	_____
6.	hope	_____	hope	+	_____
7.	drop	_____	drop	+	_____
8.	add	_____	add	+	_____
9.	point	_____	point	+	_____
10.	pat	_____	pat	+	_____
11.	shout	_____	shout	+	_____
12.	reply	_____	reply	+	_____
13.	play	_____	play	+	_____
14.	touch	_____	touch	+	_____
15.	end	_____	end	+	_____

即使不懂下列動詞的意義，也請根據學過的原則，寫出該字的 -ed 拼法與發音。

16. mop   _____   mop   +   _____

17. droop   _____   droop   +   _____

18. cope   _____   cope   +   _____

19. rant   _____   rant   +   _____

20. date   _____   date   +   _____

21. heat   _____   heat   +   _____

22. bat   _____   bat   +   _____

23. trick   _____   trick   +   _____

24. fool   _____   fool   +   _____

25. reward   _____   reward   +   _____

26. grab   _____   grab   +   _____

27. dance   _____   dance   +   _____

28. paste   _____   paste   +   _____

29. earn   _____   earn   +   _____

30. grin   _____   grin   +   _____

31. mend   _____   mend   +   _____

5-8 動詞加 -ED 和加 -ING 的拼法：雙音節的動詞

	動詞	重音			有些動詞有兩個音節。（a）中：visit 有兩個音節：vis + it。visit 的重音在第一個音節。（b）中：admit 的重音在第二個音節。
（a）	visit	**VIS** · it			
（b）	admit	ad · **MIT**			

	動詞	重音	-ED 形式	-ING 形式	以一個母音字母加一個子音字母結尾的雙音節動詞：
（c）	visit	**VIS** · it	visited	visiting	• 如果重音落於第一個音節，不必重複子音字母，如 (c) 和 (d)。
（d）	open	**O** · pen	opened	opening	
（e）	admit	ad · **MIT**	admitted	admitting	• 如果重音落於第二個音節，要重複子音字母，如 (e) 和 (f)。
（f）	occur	oc · **CUR**	occurred	occurring	

■ **練習 15**：寫出以下動詞的 -ed 和 -ing 形式。

動詞	重音	-ED 形式	-ING 形式
1. answer	**AN** · swer★	*answered*	*answering*
2. prefer	pre · **FER**	_____	_____
3. happen	**HAP** · pen	_____	_____
4. visit	**VIS** · it	_____	_____
5. permit	per · **MIT**	_____	_____
6. listen	**LIS** · ten★★	_____	_____
7. offer	**OF** · fer	_____	_____
8. occur	oc · **CUR**	_____	_____
9. open	**O** · pen	_____	_____
10. enter	**EN** · ter	_____	_____
11. refer	re · **FER**	_____	_____
12. begin	be · **GIN**	（無）★★★	_____

■ **練習 16**：以框內動詞的 -ed 形式完成下列句子。每個動詞限用一次。

admit	listen	open
✔ answer	occur	permit
happen	offer	visit

1. The teacher _____*answered*_____ a question for me in class.

2. Yesterday I _____ my aunt and uncle at their home.

3. We _____ to some music after dinner last night.

4. It was okay for the children to have some candy after lunch. Mrs. King

   _____ them to have a little candy.

5. I _____ the window because the room was hot.

   ★ *answer* 中的 *w* 不發音。
  ★★ *listen* 中的 *t* 不發音。
★★★ *begin* 是不規則動詞，沒有 -ed 形式；它的過去式是：*began*。

6. A car accident _____ at the corner of 5th Street and Main yesterday.

7. A bicycle accident _____ on Forest Avenue yesterday.

8. My friend poured a glass of water and held it toward me. She asked me if I wanted it.

   She _____ me a glass of water.

9. A man unlocked the gate and _____ the sports fans into the stadium.

ENTRANCE TO
MEMORIAL
STADIUM

ADMISSION
TICKETS

■ 練習 17 — 口語練習（闔上書本）：拼寫測驗。寫出每個動詞的 -ed 形式。

1. stop	6. rain	11. carry	16. occur
2. wait	7. permit	12. open	17. stay
3. study	8. listen	13. fold	18. help
4. smile	9. rub	14. offer	19. drop
5. enjoy	10. visit	15. happen	20. count

■ 練習 18：用括弧內的字完成下列句子，並依情況使用現在簡單式，現在進行式，或過去簡單式。請留意拼法和發音。

1. I *(walk)* _____*walked*_____ to school yesterday.

2. I *(sit)* _____*am sitting*_____ in class right now.

3. I usually *(go)* _____*go*_____ to bed at eleven o'clock every night.

4. Sally *(finish)* _____ her homework at ten o'clock last night.

5. I (study) _____ at the library yesterday.

6. I (study) _____ English every day.

7. I am in class right now. I (study) _____ English.

8. I need an umbrella because it (rain) _____ right now.

9. It (rain) _____ yesterday morning.

10. My roommate (help) _____ me with my homework last night.

11. We can go outside now. The rain (stop) _____ a few minutes ago.

12. The children are in the park. They (play) _____ baseball.

13. I (play) _____ soccer last week.

14. Yesterday morning I (brush) _____ my teeth, (wash) _____ my face, and (shave) _____ .

15. Ann is in her living room right now. She (watch) _____ television.

16. Ann usually (watch) _____ TV in the evening.

17. She (watch) _____ a good program on TV last night.

18. We (do) _____ an exercise in class right now. We (use) _____ verb tenses in sentences.

19. I (arrive) _____ in this city a month ago.

20. Matt (listen) _____ to music every morning while he's getting ready to go to school.

21. A: Where's Matt?
    B: He's in his room?

    A: What (do, he) _____ ?

    B: He (listen) _____ to music.

22. A: (you, listen) _____ to the news every day?

    B: Yes. I (like) _____ to know about events in the world.

    I usually (listen) _____ to the news on TV before I go

    to sleep at night, but last night I (listen) _____ to the news on the radio.

有些動詞沒有 *-ed* 形式，其過去式爲不規則形式。

現在式　過去式	
come – *came*	（a）I **come** to class **every day**.
do – *did*	（b）I *came* to class **yesterday**.
eat – *ate*	
get – *got*	（c）I **do** my homework **every day**.
go – *went*	（d）I *did* my homework **yesterday**.
have – *had*	
put – *put*	（e）Ann **eats** breakfast **every morning**.
see – *saw*	（f）Ann *ate* breakfast **yesterday morning**.
sit – *sat*	
sleep – *slept*	
stand – *stood*	

■ **練習 19 — 口語練習**：將下列句子改爲過去式。

1. Tom gets some mail every day.
   → *Tom got some mail yesterday.*
2. They go downtown every day.
3. We have lunch every day.
4. I see my friends every day.
5. Hamid sits in the front row every day.
6. I sleep for eight hours every night.
7. The students stand in line at the cafeteria.
8. I write a letter to my parents every week.
9. Wai-Leng comes to class late every day.
10. We do exercises in class every day.
11. I eat breakfast every morning.
12. I get up at seven every day.
13. Robert puts his books in his briefcase every day.

■ **練習 20 — 口語練習（闔上書本）**：將下列句子改爲過去式。

例： I come to class every day.
答： I came to class yesterday.

1. I eat lunch every day.
2. I see you every day.
3. I sit in class every day.
4. I write a letter every day.
5. I do my homework every day.
6. I have breakfast every day.
7. I go downtown every day.
8. I get up at eight every day.
9. I stand at the bus stop every day.
10. I sleep for eight hours every night.
11. I come to school every day.
12. I put my pen in my pocket every day.

■ **練習 21**：用括弧內的字完成下列句子，並依情況使用現在簡單式，現在進行式，或過去簡單式。請留意拼法和發音。

1. I (get) _____*got*_____ up at eight o'clock yesterday morning.

2. Mary (talk) _____ to John on the phone last night.

3. Mary (talk) _____ to John on the phone right now.

4. Mary (talk) _____ to John on the phone every day.

5. Jim and I (eat) _____ lunch at the cafeteria two hours ago.

6. We (eat) _____ lunch at the cafeteria every day.

7. I (go) _____ to bed early last night.

8. My roommate (study) _____ Spanish last year.

9. Sue (write) _____ a letter to her parents yesterday.

10. Sue (write) _____ a letter to her parents every week.

11. Sue is in her room right now. She (sit) _____ at her desk.

12. Maria (do) _____ her homework last night.

13. Yesterday I (see) _____ Fumiko at the library.

14. I (have) _____ a dream last night. I (dream) _____

    about my friends. I (sleep) _____ for eight hours.

15. A strange thing (happen) _____ to me yesterday. I couldn't
    remember my own telephone number.

16. My wife (come) _____ home around five every day.

17. Yesterday she (come) _____ home at 5:15.

18. Our teacher (stand) _____ in the middle of the room right now.

19. Our teacher (stand) _____ in the front of the room yesterday.

20. Tom (put) _____ the butter in the refrigerator yesterday.

21. He (put) _____ the milk in the refrigerator every day.

22. Pablo usually (sit) _____ in the back of the room, but yesterday

    he (sit) _____ in the front row. Today he (be) _____

    absent. He (be) _____ absent two days ago too.

5-10 過去簡單式：否定句

主詞 + DID + NOT + 主要動詞					
(a)	I	*did*	*not*	*walk*	to school yesterday.
(b)	You	*did*	*not*	*walk*	to school yesterday.
(c)	Tom	*did*	*not*	*eat*	lunch yesterday.
(d)	They	*did*	*not*	*come*	to class yesterday.

I
you
she
he } + *did not* + 主要動詞★
it   （原形）
we
they

(e) 誤： I *did not walked* to school yesterday.	注意 *did not* 後面要加原形動詞。
(f) 誤： Tom *did not ate* lunch yesterday.	

(g) I **didn't walk** to school yesterday.	否定式縮寫：
(h) Tom **didn't eat** lunch yesterday.	*did* + *not* = *didn't*

★例外：主要動詞是 *be* 動詞時，不用 *did*。請參閱表 5-2 和 5-3。
　　誤：Joe *didn't be* here yesterday.
　　正：Joe *wasn't* here yesterday.

■ **練習 22 — 口語練習（閤上書本）**：用 I don't...every day. 和 I didn't...yesterday. 造句。

例：walk to school
答：I don't walk to school every day. I didn't walk to school yesterday.

1. eat breakfast	5. study	9. do my homework
2. watch TV	6. go to the library	10. shave
3. go shopping	7. visit my friends	
4. read the newspaper	8. see (. . .)	

■ **練習 23 — 口語練習（閤上書本）**：練習現在式否定句與過去式否定句。
學生A：用 I don't 和 I didn't 造句；didn't 後面要加上適當的過去時間語詞。
學生B：將學生 A 所說的報告出來。先用 she / he doesn't 的句型說，再用 she / he didn't 加適當的過去時間語詞的方式說。

例：　walk to school every morning
學生A：I don't walk to school every morning. I didn't walk to school yesterday morning.
教　師：Tell me about (學生 A).
學生B：She / He doesn't walk to school every morning. She / He didn't walk to school yesterday morning.

1. eat breakfast every morning	6. dream in English every night
2. watch TV every night	7. visit my aunt and uncle every year
3. talk to (. . .) every day	8. write to my parents every week
4. play soccer every afternoon	9. read the newspaper every morning
5. study grammar every evening	10. pay all of my bills every month

1. I *(go, not)* _____*didn't go*_____ to a movie last night. I *(stay)*

   _____*stayed*_____ home.

2. Mike *(come, not)* _____*doesn't come*_____ to class every day.

3. I *(finish, not)* _____ my homework last night. I *(go)*

   _____ to bed early.

4. Jane *(stand, not)* _____ up right now. She *(sit)*

   _____ down.

5. It *(rain, not)* _____ right now. The rain *(stop)*

   _____ a few minutes ago.

6. The weather *(be, not)* _____ cold today, but it *(be)* _____
   cold yesterday.

7. Tina and I *(go, not)* _____ shopping yesterday. We *(go)*

   _____ shopping last Monday.

8. I *(go)* _____ to a movie last night, but I *(enjoy, not)* _____

   it. It *(be, not)* _____ very good.

9. I *(write)* _____ a letter to my girlfriend yesterday, but I *(write, not)*

   _____ a letter to her last week.

10. Sue *(read)* _____ a magazine right now. She *(watch, not)*

    _____ TV.

11. My husband (come, not) _____ home for dinner last night.

12. The children (go) _____ to bed a half an hour ago. They (sleep) _____ now.

13. We (be) _____ late for the movie last night. The movie (start) _____ at seven, but we (arrive, not) _____ until seven-fifteen.

14. Olga (ask) _____ Hamid a question a few minutes ago, but he (answer, not) _____ her question.

15. Toshi is a busy student. He usually (eat, not) _____ lunch because he (have, not) _____ enough time between classes.

16. He (eat) _____ lunch the day before yesterday, but he (eat, not) _____ lunch yesterday.

5-11 過去簡單式：YES / NO疑問句

DID + 主詞 + 主要動詞			簡答 + （完整回答）	
(a) **Did**	**Mary**	**walk** to school?	→ **Yes, she did**.	(She walked to school.)
			→ **No, she didn't**.	(She didn't walk to school.)
(b) **Did**	**you**	**come** to class?	→ **Yes, I did**.	(I came to class.)
			→ **No, I didn't**.	(I didn't come to class.)

■ **練習 25**：造疑問句並作簡答。

1. A: _____ *Did you walk downtown yesterday?* _____

   B: _____ *Yes, I did.* _____ (I walked downtown yesterday.)

2. A: _____ *Did it rain last week?* _____

   B: _____ *No, it didn't.* _____ (It didn't rain last week.)

3. A: _____

   B: _____ (I ate lunch at the cafeteria.)

4. A: _____

    B: _____ (Mr. Kwan didn't go out of town last week.)

5. A: _____

    B: _____ (I had a cup of tea this morning.)

6. A: _____

    B: _____ (Benito and I went to a party last night.)

7. A: _____

    B: _____ (Olga studied English in high school.)

8. A: _____

    B: _____ (Yoko and Ali didn't do their homework last night.)

9. A: _____

    B: _____ (I saw Gina at dinner last night.)

10. A: _____

    B: _____ (I didn't dream in English last night.)

■ 練習 26：用 was, were 或 did 完成下列句子。

1. I _____*did*_____ not go to work yesterday. I _____*was*_____ sick, so I stayed home
    from the office.

2. Tom _____ not in his office yesterday. He _____ not go to work.

3. A: _____ Mr. Chan in his office yesterday?
    B: Yes.

    A: _____ you see him about your problem?

    B: Yes. He answered all my questions. He _____ very helpful.

4. A: _____ you at the meeting yesterday?
    B: What meeting?

    A: _____ you forget about the meeting?
    B: I guess so. What meeting?
    A: The meeting with the president of the company about employee benefits.

    B: Oh. Now I remember. No, I _____ not there. _____ you?
    A: Yes. I can tell you all about it.
    B: Thanks.

5. A: Where _____ you yesterday?

   B: I _____ at the zoo.

   A: _____ you enjoy it?

   B: Yes, but the weather _____ very hot. I tried to stay out of the sun. Most

   of the animals _____ in their houses or in the shade. The sun

   _____ too hot for them, too. They _____ not want to be

   outside in the hot sun.

■ **練習 27**：造疑問句並作簡答。

   1. A: _____*Were you at home last night?*_____

      B: _____*No, I wasn't.*_____ (I wasn't at home last night.)

      A: _____*Did you go to a movie?*_____

      B: _____*Yes, I did.*_____ (I went to a movie.)

   2. A: _____

      B: _____ (It isn't cold today.)

   3. A: _____

      B: _____ (I come to class every day.)

   4. A: _____

      B : _____ (Roberto was absent yesterday.)

   5. A: _____

      B: _____ (Roberto stayed home yesterday.)

   6. A: _____

      B: _____ (I don't watch television every day.)

   7. A: _____

      B: _____ (Mohammed isn't in class today.)

      A: _____

      B: _____ (He was here yesterday.)

      A: _____

      B: _____ (He came to class the day before yesterday.)

      A: _____

      B: _____ (He usually comes to class every day.)

8. A: _____

   B: _____ (I live in an apartment.)

   A: _____

   B: _____ (I don't have a roommate.)

   A: _____

   B: _____ (I don't want a roommate.)

   A: _____

   B: _____ (I had a roommate last year.) It didn't work out.

   A: _____

   B: _____ (He was difficult to live with.)
   A: What did he do?
   B: He never picked up his dirty clothes. He never washed his dirty dishes. He was always late with his share of the rent.

   A: _____

   B: _____ (I asked him to keep the apartment clean.) He always agreed, but he never did it.

   A: _____

   B: _____ (I was glad when he left.) I like living alone.

■ 練習 28 — 口語練習（闔上書本）：詢問同學有關他 / 她今天上午的活動。

例： walk to school
學生A：Did you walk to school this morning?
學生B：Yes, I did.　或：No, I didn't.

1. get up at seven   7. smoke a cigarette
2. eat breakfast   8. go shopping
3. study English   9. have a cup of coffee
4. walk to class   10. watch TV
5. talk to (. . .)   11. listen to the radio
6. see (. . .)   12. read a newspaper

例： walk to school
學生A：Do you walk to school every day?
學生B：Yes, I do. 或：No, I don't.
學生A：Did you walk to school this morning?
學生B：Yes, I did. 或：No, I didn't.

1. go downtown
2. dream in color
3. talk to (...) on the phone
4. come to (grammar) class
5. sing in the shower
6. eat at least two pieces of fresh fruit
7. think about your family
8. cook your own dinner

9. wear （某一衣著物件）
10. laugh out loud at least two times
11. speak （某種語言）
12. go to （某處）
13. read at least one book
14. go swimming
15. go shopping

■ 練習 30 — 口語練習（闔上書本）：複習不規則動詞。用 yes 回答所有問題，並同時說出簡答與完整回答。

例： Did you come to class today?
答： Yes, I did. I came to class today.

1. Did you eat dinner last night?
2. Did (...) come to class today?
3. Did you get a letter yesterday?
4. Did (...) go shopping yesterday?
5. Did (...) do his / her homework last night?
6. Did you sleep well last night?
7. Did you have a cup of coffee this morning?
8. Did (...) go to a movie last night?
9. Did (...) sit in that chair yesterday?
10. Did you write a letter yesterday.?
11. （叫一學生站起來。） Did (...) stand up?
    （叫他 / 她坐下。） Did (...) sit down?
12. Did (...) put his / her books on his / her desk this *(morning / afternoon / evening)?*

5-12 更多的不規則動詞

bring - brought	*drive - drove*	*run - ran*
buy - bought	*read - read★*	*teach - taught*
catch - caught	*ride - rode*	*think - thought*
drink - drank		

★*read* 過去式的發音與 *red*（紅色）同。

■ **練習 31** — 口語練習（閤上書本）：練習使用不規則動詞。

例： teach-taught

教師： teach, taught. I teach class every day. I taught class yesterday. What did I do yesterday?

學生： teach, taught. You taught class.

1. *bring-brought*   I bring my book to class every day. I brought my book to class yesterday. What did I do yesterday?

2. *buy-bought*   I buy books at the bookstore. I bought a book yesterday. What did I do yesterday?

3. *teach-taught*   I teach class every day. I taught class yesterday. What did I do yesterday?

4. *catch-caught*   I catch the bus every day. I caught the bus yesterday. What did I do yesterday?

5. *think-thought*   I often think about my family. I thought about my family yesterday. What did I do yesterday?

6. 複習： What did I bring to class yesterday? What did you bring yesterday?

   What did I buy yesterday? What did you buy yesterday?

   Did you teach class yesterday? Who did?

   Did I walk to class yesterday or did I catch the bus?

   What did I think about yesterday? What did you think about yesterday?

7. *run-ran*   Sometimes I'm late for class, so I run. Yesterday I was late, so I ran. What did I do yesterday?

8. *read-read*   I like to read books. I read every day. Yesterday I read a book. What did I do yesterday? What did you read yesterday?

9. *drink-drank*   I usually drink a cup of coffee in the morning. I drank a cup of coffee this morning. What did I do this morning? Did you drink a cup of coffee this morning?

10. *drive-drove*   I usually drive my car to school. I drove my car to school this morning. What did I do this morning? Who has a car? Did you drive to school this morning?

11. *ride-rode*   Sometimes I ride the bus to school. I rode the bus yesterday morning. What did I do yesterday morning? Who rode the bus to school this morning?

12. 複習： I was late for class yesterday morning, so what did I do?

    What did I read yesterday? What did you read yesterday?

    Did you read a newspaper this morning?

    What did I drink this morning? What did you drink this morning?

    I have a car. Did I drive to school this morning? Did you?

    Did you ride the bus to school this morning?

■ **練習 32**：用括弧內的字完成下列句子。

1. A: Why are you out of breath?

   B: I *(run)* _____ to class because I was late.

2. A: *(Ms. Carter, teach)* _____ class
   yesterday?

   B: No, she didn't. Mr. Adams *(teach)* _____ our class.

3. A: I *(ride)* _____ the bus to school yesterday. How did you
   get to school?

   B: I *(drive)* _____ my car.

4. A: Did you decide to change schools?

   B: I *(think)* _____ about it, but then I decided to stay here.

5. A: *(you, go)* _____ shopping yesterday?

   B: Yes. I *(buy)* _____ a new pair of shoes.

6. A: *(you, study)* _____ last night?

   B: No, I didn't. I was tired. I *(read)* _____ a magazine and then

   (go) _____ to bed early.

7. A: Do you like milk?

   B: No. I *(drink)* _____ milk when I *(be)* _____ a child,
   but I don't like milk now.

8. A: Did you leave your dictionary at home?

   B: No. I *(bring)* _____ it to class with me.

9. A: Did you enjoy your fishing trip?

   B: I had a wonderful time! I *(catch)* _____ a lot of fish.

■ **練習 33**：用括弧內的動詞完成下列句子。

1. Ann and I *(go)* _____ to the bookstore yesterday. I *(buy)*

   _____ some stationery and a T-shirt.

2. I had to go downtown yesterday. I *(catch)* _____ the bus in front

   of my apartment and *(ride)* _____ to Grand Avenue. Then I

   (get off) _____ the bus and transferred to another one. It *(be)*

   _____ a long trip.

3. Sue *(eat)* _____ popcorn and *(drink)* _____ a

   cola at the movie theater last night. I *(eat, not)* _____ anything.
   I'm on a diet.

4. Maria (ask) _____ the teacher a question in class yesterday. The

teacher (think) _____ about the question for a few minutes and
then said, "I don't know."

5. I (want) _____ (go) _____ to the basketball

game last night, but I (stay) _____ home because I had to study.

6. Last night I (read) _____ an article in the newspaper. It (be)

_____ about the snowstorm in Moscow.

7. Yesterday Yoko (teach) _____ us how to say "thank you" in

Japanese. Kim (teach) _____ us how to say "I love you" in
Korean.

8. When Ben and I (go) _____ to the department store yesterday, I

(buy) _____ some new socks. Ben (buy, not) _____ anything.

9. Rita (pass, not) _____ the test yesterday. She (fail)

_____ it.

10. Last summer we (drive) _____ to Colorado for our vacation. We

(visit) _____ a national park, where we (camp) _____

in our tent for a week. We (go) _____ fishing one morning. I

(catch) _____ a

very big fish, but my husband

(catch, not) _____

anything. We (enjoy) _____

cooking and eating the fish for dinner.

It (be) _____ delicious.

I like fresh fish.

11. I almost *(have)* _____ an accident yesterday. A dog *(run)*

_____ into the street in front of my car. I *(slam)*

_____ on my brakes and just *(miss)* _____ the dog.

12. Yesterday I *(play)* _____ ball with my little boy. He *(catch)*

_____ the ball most of the time, but sometimes he *(drop)*

_____ it.

■ **練習 34 — 口語練習（閤上書本）**：用過去簡單式做問答練習。
學生A：用下列動詞，以過去式向同學發問。
學生B：回答問題，須同時說出簡答與完整回答。

例： drink
學生A： Did you drink a cup of coffee this morning?
學生B： Yes, I did. I drank a cup of coffee this morning. 或：No, I didn't. I didn't drink a cup of coffee this morning.

1. eat	7. drink	13. walk
2. buy	8. read	14. watch
3. get up	9. drive	15. listen to
4. have	10. sleep	16. see
5. go	11. go	17. think about
6. study	12. talk to	18. rain

■ **練習 35 — 書寫練習**：用下列語詞造句，描述自己的活動。用過去簡單式加過去時間語詞（yesterday, two days ago, last week 等）的方式造句。

例：go downtown with（某人）
答：I went downtown with Marco two days ago.

1. arrive in （本市）	12. talk to （某人） on the phone
2. write a letter to （某人）	13. go shopping
3. eat at a restaurant	14. study English
4. go to bed early	15. read a newspaper
5. buy （某物）	16. go on a picnic
6. go to bed late	17. go to a party
7. get up early	18. play （足球、彈珠台等）
8. be late for class	19. see （某人或某物）
9. have a cold	20. think about （某人或某物）
10. be in elementary school	21. do my homework
11. drink a cup of tea	22. be born

疑問句						簡答
(a)		*Did*	you	*go*	downtown?	→ Yes, I did. / No, I didn't.
(b)	**Where**	*did*	you	*go?*		→ **Downtown.**
(c)		*Did*	you	*run*	because you were late?	→ Yes, I did. / No, I didn't.
(d)	**Why**	*did*	you	*run?*		→ **Because I was late.**
(e)		*Did*	Ann	*come*	at six?	→ Yes, she did. / No, she didn't.
(f)	**When** **What time**	*did*	Ann	*come?*		→ **At six.**

比較：

(g) **What time** did Ann come? → **At six.**
　　　　　　　　　　　　　　　→ **Seven o'clock.**
　　　　　　　　　　　　　　　→ **Around 9:30.**

通常 *what time* 專門用來問鐘錶上的時間。

(h) **When** did Ann come? → **At six.**
　　　　　　　　　　　　→ **Friday.**
　　　　　　　　　　　　→ **June 15th.**
　　　　　　　　　　　　→ **Last week.**
　　　　　　　　　　　　→ **Three days ago.**

回答 *when* 可用各種不同的時間語詞。

■ **練習 36**：用 where, when, what time 或 why 造疑問句。

1. A: ___*Where did you go yesterday?*___
   B: To the zoo. (I went to the zoo yesterday.)

2. A: _____
   B: Last month. (Jason arrived in Canada last month.)

3. A: _____
   B: At 7:05. (My plane arrived at 7:05.)

4. A: _____
   B: Because I was tired. (I stayed home last night because I was tired.)

5. A: _____
   B: At the library. (I studied at the library last night.)

6. A: _____
   B: Because it's dark in here. (I turned on the light because it's dark in here.)

7. A: _____
   B: To Greece. (Sara went to Greece for her vacation.)

8. A: _____
   B: Around midnight. (I finished my homework around midnight.)

9. A: _____
   B: Five weeks ago. (I came to this city five weeks ago.)

10. A: _____
    B: Because Tony made a funny face. (I laughed because Tony made a funny face.)

11. A: _____
    B: At Emerhoff's Shoe Store. (I got my sandals at Emerhoff's Shoe Store.)

12. A: _____
    B: Upstairs. (Kate is upstairs.)

13. A: _____
    B: In the dormitory. (Ben lives in the dormitory.)

14. A: _____
    B: To the park. (I went to the park yesterday afternoon.)

15. A: _____
    B: Because he's sick. (Bobby is in bed because he's sick.)

16. A: _____
    B: Because he was sick. (Bobby stayed home because he was sick.)

17. A: _____
    B: 7:20. (The movie starts at 7:20.)

18. A: _____
    B: Two days ago. (Sara got back from Brazil two days ago.)

19. A: _____
    B: Because she wanted to talk to Joe. (Tina called because she wanted to talk to Joe.)

20. A: _____
    B: Because he wants big muscles. (Jim lifts weights because he wants big muscles.)

例： I got up at 7:30.
答： When / What time did you get up?

1. I went to the zoo.
2. I went to the zoo yesterday.
3. I went to the zoo yesterday because I wanted to see the animals.
4. (. . .) went to the park.
5. (. . .) went to the park yesterday.
6. (. . .) went to the park yesterday because the weather was nice.
7. I am in class.
8. I came to class (an hour) ago.
9. (. . .) is in class.
10. (. . .) came to class (an hour) ago.
11. (. . .) studied at the library last night.
12. (. . .) finished his / her homework around midnight.
13. (. . .) went to bed at 7:30 last night.
14. (. . .) went to bed early because he / she was tired.
15. (. . .) went to the park.
16. (. . .) went to the park yesterday.
17. (. . .) went to the park yesterday because he / she wanted to jog.
18. (. . .) is absent today because he / she is sick.
19. (. . .) is at home.
20. (. . .) stayed home because he / she is sick.

■ 練習 38：用 why didn't 爲首造疑問句完成下列對話。

1. A: *Why didn't you come to class?*
   B: Because I was sick.

2. A: _____
   B: Because I didn't have enough time.

3. A: _____
   B: Because I forgot your phone number.

4. A: _____
   B: Because I had a headache.

5. A: _____
   B: Because I wasn't hungry.

6. A: _____
   B: Because I didn't want to.

1. A: ___*Where do you want to go for your vacation?*___
   B: Hawaii.

2. A: _____
   B: Ten o'clock.

3. A: _____
   B: Because I was tired.

4. A: _____
   B: Last week.

5. A: _____
   B: South America.

6. A: _____
   B: Because I forgot.

7. A: _____
   B: Downtown.

8. A: _____
   B: Several months ago.

9. A: _____
   B: At a Chinese restaurant.

5-14 WHAT 引導的疑問句

What 用來詢問有關「事物」的問題。**Who** 用來詢問有關「人」的問題。（有關以 *who* 引導的疑問句，請參閱表 5-15。）

（疑問詞） + 助動詞 + 主詞 + 主要動詞	回答
(a) **Did** Carol **buy** a car? →	**Yes, she did.** *(She bought a car.)*
(b) **What** **did** Carol **buy**? →	**A car.** *(She bought a car.)*
(c) **Is** Fred **holding** a book? →	**Yes, he is.** *(He's holding a book.)*
(d) **What** **is** Fred **holding**? →	**A book.** *(He's holding a book.)*
主詞 動詞 受詞 (e) Carol bought **a car**. 受詞 助動詞 主詞 動詞 (f) **What** did Carol buy?	(e) 中：*a car* 是動詞的受詞。 (f) 中：*what* 是動詞 *buy* 的受詞。

1. A: _____*Did you buy a new tape recorder?*_____
   B: Yes, I did. (I bought a new tape recorder.)

2. A: _____*What did you buy?*_____
   B: A new tape recorder. (I bought a new tape recorder.)

3. A: _____
   B: Yes, she is. (Mary is carrying a suitcase.)

4. A: _____
   B: A suitcase. (Mary is carrying a suitcase.)

5. A: _____
   B: Yes, I do. (I see that airplane.)

6. A: _____
   B: An airplane. (I see an airplane.)

7. A: _____
   B: A hamburger. (Bob ate a hamburger for lunch.)

8. A: _____
   B: Yes, he did. (Bob ate a hamburger for lunch.)

9. A: _____
   B: A sandwich. (Bob usually eats a sandwich for lunch.)

10. A: _____
   B: No, he doesn't. (Bob doesn't like salads.)

■ **練習 41**：造疑問句。

1. A: _____*What did John talk about?*_____
   B: His country. (John talked about his country.)

2. A: _____*Did John talk about his country?*_____
   B: Yes, he did. (John talked about his country.)

3. A: _____
   B: A bird. (I'm looking at a bird.)

4. A: _____
   B: Yes, I am. (I'm looking at that bird.)

5. A: _____
   B: Yes, I am. (I'm interested in science.)

6. A: _____
   B: Science. (I'm interested in science.)

7. A: _____
   B: Nothing in particular. (I'm thinking about nothing in particular.)

8. A: _____
   B: English grammar. (I dreamed about English grammar last night.)

9. A: _____
   B: The map on the wall. (The teacher is pointing at the map on the wall.)

10. A: _____
    B: No, I'm not. (I'm not afraid of snakes.) Are you?

■ **練習 42 — 口語練習（閤上書本）**：用 what 以及一個過去式或現在式動詞，向同學提出問題。

例：　　　eat
學生A：　What did you eat for breakfast this morning? / What do you usually eat for
　　　　dinner? / etc.
學生A：　（自由作答）

1. eat   6. be interested in
2. wear   7. be afraid of
3. look at   8. dream about
4. study   9. have
5. think about   10. need to buy

疑問句	回答	
(a) **What** did they see? →	**A boat**. *(They saw a boat.)*	*what* 用來問有關「事物」的問題。 *who* 用來問有關「人」的問題。
(b) **Who** did they see? →	**Jim**. *(They saw Jim.)*	
(c) **Who** did they see? →	**Jim**. *(They saw Jim.)*	(c) 和 (d) 同義。 正式英文中，用 *whom* 作為動詞或介詞的受詞。 (c) 句中：日常英文通常用 *who*，而不用 *whom*。 (d) 句中：*whom* 用於非常正式的英文，極少用於日常口語中。
(d) **Whom** did they see? →	**Jim**. *(They saw Jim.)*	
受詞 (e) **Who(m)** did they see? →	受詞 **Jim**. *(They saw **Jim**.)*	(e) 句中：*who(m)* 是動詞的受詞，使用一般的疑問句字序（疑問詞＋助動詞＋主詞＋主要動詞）。
主詞 (f) **Who** came? → (g) **Who** lives there? → (h) **Who** saw Jim? →	主詞 **Mary**. (**Mary** came.) **Ed**. (**Ed** lives there.) **Ann**. (**Ann** saw Jim.)	(f), (g), 和 (h) 句中：*who* 是疑問句的主詞，不使用一般的疑問句字序。 *who* 當疑問句的主詞時： • 不用 *does, do* 或 *did* 等助動詞。 • 不改變動詞（疑問句與答句中的動詞形式相同。） 誤： *Who did come?*

■ **練習 43**：造疑問句。

1. A: _____
   B: Mary. (I saw Mary at the party.)

2. A: _____
   B: Mary. (Mary came to the party.)

3. A: _____
   B: John. (John lives in that house.)

4. A: _____
   B: John. (I called John.)

5. A: _____
   B: My aunt and uncle. (I visited my aunt and uncle.)

6. A: _____
   B: My cousin. (My cousin visited me.)

7. A: _____
   B: Bob. (Bob helped Ann.)

8. A: _____
   B: Ann. (Bob helped Ann.)

9. A: _____
   B: Yes, he did. (Bob helped Ann.)

10. A: _____
    B: No, I'm not. (I'm not confused.)

■ **練習 44**：造疑問句。

1. A: _____
   B: Ken. (I saw Ken.)

2. A: _____
   B: Ken. (I talked to Ken.)

3. A: _____
   B: Nancy. (I visited Nancy.)

4. A: _____
   B: Mary. (I'm thinking about Mary.)

5. A: _____
   B: Yuko. (Yuko called.)

6. A: _____
   B: Ahmed. (Ahmed answered the question.)

7. A: _____
   B: Mr. Lee. (Mr. Lee taught the English class.)

8. A: _____
   B: Carlos. (Carlos helped me.)

9. A: _____
   B. Gina. (I helped Gina.)

10. A: _____
    B: My brother. (My brother carried my suitcase.)

■ **練習 45**：用適當的疑問詞：where, when, what time, why, who, what 造疑問句。

1. A: _____
   B: To the zoo. (Ann went to the zoo.)

2. A: _____
   B: Yesterday. (Ann went to the zoo yesterday.)

3. A: _____
   B: Ann. (Ann went to the zoo yesterday.)

4. A: _____
   B: Ali. (I saw Ali.)

5. A: _____
   B: At the zoo. (I saw Ali at the zoo.)

6. A: _____
   B: Yesterday. (I saw Ali at the zoo yesterday.)

7. A: _____
   B: Because the weather was nice. (I went to the zoo yesterday because the weather was nice.)

8. A: _____
   B: Dr. Jones. (I talked to Dr. Jones.)

9. A: _____
   B: Dr. Jones. (Dr. Jones called.)

10. A: _____
    B: Yesterday afternoon. (Dr. Jones called yesterday afternoon.)

11. A: _____
    B: At home. (I was at home yesterday afternoon.)

12. A: _____
    B: In an apartment. (I'm living in an apartment.)

13. A: _____
    B: Grammar. (The teacher is talking about grammar.)

14. A: _____
    B: A frog. (Annie has a frog in her pocket.)

5-16 字義的詢問法

(a) **What does** "pretty" **mean**?	(a) 句和 (b) 句同義。
(b) **What is the meaning of** "pretty"?	誤： *What means "pretty"?*

■ **練習 46**：向同學詢問下列各字的意義：

1. muggy	6. listen	11. discover	16. forest
2. awful	7. supermarket	12. simple	17. possess
3. quiet	8. crowd	13. empty	18. invite
4. century	9. lend	14. enjoy	19. modern
5. finish	10. murder	15. ill	20. pretty difficult

■ **練習 47**：用自己的話造疑問句。

1. A: _____
   B: Yesterday.

2. A: _____
   B: My brother.

3. A: _____
   B: A new pair of sandals.

4. A: _____
   B: At 7:30.

5. A: _____
   B: At Rossini's Restaurant.

6. A: _____
   B: Tomorrow afternoon.

7. A: _____
   B: In an apartment.

8. A: _____
   B: My roommate.

9. A: _____
   B: Because I wanted to.

10. A: _____
    B: Ann.

11. A: _____
    B: A bird.

12. A: _____
    B: The zoo.

■ 練習 48 — 口語練習（闔上書本）：依下列回答造適當的疑問句。

例： At 7 o'clock.
答： When did you get up this morning? / What time does the movie start? / etc.

1. In an apartment.
2. Yesterday.
3. It means "wonderful."
4. (. . .).
5. At seven-thirty.
6. A shirt.
7. A hamburger.
8. No.
9. Because I wanted to.
10. Grammar.
11. Yes.
12. Nothing.
13. In the dormitory.
14. Because I was tired.
15. (. . .).
16. At nine o'clock.
17. A new pair of shoes.
18. On（某街名）
19. In（縣、市名）
20. Last night.

5-17 更多的不規則動詞

break - broke	*meet - met*	*sing - sang*
fly - flew	*pay - paid*	*speak - spoke*
hear - heard	*ring - rang*	*take - took*
leave - left	*send - sent*	*wake up - woke up*

■ 練習 49 — 口語練習（闔上書本）：練習使用不規則動詞。

例： break-broke
教 師：break, broke. Sometimes a person breaks an arm or a leg. I broke my arm five years ago. What happened five years ago?
學 生：break, broke. You broke your arm.
教 師：（對學生 A 說）Did you ever break a bone?
學生A：Yes. I broke my leg ten years ago.

1. *fly-flew*   Sometimes I fly home in an airplane. I flew home in an airplane last month. What did I do last month? When did you fly to this city?

2. *hear-heard*   I hear birds singing every morning. I heard birds singing yesterday. What did I do yesterday? What did you hear when you woke up this morning?

3. *pay-paid*   I pay the rent every month. I paid the rent last month. What did I do last month? Did you pay your rent last month?

4. *send-sent*   I send my mother a gift every year on her birthday. I sent my mother a gift last year on her birthday. What did I do last year? When did you send a gift to someone?

5. *leave-left*   I leave for school at 8:00 every morning. I left for school yesterday at 8:00 A.M. What did I do at 8:00 A.M. yesterday? What time did you leave for class this morning?

6. *meet-met*   I meet new people every week. Yesterday I met (. . .)'s friend. What did I do yesterday? Do you know (. . .)? When did you meet him / her?

7. *take-took*   I take my younger brother to the movies every month. I took my younger brother to the movies last month. What did I do last month? Who has a younger brother or sister? Where and when did you take him / her someplace?

8. *wake-woke*   I usually wake up at six. This morning I woke up at six-thirty. What time did I wake up this morning? What time did you wake up this morning?

9. *speak-spoke*   I speak to many students every day. Before class today, I spoke to (. . .). Who did I speak to? Who did you speak to before class today?

10. *ring-rang*   The phone in our apartment rings a lot. This morning it rang at six-thirty and woke me up. What happened at six-thirty this morning? Who had a telephone call this morning? What time did the phone ring?

11. *sing-sang*   I sing in the shower every morning. I sang in the shower yesterday. What did I do yesterday? Do you ever sing? When was the last time?

12. *break-broke*   Sometimes I break things. This morning I dropped a glass on the floor and it broke. What happened this morning? When did you break something?

■ **練習 50**：將框內的動詞改成正確形式，完成下列句子。

break	*meet*	*sing*
fly	*pay*	*speak*
hear	*ring*	*take*
leave	*send*	*wake*

1. A: What happened to your finger?

   B: I _____ it in a soccer game.

2. A: Who did you talk to at the director's office?

   B: I _____ to the secretary.

3. A: When did Jessica leave for Europe?

   B: She _____ for Europe five days ago.

4. A: Did you write Ted a letter?

   B: No, but I _____ him a postcard.

5. A: Do you know Meg Adams?

   B: Yes. I _____ her a couple of weeks ago.

6. A: Why did you call the police?

   B: Because I _____ a burglar!

7. A: Where did you go yesterday?

   B: I _____ the children to the zoo.

8. A: What time did you get up this morning?
   B: 6:15.
   A: Why did you get up so early?

   B: The telephone _____.

9. A: Did you enjoy the party?

   B: Yes, I had a good time. We _____ songs and danced. It was fun.

10. A: You look sleepy.

    B: I am. I _____ up before dawn this morning and couldn't get back to sleep.

11. A: Did you give the painter a check?

    B: No. I _____ him in cash.

12. A: A bird _____ into our apartment yesterday through an open window.
    B: Really? What did you do?
    A: I caught it and took it outside.

(a) 主詞 動詞 *I ate breakfast.* = 主要句子	子句：含有一個主詞和一個動詞的一組字。
(b) 主詞 動詞 ***before** I went to class* = 時間句子	主要子句是一個完整的句子。(a) 例是一完整的句子。(b) 例是不完整的句子，需和主要子句連接，如 (c) 和 (d)。

(c) 主詞 動詞
 | I ate breakfast | | ***before** I went to class.* |
 主要子句   時間子句
	before 和 *after* 可以引導時間子句。
	    before + 主詞 + 動詞 = 時間子句
	    after + 主詞 + 動詞 = 時間子句

(d) 主詞 動詞 | ***Before** I went to class,* | | I ate breakfast. | 時間子句 主要子句	
(e) | We took a walk | | ***after** we finished our walk.* | 主要子句 時間子句 (f) | ***After** we finished our work,* | | we took a walk. | 時間子句 主要子句	時間子句可接在主要子句後面，如 (c) 和 (e) 也可置於主要子句前面，如 (d) 和 (f)。(c) 句和 (d) 句之間，或 (e) 句和 (f) 句之間，意義並無差別。
(g) We took a walk | *after the movie.* | 介詞片語 (h) I had a cup of coffee | *before class.* | 介詞片語	*before* 和 *after* 並不只用來引導時間子句；它們也可作為介詞用，並在後面加名詞受詞，如 (g) 和 (h)。 有關介詞片語的資料，請參閱表 1-7 和表 4-1。

■ **練習 51**：找出下列各句的主要子句和時間子句。

1. Before I ate the banana, I peeled it.
   →   *main clause = I peeled it*
   →   *time clause = before I ate the banana*

2. We arrived at the airport before the plane landed.

3. I went to a movie after I finished my homework.

4. After the children got home from school, they watched TV.★

5. Before I moved to this city, I lived at home with my parents.

★注意：時間子句置於主要子句前面時，兩句之間要加逗號；若時間子句置於主要子句後面，則不用逗號。

■ **練習 52**：以下各題如為完整的句子，將句首第一個字母改成大寫，並於句尾加句點；如果只是時間子句，而非完整的句子，寫上 Inc. 表示不完整 Incomplete。

    1. we went home　→　*W̶we went home.*

    2. after we left my uncle's house　→　*Inc.*

    3. we went home after we left my uncle's house
       →　*W̶we went home after we left my uncle's house.*

    4. before we ate our picnic lunch

    5. we went to the zoo

    6. we went to the zoo before we ate our picnic lunch

    7. the children played games after they did their work

    8. the children played games

    9. after they did their work

  10. the lions killed a zebra

  11. after the lions killed a zebra

  12. they ate it

  13. after the lions killed a zebra, they ate it

■ **練習 53**：用 before 和 after 引導的時間子句，將兩個句子結合成一句。

   例：　I put on my coat. I went outside.
      →　*Before I went outside, I put on my coat.*
        I put on my coat before I went outside.
        After I put on my coat, I went outside.
        I went outside after I put on my coat.

1. She ate breakfast.   She went to work.

2. He did his homework.   He went to bed.

3. We bought tickets.   We entered the theater.

■ **練習 54**：利用提示造過去簡單式的句子。

例：　　after I
書寫：　I went to college after I graduated from high school.
　　　　After I finished dinner, I watched TV.
　　　　諸如此類。

1. before I came here
2. after I got home last night
3. I went . . . before I

4. after we
5. before they
6. Mr. . . . after he

5-19　WHEN 在時間子句中的用法

（a）**When** the rain stopped, we took a walk. 或： We took a walk **when** the rain stopped. （b）When **Tom** was a child, **he** lived with his aunt. 或： **Tom** lived with his aunt when **he** was a child.	*when* 可引導時間子句。 　　　　*when* ＋主詞　＋動詞　＝時間子句 （a）中：*when the rain stopped* 是時間子句。 （b）中：注意名詞 *(Tom)* 要置於代名詞 *(he)* 之 　　　前。
比較： （c）*When did the rain stop?* ＝ 疑問句 （d）*when the rain stopped* ＝ 時間子句	*when* 也可用來引導疑問句。★ 疑問句是一個完 整的句子，如（c）。時間子句不是個完整的句 子。

★*when* 在疑問句中的用法，請參閱表 2-12 和表 5-13。

■ **練習 55**：配合題。從右欄中選出適當答案以使句子完整，接著再練習改變時間子句的位置。

例：　When the phone rang,
　　　→ When the phone rang, I answered it.★
　　　　I answered the phone when it rang.

1. When the phone rang,
2. When I was in Japan,
3. Maria bought some new shoes
4. I took a lot of photographs
5. When a stranger grabbed Ann's arm,
6. Jim was a wrestler
7. When the rain stopped,
8. The antique vase broke

A. she screamed.
B. when I dropped it.
C. I closed my umbrella.
D. when he was in high school.
✔ E. I answered it.
F. when she went shopping
　　yesterday.
G. I stayed in a hotel in Tokyo.
H. when I was in Hawaii.

★注意：假如 *when* 子句引導的句子中含有兩個動作，則 *when* 子句中的動作先發生。在 *When the phone rang,*
I answered it. 一句中：電話鈴先響，然後我再接聽。*When I answered the phone, it rang.* 的說法，在邏輯上是
不可能的。

1. when did Jim arrive → *W when did Jim arrive?*

2. when Jim arrived → *Inc.*

3. when you were a child

4. when were you in Iran

5. when did the movie end

6. when the movie ended

7. when Mr. Wang arrived at the airport

8. when Khalid and Bakir went to a restaurant on First Street yesterday

9. when I was a high school student

10. when does the museum open

■ **練習 57**：利用提示造句。不要改變現有的字序。

1. When did . . . .   4. When were . . . .
2. When I . . . .   5. When the . . . .
3. I . . . when . . . .   6. The . . . when . . . .

■ **練習 58 — 複習**：用括弧內的字完成下列句子。

(1)   Yesterday *(be)* _____ a terrible day. Everything *(go)*

(2)   _____ wrong. First, I *(oversleep)* _____.

(3)   My alarm clock *(ring, not)* _____. I *(wake)*

(4)   _____ up when I *(hear)*

(5)   _____ some noise outside my window.

(6)   It was 9:15. I *(get)* _____ dressed

(7)   quickly. I *(run)* _____ to class, but

(8)   I *(be)* _____ late. The teacher

(9)   (be) _____ upset. After my classes in the morning,

(10) I (go) _____ to the cafeteria for lunch. I (have)

(11) _____ an embarrassing accident at the cafeteria. I accidentally

(12) (drop) _____ my tray of food. Some of the dishes (break)

(13) _____. When I (drop) _____ the tray,

(14) everyone in the cafeteria (look) _____ at me. I

(15) (go) _____ back to the cafeteria line and

(16) (get) _____ a second tray of food. I (pay)

(17) _____ for my lunch again. After I (sit)

(18) _____ down at a table in the corner by

(19) myself, I (eat) _____ my sandwich and

(20) (drink) _____ a cup of tea.

(21)   After lunch, I (go) _____ outside. I (sit) _____

(22) under a tree near the classroom building. I (see) _____ a friend. I

(23) (call) _____ to him. He

(24) (join) _____ me on the grass.

(25) We (talk) _____ about our

(26) classes and (relax) _____.

      Everything was fine. But when I (stand)

(27) _____ up, I (step)

(28) _____ in a hole and (break)

(29) _____ my ankle.

(30)   My friend (drive) _____ me

(31) to the hospital. We (go) _____ to

      the emergency ward. After the doctor (take)

(32) _____ X-rays of my ankle, he

(33) (put) _____ a cast on it. I

(34)　　　*(pay)* _____ my bill. Then we *(leave)* _____

(35)　　　the hospital. My friend *(take)* _____ me home and *(help)*

(36)　　　_____ me up the stairs to my apartment.

(37)　　　　　　When we *(get)* _____ to the door of my apartment, I *(look)*

(38)　　　_____ for my key. I *(look)* _____ in my

　　　purse and in my pockets. There was no key. I *(ring)*

(39)　　　_____ the doorbell. I *(think)*

(40)　　　_____ that my roommate might be

(41)　　　at home, but she *(be, not)* _____. So I *(sit)*

(42)　　　_____ down on the floor outside my

(43)　　　apartment and *(wait)* _____ for my

　　　roommate to get home.

(44)　　　　　　Finally, my roommate *(come)* _____ home and I *(get)*

(45)　　　_____ into the apartment. I *(eat)* _____

(46)　　　dinner quickly and *(go)* _____ to bed. I *(sleep)*

(47)　　　_____ for ten hours. I hope today is a better day than yesterday!

■　**練習 59 — 口語練習**：全班分為數個小組，練習敘述練習58中，主角人物 Sara 的一天。（闔上書
　　　　　　　　　　　　本，並注意動詞的過去形式。）

例：

學生A： Sara had a terrible day yesterday. Everything went wrong for her.

學生B： Yes, she had a terrible day. First she overslept and miss class.

學生C： Missed. She *missed* class.

學生B： Right. She *missed* class.

學生C： She missed class because her alarm clock didn't rang.

學生D： Didn't *ring*, not rang.

學生C： Right! Her alarm clock didn't *ring*.

學生D： She woke up when she heard some noise outside her window at 9:15. She got dressed quickly and run to class.

學生A： Excuse me, but I think you should say that she got dressed quickly and . . . .

■ **練習 60 — 書寫練習**：不要看課本，憑自己的記憶，將 Sara 的一天寫下來。

■ **練習 61 — 書寫練習**：從以下的主題中選擇一項，寫一篇有關過去事件的作文。用時間語詞（first, next, then, at...o'clock, later, after, before, when 等）表示活動發生的先後順序。

主題 1： Write about your activities yesterday, from the time you got up to the time you went to bed.

主題 2： Write about one of the best days in your life. What happened?

主題 3： Write about one of the worst days in your life. What happened?

■ **練習 62 — 書寫練習**：詢問一位你認識的人，有關他 / 她昨天早上、下午和晚上的活動。然後據此寫一篇作文。用時間語詞（first, next, then, at...o'clock, later, after, before, when 等）表示活動發生的先後順序。

■ **練習 63 — 複習**：寫出下列動詞的過去式。

1. visit	_visited_	10. pay	_____
2. fly	_flew_	11. catch	_____
3. go	_____	12. happen	_____
4. worry	_____	13. listen	_____
5. speak	_____	14. plan	_____
6. ride	_____	15. rain	_____
7. stand	_____	16. bring	_____
8. turn	_____	17. take	_____
9. hear	_____	18. write	_____

19. break	_____	25. ring	_____
20. stop	_____	26. meet	_____
21. hope	_____	27. leave	_____
22. sing	_____	28. occur	_____
23. think	_____	29. teach	_____
24. drive	_____	30. read	_____

■ **練習 64 — 複習**：利用下列動詞，以過去簡單式做問答練習。

學生A：Make up any question that includes the given verb. Use the SIMPLE PAST.
學生B：Answer the question. Give a short answer and a long answer.

例： speak
學生A：Did you speak to Mr. Lee yesterday?
學生B：Yes, I did. I spoke to him yesterday.

例： finish
學生B：What time did you finish your homework last night?
學生B：Around nine o'clock. I finished my homework around nine o'clock.

角色互換

1. drink	5. fly	9. see	13. buy
2. eat	6. talk	10. sleep	14. send
3. study	7. wake up	11. work	15. watch
4. take	8. come	12. have	16. read

■ **練習 65 — 複習**：更正下列句子的錯誤。

1. Did you went downtown yesterday?

2. Yesterday I speak to Ken before he leaves his office and goes home.

3. I heared a good joke last night.

4. When Pablo finished his work.

5. I visitted my relatives in New York City last month.

6. Where you did go yesterday afternoon?

7. Ms. Wah was flew from Singapore to Tokyo last week.

8. When I see my friend yesterday, he didn't spoke to me.

9. Why Mustafa didn't came to class last week?

10. Where were you bought those shoes? I like them.

11. Mr. Adams teached our class last week.

12. I writed a letter last night.

13. Who you wrote a letter to?

14. Who did open the door? Jack openned it.

■ **練習 66 — 複習**：用括弧內的字，以現在簡單式，現在進行式，或過去簡單式完成下列句子。其中可能包含肯定句，否定句，或疑問句的型態。

1. Tom (walk) _____ *walks* _____ to work almost every day.

2. I can see Tom from my window. He's on the street below.   He (walk)

   _____ to work right now.

3. (Tom, walk) _____ to work every day?

4. (you, walk) _____ to work every day?

5. I usually take the bus to work, but yesterday I (walk) _____ to my
   office.

6. On my way to work yesterday, I (see) _____ an accident.

7. Alex (see, not) _____ the accident.

8. (you, see) _____ the accident yesterday?

9. Tom (walk, not) _____ to work when the weather is cold. He

   (take) _____ the bus.

10. I (walk, not) _____ to work in cold weather either.

■ **練習 67 — 複習**：用括弧內的字完成下列句子。

(1)   Yesterday Fish (be) _____ in the river. He (see) _____

Bear on the bank of the river.   Here is their conversation.

   BEAR: Good morning, Fish.

(2) FISH: Good morning, Bear. How *(you, be)* _____ today?

(3) BEAR: I *(do)* _____ fine, thank you. And you?

   FISH: Fine, thanks.

(4) BEAR: *(you, would like)* _____ to get out of the river and *(sit)*

(5)   _____ with me? I *(need)* _____ someone to talk to.

(6) FISH: I *(need, not)* _____ to get out of the river for us to talk.

     We can talk just the way we are now.

   BEAR: Hmmm.

(7) FISH: Wait! What *(you, do)* _____?

(8) BEAR: I *(get)* _____ in the river to join you.

(9) FISH: Stop! This *(be)* _____ my river! I *(trust, not)* _____

(10)   _____ you. What *(you, want)* _____?

(11) BEAR: Nothing. Just a little conversation. I *(want)* _____ to tell you about

(12)   my problems. I *(have)* _____ a bad day yesterday.

FISH: Oh? What happened?

(13)   BEAR: While I was walking through the woods, I *(see)* _____ a beehive. I

(14)   *(love)* _____ honey. So I *(stop)* _____ at the

beehive. When I *(reach)*

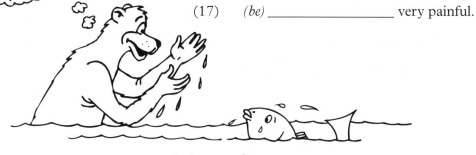

(15)   _____ inside to get

some honey, a great big bee *(come)*

(16)   _____ up behind

me and stung★ my ear. The sting

(17)   *(be)* _____ very painful.

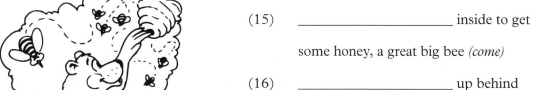

(18)   FISH: I *(believe, not)* _____ you. Bees can't hurt bears. I

(19)   *(believe, not)* _____ your story about a great big bee.

(20)   All bees *(be)* _____ the same size, and they *(be, not)* _____ big.

(21)   BEAR: But it *(be)* _____ true! Here. Come a little closer and look at

my ear. I'll show you where the big bee stung it.

(22)   FISH: Okay. Where *(it, be)* _____? Where *(the bee, sting)*

(23)   _____ you?

BEAR: Right here. See?

(24)   FISH: Stop! What *(you, do)* _____? Let go of me! Why

(25)   *(you, hold)* _____ me?

★*stung*是動詞 *sting*（叮咬）的過去式。

(26)   BEAR: I *(hold)* _____ you because I'm going to eat you for dinner.

(27)   FISH: Oh no! You *(trick)* _____ me! Your story about the great big bee

(28)   never *(happen)* _____!

(29)   BEAR: That's right. I *(get)* _____ in the river because I *(want)*

(30)   _____ *(catch)* _____ you for dinner. And I

(31)   did. I *(catch)* _____ you for dinner.

        FISH: Watch out! Behind you! Oh no! Oh no! It's a very, very big bee. It's huge! It

(32)   *(look)* _____ really angry!

(33)   BEAR: I *(believe, not)* _____ you!

(34)   FISH: But it *(be)* _____ true! A great big bee *(come)* _____

           toward you. It's going to attack you and sting you!

(35)   BEAR: What? Where? I *(see, not)* _____ a big bee! Oh no, Fish, you

(36)   are getting away from me. Oh no! I *(drop)* _____ you! Come

           back! Come back!

(37)   FISH: Ha! I *(fool)* _____ you too, Bear. Now you must find your

           dinner in another place.

(38)   BEAR: Yes, you *(trick)* _____ me too. We *(teach)* _____

           each other a good lesson today: Don't believe everything you hear.

        FISH: Thank you for teaching me that lesson. Now I will live a long and happy life.

(39) BEAR: Yes, we *(learn)* _____ a good lesson today, and that's good. But

(40) I *(be)* _____ still hungry. Hmmm. I *(have)* _____

(41) a gold tooth in my mouth. *(you, would like)* _____ to

come closer and look at it?

第六章
未來式的表達

6-1 未來式：BE GOING TO 的用法

(a) I **am going to go** downtown tomorrow. (b) Sue **is going to be** here tomorrow afternoon. (c) We **are going to come** to class tomorrow morning.	*be going to* 表示（談論）未來。 形式： $\left.\begin{array}{l} am \\ is \\ are \end{array}\right\}$ + going + 不定詞★
(d) I **'m not going to go** downtown tomorrow. (e) Ann **isn't going to study** tonight.	否定句： *be* + *not* + *going to*
(f) "**Are** you **going to come** to class tomorrow?" 　　"No, I'm not." (g) "**Is** Jim **going to be** at the meeting tomorrow?" 　　"Yes, he is." (h) "What time **are** you **going to eat** dinner tonight?" 　　"Around six."	疑問句： *be* + 主詞 + *going to* 回答含有 *be going to* 的 *yes* / *no* 問句時，用一個 *be* 動詞的形式作簡答，如 (f) 和 (g)。 （有關 *be* 動詞的簡答資料，請參閱表1-9。）

★不定詞＝ *to* + 原形動詞 *(to come, to go, to see, to study, etc.).*

■ **練習 1 — 口語練習：** 下頁列出的活動中，有哪些是你明天要做的，哪些是不要做的？兩人一組作問答練習。

　　學生A：打開書，用 Are you going to ...tomorrow? 提出問題。
　　學生B：閤上書，同時以簡答和完整答句回答問題。完整答句中要用 I'm going to ... tomorrow. 或 I'm not going to ... tomorrow. 句型。

例： go downtown

學生A： Are you going to go downtown tomorrow?

學生B： Yes, I am. I'm going to go downtown tomorrow. OR:
No, I'm not. I'm not going to go downtown tomorrow.

角色互換

1. get up before eight o'clock
2. come to class
3. stay home all day
4. eat lunch
5. eat lunch with （某人）
6. get a haircut
7. watch TV in the evening
8. do something interesting in the evening
9. go to bed early
10. go to bed late

11. get up early
12. get up late
13. walk to school
14. study grammar
15. get some physical exercise
16. eat dinner
17. eat dinner alone
18. listen to music after dinner
19. go shopping
20. do something interesting and unusual

■ 練習 2 — 口語練習（閤上書本）：回答問題。

例： tomorrow?

問學生A： What are you going to do tomorrow?

學 生A： I'm going to (go shopping).

問學生A： What is (. . .) going to do tomorrow?

學 生B： He's/She's going to go shopping.

What are you going to do:

1. tomorrow?
2. tomorrow morning?
3. tomorrow afternoon?
4. tomorrow night?
5. at 7:00 tomorrow morning?

6. at 9:00 tomorrow morning?
7. at noon tomorrow?
8. at 5:00 tomorrow afternoon?
9. around 6:30 tomorrow evening?
10. after 8:00 tomorrow night?

■ 練習 3：用 be going to + 框內語詞完成下列句子。

call the landlord	✔ go to the bookstore	see a dentist
call the police	go to an Italian restaurant	stay in bed today
get something to eat	lie down and rest for a while	take a long walk in the park
go to the beach	look it up in my dictionary	take it to the post office
go to bed	major in psychology	take them to the laundromat

1. I need to buy a book. I ____*am going to go to the bookstore*____.

2. It's midnight now. I'm sleepy. I _____.

3. Sue is hungry. She _____.

4. My clothes are dirty. I _____.

5. I have a toothache. My wisdom tooth hurts. I _____.

6. I'm writing a composition. I don't know how to spell a word. I _____

_____.

7. George has to mail a package. He _____.

8. Rosa lives in an apartment. There's a problem with the plumbing. She _____

_____.

9. Sue and I want to go swimming. We _____.

10. I have a headache. I _____.

11. It's late at night. I hear a burglar! I _____.

12. I want to be a psychologist. When I go to the university, I _____

_____.

13. I feel terrible. I think I'm getting the flu. I _____.

14. Ivan and Natasha want to go out to eat. They _____.

15. It's a nice day today. Mary and I _____.

■ **練習 4 — 口語練習（閤上書本）**：先聽教師描述一位同學的活動，在腦海裡想像其情景，然後用 be going to 說出你認為同學將要做的事。

例：（ . . . ）is carrying his / her textbooks and notebooks. He / She is walking toward the library. What is (. . .) going to do?

答：（ . . . ）is going to study at the library.

1. （ . . . ）is standing next to the chalkboard. He / She is picking up a piece of chalk. What is (. . .) going to do?

2. （ . . . ）has some letters in his / her hand. He / She is walking toward the post office. What is (. . .) going to do?

3. （ . . . ）is standing by a telephone. He / She is looking in the telephone book for (. . .)'s name. What is (. . .) going to do?

4. （ . . . ）put some water on the stove to boil. She got a cup and saucer out of the cupboard and some tea. What is (. . .) going to do?

5. （ . . . ）is putting on his / her coat. He / She is walking toward the door. What is (. . .) going to do?

6. （ . . . ）has a basket full of dirty clothes. He / She is walking toward a laundromat. What is (. . .) going to do?

7. （ . . . ）bought some meat and vegetables at the market. He / She is holding a bag of rice. He / She just turned on the stove. What is (. . .) going to do?

8. （ . . . ）and (. . .) are walking into（某餐廳）. It's seven o'clock in the evening. What are (. . .) and (. . .) going to do?

9. （ . . . ）gave (. . .) a diamond engagement ring. What are (. . .) and (. . .) going to do?

10. （ . . . ）and (. . .) have airplane tickets. They're putting clothes in their suitcases. Their clothes include swimming suits and sandals. What are (. . .) and (. . .) going to do?

■ **練習 5 — 口語練習**：用 be going to 向同學提出問題。

例： when / go downtown

學生A：When are you going to go downtown?

學生B：Tomorrow afternoon. / In a couple of days. / I don't know. / 等。

1. where / go after class today
2. what time / get home tonight
3. when / eat dinner
4. where / eat dinner
5. what time / go to bed tonight
6. what time / get up tomorrow morning
7. where / be tomorrow morning
8. when / see your family again
9. where / live next year
10. when / get married

例： You want to buy some tea. What are you going to do? What is (. . .) going to do and why?

問學生A： You want to buy some tea. What are you going to do?

學　生A： I'm going to go to the grocery store.

問學生B： What is (Student A) going to do and why?

學　生B： He / She's going to go to the grocery store because he / she wants to buy some tea.

1. You have a toothache. What are you going to do? What is (. . .) going to do and why?
2. You need to mail a package. Where are you going to go? Where is (. . .) going to go and why?
3. Your clothes are dirty.
4. It's midnight. You're sleepy.
5. It's late at night. You hear a burglar.
6. You need to buy some groceries.
7. You want to go swimming.
8. You want to go fishing.
9. You want to buy a new coat.
10. You're hungry.
11. You have a headache.
12. It's a nice day today.
13. You need to cash a check.
14. You want some *(pizza)* for dinner.
15. You're reading a book. You don't know the meaning of a word.

6-2　表示過去時間和未來時間的字詞

過去	未來	
yesterday	*tomorrow*	過去： It *rained* **yesterday**. 未來： It's *going to rain* **tomorrow**.
yesterday morning *yesterday afternoon* *yesterday evening* *last night*	*tomorrow morning* *tomorrow afternoon* *tomorrow evening* *tomorrow night*	過去： I *was* in class **yesterday morning**. 未來： I'm *going to be* in class **tomorrow morning**.
last week *last month* *last year* *last weekend* *last spring* *last summer* *last fall* *last winter* *last Monday,* 等。	*next week* *next month* *next year* *next weekend* *next spring* *next summer* *next fall* *next winter* *next Monday,* 等。	過去： Mary *went* downtown **last week**. 未來： Mary *is going to go* downtown **next week**. 過去： Bob *graduated* from high school **last spring**. 未來： Ann *is going to graduate* from high school **next spring**.
. . . minutes ago *. . . hours ago* *. . . days ago* *. . . weeks ago* *. . . months ago* *. . . years ago*	*in . . . minutes* (from now) *in . . . hours* (from now) *in . . . days* (from now) *in . . . weeks* (from now) *in . . . months* (from now) *in . . . years* (from now)	過去： I *finished* my homework **five minutes ago**. 未來： Pablo *is going to finish* his homework **in five minutes**.

■ **練習 7**：用 yesterday, last, tomorrow 或 next 完成下列句子。

1. I went swimming _____*yesterday*_____ morning.

2. Ken is going to go to the beach _____*tomorrow*_____ morning.

3. I'm going to take a trip _____ week.

4. Alice went to Miami _____ week for a short vacation.

5. We had a test in class _____ afternoon.

6. _____ afternoon we're going to go on a picnic.

7. My sister is going to arrive _____ Tuesday.

8. Sam bought a used car _____ Friday.

9. My brother is going to enter the university _____ fall.

10. _____ spring I took a trip to San Francisco.

11. Ann is going to fly to London _____ month.

12. Rick lived in Tokyo _____ year.

13. I'm going to study at the library _____ night.

14. _____ night I watched TV.

15. _____ evening I'm going to go to a baseball game.

16. Matt was at the laundromat _____ evening.

1. *ten minutes*   Class is going to end _____*in ten minutes.*_____

2. *ten minutes*   Ann's class ended _____*ten minutes ago.*_____

3. *an hour*   The post office isn't open. It closed _____

4. *an hour*   Jack is going to call us _____

5. *two more months* I'm studying abroad now, but I'm going to be back home

   _____

6. *two months*   My wife and I took a trip to Morocco _____

7. *a minute*   Karen left _____

8. *half an hour*   I'm going to meet David at the coffee shop _____

9. *one more week* The new highway is going to open _____

10. *a year*   I was living in Korea _____

1. I went to the zoo _____*last*_____ week.

2. Yolanda went to the zoo a week _____.

3. Peter Nelson is going to go to the zoo _____ Saturday.

4. We're going to go to the zoo _____ two more days.

5. My children went to the zoo _____ morning.

6. My cousin is going to go to the zoo _____ afternoon.

7. Kim Yang-Don graduated from Sogang University _____ spring.

8. I'm going to take a vacation in Canada _____ summer.

9. We're going to have company for dinner _____ night.

10. We had company for dinner three days _____.

11. We're going to have dinner at our friends' house _____ two days.

12. _____ evening we're going to go to a concert.

13. _____ Friday I went to a party.

14. _____ morning the students took a test.

15. I took a test two days _____.

16. The students are going to have another test _____ Thursday.

17. Are you going to be home _____ afternoon around three?

18. My little sister arrived here _____ month.

19. She is going to leave _____ two weeks.

20. _____ year Yuko is going to be a freshman in college.

6-3 A COUPLE OF 或 A FEW 和 AGO（過去）與 IN（未來）連用的用法

(a) Sam arrived here **one** (或：**a**) *year ago.* (b) Jack is going to be here *in **two** minutes.* (c) I talked to Ann ***three** days ago.*	時間語詞中，數目常和 *ago* 和 *in* 合用。
(d) I saw Carlos ***a couple of** months ago.* (e) He's going to return to Mexico *in **a couple of** months.* (f) I got a letter from Gina ***a few** weeks ago.* (g) I got a letter to see Gina *in **a few** weeks.*	*a couple of* 和 *a few* 也是常用的片語。*a couple of* 表示「兩個」。*a couple of months ago*＝兩個月前。 *a few* 表示「少量，數目不多」。*a few weeks ago*＝三，四，或五個星期以前。
(h) I began college last year. I'm going to graduate *in **two more** years.* My sister is almost finished with her education. She's going to graduate *in **a few more** months.* She's going to graduate *in **three more** months.*	*more* 經常用於以 *in* 開頭的未來時間語詞中。

■ **練習 10**：根據實際的生活狀況，以各題前的斜體字搭配 ago 或 in，以及數目（one, two, three, ten, sixteen 等）或 a couple of 或 a few 完成下列句子。

1. *days*   We studied Chapter 5 *a couple of days ago / three days ago / etc.*

2. *days*   We're going to finish this chapter ___*in a few more days /*___
___*in three or four days / etc.*___

3. *hours*   I ate breakfast _____

4. *hours*   I'm going to eat lunch / dinner _____

5. *minutes* We finished Exercise 9 _____

6. *minutes* This class is going to end _____

7. *years* I was born _____

8. *years* My parents got married _____

9. *years* I got / am going to get married _____

10. *weeks* ⎫ I arrived in this city _____, and I'm
    months ⎬
    years ⎭ going to leave this city _____

■ **練習 11**：用自己的話完成下列句子。例如：你幾天前做了什麼？過幾天你將做什麼？

1. _____ a few days ago.

2. _____ in a few days *(from now)*.

3. _____ in a few more minutes.

4. _____ three hours ago.

5. _____ in four more hours.

6. _____ a couple of days ago.

7. _____ in a couple of months *(from now)*.

8. _____ a few minutes ago.

9. _____ many years ago.

10. _____ in a couple of minutes *(from now)*.

6-4 TODAY, TONIGHT 和 THIS+MORNING, AFTERNOON, EVENING, WEEK, MONTH, YEAR 的用法

現在	現在是早上 10 點，我們在上英文課。 （a）We **are studying** English **this morning**.	*today* *tonight* *this morning* ⎫ *this afternoon* ⎬ 這些字可用來表 *this evening* ⎮ 示現在、過去、 *this week* ⎮ 或未來時間。 *this weekend* *this month* ⎭ *this year*
過去	現在是早上 10 點，Nancy 早上 9 點出門進城去了，她現在不在家。 （b）Nancy **went** downtown **this morning**.	
未來	現在是早上 10 點，課程 11 點結束。下課後，我要到郵局去。 （c）I**'m going to go** to the post office **this morning**.	

■ **練習 12**：用自己的話回答下列問題。

1. What is something you did earlier this year?

   → I ____came to this city_____ this year.

2. What is something you are doing this year?

   → I ____am studying English_____ this year.

3. What is something you are going to do this year?

   → I ____am going to visit my relatives in Cairo_____ this year.

4. What is something you did earlier today?

   → I _____ today.

5. What is something you are doing today, right now?

   → I _____ today.

6. What is something you are going to do later today?

   → I _____ today.

7. What is something you did earlier this morning / afternoon / evening?

   → I _____ this _____.

8. What is something you are going to do later this morning / afternoon / evening?

   → I _____ this _____.

■ **練習 13**：完成下列句子，並討論可能出現的不同動詞時態。

1. _____ today.

2. _____ this morning.

3. _____ this afternoon.

4. _____ this evening.

5. _____ tonight.

6. _____ this week.

7. _____ this month.

8. _____ this year.

■ **練習 14 — 口語練習**：三人一組，向同學提出有關未來活動的問題。

學生A：用 When are you going to ...? 提出問題。
學生B：回答學生 A 的問題。
學生A：用 When is (...)going to ...? 向學生 C 提出問題。
學生C：用完整答句回答。

例：　go downtown
學生A：When are you going to go downtown?
學生B：This weekend. (Tomorrow morning. / In a couple of days. / 等。)
學生A：When is (. . .) going to go downtown?
學生C：He / She is going to go downtown this weekend.

1. study at the library
2. go shopping
3. go to （某堂課）
4. have dinner
5. do your grammar homework
6. get married
7. go on a picnic
8. visit（本市某處）

9. call (. . .) on the phone
10. go to（某餐廳）for dinner
11. see your family again
12. quit smoking
13. buy a car
14. see (. . .)
15. go to（本市某處）
16. take a vacation

■ **練習 15 — 口語練習**：兩人一組，用提示的字做問答練習。

例：　tomorrow morning
學生A：Are you going to come to class tomorrow morning?
學生B：Yes, I am.　或：No, I'm not.
例：　yesterday morning
學生A：Did you eat breakfast yesterday morning?
學生B：Yes, I did.　或：No, I didn't.

角色互換

1. last night
2. tomorrow night
3. tonight
4. tomorrow afternoon
5. yesterday afternoon
6. this afternoon
7. last Friday
8. next Friday
9. next week

10. last week
11. this week
12. yesterday morning
13. tomorrow morning
14. this morning
15. later today
16. a couple of hours ago
17. in a couple of hours *(from now)*
18. this evening

直述句	(a) Mike **will go** to the library tomorrow. (b) Mike **is going to go** to the library tomorrow.	(a) 句和 (b) 句基本上同義。
	(c) 誤： *Mike will* **goes** *there.*	*will* 後面要接原形動詞。 (c) 句中：*goes* 是不正確的。
	(d) 誤： *Mike will***s** *go there.*	表示未來式的 *will*，字尾不可加 -s。
	(e) 誤： *Mike will* **to** *go there.*	*will* 後面不可加含有 *to* 的不定詞。
縮寫形式	(f) I will come. = **I'll** come. You will come. = **You'll** come. She will come. = **She'll** come. He will come. = **He'll** come. It will come. = **It'll** come. We will come = **We'll** come. They will come. = **They'll** come.	*will* 可以和主詞代名詞縮寫成 *'ll*。★這種縮寫方式常見於口語和書寫中。
否定句	(g) Bob **will not be** here tomorrow. (h) Bob **won't be** here tomorrow.	否定式縮寫： *will + not = won't*

★*will* 在口語中（書寫中不可）也經常和名詞縮寫在一起。
   書寫： *Tom will be here at ten.*
   口語： *"Tom'll" be here at ten.*

■ **練習 16 — 口語練習**：用 will 表示未來時間，改寫下列句子。

1. I'm going to arrive around six tomorrow.
   → *I'll arrive around six tomorrow.*
2. Fred isn't going to come to our party.
3. He's going to be out of town next week.
4. Sue is going to be in class tomorrow.
5. She has a cold, but she isn't going to stay home.
6. Jack and Peggy are going to meet us at the movie theater.
7. They're going to be there at 7:15.
8. Tina is going to stay home and watch TV tonight.★
9. This is an important letter. I'm going to send this letter by express mail.

★用 *and* 連接兩個動詞時，通常不重複助動詞 *be going to* 和 *will*。例如：
I'm going to lock the doors and ~~am going to~~ turn out the lights.
I'll lock the doors and ~~will~~ turn out the lights.

10. My parents are going to stay at a hotel in Honolulu.
11. Hurry up, or we're going to be late for the concert.
12. I'm not going to be at home this evening.
13. I'm going to wash the dishes and clean the kitchen after dinner.
14. Be careful with those scissors! You're going to hurt yourself!

6-6 用 WILL 造問句

疑問句						回答
（疑問詞） +	WILL +	主詞 +	主要動詞			
(a)	*Will*	*Tom*	*come*	tomorrow?	→	*Yes, he will.*★ *No, he won't.*
(b)	*Will*	*you*	*be*	at home tonight?	→	*Yes, I will.*★ *No, I won't.*
(c) When	*will*	*Ann*	*arrive?*		→	*Next Saturday.*
(d) What time	*will*	*the plane*	*arrive?*		→	*Three-thirty.*
(e) Where	*will*	*you*	*be*	tonight?	→	*At home.*

★注意：簡答中，*will* 不可和代名詞縮寫。有關簡答中的縮寫式用法，請參閱表 1-9。

■ **練習 17**：造疑問句。

1. A: _____*Will you be at home tomorrow night?*_____

    B: Yes, _____*I will.*_____ (I'll be at home tomorrow night.)

2. A: _____*Will Ann be in class tomorrow?*_____

    B: No, _____*she won't.*_____ (Ann won't be in class tomorrow.)

3. A: _____*When will you see Mr. Pong?*_____

    B: Tomorrow afternoon. (I'll see Mr. Pong tomorrow afternoon.)

4. A: _____

    B: Yes, _____ (The plane will be on time.)

5. A: _____

    B: Yes, _____ (Dinner will be ready in a few minutes.)

6. A: _____

    B: In a few minutes. (Dinner will be ready in a few minutes.)

7. A: _____

    B: Next year. (I'll graduate next year.)

8. A: _____

    B: At the community college. (Mary will go to school at the community college next year.)

9. A: _____

    B: No, _____ (Jane and Mark won't be at the party.)

10. A: _____

    B: Yes, _____ (Mike will arrive in Chicago next week.)

11. A: _____

    B: In Chicago. (Mike will be in Chicago next week.)

12. A: _____

    B: No, _____ (I won't be home early tonight.)

13. A: _____

    B: In a few minutes. (Dr. Smith will be back in a few minutes.)

14. A: _____

    B: Yes, _____ (I'll be ready to leave at 8:15.)

    A: Are you sure?

6-7 動詞摘要：現在、過去和未來

	肯定句	否定句	疑問句
現在簡單式	I *eat* lunch every day. He *eats* lunch every day.	I *don't eat* breakfast. She *doesn't eat* breakfast.	*Do* you *eat* breakfast? *Does* she *eat* lunch?
現在進行式	I *am eating* an apple right now. She *is eating* an apple. They *are eating* apples.	I'*m not eating* a pear. She *isn't eating* a pear. They *aren't eating* pears.	*Am* I *eating* a banana? *Is* he *eating* a banana? *Are* they *eating* bananas?
過去簡單式	He *ate* lunch yesterday.	He *didn't eat* breakfast.	*Did* you *eat* breakfast?
BE GOING TO	I *am going to eat* lunch at noon. She *is going to eat* lunch at noon. They *are going to eat* lunch at noon.	I'*m not going to eat* breakfast tomorrow. She *isn't going to eat* breakfast tomorrow. They *aren't going to eat* breakfast tomorrow.	*Am* I *going to see* you tomorrow? *Is* she *going to eat* lunch tomorrow? *Are* they *going to eat* lunch tomorrow?
WILL	He *will eat* lunch tomorrow.	He *won't eat* breakfast tomorrow.	*Will* he *eat* lunch tomorrow?

■ **練習 18 — 複習動詞：**用括弧內的動詞完成下列句子。

1.　Right now, Anita *(sit)* _____*is sitting*_____ at her desk.

2.　She *(do, not)* _____ homework.　She *(write)*

　　_____ a letter to her parents.

3. She *(write)* _____ to her parents every week.

4. She *(write, not)* _____ a letter every day.

5. Her parents *(expect, not)* _____ to get a letter every day.

6. Last night Anita *(write)* _____ a letter to her brother. Then she

 (start) _____ to write a letter to her sister.

7. While Anita was writing a letter to her sister last night, her phone *(ring)*

 _____ . It *(be)* _____ her sister!

8. Anita *(finish, not)* _____ the letter to her sister last night.

 After she *(talk)* _____ to her sister, she *(go)* _____

 to bed.

9. Tomorrow she *(write)* _____ a letter to her cousin in Brazil.

10. Anita *(write, not)* _____ a letter to her parents tomorrow.

11. *(you, write)* _____ a letter to someone every day?

12. *(you, write)* _____ a letter to someone yesterday?

13. *(you, write)* _____ a letter to someone tomorrow?

6-8　動詞摘要：BE 動詞的形式

	肯定句	否定句	疑問句
現在簡單式	I **am** from Korea. He **is** from Egypt. They **are** from Venezuela.	I **am not** from Jordan. She **isn't** from China. They **aren't** from Italy.	**Am** I in the right room? **Is** she from Greece? **Are** they from Kenya?
過去簡單式	Ann **was** late yesterday. They **were** late yesterday.	She **wasn't** on time. They **weren't** on time.	**Was** she in class? **Were** they in class?
BE GOING TO	I **am going to be** late. She **is going to be** late. They **are going to be** late.	I**'m not going to be** on time. She **isn't going to be** on time. They **aren't going to be** on time.	**Am** I **going to be** late? **Is** she **going to be** late? **Are** they **going to be** late tomorrow?
WILL	He **will be** at home tomorrow.	He **won't be** at work tomorrow.	**Will** he **be** at work next week?

1. I *(be)* _____ in class right now. I *(be, not)* _____

   _____ here yesterday. I *(be)* _____ absent

   yesterday. *(you, be)* _____ in class yesterday? *(Carmen, be)*

   _____ here yesterday?

2. Carmen and I *(be)* _____ absent from class yesterday. We

   (be, not) _____ here.

3. My friends *(be)* _____ at Fatima's apartment tomorrow

   evening. I *(be)* _____ there too. *(you, be)* _____

   there? *(Yuko, be)* _____ there?

4. A whale *(be, not)* _____ a fish. It *(be)* _____ a

   mammal. Dolphins *(be, not)* _____ fish either. They

   (be) _____ mammals.

   DOLPHIN

■ 練習 20 — 複習動詞：用括弧內的動詞完成下列句子；必要時，請作簡答。

1. A: *(you, have)* _____*Do you have*_____ a bicycle?

   B: Yes, I *(do)* _____*do*_____. I *(ride)* _____*ride*_____ it to work
      every day.

2. A: *(you, walk)* _____ to work yesterday?

   B: No, I _____. I *(ride)* _____ my bicycle.

3. A: *(you, know)* _____ Mr. Park?

   B: Yes, I _____.

   A: Where *(you, meet)* _____ him?

   B: I *(meet)* _____ him at a dinner party at my uncle's house.

4. A: What time *(you, get up)* _____ every day?
   B: Between six and seven.

   A: What time *(you, get up)* _____ tomorrow?
   B: Six-thirty.

5. A: Where *(you, study, usually)* _____?
   B: In my room.

   A: *(you, go)* _____ to the library to study sometimes?

   B: No. I *(like, not)* _____ to study at the library.

6. A: *(you, be)* _____ in class tomorrow?

   B: Yes, I _____. But I *(be, not)* _____ in class
      the day after tomorrow.

7. A: *(Yuko, call)* _____ you last night?

   B: Yes, she _____. We *(talk)* _____ for a few minutes.

   A: *(she, tell)* _____ you about her brother?

   B: No, she _____. She *(say, not)* _____
      anything about her brother. Why?

   A: Her brother *(be)* _____ in an accident.
   B: That's too bad. What happened?

A: A dog *(run)* _____ in front of his bicycle. Her brother *(want, not)*

_____ to hit the dog. When he *(try)* _____

to avoid the dog, his bike *(run)* _____ into a truck. It was an
unfortunate accident.

B: *(he, be)* _____ in the hospital now?

A: No, he _____. He *(be)* _____ at home.

8. A: *(whales, breathe)* _____ air?

B: Yes, they _____.

A: *(a whale, have)* _____ lungs?

B: Yes, it _____.

A: *(a whale, be)* _____ a fish?

B: No, it _____. It *(be)* _____ a mammal.

9. A: *(you, watch)* _____ *Star Trek* on TV last night?
   B: What's *Star Trek*?

A: It *(be)* _____ a TV show about

the future. It *(be)* _____ a
science fiction show. *(you, like)*

_____
science fiction?

B: Yes, I _____. I *(read)* _____ science fiction books

often. When *(Star Trek, be)* _____
on TV again?
A: Next week, on Thursday at nine o'clock.

B: I *(try)* _____ to watch it. I might like it. What *("trek," mean)*

_____?

A: "Trek" *(mean)* _____ a long and difficult journey.

B: What *("journey," mean)* _____?

A: "Journey" *(mean)* _____ that you travel from one place to another
place. *Star Trek* is the story of people who travel in outer space among the stars.

描述 1： 假設以下圖片表示 Alex 正在做，或每天做的事，根據圖片用現在式描述 Alex 的一
些活動。

描述 2： 假設以下圖片表示 Alex 明天將做的事，請描述這些活動。

描述 3： 假設以下圖片表示 Alex 昨天做過的事，請描述這些活動。

6-9 WHAT + DO 的某一形態之用法

現在			what + 一種 do 的形式可用來詢問有關活動的問題。
（a） *What **do** you **do*** every day?	→	I *work* every day.	
（b） *What **are** you **doing*** right now?	→	I'm *studying English*.	
過去			
（c） *What **did** you **do*** yesterday?	→	I *went to school* yesterday.	
未來			
（d） *What **are** you **going to do*** tomorrow?	→	I'm *going to go downtown* tomorrow.	
（e） *What **will** we **do*** if it rains tomorrow?	→	We'll *stay home* if it rains tomorrow.	

■ **練習 22**：用括弧內的字完成下列句子。

1. A: What *(you, do)* _____ do you do _____ every Friday?

   B: I *(come)* _____ come _____ to class.

2. A: What *(you, do)* _____ last Friday?

   B: I *(come)* _____ to class.

3. A: What *(you, do)* _____ next Friday?

   B: I *(come)* _____ to class.

4. A: What *(you, do)* _____ yesterday evening?

   B: I *(watch)* _____ TV.

5. A: What *(you, do)* _____ every evening?

   B: I *(watch)* _____ TV.

6. A: What *(you, do)* _____ tomorrow evening?

   B: I *(watch)* _____ TV.

7. A: What *(you, do)* _____ right now?

   B: I *(do)* _____ a grammar exercise.

8. A: What *(Maria, do)* _____ every morning?

   B: She *(go)* _____ to work.

9. A: What *(the students, do)* _____ right now?

   B: They *(work)* _____ on this exericse.

10. A: What *(they, do)* _____ in class tomorrow?

    B: They *(take)* _____ a test.

11. A: What *(Boris, do)* _____ last night?

    B: He *(go)* _____ to a movie.

12. A: What *(the teacher, do)* _____ every day at the beginning of class?

    B: She *(put)* _____ her books on her desk, *(look)* _____

    at the class, and *(say)* _____ , "Good morning."

■ **練習 23 — 口語練習**：用 What + 一種 do 的形式，加上提示的時間語詞，向同學提出問題。

例： yesterday
學生A： What did you do yesterday?
學生B：（自由作答）

1. last night
2. every day
3. right now
4. tomorrow
5. yesterday afternoon
6. tomorrow morning
7. every morning

角色互換
8. right now
9. last Saturday
10. next Saturday
11. this morning
12. this afternoon
13. tonight
14. next week

6-10 MAY / MIGHT 和 WILL 的比較

(a) It **may rain** *tomorrow*. (b) Anita **may be** at home *now*.	*may* + 動詞（原形）表示未來的可能性，如 (a) 句；或現在的可能性，如 (b) 句。
(c) It **might rain** *tomorrow*. (d) Anita **might be** at home *now*.	*might* 和 *may* 意義相同。(a) 句和 (c) 同義。
(e) Tom **will be** at the meeting tomorrow. (f) Ms. Lee **may / might be** at the meeting tomorrow.	(e)句中：說者用 *will* 表示他確定 *Tom* 明天會出席會議。 (f)句中：說者用 *may / might* 表示「我不知道 *Ms. Lee* 是否會出席會議，不過有此可能。」
(g) Ms. Lee **may / might not be** at the meeting tomorrow.	否定式： *may / might* + *not* 注意：(f) 句和 (g) 句基本上同義：*Ms Lee* 明天可能會也可能不會出席會議。
(h) 誤：*Ms. Lee **may will** be at the meeting tomorrow.* 誤：*Ms. Lee **might will** be at the meeting tomorrow.*	*may* 和 *might* 不可和 *will* 合用。

■ **練習 24**：如果是你確定的事，就用 will 或 won't 完成下列句子；如果不確定，就用 may / might。

1. I _____ be in class next Monday.
   → *I **will be** in class next Monday.* = 你確定。
   → *I **will not (won't) be** in class next Monday.* = 你確定。
   → *I **may / might be** in class next Monday* (或 *I **may / might not be** in class next Monday).* = 可能，但你不確定。

2. I _____ eat breakfast tomorrow morning.

3. I _____ be in class tomorrow.

4. I _____ get a letter from a friend of mine tomorrow.

5. I _____ watch TV for a little while after dinner tonight.

6. We _____ have a grammar test in class tomorrow.

7. I _____ eat dinner at a restaurant tonight.

8. It _____ be cloudy tomorrow.

9. The sun _____ rise tomorrow morning.

10. I _____ choose a career in music after I finish school.

11. There _____ be another earthquake in Japan in the next few months.

12. The population of the earth _____ continue to grow.

13. Cities _____ become more and more crowded.

14. We _____ communicate with beings from outer space before the end of the 21st century.

15. Do you think we _____ communicate with other beings through music?

■ **練習 25 ― 書寫練習：**用 be going to 和 may / might 寫出自己明天的活動。

1. I'm going to get up at . . . tomorrow morning.
2. Then . . . .
3. After that . . . .
4. Around . . . o'clock . . . .
5. Later . . . .

6. At . . . o'clock . . . .
7. Then . . . .
8. After that . . . .
9. Next . . . .
10. Then at . . . o'clock . . . .

■ **練習 26 ― 書寫練習：**寫出你昨天的活動。

1. I got up at . . . yesterday morning.
2. I . . . and . . . .
3. Then I . . . .
4. I didn't . . . because . . . .
5. Later . . . .
6. Around . . . o'clock . . . .
7. Then . . . .

8. After that . . . .
9. At . . . o'clock . . . .
10. I didn't . . . because . . . .
11. At . . . I . . . .
12. . . . after that.
13. Then at . . . .

6-11　MAYBE（一個字）和 MAY BE（兩個字）的比較

(a)	"Will Abdullah be in class tomorrow?" "I don't know. ***Maybe. Maybe Abdullah will be*** in class tomorrow, and ***maybe he won't.***"	*maybe*（一個字）為一副詞，意為「可能的」。
(b)	⎴ ***Maybe*** ⎴ ⎴ Abdullah ⎴ ⎴ will be ⎴　here. 　副詞　　　　　主詞　　　　　動詞	*maybe* 置於主詞和動詞之前。 *may be*（兩個字）做為句子的動詞。
(c)	⎴ Abdullah ⎴ ⎴ ***may be*** ⎴　here tomorrow. 　主詞　　　　　動詞	

■ **練習 27**：找出句中 maybe 作副詞用，與 may 做為動詞的部份。

1. Maybe it will rain tomorrow. → ***maybe*** = 副詞

2. It may rain tomorrow. → ***may rain*** = 動詞；may 是動詞的一部分

3. We may go to the art museum tomorrow.

4. Maybe Ann would like to go to the museum with us.

5. She may like to go to art museums.

6. It's cold and cloudy today. It may be cold and cloudy tomorrow. Maybe the weather will be warm and sunny this weekend.

■ **練習 28**：填入 maybe 或 may / might。

1. A: Is David going to come to the party?

   B: I don't know. ____*Maybe*____.

2. A: What are you going to do tomorrow?

   B: I don't know. I ____*may / might*____ go swimming.

3. A: What are you going to do tomorrow?

   B: I don't have any plans. _____ I'll go swimming.

4. A: Where is Robert?

   B: I don't know. He _____ be at his office.

5. A: Where is Robert?

   B: I don't know. _____ he's at his office.

6. A: Are Kate and Steve going to get married?

   B: _____. Who knows?

7. A: Are you going to move to Portland or to Seattle?

   B: I don't know. I _____ move to San Francisco.

8. A: Where are you planning to go on your vacation?

   B: _____ we'll go to Mexico. We haven't decided yet. We

      _____ go to Florida.

9. A: Is Amanda married?

   B: Hmmm. I'm not sure. _____ she is, and

      _____ she isn't.

10. A: Do you think it will rain tomorrow?

    B: I have no idea. _____ it will, and _____ it
       won't.

11. A: Are you going to study English next semester?

    B: _____. Are you?

12. A: I'd like to have a pet.

    B: Oh? What kind of pet would you like to get?

    A: Oh, I don't know. I haven't decided yet. _____ I'll get a

       canary. Or _____ I'll get a snake. I'm not sure. I

       _____ get a frog. Or I _____ get a turtle.

    B: What's wrong with a cat or dog?

■ 練習 29：用 maybe 或 may be 完成下列句子。

1. A: I _____ *may be* _____ a little late tonight.
   B: That's okay. I won't worry about you.

2. A: Will you be here by seven o'clock?

   B: It's hard to say. _____ *Maybe* _____ I'll be a little late.

3. A: It _____ cold tomorrow.
   B: That's okay. Let's go to the beach anyway.

4. A: Will the plane be on time?

    B: I think so, but it _____ a few minutes late.

5. A: Do you want to go to the park tomorrow?
    B: Sure. That sounds like fun.

    A: Let's talk to Carlos too. _____ he would like to go with us.

6. A: Where's Mr. Chu?

    B: Look in Room 506 down the hall. I think he _____ there.

    A: No, he's not there. I just looked in Room 506.

    B: _____ he's in Room 508.

■ 練習 30 — 口語練習（閤上書本）：用 I don't know + maybe 或 may / might 回答下列問題。

例： What are you going to do tonight?
答： I don't know. Maybe I'll watch TV. / I may watch TV. / I might watch TV.

1. What are you going to do tonight?
2. What are you going to do tomorrow?
3. What are you going to do after class today?
4. What are you going to do this weekend?
5. What are you going to do this evening?
6. Who is going to go shopping tomorrow? What are you going to buy?
7. Who is going to go out to eat tonight? Where are you going to go?
8. Who is going to get married? When?
9. Who is going to watch TV tonight? What are you going to watch?
10. Who is absent today? Where is he / she?
11. Is it going to rain tomorrow? What is the weather going to be like tomorrow?
12. Who is planning to go on a vacation? Where are you going to go?
13. Who wants to have a pet? What kind of pet are you going to get?

■ 練習 31 — 口語練習（閤上書本）：以 may / might 和 maybe 作猜測。

例： (. . .) is absent today. Why? Do you have any possible explanations?
    → *He / She* **may be** *sick. He / She* **might be** *out of town today.* **Maybe** *he /
    she is late today and will come soon.*

1. What is (. . .) going to do after class today?
2. (. . .) said, "I have very exciting plans for this weekend." What is he / she going to
    do this weekend?
3. (. . .) has an airplane ticket in his pocket. I saw it. Do you know where he / she is
    going to go?

4. (. . .) said, "I don't like it here in this city." Why doesn't (. . .) like it here? Do you have any idea?

5. (. . .) doesn't like it here. What is he / she going to do?

6. (. . .) has something very special in his / her pocket, but he / she won't show anyone what it is. What do you suppose is in his / her pocket?

7. Can you think of some good things that may happen to you this year?

8. What are some good things that might happen to (. . .) this year or next year?

9. Can you think of some bad things that might happen in this world this year or next?

10. What are some good things that may happen in the world this year?

11. What new inventions do you think we may have in the future to make our lives easier?

6-12 含有 BEFORE, AFTER 和 WHEN 的未來時間子句

(a) *Before Ann* **goes** *to work tomorrow,* she will eat breakfast. (b) 誤： *Before Ann* **will go** *to work tomorrow, she will eat breakfast.* 誤： *Before Ann* **is going to go** *to work tomorrow, she will eat breakfast.*	(a) 句中：*Before Ann goes to work tomorrow* 是未來時間子句。★ 未來時間子句用現在簡單式表示，不要用*will* 或 *be going to*。
(c) I'm going to finish my homework *after I* **eat** *dinner tonight.* (d) *When I* **go** *to New York next week*, I'm going to stay at the Hilton Hotel.	(c) 句中：*after I eat dinner tonight* ＝未來時間子句。 (d) 句中：*When I go to New York next week* ＝未來時間子句。

★有關時間子句的資料，請參閱表 5-18。

■ **練習 32**：找出下列句子的時間子句。

1. When we go to the park tomorrow, we're going to go to the zoo.
   → *When we go to the park tomorrow* ＝時間子句

2. After I get home tonight, I'm going to make an overseas call to my parents.

3. Mr. Kim will finish his report before he leaves the office today.

4. I'll get some fresh fruit when I go to the market tomorrow.

5. Before I go to bed tonight, I'm going to write a letter to my brother.

6. I'm going to look for a job at a computer company after I graduate next year.

1. Before I *(go)* _____go_____ to bed tonight, I *(watch)*

   _____am going to watch/will watch_____ my favorite show on TV.

2. I *(buy)* _____ a new coat when I *(go)* _____
   shopping tomorrow.

3. After I *(finish)* _____ my homework this evening, I *(take)*

   _____ a walk.

4. When I *(see)* _____ Eduardo tomorrow, I *(ask)* _____
   him to join us for dinner this weekend.

5. When I *(go)* _____ to Australia next month, I *(meet)*

   _____ my Aunt Emily for the first time.

6. Mrs. Polanski *(change)* _____ her clothes before she *(work)*

   _____ in her garden this afternoon.

例： Who's going to go shopping later today? What are you going to do after you go shopping?

教　師： Who's going to go shopping later today?

學生A： （學生 A 舉起手。）

教　師： What are you going to do after you go shopping?

學生A： After I go shopping, I'm going to go home. 或：
　　　　 I'm going to go home after I go shopping.

教　師： What is (. . .) going to do after he / she goes shopping?

學生B： After (. . .) goes shopping, he / she is going to go home. 或：
　　　　 (. . .) is going to go home after he / she goes shopping.

1. Who's going to study tonight? What are you going to do after you study tonight?

2. Who else is going to study tonight? What are you going to do before you study?

3. Who's going to watch TV tonight? What are you going to do before you watch TV?

4. Who's going to watch TV tonight? What are you going to do after you watch TV?

5. Who's going to go shopping tomorrow? What are you going to buy when you go shopping tomorrow?

6. (. . .), what are you going to do tonight? What are you going to do before you . . . ? What are you going to do after you . . . tonight?

7. (. . .), what are you going to do tomorrow? What are you going to do before you . . . tomorrow? What are you going to do after you . . . tomorrow?

8. Who's going out of town soon? Where are you going? What are you going to do when you go to （某處）?

9. Who's going to eat dinner tonight? What are you going to do before you eat dinner? What are you going to do after you eat dinner? What are you going to have when you eat dinner?

10. (. . .), what time are you going to get home today? What are you going to do before you get home? What are you going to do when you get home? What are you going to do after you get home?

6-13　含有 IF 的子句

(a)	**If it rains tomorrow,** if-子句	we will stay home. 主要子句	if - 子句是以 if 引導的子句，其中含有一個主詞和一個動詞。
(b)	We will stay home 主要子句	**if it rains tomorrow.** if-子句	if - 子句可置於主要子句之前或之後。
(c)	**If it rains** tomorrow, we won't go on a picnic.		if - 子句用現在簡單式表示未來時間（不用 will 或 be going to）。
(d)	I'm going to buy a new car next year **if I have** enough money. **If I don't have** enough money for a new car next year, I'm going to buy a used car.		

■ **練習 35**：用括弧內的字完成下列句子。

1. If Ali *(be)* _____*is*_____ in class tomorrow, I *(ask)*

   ___*am going to/will ask*___ him to join us for coffee after class.

2. If the weather *(be)* _____ nice tomorrow, I *(go)*

   _____ to Central Park with my friends.

3. I *(stay, not)* _____ home tomorrow if the weather *(be)*

   _____ nice.

4. If I *(feel, not)* _____ well tomorrow, I *(go, not)*

   _____ to work.

5. Masako *(stay)* _____ in bed tomorrow if she *(feel, not)*

   _____ well.

6. I *(stay)* _____ with my aunt and uncle if I *(go)*

   _____ to Miami next week.

7. If my friends *(be)* _____ busy tomorrow, I *(go)*

   _____ to a movie by myself.

8. If we *(continue)* _____ to pollute the land and oceans with poisons

   and waste, future generations *(suffer)* _____.

學生A：書本打開，用 What are you going to do...? 提出問題。
學生B：闔上書本，以含有 if-子句的句子回答問題。

例： . . . if the weather is nice tomorrow?
學生A：What are you going to do if the weather is nice tomorrow?
學生B：If the weather is nice tomorrow, I'm going to sit outside in the sun.
或： I'm going to sit outside in the sun if the weather is nice tomorrow.

1. . . . if the weather is cold tomorrow?
2. . . . if the weather is hot tomorrow?
3. . . . if you don't understand a question that I ask you?
4. . . . if class is canceled tomorrow?
5. . . . if you don't feel well tomorrow?
6. . . . if you go to （某處） tomorrow?

角色互換

7. . . . if it rains tonight?
8. . . . if you're hungry after class today?
9. . . . if you go to （某處） tomorrow?
10. . . . if you don't study tonight?
11. . . . if you lose your grammar book?
12. . . . if someone steals your （某物：*bicycle, wallet*, 等）？

■ 練習 37：兩人一組練習。

學生A： 在行事曆中填入你下週的活動。（假如你的既定活動不多，就自創一些有趣的活動。）
然後，將你的行事曆交給學生 B。

學生B： 以書寫方式，描述學生 A 下週的活動。盡量寫出以 when, after 和 before 引導的時間子句。你也可以詢問學生 A 有關他／她的行事曆的問題，以獲得更多的資料。

例： （學生 A 是 Ali。）

SUNDAY

7:00 tennis with Talal
9:00 breakfast with Talal
1:00 meet Ivan at Cozy's before game
2:00 Memorial Stadium

7-9 Study

學生 B 了解學生 A 的行事曆後，寫下：
On Sunday, Ali is going to play tennis with Talal early in the morning. They're going to play on the tennis courts here at this school. After they play tennis, they're going to have breakfast. In the afternoon, Ali is going to meet Ivan at Cozy's. Cozy's is a cafe. They're going to have a sandwich and a cup of coffee before they go to the soccer game at Memorial Stadium. Ali will study in the evening before he watches TV and goes to bed.

將你下週的活動填入此行事曆。

MONDAY	THURSDAY
TUESDAY	**FRIDAY**
WEDNESDAY	**SATURDAY**

6-14　時間子句和 IF 子句表達習慣性現在式的用法

(a) 未來式	After Ann *gets* to work today, she *is going to have* a cup of coffee.	(a) 句表示未來的某一特定活動；時間子句用現在簡單式，主要子句用 *be going to*。
(b) 習慣性現在式	After Ann *gets* to work (every day), she always *has* a cup of coffee.	(b) 句表示習慣性活動，因此時間子句和主要子句都用現在簡單式。
(c) 未來式	If it *rains* tomorrow, I *am going to* wear my raincoat to school.	(c) 句表示未來的某一特定活動；*if*-子句用現在簡單式，主要子句用 *be going to*。
(d) 習慣性現在式	If it *rains*, I *wear* my raincoat.	(d) 句表示習慣性活動，因此 *if*-子句和主要子句都用現在簡單式。

1. When I *(go)* _____ to Miami, I *(stay, usually)* _____ with my aunt and uncle.

2. When I *(go)* _____ to Miami next week, I *(stay)* _____ with my aunt and uncle.

3. Before I *(go)* _____ to class today, I *(have)* _____ a cup of tea.

4. Before I *(go)* _____ to class, I *(have, usually)* _____ a cup of tea.

5. I'm often tired in the evening after a long day at work. If I *(be)* _____ tired in the evening, I *(stay, usually)* _____ home and *(go)* _____ to bed early.

6. If I *(be)* _____ tired this evening, I *(stay)* _____ home and *(go)* _____ to bed early.

7. After I *(get)* _____ home in the evening, I *(sit, usually)* _____ in my favorite chair and *(read)* _____ the newspaper.

8. After I *(get)* _____ home tonight, I *(sit)* _____ in my favorite chair and *(read)* _____ the newspaper.

9. We *(go)* _____ swimming tomorrow if the weather *(be)* _____ warm.

10. My friends and I *(like)* _____ to go swimming if the weather *(be)* _____ warm.

11. People *(yawn, often)* _____ and *(stretch)* _____ when they *(wake)* _____ up.

12. I *(buy)* _____ some stamps when I *(go)* _____ to the post office this afternoon.

13. Before the teacher *(walk)* _____ into the room every day, there *(be)* _____ a lot of noise in the classroom.

14. When I *(go)* _____ to Taiwan next month, I *(stay)* _____

    with my friend Mr. Chu. After I *(leave)* _____ Taiwan, I *(go)*

    _____ to Hong Kong.

15. Ms. Wah *(go)* _____ to Hong Kong often. When she *(be)*

    _____ there, she *(like)* _____ to take the ferry across

    the bay, but sometimes she *(take)* _____ the subway under the bay.

■ **練習 39 — 口語練習（闔上書本）**：用完整答句回答下列問題。

1. What do you do when you get up in the morning?
2. What are you going to do when you get up tomorrow morning?
3. What do you usually do before you go to bed?
4. What are you going to do before you go to bed tonight?
5. What are you going to do after you eat dinner tonight?
6. What do you usually do after you eat dinner?
7. What do you like to do if the weather is nice?
8. What are you going to do if the weather is nice tomorrow?

■ **練習 40**：用自己的話完成下列句子。

1. Before I go to bed tonight, ...
2. Before I go to bed, I usually . . . .
3. I'm going to . . . tomorrow after I . . . .
4. When I go to . . . , I'm going to . . . .
5. When I go to . . . , I always . . . .
6. If the weather . . . tomorrow, I . . . .
7. I will visit . . . when I . . . .
8. I'll . . . if I . . . .
9. If the weather . . . tomorrow, . . . you going to . . . ?
10. Are you going to . . . before you . . . ?
11. Do you . . . before you . . . ?
12. After I . . . tonight, I . . . .

■ **練習 41 — 複習（口語／書寫練習）**：假裝你將著手訂定來年的自我改善計畫，說出／寫出這一年
內你將做什麼來改善自己和自己的生活？例如：I will stop
smoking. I am going to get more exercise.等。

■ 練習 42 — 複習（口語／書寫練習）：未來 50 年，你同學的生活將會是什麼情形？請對同學的未來做預測。例如：Heidi is going to become a famous research scientist. Ali will have a happy marriage and lots of children. Carlos will live in a quiet place and write poetry.

■ 練習 43 — 複習（口語／書寫練習）：假設你收到一封銀行的來信，裡面告訴你，只要遵循信中的指示，你便可獲得一大筆錢。（全班一起決定此金額。）以下有六種不同的信文，從中選擇一封（或多封），然後描述你將要做的事。

信文 1： You have to spend the money on a wonderful vacation. What are you going to do?

信文 2： You have to spend the money to help other people. What are you going to do?

信文 3： You have to spend the money to improve your school or place of work. What are you going to do?

信文 4： You have to spend the money on your family. What are you going to do?

信文 5： You have to spend the money to make the world a better place. What are you going to do?

信文 6： You have to spend the money to improve your country. What are you going to do?

6-15 更多的不規則動詞

begin – began	*say – said*	*tell – told*
find – found	*sell – sold*	*tear – tore*
lose – lost	*steal – stole*	*wear – wore*
hang – hung		

■ 練習 44 — 口語練習（闔上書本）：練習使用上表中的不規則動詞。

1. *begin–began* Our class begins at (9:00) every day. Class began at (9:00 this morning). When did class begin (this morning)?
   → *It began at (9:00).*

2. *lose–lost* Sometimes I lose things. Yesterday I lost my keys. What did I do yesterday?

3. *find–found* Sometimes I lose things. And then I find them. Yesterday I lost my keys, but then I found them in my jacket pocket. What did I do yesterday?

4. *tear–tore* If we make a mistake when we write a check, we tear the check up. Yesterday I made a mistake when I wrote a check, so I tore it up and wrote a new check. What did I do yesterday?

5. *sell–sold* People sell things that they don't need anymore. (. . .) has a new bicycle, so he / she sold his / her old bicycle. What did (. . .) do?

6. *hang–hung* I like to hang pictures on my walls. This morning I hung a new picture in my bedroom. What did I do this morning?

7. *tell–told* The kindergarten teacher likes to tell stories to her students. Yesterday she told a story about a little red train. What did the teacher do yesterday?

8. *wear–wore* I wear a sweater to class every evening. Last night I wore a jacket as well. What did I wear last night?

9. *steal–stole* Thieves steal money and other valuables. Last month a thief stole my aunt's pearl necklace. What did a thief do last month?

10. *say–said* People usually say "hello" when they answer a phone. When (. . .) answered his / her phone this morning, he / she said "hello." What did (. . .) do this morning?

■ **練習 45**：用框內的動詞完成下列句子。

begin	*say*	*tear*
find	*sell*	*tell*
hang	*steal*	*wear*
lose		

1. A: Did you go to the park yesterday?

   B: No. We stayed home because it _____ to rain.

2. A: Susie is in trouble.
   B: Why?

   A: She _____ a lie. Her mom and dad are upset.

3. A: Where did you get that pretty shell?

   B: I _____ it on the beach.

SHELLS

4. A: May I please have your homework?

   B: I don't have it. I _____ it.
   A: You what!?
   B: I can't find it anywhere.

5. A: Where's my coat?

   B: I _____ it up in the closet for you.

6. A: What happened to your sleeve?

   B: I _____ it on a nail.
   A: That's too bad.

7. A: Do you still have your bicycle?

   B: No. I _____ it because I needed some extra money.

8. A: It's hot in here.
   B: Excuse me? What did you say?

   A: I _____ , "It's hot in here."

9. A: Why did you take the bus to work this morning? Why didn't you drive?

   B: Because somebody _____ my car last night.
   A: Did you call the police?
   B: Of course I did.

10. A: Did you wear your blue jeans to the job interview?

    B: Of course not! I _____ a suit.

■ **練習 46**：利用括弧內的字，以適當的動詞形式完成下列句子。

1. A: *(you, be)* _____ at home tomorrow morning around ten?

   B: No. I *(be)* _____ out.

2. A: I *(lose)* _____ my sunglasses yesterday.
   B: Where?

   A: I *(think)* _____ that I *(leave)* _____ them on a table at the restaurant.

3. A: How are you getting along?

   B: Fine. I'm making a lot of friends, and my English *(improve)* _____ .

4. A: Sometimes children tell little lies. You talked to Annie. *(she, tell)* _____ _____ the truth, or *(she, tell)* _____ a lie?

   B: She *(tell)* _____ the truth. She's honest.

5. A: *(you, write)* _____ a letter to George yesterday?

   B: Yes, I did. I *(send)* _____ him a letter yesterday.

6. A: May I see the classified section of the newspaper?
   B: Sure. Here it is.

   A: Thanks. I *(want)* _____ *(look)* _____ at the want ads. I

   (need) _____ *(find)* _____ a new apartment.


```
┌─────────────────────────────────────┐
│  APTS., UNFURN.                       │
│  ─────────────────                    │
│  2 BR. $725/mo. Lake St.              │
│  Near bus. All utils. incl.           │
│  No pets. 361-3663. eves.             │
└─────────────────────────────────────┘
```


7. A: Where *(you, go)* _____ yesterday?

   B: I *(go)* _____ to my cousin's house. I *(see)* _____

   Jean there and *(talk)* _____ to her for a while. And I *(meet)*

   _____ my cousin's neighbors, Mr. and Mrs. Bell. They're nice
   people. I like them.

8. A: What are you going to do tonight? *(you, study)* _____?

   B: No. I don't think so. I'm tired. I think I *(watch)* _____

   TV for a while, or maybe I *(listen)* _____ to some

   music. Or I might read a novel. But I *(want, not, study)* _____

   _____ tonight.

9. A: *(you, do)* _____ your homework last night?

   B: No. I *(be)* _____ too tired. I *(go)* _____ to bed early

   and *(sleep)* _____ for nine hours.

10. A: Good morning.
    B: Excuse me?

    A: I *(say)* _____, "Good morning."

    B: Oh! Good morning! I'm sorry. I *(understand, not)* _____
      you at first.

11. A: What did you do yesterday?

   B: Well, I *(wake up)* _____ around nine and *(go)*

      _____ shopping. While I was downtown, someone *(steal)*

      _____ my purse. I *(take)* _____ a taxi home. When

      I *(get)* _____ out of the taxi, I *(tear)* _____ my

      blouse. I *(borrow)* _____ some money from my roommate to
      pay the taxi driver.
   A: Did anything good happen to you yesterday?

   B: Hmmm. Let me think. Oh yes. I *(lose)* _____ my grammar book,

      but I *(find)* _____ it later.

6-16 　更多的不規則動詞

cost – cost	*hit – hit*	*spend – spent*
cut – cut	*hurt – hurt*	*understand – understood*
forget –forgot	*lend – lent*	
give – gave	*make – made*	

■ **練習 47 ─ 口語練習（闔上書本）**：練習使用上表中的不規則動詞。

1. *cost-cost*　　　I bought a hat yesterday. I paid (twenty dollars) for it. It cost (twenty dollars). What did I buy yesterday? How much did it cost?
   → *You bought a hat. It cost (twenty dollars).*

2. *give-gave*　　　People give gifts when someone has a birthday. Last week, (. . .) had a birthday. I gave him / her（某物）. What did I do?

3. *make-made*　　I make good chocolate cake. Last week I made a cake for (. . .)'s birthday. What did I do last week?

4. *cut-cut*　　　　(. . .) cuts vegetables when he / she makes a salad. Two nights ago, while he / she was making a salad, he / she cut his / her finger with the knife. What happened two nights ago?

5. *hurt-hurt*　　　When I have a headache, my head hurts. Yesterday I had a headache. My head hurt yesterday. How did my head feel yesterday? How does your head feel when you have a headache?

6. *lend-lent*　　　I lend money to my friends if they need it. Yesterday I lent（一筆錢） to (. . .). What did I do?

7. *forget-forgot*　Sometimes I forget my wallet. Last night, I forgot it at a restaurant. What did I do last night?

8. *spend-spent*　　I usually spend Saturdays with my parents. Last Saturday, I spent the day with my friends instead. What did I do last Saturday?

9. *shut-shut*   I shut the garage door every night at 10:00 P.M. I shut it early last night. What did I do last night?

10. *understand-understood*   I always understand (. . .) when he / she speaks. He / She just said something and I understood it. What just happened?

11. *hit-hit*   (. . .) lives in an apartment. His / Her neighbors are very noisy. When they make too much noise, (. . .) hits the wall with his/her hand. Last night he / she couldn't get to sleep because of the noise, so he / she hit the wall with his / her hand. What did (. . .) do last night? What does he / she usually do when his / her neighbors make too much noise?

■ **練習 48**：用括弧內的字完成下列句子。

1. A: How much *(a new car, cost)* _____?

   B: It *(cost)* _____ a lot! New cars are expensive.

2. A: Did you get a ticket for the rock concert?

   B: Yes, and it was really expensive! It *(cost)* _____ fifty dollars.

3. A: Where's your dictionary?

   B: I *(give)* _____ it to Robert.

4. A: I had a car accident yesterday morning.
   B: What happened?

   A: I *(hit)* _____ a telephone pole.

5. A: May I have your homework, please?

   B: I'm sorry, but I don't have it. I *(forget)* _____ it.

   A: You *(forget)* _____ it!?

6. A: Did you eat breakfast?

   B: Yeah. I *(make)* _____ some scrambled eggs and toast for myself.

7. Jack *(put)* _____ on his clothes every morning.

8. Jack *(put)* _____ on his clothes this morning after he got up.

9. A: Did you enjoy going into the city to see a show?

   B: Yes, but I *(spend)* _____ a lot of money. I can't afford to do that very often.

10. A: May I see your dictionary?

    B: I don't have it. I *(lend)* _____ it to George.

11. A: Is that knife sharp?

   B: It's very sharp. It *(cut)* _____ anything easily.

12. A: I went to a barber this morning. He *(cut)* _____ my hair too short.
   B: It looks fine.

■ **練習 49 — 口語練習（閤上書本）**：拼唸出下列動詞的過去式，然後再以此過去式動詞造句。

例：come
答：came . . . C–A–M–E . . . I came to class this morning.

1. come	19. meet	37. forget
2. eat	20. speak	38. drive
3. stand	21. take	39. ride
4. understand	22. wear	40. run
5. drink	23. write	41. go
6. break	24. fly	42. see
7. hear	25. leave	43. sit
8. lose	26. pay	44. cut
9. find	27. cost	45. hit
10. begin	28. spend	46. sing
11. put	29. sell	47. bring
12. shut	30. buy	48. read
13. hang	31. ring	49. teach
14. tell	32. make	50. think
15. tear	33. do	51. have
16. get	34. say	52. sleep
17. wake up	35. catch	53. give
18. steal	36. send	54. lend

■ **練習 50 — 複習**：利用括弧內的字，以適當的動詞形式完成下列句子。

1. A: I *(cut)* _____ class tomorrow.
   B: Why?
   A: Why not?
   B: That's not a very good reason.

2. A: How did you get here?

   B: I *(take)* _____ a plane. I *(fly)* _____ here from Bangkok.

3. A: How do you usually get to class?

   B: I (walk, usually) _____, but sometimes I (take)

   _____ the bus.

4. A: Where (you, meet) _____ your wife?

   B: I (meet) _____ her at a party ten years ago.

5. A: Did you see that?
   B: What?

   A: The man in the red shirt (hit) _____ the man in the blue shirt.
   B: Really?

6. A: Were you late for the movie?

   B: No. The movie (begin) _____ at 7:30, and we (get) _____
      to the theater at 7:26.

7. A: What time (the movie, begin) _____ last
      night?
   B: 7:30.

   A: (you, be) _____ late?

   B: No. We (make) _____ it in time.

8. A: Do you hear that noise?
   B: What noise?

   A: (you, listen) _____?

9. A: Where's your homework?

   B: I (lose) _____ it.
   A: Oh?

   B: I (forget) _____ it.
   A: Oh?

   B: I (give) _____ it to Roberto to give to you, but he (lose)

   _____ it.
   A: Oh?

   B: Someone (steal) _____ it.
   A: Oh?

   B: Well, actually I (have, not) _____ enough time to
      finish it last night.
   A: I see.

10. A: Where's my book! Someone *(steal)* _____ it!

    B: Take it easy. Your book *(be)* _____ right here.
    A: Oh.

11. A: *(you, stay)* _____ here during vacation next week?

    B: No. I *(take)* _____ a trip to Miami. I *(visit)*

    _____ my aunt and uncle.

    A: How long *(you, be)* _____ away?
    B: About five days.

12. A: Why *(you, wear)* _____ a cast on your foot?

    B: I *(break)* _____ my ankle.
    A: How?

    B: I *(step)* _____ in a hole while I was running in the park.

13. A: *(you, want, go)* _____ to the zoo this afternoon?
    B: I'd like to go, but I can't because I have to study.
    A: That's too bad.

    B: *(you, go)* _____ to the zoo?

    A: Yes. The weather is perfect, and I *(want)* _____ *(get)*

    _____ outside and *(enjoy)* _____ it.

14. A: *(you, see)* _____ Randy yesterday?

    B: No, but I *(speak)* _____ to him on the phone. He *(call)*

    _____ me yesterday evening.
    A: Is he okay?
    B: Yes. He still has a cold, but he's feeling much better.
    A: That's good.

15. A: Is Carol here?

    B: No, she *(be, not)* _____. She *(leave)* _____ a few minutes ago.

    A: *(she, be)* _____ back soon?
    B: I think so.

    A: Where *(she, go)* _____?

    B: She *(go)* _____ to the drugstore.

1. "Are you going to go to the baseball game tomorrow afternoon?"

   "I don't know. I _____."
       A. will   B. am going to   C. maybe   D. might

2. "Are Jane and Eric going to be at the meeting?"

   "No, they're too busy. They _____ be there."
       A. don't   B. won't   C. will   D. may

3. "Are you going to go to the market today?"

   "No. I went there _____ Friday."
       A. yesterday   B. next   C. last   D. ago

4. "When are you going to go to the bank?"

   "I'll go there before I _____ to the post office tomorrow morning."
       A. will go   B. go   C. went   D. am going

5. "Why is the teacher late today?"

   "I don't know. _____ he slept late."
       A. May   B. Did   C. Maybe   D. Was

6. "Do you like to go to New York City?"

   "Yes. When I'm in New York, I always _____ new things to do and places to go."
       A. found   B. find   C. will find   D. am finding

7. "Is Ken going to talk to us this afternoon about our plans for tomorrow?"

   "No. He'll _____ us this evening."
       A. calls   B. calling   C. call   D. called

8. "_____ are you going to do after class today?"
   "I'm going to go home."
       A. When   B. Where   C. What   D. What time

9. "Where _____ Ivonne live before she moved into her new apartment?"
   "She lived in a dormitory at the university."
       A. did   B. does   C. is   D. was

10. "What time _____ Olga and Boris going to arrive?"
    "Six."
        A. is   B. do   C. will   D. are

1. Is Ivan will go to work tomorrow?

2. When you will call me?

3. Will Tom to meet us for dinner tomorrow?

4. We went to a movie yesterday night.

5. If it will be cold tomorrow morning, my car won't start.

6. We maybe late for the concert tonight.

7. Did you found your keys?

8. What time you are going to come tomorrow?

9. My sister is going to meet me at the airport. My brother won't to be there.

10. Fatima will call us tonight when she will arrive home safely.

11. Mr. Wong will sells his business and retires next year.

12. Do you will be in Venezuela next year?

13. Emily may will be at the party.

14. I'm going to return home in a couple of month.

15. When I'll see you tomorrow, I'll return your book to you.

16. I saw Jim three day ago.

17. I may to don't be in class tomorrow.

18. Ahmed puts his books on his desk when he walked into his apartment.

19. A thief stoled my bicycle.

20. I'll see my parents when I will return home for a visit next July.

(1)　　　　　*Peter and Rachel are brother and sister. Right now their parents* (be) _____

(2)　*abroad on a trip, so they* (stay) _____ *with their grandmother. They*

(3)　(like) _____ *to stay with her. She* (make, always) _____

(4)　*wonderful food for them. And she* (tell) _____ *them stories every night before they*

(5)　(go) _____ *to bed.*

(6)　　　　　*Before Peter and Rachel* (go) _____ *to bed last night, they* (ask)

(7)　_____ *Grandma to tell them a story. She* (agree) _____. *The*

(8)　*children* (put) _____ *on their pajamas,* (brush) _____ *their teeth, and*

(9)　(sit) _____ *with their grandmother in her big chair to listen to a story.*

GRANDMA:　That's good. Sit here beside me and get comfortable.

(10)　CHILDREN:　What *(you, tell)* _____ us about tonight,

　　　Grandma?

(11)　GRANDMA:　Before I *(begin)* _____ the story, I *(give)* _____

　　　each of you a kiss on the forehead because I love you very much.

(12)　CHILDREN:　We *(love)* _____ you, too, Grandma.

(13)   GRANDMA: Tonight I *(tell)* _____ you a story about Rabbit and

Eagle. Ready?

      CHILDREN: Yes!

      GRANDMA: Rabbit had light gray fur and a white tail. He lived with his family in a hole

(14)   in a big, grassy field. Rabbit *(be)* _____ afraid of many things, but he

(15)   *(be)* _____ especially afraid of Eagle. Eagle liked to eat rabbits for dinner.

(16)   One day while Rabbit was eating grass in the field, he *(see)* _____ Eagle in

(17)   the sky above him. Rabbit *(be)* _____ very afraid and *(run)* _____

(18)   home to his hole as fast as he could. Rabbit *(stay)* _____ in his hole day

(19)   after day because he *(be)* _____ afraid to go outside. He *(get)* _____

(20)   very hungry, but still he *(stay)* _____ in his hole. Finally, he *(find)*

(21)   _____ the courage to go outside because he *(need)* _____

(22)   *(eat)* _____.

(23)   Carefully and slowly, he *(put)* _____ his little pink nose outside the

(24)   hole. He *(smell, not)* _____ any dangerous animals.

(25)   And he *(see, not)* _____ Eagle anywhere, so he *(hop)*

(26)   _____ out and *(find)* _____ some delicious new

(27)   grass to eat. While he was eating the grass, he *(see)* _____ a shadow on the

(28)   field and *(look)* _____ up. It was Eagle! Rabbit said, "Please don't eat

me, Eagle! Please don't eat me, Eagle!"

On this sunny afternoon, Eagle was on her way home to her nest when she

(29) *(hear)* _____ a faint sound below her. "What is that sound?" Eagle said

(30) to herself. She looked around, but she *(see, not)* _____

(31) anything. She *(decide)* _____ to ignore the sound and go home.

(32) She was tired and *(want)* _____ *(rest)* _____ in

her nest.

(33) Then below her, Rabbit *(say)* _____ again in a very loud voice,

"Please don't eat me, Eagle! Please don't eat me, Eagle." This time Eagle *(hear)*

(34) _____ Rabbit clearly. Eagle *(spot)* _____ Rabbit in

(35) the field, *(fly)* _____ down, and *(pick)* _____ Rabbit

up in her talons.

"Thank you, Rabbit," said Eagle. "I was hungry and *(know, not)*

(36) _____ where I could find my dinner. It's a good thing

(37) you called to me." Then Eagle *(eat)* _____ Rabbit for dinner.

(38) There's a lesson to learn from this story, children. If you *(be)* _____

afraid and expect bad things to happen, bad things will happen. The opposite is also

(39) true. If you *(expect)* _____ good things to happen, good things will happen.

(40) *(you, understand)* _____? Now it's time for bed.

CHILDREN: Please tell us another story!

(41) GRANDMA: Not tonight. I'm tired. After I *(have)* _____ a warm drink, I

(42) *(go)* _____ to bed. All of us need *(get)* _____ a

(43) good night's sleep. Tomorrow *(be)* _____ a busy day.

(44) CHILDREN: What *(we, do)* _____ tomorrow?

(45) GRANDMA: After we *(have)* _____ breakfast, we *(go)* _____

(46) to the zoo at Woodland Park. When we *(be)* _____ at the zoo, we

(47) *(see)* _____ lots of wonderful animals. Then in the afternoon

(48) we *(see)* _____ a play at the Children's Theater. But before we

(49) *(see)* _____ the play, we *(have)* _____

a picnic lunch in the park.

(50) CHILDREN: Wow! We *(have)* _____ a wonderful day tomorrow!

GRANDMA: Now off to bed! Goodnight, Rachel and Peter. Sleep tight.★

CHILDREN: Goodnight, Grandma. Thank you for the story!

★ *Sleep tight* 意思就是睡得好；整夜熟睡： *sleep well; have a good night's sleep*。

第七章
能力的表達

7-1 CAN 的用法

(a) I have some money. I **can buy** a book. (b) We have time and money. We **can go** to a movie. (c) Tom is strong. He **can lift** the heavy box.	*can* 表示能力和可能性。
(d) 正： Yuko *can* **speak** English.	*can* 後面要加主要動詞的原形。(d) 句中：*speak* 是主要動詞。
(e) 誤： *Yuko can* **to** *speak English.*	*can* 後面不可接含有 *to* 的不定詞。 (e) 句中：*to speak* 是錯誤的。
(f) 誤： *Yuko can speak***s** *English.*	主要動詞的字尾不可加 *-s*。 (f) 句中：*speaks* 是錯誤的。
(g) Alice **can not** come. Alice **cannot** come. Alice **can't** come.	否定形式： *can + not = can not* 或：*cannot* 縮寫形式： *can + not = can't*

■ **練習 1— 口語練習**：用 can 或 can't 及提示的語詞，完成下列句子。

例：A bird \ sing
答：A bird can sing.

例：A horse \ sing
答：A horse can't sing.

1. A bird \ fly
2. A cow \ fly
3. A child \ drive a car
4. An adult \ drive a car
5. A newborn baby \ walk
6. A fish \ breathe air
7. A fish \ swim
8. A deaf person \ hear
9. A blind person \ see
10. An elephant \ swim
11. An elephant \ climb trees
12. A cat \ climb trees
13. A boat \ float on water
14. A rock \ float on water

■ **練習 2 — 口語練習**：用 I can 或 I can't 造句。

例：speak Chinese
答：I can speak Chinese. 或：I can't speak Chinese.

1. whistle
2. ride a bicycle
3. touch my ear with my elbow
4. play the piano★
5. play the guitar
6. lift a piano
7. drive a stick-shift car
8. fix a flat tire
9. swim
10. float on water
11. ski
12. do arithmetic
13. make a paper airplane
14. sew a button on a shirt
15. eat with chopsticks
16. wiggle my ears

7-2　CAN 的用法：疑問句

（疑問詞）　+　　CAN + 主詞　+　　主要動詞				回答
(a)　　　　　　　**Can**　　**you**　　　**speak**　Arabic?			→	**Yes, I can.**
			→	**No, I can't.**
(b)　　　　　　　**Can**　　**Marge**　**come**　to the party?			→	**Yes, she can.**
			→	**No, she can't.**
(c)　**Where**　**can**　**I**　　　**buy**　a hammer?			→	**At a hardware store.**
(d)　**When**　　**can**　**you**　　**help**　me?			→	**Tomorrow afternoon.**

■ **練習 3**：造 yes / no 問句，並作簡答。

1. A: _____*Can Jean speak English?*_____

   B: _____*Yes, she can.*_____ (Jean can speak English.)

2. A: _____*Can you speak French?*_____

   B: _____*No, I can't.*_____ (I can't speak French.)

3. A: _____

   B: _____ (Jim can't play the piano.)

4. A: _____

   B: _____ (I can whistle.)

_____
★*play* 與 *the* 組成的語詞中，*the* 通常和樂器併用：*play the piano, play the guitar, play the violin* 等。

5. A: _____

   B: _____ (I can go shopping with you this afternoon.)

6. A: _____

   B: _____ (Carmen can't ride a bicycle.)

7. A: _____

   B: _____ (Elephants can swim.)

8. A: _____

   B: _____ (The students can finish this exercise quickly.)

9. A: _____

   B: _____
   (I can stand on my head.)

10. A: _____

    B: _____
    (The doctor can see you tomorrow.)

11. A: _____

    B: _____
    (We can't have pets in the dormitory.)

■ **練習 4 — 口語練習：**兩人一組練習。

    學生A： 打開書，用 Can you...? 提出問題。
    學生B： 閣上書，回答問題。

    例：   speak Arabic
    學生A： Can you speak Arabic?
    學生B： Yes, I can. 或：No, I can't.

角色互換

1. ride a bicycle
2. ride a motorcycle
3. ride a horse
4. play the piano
5. play the guitar
6. touch the ceiling of this room
7. cook（某國）food
8. sing
9. whistle
10. float on water
11. spell Mississippi
12. see the back of (. . .)'s head
13. count to five in（某語言）
14. stand on your head
15. touch your knee with your nose
16. touch your ear with your elbow
17. play the violin
18. drive a stick-shift car
19. fix a flat tire
20. ski

學生A：打開書，用 Where Can I ...? 提出問題。

學生B：閣上書，回答問題。

例： buy a notebook

學生A：Where can I buy a notebook?

學生B：At the bookstore. / At （店名）. / 諸如此類。

角色互換

1. buy a camera
2. get a dozen eggs
3. buy a window fan
4. get a good dinner
5. go swimming
6. play tennis
7. catch a bus
8. mail a package

9. buy a diamond ring
10. buy a hammer
11. see a zebra
12. get a newspaper
13. find an encyclopedia
14. get a taxi
15. get a sandwich
16. cash a check

7-3 KNOW HOW TO 的用法

(a) I can swim.	(a) 句和 (b) 句基本上同義。*know how to* 表示能力。
(b) I *know how to swim*.	(c) 句和 (d) 句基本上同義。
(c) Can you cook?	
(d) *Do* you *know how to cook*?	

■ 練習 6 — 口語練習：兩人一組練習。

學生A：打開書，用 know how to 提出問題。

學生B：閣上書，回答問題。

例： swim

學生A：Do you know how to swim?

學生B：Yes, I do. 或：No, I don't.

角色互換

1. cook
2. dance
3. play the piano
4. get to the post office from here
5. fix a flat tire
6. drive a stick-shift car
7. wiggle your ears
8. sew

9. play the guitar
10. get to the airport from here
11. get to（某商店）from here
12. use a hammer
13. use a screwdriver
14. count to five in（某語言）
15. add, subtract, multiply, and divide
16. find the square root of nine

■ **練習 7**— 口語練習／書寫練習：同學互相詢問，找出具有下列能力的同學，並提出有關其能力的問題。然後根據所得資料寫一篇報告。

1. play a musical instrument
2. play a sport
3. speak three or four languages
4. cook
5. sing
6. sew
7. fix a car
8. draw
9. swim
10. eat with chopsticks

7-4 COULD 的用法：CAN 的過去式

（a） I am in Hawaii. I can go to the beach every day. （b） I was in Hawaii **last month**. I **could go** to the beach every day when I was there.	*could* ＝ *can* 的過去式。
（c） I can't go to the movie today. I have to study. （d） I $\begin{Bmatrix} \textbf{\textit{couldn't go}} \\ \textbf{\textit{could not go}} \end{Bmatrix}$ to the movie **last night**. I had to study.	否定形式： *could* + *not* = *couldn't*
（e） **Could** *you* **speak** English before you came here?	疑問句： *could* + 主詞 + 主要動詞

■ **練習 8**：用 couldn't 及框內的語詞或自己的話完成下列句子。

call you	*go to the movie*
come to class	*light the candles*
✔ *do my homework*	*listen to music*
get into my car	*wash his clothes*
go swimming	*watch TV*

1. I _____*couldn't do my homework*_____ last night because I was too tired.

2. I _____ yesterday because I lost your telephone number.

3. I _____ last night because my TV set is broken.

4. Tom _____ because he didn't have any matches.

5. The teacher _____ yesterday because he was sick.

6. I _____ last night because my radio doesn't work.

7. Ken _____ because he didn't have any laundry soap.

8. We _____ yesterday because the water was too cold.

9. I _____ yesterday because I locked all the doors and left the keys inside.

10. I _____ last night because I had to study.

■ **練習 9 — 口語練習（閤上書本）**：用 No, I couldn't ...because .... 回答下列問題。

例：Did you finish your homework last night?
答：No, I couldn't finish my homework because (I had a headache, etc.).

1. go shopping yesterday
2. study last night
3. go swimming yesterday
4. watch TV last night

5. go to (. . .)'s party last night
6. come to class yesterday
7. go downtown yesterday afternoon
8. wash your clothes yesterday

■ **練習 10 — 口語練習（閤上書本）**：用 can't 或 couldn't 說出以下情況會造成何種否定的結果。

例：There's no chalk in the classroom.
答：We can't write on the board.

例：There was no chalk in the classroom yesterday.
答：The teacher couldn't write on the board.

1. (. . .) has a broken leg.
2. (. . .) had the flu last week.
3. (. . .) has only（一小筆錢）in his pocket / in her purse today.
4. (. . .) doesn't know how to use a computer.
5. Your parents had rules for you when you were a child.
6. All of you are adults. You are not children.
7. You didn't know any English last year.
8. Millions of people in the world live in poverty.

1. Could you to drive a car when you were thirteen years old?

2. If your brother goes to the graduation party, he can meets my sister.

3. Mr. Lo was born in Hong Kong, but now he lives in Canada. He cannot understand spoken English before he moved to Canada, but now he speak and understand English very well.

4. I couldn't opened the door because I didn't have a key.

5. When Ernesto arrived at the airport last Tuesday, he can't find the right gate.

7-5 VERY 和 TOO + 形容詞的用法

(a) The box is ***very*** heavy, but Tom ***can*** lift it. (b) The box is ***too*** heavy. Bob ***can't*** lift it. (c) The coffee is ***very*** hot, but I ***can*** drink it. (d) The coffee is ***too*** hot. I ***can't*** drink it.	*very* 和 *too* 置於形容詞之前；*heavy* 和 *hot* 是形容詞。 *very* 和 *too* 不同義。 (a) 句中：*very heavy* = 雖困難，但 *Tom* 還是可以舉起箱子。 (b) 句中：*too heavy* = *Bob* 不可能舉起箱子來。

(e) The coffee is ***too*** hot.
  否定的結論： I can't drink it.
(f) The weather is ***too*** cold.
  否定的結論： We can't go to the beach.
	說話者用 *too* 表示其心中持有否定的結論。

TOM

BOB

> | | |
> |---|---|
> | *buy it* | *lift it* |
> | *do his homework* | *reach the cookie jar* |
> | *eat it* | *sleep* |
> | *go swimming* | *take a break* |

1. The soup is too hot. I can't _____

2. The diamond ring is too expensive. I can't _____

3. The weather is too cold. We can't _____

4. Peggy is too short.

   She can't _____

5. Ali is too tired.

   He can't _____

6. I am too busy.

   I can't _____

7. It's too noisy in the dorm at night.

   I can't _____

8. A piano is too heavy.

   I can't _____

■ 練習 **13**：用 too 加框內的形容詞或自己的話，完成下列句子。

> | | |
> |---|---|
> | *cold* | *small* |
> | *expensive* | *tall* |
> | *heavy* | *tired* |
> | *noisy* | *young* |

1. You can't lift a car. A car is _____

2. Jimmy is ten. He can't drive a car. He's _____

3. I can't study in the dorm at night. It's _____

4. I don't want to go to the zoo. The weather is _____

5. Ann doesn't want to play tennis this afternoon. She's _____

6. I can't buy a new car. A new car is _____

7. John has gained weight. He can't wear his old shirt. It's _____

8. The basketball player can't stand up straight in the subway. He's _____

■ **練習 14**：用 too 或 very 完成下列句子。

1. The tea is _____*very*_____ hot, but I can drink it.

2. The tea is _____*too*_____ hot. I can't drink it.

3. I can't put my dictionary in my pocket. My dictionary is _____ big.

4. An elephant is _____ big. A mouse is _____ small.

5. I can't buy a boat because it's _____ expensive.

6. A sports car is _____ expensive, but Anita can buy one if she wants to.

7. We went to the Rocky Mountains for our vacation. The mountains are

   _____ beautiful.

8. I can't eat this food because it's _____ salty.

9. Amanda doesn't like her room in the dorm. She thinks it's _____ small.

10. I lost your dictionary. I'm _____ sorry. I'll buy you a new one.

11. A: Do you like your math course?

    B: Yes. It's _____ difficult, but I enjoy it.

12. A: Do you like your math course?

    B: No. It's _____ difficult. I don't like it because I can't understand the math.

13. A: It's seven-thirty. Do you want to go to the movie?

    B: We can't. It's _____ late. The movie started at seven.

14. A: Did you enjoy your dinner last night?

    B: Yes. The food was _____ good!

15. A: Are you going to buy that dress?

    B: No. It doesn't fit. It's _____ big.

16. A: Do you think Carol is smart?

    B: Yes, I do. I think she's _____ intelligent.

17. A: My daughter wants to get married.

    B: What? But she can't! She's _____ young.

18. A: Can you read that sign across the street?

    B: No, I can't. It's _____ far away.

7-6 TOO MANY 和 TOO MUCH + 名詞的用法

My stomach doesn't feel good. (a) I ate **too many sandwiches**. (b) I ate **too much food**.	*too* 經常和 *many* 及 *much* 連用。 *too many* 置於可數名詞之前，如 (a)。 *too much* 置於不可數名詞之前，如 (b)。★

★有關可數名詞和不可數名詞的資料，請參閱表 4-6。

■ **練習 15**：填入 too many 或 too much 完成下列句子。too many 和複數可數名詞連用；too much 和不可數名詞連用。

1. I can't go to the movie tonight. I have _____*too much*_____ homework to do.

2. Mr. and Mrs. Smith have six cars. They have _____*too many*_____ cars.

3. Alex is nervous and jumpy. He drinks _____ coffee.

4. There are _____ students in my chemistry class. I can't remember all of their names.

5. Fred is a commuter. He drives to and from work every day. Yesterday afternoon he

   tried to get home early, but he couldn't because there was _____

   traffic. There were _____ cars on the highway during
   rush hour.

6. You use _____ salt on your food. A lot of salt isn't good for you.

7. It's not possible for a person to have _____ friends.

8. The restaurant was crowded, so we left. There were _____
   people at the restaurant.

9. This food is too hot! I can't eat it. There's _____ pepper in it.

10. Mike is gaining weight because he eats _____ food.

11. I can't buy this watch. It costs _____ money.

12. Ann doesn't study because she's always busy. She has _____
    boyfriends.

13. I have to study for eight hours every night. My teachers assign _____
    homework.

14. I invited three friends to my house for lunch. I made twelve sandwiches for them, but

    they ate only six. I made _____ sandwiches. I made

    _____ food for my guests.

例：You had too much homework last night. What was the result?
答：I couldn't finish it. / I didn't get to bed until after midnight. / 諸如此類。

1. (. . .) wants to buy（某物）, but it costs too much money. What's the result?

2. (. . .) tried to read an article in the newspaper about（某流行話題）, but there was too much vocabulary that he didn't know. What was the result?

3. (. . .) and (. . .) wanted to eat at（某餐廳）last night, but there were too many people there. What was the result?

4. (. . .) likes to study in peace and quiet. His / Her roommate likes to listen to loud music and makes too much noise. What's the result?

5. (. . .) wants to（做某事）today, but the weather is too (hot / cold / humid / cloudy / wet / etc.). What's the result?

6. (. . .) invited (. . .) to（做某事）last night, but (. . .) was too busy. He / She had too much homework. What was the result?

7. Sometimes (. . .) drinks too much coffee. What's the result?

8. (. . .) wants to climb（某座山）, but the mountain is too steep and too high. The climb is too difficult for (. . .) because he / she is an inexperienced climber. What is the result?

9. (. . .) took the bus yesterday. He / She was very tired and needed to sit down, but there were too many people on the bus. What was the result?

10. (. . .) made a cup of coffee for (. . .), but it was too strong. It tasted bitter. What was the result?

11. At the present rates of population growth, someday there will be too many people on earth. What will be the result?

12. (. . .)'s apartment is too small for him / her and his / her wife / husband (and their children). What's the result?

13. (. . .) took a trip to（某地方）last month. He / She took six big suitcases. In other words, he / she had too many suitcases. What was the result?

(a) Susie can't go to school because she is too young. (b) Susie is **too young to go** to school.	(a) 句和 (b) 同義。
TOO + 形容詞 + 不定詞 (c) Susie is **too** **young** **to go** to school. (d) Peggy is **too** **short** **to reach** the cookie jar. (e) Bob is **too** **tired** **to do** his homework.	

■ **練習 17**：用 too + 形容詞 + 不定詞的句型，造與題目同義的句子。

1. Mr. Cook is old. He can't drive a car anymore.

    → Mr. Cook is ⌊___*too*___⌋ ⌊_____*old*_____⌋ ⌊_____*to drive*_____⌋ a car.
                     too   +   形容詞   +   不定詞

2. Susie doesn't want to go to the party because she is tired.

    → Susie is ⌊_____⌋ ⌊_____⌋ ⌊_____⌋ to the party.
                 too   +   形容詞   +   不定詞

3. Robert is short. He can't touch the ceiling.

    → Robert is ⌊_____⌋ ⌊_____⌋ ⌊_____⌋ the ceiling.
                 too   +   形容詞   +   不定詞

4. I couldn't finish my work because I was sleepy.

    → I was ⌊_____⌋ ⌊_____⌋ ⌊_____⌋ my work.
              too   +   形容詞   +   不定詞

5. Jackie is young. She can't get married.

    → Jackie is too . . . .

6. Sam didn't want to go to the zoo because he was busy.

    → Sam . . . .

7. I'm full. I can't eat another sandwich.

    → I . . . .

8. I don't want to clean up my apartment today. I'm lazy.

    → I . . . .

7-8 TOO + 形容詞 + FOR（某人）+ 不定詞的用法

(a)	Bob can't lift the box because it is too heavy.		(a) 句和 (b) 同義。
(b)	The box is *too heavy for Bob to lift*.		

		TOO + 形容詞	+	FOR（某人）	+	不定詞
(c)	The box is	**too** **heavy**		**for** **Bob**		**to lift**.
(d)	The dorm is	**too** **noisy**		**for** **me**		**to study**.

■ **練習 18**：用 too + 形容詞 + for（某人）+ 不定詞的句型，造與題目同義的句子。

1. Robert can't touch the ceiling because it's too high.

   → The ceiling is ⌊___*too*___⌋ ⌊___*high*___⌋ ⌊___*for Robert*___⌋ ⌊___*to touch*___⌋.

   too + 形容詞 + for 某人 + 不定詞

2. I can't do the homework because it's too difficult.

   → The homework is ⌊_____⌋ ⌊_____⌋ ⌊_____⌋ ⌊_____⌋.

   too + 形容詞 + for 某人 + 不定詞

3. Rosa can't drink this coffee because it's too hot.

   → This coffee is ⌊_____⌋ ⌊_____⌋ ⌊_____⌋ ⌊_____⌋.

   too + 形容詞 + for 某人 + 不定詞

4. We can't go to the movie because it's too late.

   → It's ⌊_____⌋ ⌊_____⌋ ⌊_____⌋ ⌊_____⌋.

   too + 形容詞 + for 某人 + 不定詞

5. Ann can't carry that suitcase because it's too heavy.

   → That suitcase is too . . . .

6. I can't buy this book because it's too expensive.

   → This book . . . .

7. We can't go swimming because the weather is too cold.

   →

8. Mrs. Rivers can't swallow the pill. It's too big.

   →

用 no 回答，並以 too + 不定詞的完整答句解釋原因。

例：The coffee is too hot. Can you drink it? Can (. . .) drink it?

答：No. The coffee is too hot (for me) to drink. I think it's also too hot for (. . .) to drink.

1. *(This desk | A piano)* is heavy. Can you lift it? Can (. . .)?
2. (. . .)'s shoe is small. Can you wear it? Can (. . .) wear it?
3. (. . .)'s shoe is big. Can you wear it? Can (. . .) wear it?
4. Who wants to buy his or her own private airplane? How much does one cost? Can you buy one? Can (. . .) buy one?
5. Who is a parent? Has a son or daughter? How old? Can he / she walk / read / go to college / get a job / get married?
6. Antarctica is very, very cold. Do people live there?
7. There are many, many stars in the universe. Can we see all of them?
8. An elephant is a large animal. Can an elephant walk through that door?
9. The Sahara Desert is very dry. Do farmers grow (crops, rice, vegetables) there?
10. An apple is about the same size as my fist. Can you swallow a whole apple all at once? Can anyone swallow a whole apple all at once?

7-9　形容詞 + ENOUGH 的用法

（a） Peggy can't go to school. She is too young. （b） Peggy can't go to school. She is not **old enough**.	(a) 句和 (b) 句同義。注意：*enough* 位於形容詞之後。
（c） I can't hear the radio. It's not **loud enough**. （d） Bobby can read. He's **old enough**. （e） We can go swimming. The weather is **warm enough**.	形容詞　+　ENOUGH 　old　　　enough 　loud　　　enough 　warm　　　enough

■ **練習 20**：用 too 或 enough 加括弧內的字完成下列句子。

1. *(young, old)*　Susie can't go to school. She's ____*too young*____. She's not ____*old enough*____.

2. *(loud, soft)*　I can't hear the music. It's _____. It's not _____.

3. *(big, small)*　Jack is gaining weight. He can't wear his old coat. It's _____. It's not _____.

4. *(short, tall)*   Cindy can't reach the book on the top shelf. She's

_____ . She's not _____ .

5. *(cold, hot)*   I don't want to finish my coffee because it's _____ .

It's not _____ .

6. *(weak, strong)*   Ron can't lift the heavy box. He's not _____ .

He's _____ .

7. *(sweet, sour)*   I don't want to finish eating this orange. It's _____ .

It's not _____ .

8. *(old, fresh)*   Don't buy that fruit. It's _____ . It's not

_____ .

9. *(young, old)*   Jimmy is an infant. He can't talk yet. He's not _____ .

He's _____ .

10. *(strong, weak)*   This coffee looks like dirty water. It's _____ . It's

not _____ .

11. *(big, small)*   I can put my dictionary in my shirt pocket. My pocket is

_____ . It's not _____ .

12. *(comfortable,*   I don't want to sit in that chair. It's _____ .
    uncomfortable)

It's not _____ .

13. *(wide, narrow,*   Anne and Sue can't carry the love
    large, small)   seat through the door. The door is

_____ . The door

isn't _____ . The

love seat is _____ . The

love seat isn't _____ .

14. *(warm, cold)*   We can go to the beach today. The weather is _____.

    It's not _____.

■ **練習 21 — 口語練習（闔上書本）**：用 no 回答，並且用 enough 解釋原因。

例：Can you touch the ceiling?
答：No, I'm not tall enough to touch the ceiling.

1. Can an elephant walk through that door?
2. Can ten-year-old children go to college?
3. Can you touch（某位離自己稍遠的同學）without standing up?
4. Can you put your grammar book in your shirt pocket?
5. Can a dog learn to read?
6. Can you eat *(four hamburgers)* right now?
7. Can you read a book by moonlight?
8. Can you understand every word an English-speaking TV newscaster says?
9. Can a turtle win a race with a rabbit?
10. （在黑板上寫極細小的字）Can you read these letters?
11. Can this room hold *(two hundred)* people?
12. Can you cut a piece of paper with your fingernail?

7-10 ENOUGH + 名詞和 MORE + 名詞的用法

(a) I can't buy this book. I need ***more money***. (b) I can't buy this book. I don't have ***enough money***.	*more* = 額外的 *enough* = 足夠的
(c) I can't finish my work. I need some ***more time***. (d) I can't finish my work. I don't have ***enough time***.	注意：*more* 置於名詞之前。 MORE + 名詞 *more* *money* *more* *time* 注意：*enough* 置於名詞之前。★ ENOUGH + 名詞 *enough* *money* *enough* *time*

★*enough* 也可置於名詞之後：*I don't have money enough.* 日常英文中，*enough* 通常置於名詞之前。

■ **練習 22**：用自己的話完成下列句子。

1. I can't _____ because I don't have
    enough money.

2. I can't _____ because I don't have
    enough time.

3. I couldn't _____ because I didn't have enough money.

4. I couldn't _____ because I didn't have enough time.

5. I don't want to _____ because I don't have enough time.

6. I would like to _____, but I can't because I don't have enough money.

■ **練習 23**：用 more 或 enough 加框內的字完成下列句子，必要時可用複數形式。

✔ *bread*	*light*	*time*
desk	*minute*	*vocabulary*
✔ *egg*	*sugar*	
gas	*tea*	

1. I'm hungry. I want to make a sandwich, but I can't. There isn't

    _____*enough bread*_____.

2. According to the cake recipe I need three eggs, but I have only one. I need two

    _____*more eggs*_____.

3. Ken isn't finished with his test. He needs ten _____.

4. I can't go skiing Saturday. I'm too busy. I don't have _____.

5. My tea isn't sweet enough. I need some _____.

6. There are fifteen students in the class, but there are only ten desks. We need five

    _____.

7. I can't understand the front page of the newspaper because I don't know

    _____.

8. It's too dark in here. I can't read my book. There isn't _____.

9. A: Do we have _____?
   B: No. We have to stop at a gas station.

10. A: Would you like _____?
    B: Yes, thank you. I'd like one more cup.

(a)　Peggy can go to school because she is old enough.	(a) 句和 (b) 句同義。
形容詞 ＋ ENOUGH ＋ 不定詞	
(b)　Peggy is **old** **enough** **to go** to school.	
(c)　I can't buy this book because I don't have enough money.	(c) 句和 (d) 句同義。
ENOUGH ＋ 名詞 ＋ 不定詞	
(d)　I don't have **enough** **money** **to buy** this book.	

■ **練習 24**：用不定詞造同義的句子。

1. Ken can reach the top shelf because he's tall enough.
   → *Ken is tall enough to reach the top shelf.*

2. I can't finish my work because I don't have enough time.

3. Mustafa can buy a new car because he has enough money.

4. Johnny can't get married because he isn't old enough.

5. Mr. and Mrs. Forest can't feed their family because they don't earn enough money.

6. I can eat a horse. I'm hungry enough.★

7. Sally bought enough food. She can feed an army.

8. Did you finish your homework last night? Did you have enough time?

9. Can you buy a ticket to the show? Do you have enough money?

10. I can't understand this article in the newspaper because I don't know enough vocabulary.

★*I'm hungry enough to eat a horse* 是一句英文俚語。說者的意思是 I'm very hungry.而非眞的要吃下一匹馬。
其他的俚語有：
I put my foot in my mouth. ＝ I said something stupid. （我說了一些傻話。）也就是，我在不適當的時候，
對不該說的人，說了一些話。
Watch your step. ＝ Be careful. （當心）
It's raining cats and dogs. ＝ It's raining hard. （下傾盆大雨）
每種語言都有俚語。俚語是用來表達特殊意義的慣用說法。

1. I'm old enough to _____

2. I'm strong enough to _____

3. I'm not strong enough to _____

4. I'm not hungry enough to _____

5. I have enough money to _____

6. I don't have enough money to _____

7. I have enough time to _____

8. I don't have enough time to _____

9. I know enough English to _____

10. I don't know enough English to _____

■ 練習 26 — 口語練習（閤上書本）：用 no 回答，並用 too 或 enough 解釋原因。

例：Is the weather perfect today?
答：No, it's too cold. / No, it's not warm enough. / 諸如此類。

1. I have a daughter. She's two years old. Can she go to school?
2. I'm making a noise（指非常細小的聲音）. Can you hear it?
3. Bobby is fifteen years old. He's in love. He wants to get married. Is that a good idea?
4. Can you put my briefcase / purse / etc. in your pants pocket / handbag / etc.?
5. Can you understand everything on the front page of a newspaper?
6. Can an elephant sit in that chair?
7. Do you like the weather（指本市）in the winter / summer?
8. Did you finish your homework last night?
9. Do you want to go on a picnic Saturday?
10. Would you like to eat your lunch on the floor of this room?
11. Can you buy a hotel?
12. Here's an arithmetic problem. You have three seconds to solve it（指不用計算機）. Multiply 673 by 897. Could you solve it in three seconds?

7-12 BE ABLE TO 的用法

現在	(a) I *am able to touch* my toes. (b) I *can touch* my toes.	(a) 句和 (b) 句基本上同義。
未來	(c) I *will be able to go* shopping tomorrow. (d) I *can go* shopping tomorrow.	(c) 句和 (d) 基本上同義。
過去	(e) I *wasn't able to finish* my homework last night. (f) I *couldn't finish* my homework last night.	(e) 句和 (f) 句基本上同義。

■ 練習 27 — 口語練習：用 be able to 造與題目同義的句子。

1. I can be here tomorrow at ten o'clock.
   → *I'll (I will) be able to be here tomorrow at ten o'clock.*
2. Two students couldn't finish the test.
   → *Two students weren't able to finish the test.*
3. Mark is bilingual. He can speak two languages.
4. Sue can get her own apartment next year.
5. Animals can't speak.
6. Can you touch your toes without bending your knees?
7. Jack couldn't describe the thief.
8. Could you do the homework?
9. I couldn't sleep last night because my apartment was too hot.
10. My roommate can speak four languages. He's multilingual.
11. I'm sorry that I couldn't call you last night.
12. I'm sorry, but I can't come to your party next week.
13. Can we take vacations on the moon in the 22nd century?

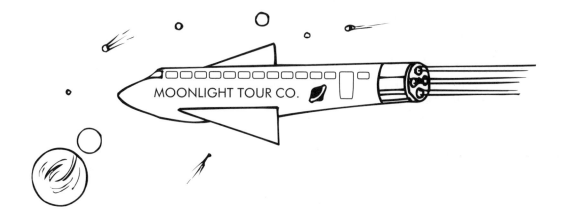

MOONLIGHT TOUR CO.

1. I wasn't able to _____ last night because

_____ .

2. We'll be able to _____ in the 22nd century.

3. I'm sorry, but I won't be able to _____ .

4. Birds are able to _____ .

5. My friend is multilingual. She's able to _____ .

6. I'm bilingual. I'm able to _____ .

7. The students weren't able to _____ in class

yesterday because _____ .

8. Will you be able to _____ tomorrow?

9. _____ wasn't able to _____ because

_____ .

10. _____ isn't able to _____

because _____ .

11. _____ won't be able to _____

because _____ .

7-13 禮貌性的疑問句：MAY I, COULD I 和 CAN I

(a) ***May I borrow*** your pen? (b) ***Could I borrow*** your pen? (c) ***Can I borrow*** your pen?	(a) 句，(b) 句和 (c) 句同義，即：*I want to borrow your pen.* 我客氣地向你借筆。
(d) *May I **please** borrow* your pen? (e) *Could I **please** borrow* your pen? (f) *Can I **please** borrow* your pen?	*please* 經常用於禮貌性的疑問句。
典型回答 (g) ***Yes, of course.*** (h) ***Of course.*** (i) ***Certainly.*** (j) ***Sure.*** （非正式說法）★ (k) ***No problem.*** （非正式說法）★	典型對話 A: *May I please borrow your pen?* B: ***Yes, of course.*** *Here it is.* A: *Thank you. / Thanks.*

★非正式英文通常用在朋友或家人間的對話。

■ **練習 30 — 口語練習（閤上書本）**：和同學用 May I, Can I 或 Could I 做禮貌性疑問句的問答練習。

例：　　　（ . . .) has a pencil. You want to borrow it.
學生A：（ . . .), may I (please) borrow your pencil?
學生B：Certainly. Here it is.
學生A：Thank you.

1. (. . .) has a dictionary. You want to borrow it.
2. (. . .) has a pen. You want to use it for a minute.
3. (. . .) has an eraser. You want to use it for a minute.
4. (. . .) has a pencil sharpener. You want to borrow it.
5. (. . .) has a book. You want to see it.
6. (. . .) has a dictionary. You want to see it.
7. You are at (. . .)'s home. You want to use the phone.
8. You are at (. . .)'s home. You want a glass of water.
9. You are at a restaurant. (. . .) is a waiter / waitress. You want to have a cup of coffee.
10. (. . .) is a waiter / waitress. You want to have the check.

7-14　禮貌性的疑問句：COULD YOU 和 WOULD YOU

(a) ***Could you (please) open*** the door? (b) ***Would you (please) open*** the door?	(a) 句和 (b) 句同義，即：*I want you to open the door.* 我客氣地請你打開門。
典型回答 (c) ***Yes, of course.*** (d) ***Certainly.*** (e) ***I'd be glad to.*** (f) ***I'd be happy to.*** (g) ***Sure.***（非正式說法） (h) ***No problem.***（非正式說法）	典型對話 A: *Could you please open the door?* B: ***I'd be glad to.*** A: *Thank you. / Thanks.*

304 ■ 第七章

1. A: Excuse me, sir. _____

   B: _____

   A: _____

2. A: _____

   B: Excuse me? I didn't understand what you said.

   A: _____

   B: _____

例： You want (. . .) to open the window.
學生A： (. . .), could you (please) open the window?
學生B： Certainly.
學生A： Thank you.

1. You want (. . .) to close the door.
2. You want (. . .) to turn on the light.
3. You want (. . .) to turn off the light.
4. You want (. . .) to pass you the salt and pepper.
5. You want (. . .) to hand you that book.
6. You want (. . .) to translate a word for you.
7. You want (. . .) to tell you the time.
8. You want (. . .) to open the window.
9. You want (. . .) to hold your books for a minute.
10. You want (. . .) to lend you（一筆錢）.

■ 練習 33 — 口語練習：兩人一組，練習在下列情況中，人們可能會問的禮貌性問題，並將你們的對話和班上其他各組分享。

學生A： 提出禮貌性的問題。
學生B： 回答問題。

例： 情況：教授的辦公室。學生 A 扮學生，學生 B 扮教授。
學生A： (Knock, knock). May I come in?
學生B： Certainly. Come in. How are you today?
學生A： Fine, thanks.

或：
學生A： Hello, Professor Alvarez. Could I talk to you for a few minutes? I have some questions about the last assignment.
學生B： Of course. Have a seat.
學生A： Thank you.

情況1.： a restaurant. Student A is a customer. Student B is a waitress / waiter.
情況2.： a classroom. Student A is a teacher. Student B is a student.
情況3.： a kitchen. Student A is a visitor. Student B is at home.
情況4.： a clothing store. Student A is the customer. Student B is a salesperson.
情況5.： an apartment. Student A and B are roommates.
情況6.： a car. Student A is a passenger. Student B is the driver.
情況7.： an office. Student A is a boss. Student B is an employee.
情況8.： a telephone conversation. Student B answers the phone. Student A wants to talk to（某人）.

(a)	"**Close** the door, Jimmy. It's cold outside." "Okay, Mom."	(a) 句中：*Close the door* 是祈使句，意爲 *Jimmy, I want you to close the door. I am telling you to close the door.*（我要你現在去把門關起來。）
(b) (c)	**Sit** down. **Be** careful!	祈使句要用原形動詞（*close, sit, be* 等）。
(d) (e)	**Don't open** the window. **Don't be** late.	否定句：*don't* + 原形動詞
(f) (g) (h) (i)	命令：　**Stop**, thief! 指示：　**Open** your books to page 24. 建議：　**Don't worry**. 請求：　**Please close** the door.	祈使句用來表達命令、指示和建議。祈使句加上 *please*，如 (i) 句，表示禮貌的請求。

■ **練習 34**：將對話中的使役動詞畫線。

1. CINDY: We're leaving.
   BETH: <u>Wait</u> for me!
   CINDY: <u>Hurry</u> up! We'll be late.
   BETH: Okay. Okay. I'm ready. Let's go.

2. MICHELLE: （敲門聲）　May I come in?
   PROFESSOR: Certainly. Come in. Please have a seat.
   MICHELLE: Thanks.
   PROFESSOR: How can I help you?
   MICHELLE: I need to ask you a question about yesterday's lecture.
   PROFESSOR: Okay. What's the question?

3. MARY: We need to leave soon.
   IVAN: I'm ready.
   MARY: Don't forget your house key.
   IVAN: I have it.
   MARY: Okay.

4. TOM: What's the matter?
   JIM: I have the hiccups.
   TOM: Hold your breath.
   BOB: Drink some water.
   JOE: Breathe into a paper bag.
   KEN: Eat a piece of bread.
   JIM: It's okay. The hiccups are gone.

5. STUDENT: Do we have any homework for tomorrow?
   TEACHER: Yes. Read pages 24 through 36, and answer the questions on page 37, in writing.
   STUDENT: Is that all?
   TEACHER: Yes.

6. YUKO: How do I get to the post office from here?
   ERIC: Walk two blocks to 16th Avenue. Then turn right on Forest Street. Go two more blocks to Market Street and turn left. The post office is halfway down the street on the right-hand side.
   YUKO: Thanks.

7. ANDY: Bye, Mom. I'm going over to Billy's house.
   MOM: Wait a minute. Did you clean up your room?
   ANDY: I'll do it later.
   MOM: No. Do it now, before you leave.
   ANDY: Do I have to?
   MOM: Yes.
   ANDY: What do I have to do?
   MOM: Hang up your clothes. Make your bed. Put your books back on the shelf. Empty the wastepaper basket. Okay?
   ANDY: Okay.

8. HEIDI: Please close the window, Mike. It's a little chilly in here.
   MIKE: Okay. Is there anything else I can do for you before I leave?
   HEIDI: Could you turn off the light in the kitchen?
   MIKE: No problem. Anything else?
   HEIDI: Ummm, please hand me the remote control for the TV. It's over there.
   MIKE: Sure. Here.
   HEIDI: Thanks.
   MIKE: I'll stop by again tomorrow. Take care of yourself. Take good care of that broken leg.
   HEIDI: Don't worry. I will. Thanks again.

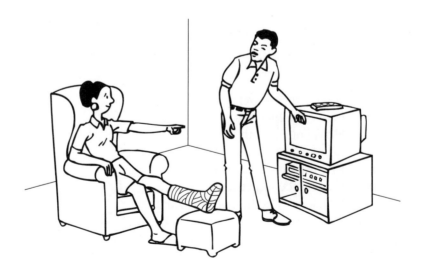

■ **練習 35**：在圖中說話者上方的空格內填入祈使句。

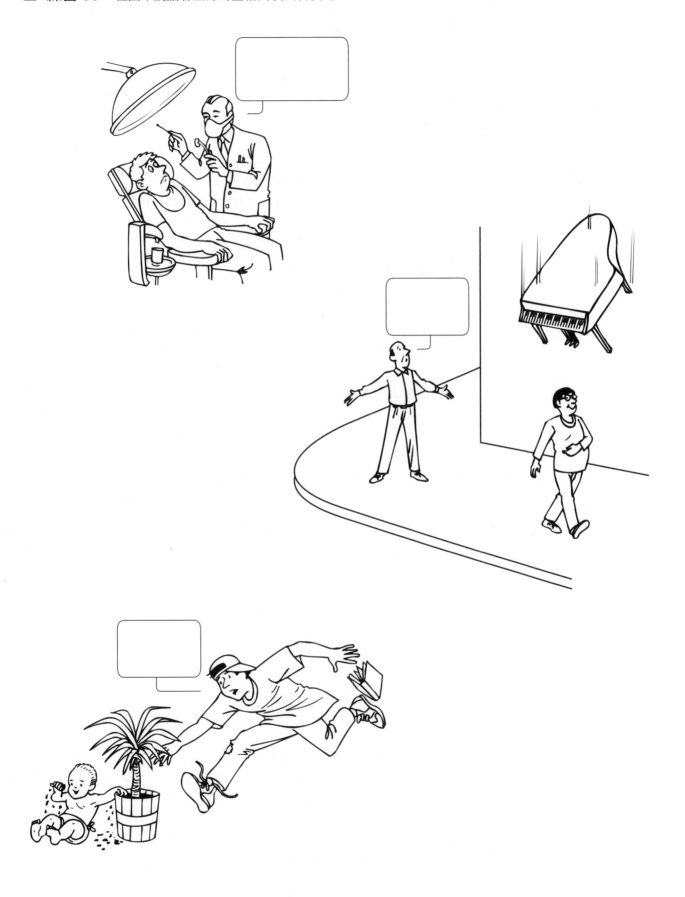

例： (...) is your friend. He / She has a headache. What are some typical imperative sentences for this situation?

答： Take an aspirin.
Lie down and close your eyes for a little while.
Put a cold cloth across your forehead.
Take a hot bath and relax.
依此類推。

1. You are the teacher of this class. You are assigning homework for tomorrow. What are some typical imperative sentences for this situation?

2. Your friend (...) has the hiccups. What are some typical imperative sentences for this situation?

3. (...) is your eight-year-old son / daughter. He / She is walking out the door to go to school. What are some typical imperative sentences for this situation?

4. (...) wants to improve his / her health. Tell him / her what to do and what not to do.

5. (...) is going to cook rice for the first time tonight. Tell him / her how to cook rice.

6. (...) is going to visit your country for the first time next month. Tell him / her what to do and what to see as a tourist in your country.

7-16 TWO, TOO 和 TO 的用法

			two, too 和 *to* 發音相同。
TWO	(a)	I have **two** children.	(a) 句中：*two* ＝ 數目。
TOO	(b)	Timmy is **too** young. He can't read.	(b) 句中：*too young* ＝ *not old enough* （年紀太輕）。
	(c)	Ann saw the movie. I saw the movie **too**.	(c) 句中：*too* ＝ *also* （也）。
TO	(d)	I talked **to** Jim.	(d) 句中：*to* ＝ 介系詞。
	(e)	I want **to** watch television.	(e) 句中：*to* ＝ 不定詞的一部份。

■ 練習 37：用 two, too 或 to 完成下列句子。

1. I'd like a cup of coffee. Bob would like a cup ___*too*___.

2. I had _____ cups of coffee yesterday.

3. I can't drink my coffee. It's _____ hot. The coffee is _____ hot for me _____ drink.

4. I talked _____ Jim. Jane wants _____ talk _____ Jim _____.

5. I walked _____ school today. Alex walked _____ school today _____.

6. I'm going _____ take the bus _____ school tomorrow.

7. Shh. I want _____ listen _____ the news broadcast.

8. I can't study. The music is _____ loud.

9. The weather is _____ cold for us _____ go _____ the beach.

10. I have _____ apples. Ken wants _____ have _____ apples _____.

7-17 詳述介系詞：表示地方的 AT 和 IN

(a) Olga is **at** home. Ivan is **at** work. Yoko is **at** school.	(a) 句中：at 和 *home, work* 及 *school* 連用。
(b) Sue is **in** bed. Tom is **in** class. Paul is **in** jail / prison. Mr. Lee is **in** (the) hospital.	(b) 句中：in 和 *bed, class, jail / prison* 及 *hospital* 連用。 注意： 美式英文 = *in the hospital.* 　　　英式英文 = *in hospital.*
(c) Ahmed is **in** the kitchen.	(c) 句中：in 和房間連用：*in the kitchen, in the classroom, in the hall, in my bedroom* 等。
(d) David is **in** Mexico City.	(d) 句中：in 和城市、州／省 、國及洲連用：*in Mexico City, in Florida, in Italy, in Asia* 等。
(e) A: Where's Ivan? B: He isn't here. He's **at** the bank.	(e) 句中：at 和城市中的位置連用：*at the post office, at the bank , at the library, at the bookstore, at the park, at the theater , at the restaurant, at the football stadium* 等。
比較 (f) In Picture 2, Ivan is **in** the bank. He is not outside the bank.	(f) 句中：有必要表明某人是在建築物裡面，而非外面時，說話者會用 in 加建築物。一般情況說話者會以 at 和建築物連用。 *in the bank* = 在銀行的裡面。

Ivan is **at** the bank.

Ivan is **at** the bank.
Ivan is **in** (**inside**) the bank.

1. A: Is Jennifer here?

   B: No, she's ___*at*___ the bookstore.⋆

2. A: Where's Jack?

   B: He's ___*in*___ his room.

3. When I was _____ work yesterday, I had an interesting telephone call.

4. Poor Anita. She's _____ the hospital again for more surgery.

5. Mr. Gow wasn't _____ class yesterday. He was _____ home. He wasn't feeling well.

6. Last year at this time, Eric was _____ Korea. This year he's _____ Spain.

7. A: Where's Donna?

   B: She's _____ New York. She's attending a conference.

8. There's a fire extinguisher _____ the hall.

9. The children are _____ home this morning. They aren't _____ school.

10. A: Where's Olga? I was supposed to meet her here at five.

    B: She's _____ the library. She's studying for a test.
    A: Oh. Maybe she forgot that she was supposed to meet me here.

11. A: Where's Robert?

    B: He's _____ the computer room.

12. A: Where's Fatima?

    B: She's _____ the supermarket.

13. We ate _____ a good restaurant last night. The food was delicious.

14. A thief broke the window of a jewelry store and stole some valuable jewelry. The police caught him. Now he's _____ jail. He's going to be _____ prison for a long time.

15. Singapore is _____ Asia.

16. We had a good time _____ the zoo yesterday.

⋆亦可說：*She's in the bookstore*，但只用在說話者想表明她在書店的裡面，而不是外面的時候。通常說話者會用 *at* + 建築物來表明某人的所在位置。

17. There are thirty-seven desks _____ our classroom.

18. A: Where can I get some fresh tomatoes?

    B: _____ the market on Waterfront Street.

19. A: Here's your hotel key, Ms. Fox. You're _____ Room 609.
    B: Thank you. Where are the elevators?

20. A: Is Mike up?

    B: No, he's _____ bed.
    A: Well, it's time to get up. I'm going to wake him up. Hey, Mike! You can't sleep all day! Get up!
    C: Go away!

■ **練習 39 — 口語練習（閤上書本）：** 用提示的字加上正確的介詞 at 或 in，完成 I was... yesterday. 的句子。

例：work
答：I was at work yesterday.

1. class   7. work
2. the library   8. Room 206
3. （某市）   9. a hotel
4. home   10. （某洲）
5. this room   11. (. . .)'s living room
6. the bookstore   12. （某建築物）

■ **練習 40 — 口語練習（閤上書本）：** 做有關位置的問答練習。
學生A：用 Where were you . . . . ? 提出問題。
學生B：用 at 或 in 回答問題。

例：   yesterday afternoon
學生A：Where were you yesterday afternoon?
學生B：I was in class.

1. at nine o'clock last night
2. at two o'clock yesterday afternoon
3. after class yesterday
4. this morning at six o'clock
5. six weeks ago
6. five years ago
7. on your last vacation
8. when you were ten years old

以下的人、動物、物品能 (can) 做什麼或不能 (can't) 做什麼？能的原因或不能的原因為何？以小組方式討論下列主題，並向其他組提出報告。

例： a tiger
答： A tiger can kill a water buffalo because a tiger is very strong and powerful.
A tiger can sleep in the shade of a tree all day if it wants to. It doesn't have a job, and it doesn't go to school.
A tiger can't speak (a human language). It's an animal.
A tiger can communicate with other tigers. Animals can talk to each other in their own languages.

1. the students in this class
2. small children
3. a monkey
4. （同學的名字）
5. international students who live in （本國）
6. teenagers
7. people who live in （本市）
8. people who are illiterate
9. money
10. computers
11. （本班的教師）
12. （本國或某國的領袖）

■ 練習 42 — 複習：選出正確答案完成下列句子。

1. _____ play a musical instrument?
    A. Do you can   B. Can you   C. Do you be able to   D. Can you to

2. Jack was _____ sick to go to work yesterday morning. He stayed home.
    A. very   B. enough   C. too   D. too much

3. I was too sleepy _____ last night.
    A. to studying   B. for studying   C. to study   D. for study

4. *(Knock, knock.)* Hello? _____ come in? Thanks.
    A. Could I to   B. Will I   C. Can I too   D. May I

5. I don't know how _____ to the Palace Hotel from here.
    A. do I get   B. get   C. getting   D. to get

6. Gina _____ understand the speaker at the lecture last night.
    A. couldn't   B. might not   C. isn't able to   D. can't

7. In my life right now, I have _____ problems. I can't solve all of them.
    A. very much   B. too many   C. too much   D. very

8. I can't reach the eraser on my friend's desk. My arms aren't _____.
    A. long enough   B. too long   C. enough long   D. too much long

9. My uncle can't _____ English.
    A. to speak   B. speaking   C. speaks   D. speak

10. I'm sorry. I can't hear what you're saying. _____ speak a little louder?
    A. May you   B. Could you   C. Don't   D. Can

11. An encyclopedia is too difficult _____.
    A. for to read a child   C. for a child to read
    B. to read a child   D. to for a child read

12. Rosa works for a computer company _____ Taipei.
    A. on   B. at   C. in   D. to

■ **練習 43 — 複習**：更正下列句子的錯誤。

1. My brother wasn't able calling me last night.

2. Don't to interrupt. It's not polite.

3. May I please to borrow your dictionary? Thank you.

4. We will can go to the museum tomorrow afternoon.

5. We can't count all of the stars in the universe. There are to many.

6. The diamond ring was to buy too expensive for John.

7. Can you to stand on your head?

8. My son isn't enough old too go to school. He's only too years old.

9. I saw a beautiful vase at a store yesterday, but I couldn't bought it.

10. We have too many homeworks.

11. Closing the door please. Thank you.

12. Robert was to tired to go two his class at to o'clock.

(1)   *Once upon a time there* (be) _____ *a mouse named Young Mouse. He lived near a river with his family and friends. Every day he and the other mice did the same things.*

(2)   *They* (hunt) _____ *for food and* (take) _____ *care of their*

(3)   *mouse holes. In the evening they* (listen) _____ *to stories around a fire. Young Mouse especially liked to listen to stories about the Far Away Land. He* (dream)

(4)   _____ *about the Far Away Land. It sounded wonderful. One day he*

(5)   (decide) _____ *to go there.*

YOUNG MOUSE: Goodbye, Old Mouse. I'm leaving now.

(6)   OLD MOUSE: Why *(you, leave)* _____? Where

(7)   *(you, go)* _____?

(8)   YOUNG MOUSE: I *(go)* _____ to a new and different place. I *(go)*

(9)   _____ to the Far Away Land.

(10)   OLD MOUSE: Why *(you, want)* _____ *(go)* _____ there?

(11)   YOUNG MOUSE: I *(want)* _____ *(experience)* _____

(12)   all of life. I *(need)* _____ *(learn)* _____ about everything.

(13)   OLD MOUSE: You *(can learn)* _____ many things if you *(stay)*

(14)   _____ here with us. Please *(stay)* _____ here with us.

(15)   YOUNG MOUSE: No, I *(can stay, not)* _____ here by the

(16)   river for the rest of my life. There *(be)* _____ too much to learn about in the world. I must go to the Far Away Land.

OLD MOUSE: The trip to the Far Away Land is a long and dangerous journey. You *(have)*

(17)   _____ many problems before you *(get)* _____

(18)   there. You *(face)* _____ many dangers.

YOUNG MOUSE: I understand that, but I need to find out about the Far Away Land.

(19)   Goodbye, Old Mouse. Goodbye, everyone! I *(may see, never)* _____

(20)   any of you again, but I *(try)* _____ to return from the
Far Away Land someday. Goodbye!

*So Young Mouse left to fulfill his dream of going to the Far Away Land. His first problem
was the river. At the river, he met a frog.*

(21)   MAGIC FROG: Hello, Young Mouse. I'm Magic Frog. *(you, have)* _____
a problem right now?

(22)   YOUNG MOUSE: Yes. How *(I, can cross)* _____ this river?

(23)   I *(know, not)* _____ how to swim. If I

(24)   *(can cross, not)* _____ this

(25)   river, I *(be, not)* _____

able to reach the Far Away Land.

(26)   MAGIC FROG: I *(help)* _____

you to cross the river. I *(give)*

(27)   _____ you

the power of my legs so you *(can jump)*

(28)   _____ across the river. I *(give, also)* _____
you a new name. Your new name will be Jumping Mouse.

JUMPING MOUSE: Thank you, Magic Frog.

MAGIC FROG: You are a brave mouse, Jumping Mouse, and you have a good heart. If you

(29)   *(lose, not)* _____ hope, you *(reach)* _____
the Far Away Land.

*With his powerful new legs, Jumping Mouse jumped across the river. He traveled fast for
many days across a wide grassland. One day he met a buffalo. The buffalo was lying on the
ground.*

JUMPING MOUSE: Hello, Buffalo. My name is Jumping Mouse. Why *(you, lie★)*

(30)   _____ on the ground? *(you, be)* _____ ill?

_____
★*lie* 的 *-ing* 形式拼作 *lying*。

(31) BUFFALO: Yes. I *(can see, not)* _____. I *(drink)*

(32) _____ some poisoned water, and now I *(be)* _____

(33) blind. I *(die)* _____ soon because I *(can find, not)*

(34) _____ food and water without my eyes.

(35) JUMPING MOUSE: When I started my journey, Magic Frog *(give)* _____
      me her powerful legs so I could jump across the river. What *(I, can give)*

(36) _____ you to help you? I know! I *(give)*

(37) _____ you my sight so you can see to find food and water.

BUFFALO: Are you really going to do that? Jumping Mouse, you are very kind! Ah! Yes,

(38) I *(can see)* _____ again. Thank you! But now you

(39) *(can see, not)* _____. How *(you, find)* _____

(40) _____ the Far Away Land? I know. *(jump)*

(41) _____ onto my back. I *(carry)* _____
      you across this land to the foot of the mountain.

JUMPING MOUSE: Thank you, Buffalo.

So Jumping Mouse found a way to reach the mountain. When they reached the mountain, Jumping Mouse and Buffalo parted.

(42) BUFFALO: I don't live in the mountains, so I *(can go, not)* _____
      any farther.

(43) JUMPING MOUSE: What *(I, do)* _____? I *(have)*

(44) _____ powerful legs, but I can't see.

(45)   BUFFALO: *(keep)* _____ your hope alive. You *(find)* _____
       a way to reach the Far Away Land.

Jumping Mouse was very afraid. He didn't know what to do. Suddenly he heard a wolf.

(46)   JUMPING MOUSE: Hello? Wolf? I *(can see, not)* _____ you,

(47)   but I *(can hear)* _____ you.

(48)   WOLF: Yes, Jumping Mouse. I'm here, but I *(can help, not)* _____

(49)   you because I *(die★)* _____.

(50)   JUMPING MOUSE: What's wrong? Why *(you, die)* _____?

(51)   WOLF: I *(lose)* _____ my sense of smell many weeks ago, so now I

(52)   *(can find, not)* _____ food. I *(starve)*

(53)   _____ to death.

(54)   JUMPING MOUSE: Oh, Wolf, I *(can help)* _____ you. I *(give)*

(55)   _____ you my ability to smell.

(56)   WOLF: Oh, thank you, Jumping Mouse. Yes, I *(can smell)* _____
       again. Now I'll be able to find food. That is a wonderful gift! How *(I, can help)*

(57)   _____ you?

(58)   JUMPING MOUSE: I *(try)* _____ to get to the Far Away Land.

(59)   I *(need)* _____ *(go)* _____ to the top of the mountain.

(60)   WOLF: *(come)* _____ over here. I *(put)* _____

(61)   you on my back and *(take)* _____ you to the top of the mountain.

★*die* 的 *-ing* 形式拼作 *dying*。

So Wolf carried Jumping Mouse to the top of the mountain. But then Wolf left.   Jumping

(62)   *Mouse was all alone. He* (can see, not) _____

(63)   *and he* (can smell, not) _____ *, but he still had powerful legs.*

(64)   *He almost* (lose) _____ *hope. Then suddenly, he* (hear) _____ *Magic Frog.*

(65)   JUMPING MOUSE: Is that you, Magic Frog? Please *(help)* _____ me. I'm all alone and afraid.

(66)   MAGIC FROG: *(cry, not)* _____, Jumping Mouse. You have a

(67)   generous, open heart. You *(be, not)* _____ selfish. You help others. Your unselfishness caused you suffering during your journey, but you

(68)   *(lose, never)* _____ hope. Now you are in the Far

(69)   Away Land. *(jump)* _____, Jumping Mouse. *(use)* _____ your powerful legs to jump high in the air. Jump! Jump!

Jumping Mouse jumped as high as he could, up, up, up.
He reached his arms out to his sides and started to fly.
He felt strong and powerful.

JUMPING MOUSE: I can fly! I can fly! I *(fly)*

(70)   _____!

MAGIC FROG: Jumping Mouse, I am going to give you a new name. Now your name is Eagle!

So Jumping Mouse became the powerful Eagle and fulfilled his dream of reaching the Far Away Land and experiencing all that life has to offer.★

★此寓言源自美國的一個本土故事，節錄自 *John Steptoe* 所寫的 *The Story of Jumping Mouse*；
© *Lothrop, Lee & Shepard Books, 1984*。

■ **練習 45**：六人一組，以跳跳鼠的故事演一齣戲。戲中要有五個角色：跳跳鼠 (Jumping Mouse)，大老鼠 (Old Mouse)，神奇蛙 (Magic Frog)，水牛 (Buffalo)，以及野狼 (Wolf)。另外，一位組員擔任旁白，說出練習 44 的故事中，斜體字的部份。

7-18 更多的不規則動詞

blow – blew	*keep – kept*
draw – drew	*know - knew*
fall – fell	*swim – swam*
feel – felt	*throw – threw*
grow – grew	*win – won*

■ **練習 46 — 口語練習（闔上書本）**：練習使用上表中的不規則動詞。

例：*fall-fell* Rain falls. Leaves fall. Sometimes people fall. Yesterday I fell down. I hurt my knee. How did I hurt my knee yesterday?

答：You fell (down).

1. *blow-blew* The sun shines. Rain falls. Wind blows. Last week we had a storm. It rained hard, and the wind blew hard. Tell me about the storm last week.

2. *draw-drew* I draw once a week in art class. Last week I drew a portrait of myself. What did I do in art class last week?

3. *feel-felt* You can feel an object. You can also feel an emotion or a sensation. Sometimes I feel sleepy in class. I felt tired all day yesterday. How did I feel yesterday? How did you feel yesterday?

4. *fall-fell* Sometimes I fall down. Yesterday I fell down. I felt bad when I fell down. What happened to me yesterday?

5. *grow-grew* Trees grow. Flowers grow. Vegetables grow.   Usually I grow vegetables in my garden, but last year I grew only flowers. What did I grow in my garden last year?

6. *keep-kept* Now I keep my money in（某銀行）. Last year I kept my money in （另一銀行）. Where did I keep my money last year?

7. *know-knew* (. . .) knows a lot about English grammar. On the grammar test last week, s/he knew all the answers. What did (. . .) know last week?

8. *swim-swam* I swim in（湖、海、洋或當地游泳池）every summer. I swam in（湖、海洋或當地游泳池）last summer. What did I do last summer?

9. *throw-threw*   I can hand you this (piece of chalk) or I can throw it to you. I just threw this (piece of chalk) to (. . .). What did I just do?
10. *win-won*   You can win a game or lose a game. Last weekend（某球隊）won a game / match against（另一球隊）. How did（球隊名）do last weekend? Did they win or lose?

■ **練習 47**：用框內動詞的過去式完成下列句子。

blow	*grow*	*swim*
draw	*hurt*	*throw*
fall	*keep*	*win*
feel	*know*	

1. A: Did you enjoy your tennis game with Jackie?

   B: Yes, but I lost. Jackie _____.

2. A: How did you break your leg?

   B: I _____ down on the ice on the sidewalk.

3. A: Ouch!
   B: What's the matter?

   A: I _____ my finger.
   B: How?
   A: I pinched it in the door.

4. A: Did you give the box of candy to your girlfriend?

   B: No, I didn't. I _____ it and ate it myself.

5. A: That's a nice picture.

   B: I agree. Anna _____ it. She's a good artist.

6. A: Did you have a garden when you lived at home?

   B: Yes. I _____ vegetables and flowers.

7. A: Did you finish the test?

   B: No. I didn't have enough time. I _____ all of the answers but I ran out of time.

8. A: Did you have fun at the beach?

   B: Lots of fun. We sunbathed and _____ in the ocean.

9. A: I burned my finger.

   B: Did you put ice on it?

   A: No. I _____ on it.

10. A: What's the matter? You sound like you have a frog in your throat.

    B: I think I'm catching a cold. I _____ okay yesterday, but I don't feel very good today.

11. A: How did you break the window, Tommy?

    B: Well, I _____ a ball to Annie, but I missed Annie and hit the window instead.

■ **練習 48**：用框內動詞的過去式完成下列句子。

begin	*fly*	*make*	*take*
break	*grow*	*meet*	*tell*
catch	*know*	*sing*	*throw*
cost	*leave*	*spend*	*wear*
fall	*lose*	*steal*	*win*

1. When I went to the airport yesterday, I _____ a taxi.

2. I _____ my winter jacket yesterday because the weather was cold.

3. Tom bought a new tie. It _____ a lot because it was a hand-painted silk tie.

4. Laurie doesn't feel good. She _____ a cold a couple of days ago.

5. Leo could read the story easily. The words in the story weren't new for him. He

   _____ the vocabulary in the story.

6. I know Ronald Sawyer. I _____ him at a party a couple of weeks ago.

7. My hometown is Ames, Iowa. I _____ up there.

8. I dropped my book. It _____ to the floor.

9. Ken couldn't get into his apartment because he _____ his keys.

10. We _____ a lot of money at the restaurant last night. The food was good, but expensive.

11. The baseball player _____ the ball to the catcher.

12. I wrote a check yesterday. I _____ a mistake on the check, so I tore it up and wrote another one.

13. Someone _____ my bicycle, so I called the police.

14. Maggie didn't tell a lie. She _____ the truth.

15. Rick _____ his arm when he fell on the ice.

16. We were late for the movie. It _____ at 7:00, but we didn't get there until 7:15.

17. We _____ songs at the party last night and had a good time.

18. I _____ to Chicago last week. The plane was only five minutes late.

19. My plane _____ at 6:03 and arrived at 8:45.

20. We played a soccer game yesterday. The other team _____. We lost.

第八章
名詞、代名詞和形容詞

■ **練習 1**：分辨下列的字是名詞 (NOUN)，或形容詞 (ADJ)，並用該字造句。

1. busy   NOUN   (ADJ)
   → *I'm too busy to go to the zoo.*

2. computer   (NOUN)   ADJ
   → *Computers are machines*

3. tall   NOUN   ADJ

4. apartment   NOUN   ADJ

5. Tom   NOUN   ADJ

6. intelligent   NOUN   ADJ

7. hand   NOUN   ADJ

8. good   NOUN   ADJ

9. monkey   NOUN   ADJ

10. young   NOUN   ADJ

11. music   NOUN   ADJ

12. expensive   NOUN   ADJ

13. grammar   NOUN   ADJ

8-1　用形容詞和名詞修飾名詞

(a)　I bought an *expensive* book. 　　　　　　　　形容詞　＋　名詞	形容詞可以修飾名詞，如 (a)。常用的形容詞，請參閱表 4-2。
(b)　I bought a *grammar* book 　　　　　　　名詞　＋　名詞	名詞可以修飾其他名詞。(b) 句中：*grammar* 是名詞，但有形容詞的作用，用來修飾另一個名詞 (*book*)。
(c)　He works at a *shoe* store. 　　　　　　　名詞　＋　名詞 (d)　誤： *He works at a shoes store.*	名詞作形容詞用時，要用單數形式。(c) 句中：這家店賣的鞋子是複數 (*the store sells shoes*)，但鞋店要說成 *shoe*（單數）*store*。
(e)　I bought an *expensive* *grammar* book. 　　　　　形容詞　＋　名詞　＋　名詞 (f)　誤： *I bought a grammar expensive book.*	同時用一個形容詞和一個名詞，修飾另一個名詞時，先寫形容詞，再寫名詞。

■ **練習 2**：找出下列句子中的形容詞，並指出該形容詞所修飾的名詞。

1. I drank some hot tea.

2. My grandmother is a wise woman.

3. English is not my native language.

4. The busy waitress poured coffee into the empty cup.

5. A young man carried the heavy suitcase for Fumiko.

6. I sat in an uncomfortable chair at the restaurant.

7. There is international news on the front page of the newspaper.

8. My uncle is a wonderful man.

■ **練習 3**：找出下列句子中有形容詞作用的名詞，並指出該字所修飾的名詞。

1. We sat at the kitchen table.

2. I bought some new CDs at the music store.

3. We met Jack at the train station.

4. Vegetable soup is nutritious.

5. The movie theater is next to the furniture store.

6. The waiter handed us a lunch menu.

7. The traffic light was red, so we stopped.

8. Ms. Bell gave me her business card.

■ **練習 4**：依各題前半句的資料，用名詞修飾名詞的句型完成下列句子。

1. Vases that are used for flowers are called _____*flower vases.*_____

2. A cup that is used for coffee is called _____*a coffee cup.*_____

3. A story that appears in a newspaper is called _____

4. Rooms in hotels are called _____

5. Soup that is made of beans is called _____

6. A worker in an office is called _____

7. A room that contains computers is called _____

8. Seats on airplanes are called _____

9. A bench that is found in a park is called _____

10. A tag that gives the price of something is called _____

　　　　例如：第一句的答案可以是 a university education, a high school education 以及 a college education。

class	official	soup
✔ education	program	store
keys	race	tickets
number	room	trip

1. Jane has a { university / high school / college } _education._____

2. We went to a { furniture / shoe / clothing } _____

3. I took a { history / math / science } _____

4. We watched a { horse / car / foot } _____

5. I talked to a { government / city / school } _____

6. Mom made some { vegetable / bean / chicken } _____

7. He told me about a { radio / television / computer } _____

8. We took a / an { boat / bus / airplane } _____

9. I couldn't find my { car / house / door } _____

10. What is your { telephone / apartment / license plat } _____

11. We bought some
$$\begin{Bmatrix} \text{theater} \\ \text{concert} \\ \text{airplane} \end{Bmatrix}$$
_____

12. We visited Sue in her
$$\begin{Bmatrix} \text{hospital} \\ \text{hotel} \\ \text{dormitory} \end{Bmatrix}$$
_____

■ **練習 6**：將指定的名詞和形容詞，依正確的順序填入空格中。

1. *homework*
   long
   assignment

   The teacher gave us a ___*long homework assignment.*___

2. *program*
   good
   television

   I watched a _____

3. *road*
   mountain
   dangerous

   We drove on a _____

4. *automobile*
   bad
   accident

   Janet was in a _____

5. *article*
   magazine
   interesting

   I read an _____

6. *delicious*
   vegetable
   soup

   Mrs. Green made some _____

7. *card*
   funny
   birthday

   My sister gave me a _____

8. *narrow*
   seats
   airplane

   People don't like to sit in _____

(a) a **large red** car (b) 誤： *a red large car*	(a) 中：兩個形容詞 *(large* 和 *red)* 一同修飾名詞 *(car)*。形容詞有其特定的字序。(a) 中，描述大小尺寸的形容詞 *(large)* 位於顏色形容詞 *(red)* 的前面。
(c) a **beautiful young** woman (d) a **beautiful red** car (e) a **beautiful Greek** island	形容詞 *beautiful* 表達出一種意見、看法。 意見形容詞通常置於其他形容詞之前。 (c) 中：意見先於年齡 (d) 中：意見先於顏色 (e) 中：意見先於國籍
(f) 表達意見的形容詞 *dangerous favorite important* *difficult good interesting* *dirty happy strong* *expensive honest wonderful*	意見形容詞很多。(f) 內的字是一些常見的意見形容詞。

一般的形容詞字序

(1) 意見 *beautiful* *delicious* *kind*	(2) 大小 *large* *tall* *little*	(3) 年齡 *young* *old* *middle-aged*	(4) 顏色 *red* *blue* *black*	(5) 國籍* *Greek* *Chinese* *Mexican*	(6) 材質 *metal* *glass* *plastic*

(g) some **delicious Mexican** food (h) a **small glass** vase (i) a **kind old Chinese** man	一個名詞通常只用一、二個形容詞來修飾，偶爾可見用三個形容詞的情形。
(j) 罕見情形： a *beautiful small old brown Greek metal coin*	名詞前面少見一長串的形容詞。

*描述國籍的形容詞須大寫：*Korean, Venezuelan, Saudi Arabian* 等。

■ **練習 7**：將各題前的形容詞依正確字序填入空格內。

1. *glass*
   tall

   a   *tall glass*   vase

2. *delicious*
   Thai

   some   food

3. *red*
   small

   some   tomatoes

4. *old*
   big
   brown

   some _____ cows

5. *narrow*
   dirt

   a _____ road

6. *young*
   serious

   a _____ woman

7. *long*
   black
   beautiful

   _____ hair

8. *Chinese*
   famous
   old

   a / an _____ work of art

9. *leather*
   brown
   thin

   a _____ belt

10. *wonderful*
    old
    Native American

    a / an _____ story

■ **練習 8**：用框內的字完成下列句子。

Asian	✔ *cotton*	*polite*
brick	*important*	*soft*
Canadian	*leather*	*unhappy*
coffee		

1. Jack is wearing a white _____*cotton*_____ shirt.

2. Hong Kong is an important _____ city.

3. I'm wearing some comfortable old _____ shoes.

4. Tommy was a / an _____ little boy when he broke his favorite toy.

5. Ann has a / an _____ wool blanket on her bed.

6. Our dorm is a tall red _____ building.

7. The computer is a / an _____ modern invention.

8. My nephew has good manners. He is always a / an _____ young man, especially to his elders.

9. Jack always carries a large blue _____ cup with him.

10. Ice hockey is a popular _____ sport.

■ **練習 9**：在下列空格中填入形容詞或具有形容作用的名詞。

1. We had some hot _____ food.

2. My dog, Rover, is a / an _____ old dog.

3. We bought a blue _____ blanket.

4. Alice has _____ gold earrings.

5. Tom has short _____ hair.

6. Mr. Lee is a / an _____ young man.

7. Jack lives in a large _____ brick house.

8. I bought a big _____ suitcase.

9. Sally picked a / an _____ red flower.

10. Ali wore an old _____ shirt to the picnic.

1. Ms. Lane has ~~a wood old~~ *an old wood* desk in her office.

2. She put the flowers in a blue glass vase. （不須修改）

3. The Great Wall is a Chinese landmark famous.

4. I read a newspaper article interesting this morning.

5. Spiro gave me a wonderful small black Greek box as a birthday present.

6. Alice reached down and put her hand in the mountain cold stream.

7. Pizza is my favorite food Italian.

8. There was a beautiful flower arrangement on the kitchen table.

9. Jack usually wears brown old comfortable shoes leather.

10. Gnats are black tiny insects.

11. I used a box brown cardboard to mail a gift to my sister.

12. Tony has a noisy electric fan in his bedroom window.

13. James is a middle-aged handsome man with brown short hair.

14. When Jane was on her last business trip, she had a cheap rental car, but she stayed in a room expensive hotel.

學生A：打開書，唸出下列各題的字，尾音不要下降好讓學生 B 接下去完成詞語。

學生B：闔上書，用一個名詞完成學生 A 的詞語。將你想到的名詞盡快說出來。

例：　　a dark . . .

學生A：a dark

學生B：night (room, building, day, cloud, etc.)

例：　　some ripe . . .

學生A：some ripe

學生B：soup

學生A：some ripe soup? I don't think soup can be called ripe.

學生B：Okay. How about "some ripe fruit"? or "some ripe bananas"?

學生A：That's good. Some ripe fruit or some ripe bananas.

1. a kitchen . . .	11. a birthday . . .
2. a busy . . .	12. a computer . . .
3. a public . . .	13. a baby . . .
4. a true . . .	14. a soft . . .
5. some expensive . . .	15. an easy . . .
6. an interesting old . . .	16. a government . . .
7. an airplane . . .	17. some hot . . .
8. a dangerous . . .	18. a flower . . .
9. a beautiful Korean . . .	19. a bright . . .
10. some delicious Mexican . . .	20. some small round . . .

角色互換

21. a telephone . . .	31. some great old . . .
22. a fast . . .	32. a television . . .
23. some comfortable . . .	33. a very deep . . .
24. a foreign . . .	34. an office . . .
25. a famous Italian . . .	35. a gray wool . . .
26. a bus . . .	36. an afternoon . . .
27. a history . . .	37. an empty . . .
28. a rubber bicycle . . .	38. a wonderful South American . . .
29. a hospital . . .	39. a bedroom . . .
30. a movie . . .	40. a science . . .

8-3 數量的表達：ALL OF, MOST OF, SOME OF

（a） Rita ate ***all of*** *the food* on her plate. （b） Mike ate ***most of*** *his food.* （c） Susie ate ***some of*** *her food.*	*all of, most of* 和 *some of* 表示數量。 　　*all of* = 全部 (100%) 　　*most of* = 大部份，但非全部 　　*some of* = 小部份或中等部份
（d） Matt ate ***almost all of*** his food. （e） 誤： *Matt ate almost of his food.*	*all of* = 全部 (100%) *almost all of* = 95% – 99% *almost* 和 *all* 連用；*all* 不可省略。

■ **練習 12**：用 (almost) all of, most of 或 some of 完成下列句子。

1. 2, 4, 6, 8: _____*All of*_____ these numbers are even.

2. 1, 3, 5, 7: _____these numbers are odd.

3. 1, 3, 4, 6, 7, 9: _____ these numbers are odd.

4. 1, 3, 4, 6, 7, 8: _____ these numbers are odd.

5. 1, 3, 4, 5, 7, 9: _____ these numbers are odd.

6. _____ the birds in Picture A are flying.

7. _____ the birds in Picture B are flying.

8. _____ the birds in Picture C are flying.

9. _____ the birds in Picture D are flying.

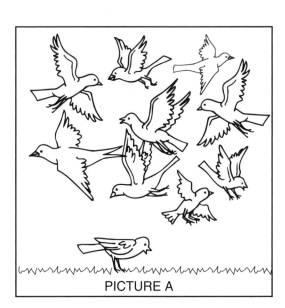

PICTURE A

PICTURE B

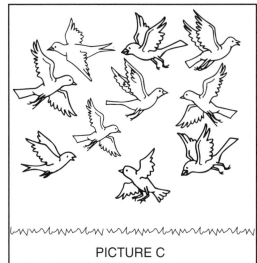

PICTURE C

PICTURE D

10. _____ the students in this class have dark hair.

11. _____ the students in this class are using pens rather than pencils to do this exercise.

12. _____ the students in this class wear glasses.

13. _____ the students in this class can speak English.

(a) *All of my **work is** finished.* (b) *All of my **friends are** kind.* (c) *Some of my **homework is** finished.* (d) *Some of my **friends are** coming to my birthday party.*	(a) 中：*all of* + 單數名詞 + 單數動詞 (b) 中：*all of* + 複數名詞 + 複數動詞 (c) 中：*some of* + 單數名詞 + 單數動詞 (d) 中：*some of* + 複數名詞 + 複數動詞
	主詞中含有數量語詞時，動詞須與 *of* 後面的名詞一致。

常用的數量語詞		
all of	*most of*	*half of*
almost all of	*a lot of*	*some of*

■ **練習 6**：選擇正確動詞。

1. All of that money _____*is*_____ mine.
   (is \ are)

2. All of the windows _____ open.
   (is \ are)

3. We saw one movie. Some of the movie _____ interesting.
   (was \ were)

4. We saw five movies. Some of the movies _____ interesting.
   (was \ were)

5. Half of the glasses _____ empty,
   (is \ are)

   and half of the glasses _____ full.
   (is \ are)

6. Half of the glass

   _____ empty.
   (is \ are)

IT'S HALF EMPTY.   IT'S HALF FULL.

Pessimist   Optimist

7. A lot of those words _____ new to me.

    (is \ are)

8. A lot of that vocabulary _____ new to me.

    (is \ are)

9. Almost all of the air in the city _____ polluted.

    (is \ are)

10. Almost all of the oceans in the world _____ polluted.

    (is \ are)

11. Most of the students _____ on time.

    (arrives \ arrive)

12. Most of our mail _____ in the morning.

    (arrives \ arrive)

8-5　數量的表達：ONE OF, NONE OF

(a) ONE OF ＋ 複數名詞 Sam is **one** of my **friends**. (b) 誤： *Sam is one of my friend.*	*one of* 後面要接一特定之複數名詞，如 (a)。 *one of* 後面加單數名詞是錯誤的，如 (b)。
ONE OF ＋ 複數名詞 ＋ 單數動詞 (c) **One** of my **friends** **is** here. (d) 誤： *One of my friends are here.*	句子的主詞是 *one of* ＋ 一個複數名詞時，後面的動詞用單數動詞。
(e) **None of** the students **was** late. (f) **None of** the students **were** late.	(e) 中：沒有一個學生遲到。 　　*none of = not one of*（沒有一個） 接在 *none of* ＋ 複數名詞之後的動詞可以是單數動詞，如 (e)，也可以是複數動詞，如 (f)。兩者皆正確。★

★非常正式的英文中 *none of* ＋ 複數名詞的後面要用單數動詞：*None of the students **was** late.* 日常英文中，單數動詞與複數動詞皆可用。

■ **練習 14**：用提示的字和語詞造句。

1. One of my \ teacher \ be \（教師名）

    ____One of my teachers is Ms. Lopez._____

2. （學生名）\ be \ one of my \ classmate

    _____

3. one of my \ book \ be \ red

_____

4. one of my \ book \ have \ a green cover

_____

5. （某地名）\ be \ one of my favorite \ place \ in the world

_____

6. one of the \ student \ in my class \ always come \ late

_____

7. （某人）\ be \ one of my best \ friend

_____

8. one of my \ friend \ live \ in（某地）

_____

9. （某電視節目）\ be \ one of the best \ program \ on TV

_____

10. （某人）\ be \ one of the most famous \ people★ \ in the world

_____

11. one of my biggest \ problem \ be \ my inability to understand spoken English

_____

12. （某報紙）\ be \ one of the \ leading newspaper \ in（某市）

_____

13. none of the \ student \ in my class \ speak \（某一語言）

_____

14. none of the \ furniture \ in this room \ be \ soft and comfortable

_____

_____
★*people* 雖然字尾不加 -s，卻是個複數名詞。

1. One of my favorite _____ is _____.

2. _____ is one of the most interesting _____ in the world.

3. One of the _____ in my _____ is _____.

4. _____ is one of my best _____.

5. One of _____.

6. None of _____.

■ **練習 16**：選出正確動詞。

1. My grammar book _____*is*_____ red.
   (is \ are)

2. Some of my books _____ on my desk.
   (is \ are)

3. One of my books _____ blue and green.
   (is \ are)

4. My favorite colors _____ red and yellow.
   (is \ are)

5. Sue's favorite color _____ green.
   (is \ are)

6. One of my favorite colors _____ red.
   (is \ are)

7. My best friends _____ in Brazil.
   (lives \ live)

8. One of my best friends _____ in Australia.
   (lives \ live)

9. Some of the students in my class _____ lap-top computers.
   (has \ have)

10. One of the students in Pablo's class _____ a mustache.
    (has \ have)

11. None of these letters _____ for you.
    (is \ are)

12. None of this mail _____ for you.
    (is \ are)

1. Some of the children's toys _____*are*_____ broken.

2. Most of my classmates _____ always on time for class.

3. One of my classmates _____ always late.

4. All of my friends _____ kind people.

5. One of my friends _____ Sam Brown.

6. Most of the rivers in the world _____ polluted.

7. Some of the Pacific Ocean _____ badly polluted.

8. Most of this page _____ white.

9. Most of the pages in this book _____ full of grammar exercises.

10. One of the pages in this book _____ the title page.

■ **練習 18 — 口語練習（闔上書本）**：用數量詞（all of, most of, some of, a lot of, one of, three of 等）以及完整答句，回答下列句子。

例：How many of the people in this room are wearing shoes?
答：All of the people in this room are wearing shoes.

例：How many of us are wearing blue jeans?
答：Some of us are wearing blue jeans.

1. How many people in this room have (short) hair?
2. How many of the students in this class have red grammar books?
3. How many of us are sitting down?
4. How many of your classmates are from（某縣市）?
5. How many of the people in this room can speak（某語言）?
6. How many of the women in this room are wearing earrings? How many of the men?
7. What is one of your favorite TV programs?
8. How many of the people in this city are friendly?
9. Who is one of the most famous people in the world?
10. How many of the married women in your country work outside the home?

8-6 EVERY 的用法

(a) **Every student** has a book. (b) *All of the students* have books.	(a) 句和 (b) 句基本上同義。 (a) 句中：*every* + 單數名詞 + 單數動詞。
(c) 誤： *Every of the students* *has a book.* (d) 誤： *Every students have books.*	*every* 後面不可直接加 *of*。 *every* 後面須直接加單數名詞，不可加複數名詞。
(e) **Everyone has** a book. (f) **Everybody has** a book.	(e) 句和 (f) 句同義。 *everyone* 和 *everybody* 後面要加單數動詞。
(g) I looked at **everything** in the museum.	(g) 句中：*everything* = 每一件東西 (*each thing*)。
(h) **Everything is** okay.	(h) 句中：*everything* 後面加單數動詞。

■ **練習 19**：選擇正確答案完成下列句子。

1. All of the _____*books*_____ on this desk _____*are*_____ mine.
   (book \ books)　　　　　　　　　　　(is \ are)

2. Every _____ on this desk _____ mine.
   (book \ books)　　　　　　　　　　　(is \ are)

3. All of the _____ _____ here today.
   (student \ students)　　　　(is \ are)

4. Every _____ _____ here today.
   (student \ students)　　　　(is \ are)

5. Every _____ at my college _____ tests regularly.
   (teacher \ teachers)　　　　　　　　　(gives \ give)

6. All of the _____ at my college _____ a lot of tests.
   (teacher \ teachers)　　　　　　　　　(gives \ give)

7. Every _____ in my country _____ bedtime stories.
   (child \ children)　　　　　　　　　(likes \ like)

8. All of the _____ in my country _____ that story.
   (child \ children)　　　　　　　　　(knows \ know)

9. All of the _____ in this class _____ studying English.
   (person \ people)　　　　　　　　(is \ are)

10. Everyone in this class _____ to learn English.
    (wants \ want)

11. _____ all of the _____ in this class speak English well?
    (Does \ Do)   (student \ students)

12. _____ every _____ in the world like to listen to music?
    (Does \ Do)   (person \ people)

13. _____ all of the _____ in the world enjoy dancing?
    (Does \ Do)   (person \ people)

14. _____ everybody in the world have enough to eat?
    (Does \ Do)

15. Every _____ in Sweden _____ a good transportation system.
         (city \ cities)   (has \ have)

■ **練習 20 — 錯誤分析**：找出句子的錯誤並更正。

1. I work hard every days.

2. I live in an apartment with one of my friend.

3. We saw a pretty flowers garden in the park.

4. Almost of the students are in class today.

5. Every people in my class are studying English.

6. All of the cities in North America has traffic problems.

7. One of my books are green.

8. Nadia drives a blue small car.

9. Istanbul is one of my favorite city in the world.

10. Every of students in the class have a grammar book.

11. The work will take a long time. We can't finish every things today.

12. Everybody in the world want peace.

	單數名詞	名詞所有格	要表示某人擁有某物，在單數名詞字尾加縮寫符號 (') 和 -s。
(a)　My *friend* has a car. My ***friend's*** car is blue.	**friend**	**friend's**	名詞所有格，單數形式： 　　名詞 + 縮寫符號 (') + **-s**
(b)　The *student* has a book. The ***student's*** book is red.	**student**	**student's**	

	複數名詞	名詞所有格	複數名詞字尾（**-s** 後面）加縮寫符號 (')。
(c)　The *students* have books. The ***students'*** books are red.	**students**	**students'**	名詞所有格，複數形式： 　　名詞 + **-s** + 縮寫符號 (')
(d)　My *friends* have a car. My ***friends'*** car is blue.	**friends**	**friends'**	

■ **練習 21**：將下列句子中的名詞所有格加上縮寫符號。

　　　　　　　　　Jim's
1. Jims 　∧　 last name is Smith.

2. Bobs cat likes to sleep on the sofa.

3. My teachers names are Ms. Rice and Mr. Molina.

4. My mothers first name is Marika.

5. My parents telephone number is 555-9876.

6. My Uncle George is my fathers brother.

7. Nicole is a girls name.

8. Erica and Heidi are girls names.

9. Do you like Toms shirt?

10. Do you know Anitas brother?

11. The teacher collected the students test papers at the end of the period.

12. Alexs friends visited him last night.

13. How long is an elephants trunk?

14. A monkeys hand looks like a human hand.

15. Monkeys hands have thumbs.

■ **練習 22**：填上同學的名字完成下列各句。

1. _____ hair is short and straight.

2. _____ grammar book is on her desk.

3. _____ last name is _____.

4. I don't know _____ address.

5. _____ eyes are gray.

6. _____ shirt is blue.

7. _____ briefcase is on the floor.

8. I need to borrow _____ dictionary.

9. Do you like _____ mustache?

10. Do you know _____ wife?

■ 練習 **23** — **書寫練習**：寫出有關同學擁有物的句子。

　　例： Kim's book is on his desk.　Anna's purse is brown.　Pablo's shirt is green.

■ 練習 **24**：完成下列句子。

1. My husband's _____ *brother* _____ is my brother-in-law.

2. My father's _____ is my uncle.

3. My mother's _____ is my grandmother.

4. My sister's _____ are my nieces and nephews.

5. My aunt's _____ is my mother.

6. My wife's _____ is my mother-in-law.

7. My brother's _____ is my sister-in-law.

8. My father's _____ and _____
　are my grandparents.

9. My niece is my brother's _____.

10. My nephew is my sister's _____.

8-8　所有格：不規則複數名詞

(a)　The ***children's*** *toys* are on the floor.	不規則複數名詞 *(children, men, women, people)* 具有不規則的複數名詞所有格。縮寫符號 (') 要置於字尾的 *-s* 前面。
(b)　The store sells ***men's*** *clothing*.	
(c)　That store sells ***women's*** *clothing*.	規則的複數名詞所有格： 　　　the ***students'*** *books* 不規則的複數名詞所有格： 　　　the ***women's*** *books*
(d)　I like to know about other ***people's*** *lives*.	

■ 練習 **25**：用正確的所有格形式完成下列句子。

1. *children* 　　That store sells _____ *children's* _____ books.

2. *girl* 　　Mary is a _____ name.

3. *girls* 　　Mary and Sue are _____ names.

4. *women* 　　Mary and Sue are _____ names.

5. *uncle* Robert is living at his _____ house.

6. *person* A biography is the story of a _____ life.

7. *people* Biographies are the stories of _____ lives.

8. *students* _____ lives are busy.

9. *brother* Do you know my _____ wife?

10. *brothers* Do you know my _____ wives?

11. *wife* My _____ parents live in California.

12. *dog* My _____ name is Fido.

13. *dogs* My _____ names are Fido and Rover.

14. *men* Are Jim and Tom _____ names?

15. *man, woman* Chris can be a _____ nickname or a

_____ nickname.

16. *children* Our _____ school is near our house.

■ **練習 26**：加上必要的縮寫符號和字尾 -s，改成名詞所有格。

1. Someone stole Paul ∧ bicycle.
    Paul's

2. Do you know Yuko roommate?

3. Does that store sell women clothes?

4. My roommate desk is always a mess.

5. What is your parent new address?

6. I have my father nose.★

7. Where is Rosa apartment?

8. I can't remember all of my classmate names.

Tina's Boutique

Women's Clothing   Girls' Clothing

★*I have my father's nose* = My nose looks like my father's nose（我的鼻子長得像父親的鼻子）；我的鼻型遺傳自我的父親。

9. It's important to respect other people opinions.

10. My husband sister is visiting us this week.

11. Excuse me. Where is the men room?

12. That store sells children toys.

8-9　所有格代名詞：MINE, YOURS, HIS, HERS, OURS, THEIRS 的用法

| (a) | This book belongs to me.
It is **my** book.
It is **mine**.
(b)　That book belongs to you.
It is **your** book.
It is **yours**. | 所有格
形容詞

my
your
her
his
our
their | 所有格
代名詞

mine
yours
hers
his
ours
theirs | 所有格形容詞位於名詞之前：*my* *book*。

所有格代名詞單獨使用，後面不加名詞：
　That book is **mine**.

誤：　*That is mine book.* |

■ **練習 27**：用受格代名詞，所有格形容詞，和所有格代名詞完成下列句子。

1. **I** own this book.

   This book belongs to ____me____.

   This is ____my____ book.

   This book is ____mine____.

2. **They** own these books.

   These books belong to _____.

   These are _____ books.

   These books are _____.

3. **You** own that book.

   That book belongs to _____.

   That is _____ book.

   That book is _____.

4. **She** owns this pen.

   This pen belongs to _____.

   This is _____ pen.

   This pen is _____.

5. **He** owns that pen.

   That pen belongs to _____.

   That is _____ pen.

   That pen is _____.

6. **We** own those books.

   Those books belong to _____.

   Those are _____ books.

   Those books are _____.

■ **練習 28**：將句前的斜體字改成正確的所有格形式，完成下列句子。

1. *I*   a. This bookbag is _____mine_____.

    Sue   b. That bookbag is _____Sue's_____.

    I   c. _____My_____ bookbag is red.

    she   d. _____Hers_____ is green.

2. *we*   a. These books are _____.

    they   b. Those books are _____.

    we   c. _____ books are on the table.

    they   d. _____ are on the desk.

3. *Tom*   a. This raincoat is _____.

    Mary   b. That raincoat is _____.

    he   c. _____ is light brown.

    she   d. _____ is light blue.

4. *I*   a. This notebook is _____.

    you   b. That one is _____.

    I   c. _____ has _____ name on it.

    you   d. _____ has _____ name on it.

5. *Jim*   a. _____ apartment is on Pine Street.

    we   b. _____ is on Main Street.

    he   c. _____ apartment has three rooms.

    we   d. _____ has four rooms.

6. *I*   a. This is _____ pen.

    you   b. That one is _____.

    I   c. _____ is in _____ pocket.

    you   d. _____ is on _____ desk.

7. *we*   a. _____ car is a Chevrolet.

   they   b. _____ is a Volkswagen.

   we   c. _____ gets 17 miles to the gallon.

   they   d. _____ car gets 30 miles to the gallon.

8. *Ann*   a. These books are _____.

   Paul   b. Those are _____.

   she   c. _____ are on _____ desk.

   he   d. _____ are on _____ desk.

■ **練習 29**：選出正確答案。

1. Is this _____*your*_____ pen?
          (your \ yours)

2. Please give this dictionary to Olga. It's _____.
                                  (her \ hers)

3. A: Don't forget _____ hat. Here.
                    (your \ yours)

   B: No, that's not _____ hat. _____ is green.
                       (my \ mine)   (My \ Mine)

4. A: Please take this wood carving as a gift from me. Here. It's _____.
                                                     (your \ yours)

   B: Thank you. You're very thoughtful.

5. A: Isn't that the Smiths' car? That one over there. The blue one.

   B: No, that's not _____. _____ car is dark blue.
                     (their \ theirs)   (Their \ Theirs)

6. A: Jim and I really like _____ new apartment. It has lots of
                            (our \ ours)

     space. How do you like _____?
                         (your \ yours)

   B: _____ is small, but it's comfortable.
     (Our \ Ours)

7. A: Excuse me. Is this _____ umbrella?
                      (your \ yours)

   B: I don't have an umbrella. Ask Ken. Perhaps it is _____.
                                           (him \ his)

8. A: When do _____ classes begin?
      (your \ yours)

   B: September second. How about _____? When do
                                    (your \ yours)

      _____ begin?
       (your \ yours)

   A: _____ begin August twenty-ninth.
       (My \ Mine)

9. A: Maria, _____ spaghetti sauce is delicious!
             (your \ yours)

   B: Thank you, but it's not as good as _____.
                                          (your \ yours)

   A: Oh, no. _____ is much better! It tastes just as good as Anna's.
               (Your \ Yours)

   B: Do you like Anna's spaghetti sauce? I think _____ is too salty.
                                                    (her \ hers)

   A: Maybe. _____ husband makes good spaghetti sauce too.
              (My \ Mine)

      _____ is thick and rich.
       (His \ He)

   B: In truth, making spaghetti sauce is easy, but everyone's sauce is just a little different.

8-10 WHOSE 引導的疑問句

(a)	**Whose book** is this?	→ Mine. → It's mine. → It's my book.	*whose* 用來問擁有的狀況。 *whose* 經常和名詞連用（例如：*whose book*），如 (a) 和 (b)。
(b)	**Whose books** are these?	→ Rita's. → They're Rita's. → They're Rita's books.	
(c)	**Whose** is this? （說者指著一本書。）		意義明確時，*whose* 也可以不加名詞， 如 (c) 和 (d)。
(d)	**Whose** are these? （說者指著數本書。）		

WHOSE IS THIS? THERE'S NO NAME ON IT. WHO'S THE ARTIST?

■ **練習 30**：選擇正確答案完成句子。

1. Whose watch ____*is*____ ____*this*____?

                 (is \ are)   (this \ these)

2. Whose glasses _____ _____?

                     (is \ are)   (that \ those)

3. Whose keys _____ _____?

                (is \ are)   (this \ these)

4. Whose hat _____ _____?

             (is \ are)   (that \ those)

5. Whose shoes _____ _____?

             (is \ are)   (that \ those)

6. Whose handbag _____ _____?

               (is \ are)   (this \ these)

■ **練習 31**：指出或觸摸教室內屬於某人的物品，並用 whose 提出問題。

> 例： (Student A points to or touches a grammar book.)
> 學生A： Whose book is this?
> 學生B： It's mine. / Mine. / It's my book.
> 學生A： Whose book is that?
> 學生B： It's Po's. / Po's. / It's Po's book.

8-11 摘要：所有格符號的用法

(a)	***I'm*** happy. （誤： *I'am happy.*） ***She's*** happy. ***We're*** happy.	縮寫符號的用法 • 用於代名詞與 *am, is* 和 *are* 的縮寫。參閱表 1-4。
(b)	***Tom's*** happy.	• 用於名詞和 *is* 的縮寫。 (b) 句中，*Tom's = Tom is*★
(c)	***That's*** my notebook.	• 用於 *that* 和 *is* 的縮寫。
(d)	***There's*** a book on the table. ***There're*** some books on the table.	• 用於 *there* 和 *is/are* 的縮寫。
(e)	***What's*** this? ***Where's*** Anna?	• 用於一些疑問詞和 *is* 的縮寫。 比較
(f)	***Who's*** that? → It's *Mike*.	(f) 中： *Who's = who is*
(g)	***Whose*** is that? → It's *Mike's*.	(g) 中： *Whose* = 用來問擁有狀況的疑問詞，不可用縮寫符號。
(h)	Tina ***isn't*** here.	• 用於否定的縮寫： *isn't, aren't, wasn't, weren't, doesn't, don't, won't, can't.*
(i)	***Tom's*** hair is brown.	• 用於名詞所有格，如 (i) 和 (j)。參閱表 8-7 和 8-8。縮寫符號不可用於所有格代名詞。(1) 中：*hers* 加縮寫符號 (*her's*) 是錯誤的。
(j)	My ***parents'*** house is white.	
(k)	This pen belongs to Ann. It is ***hers***.	
(l)	誤： *It is her's.*	
(m)	***It's*** sunny today.	比較：(m) 中： *it's = it is.*
(n)	I'm studying about India. I'm interested in ***its*** history.	(n) 中：its = 所有格形容詞： *its history = India's history*。所有格形容詞不用縮寫符號。
(o)	誤： *I'm interested in it's history.*	

★口語英文中，名詞通常會和 *is* 縮寫。書寫英文中，名詞和 *is* 的縮寫（例如： *Tom's happy*）只見於非正式的英文（例如：朋友間的書信），而不見於正式的英文（例如：學術性的報告）。通常，動詞的縮寫（*I'm, you're, isn't, there's* 等）用於非正式英文中，不用於正式英文中。

1. Thats Anns book. → *That's Ann's book.*

2. That book is hers. → （不須修改）

3. Jims car is small.

4. Jims in New York this week.

5. Hes visiting his brother.

6. Im a little hungry this morning.

7. Tonys my neighbor.

8. Tonys apartment is next to mine.

9. Whos that woman?

10. Shes Bobs wife.

11. Whose book is that?

12. Is it yours?

13. Its Ginas book.

14. Wheres your dictionary?

15. Amy wont go to the movie with us.   She doesnt have enough money.

16. Paris is a popular tourist destination. Its most famous attraction is the Eiffel Tower.

   Its most famous building is the Louvre Museum. Its also famous for its night life.

■ 練習 33：在必要處加上縮寫符號。

1. Yokos ^Yoko's last name is Yakamoto.

2. Yokos a student in my English class.

3. Pablo is a student. Hes in my class. His last name is Alvarez.

4. Pablos full name is Pablo Alvarez.

5. Youre a student. Your name is Ali.

6. Im a student. I am in Mr. Lees English class.

7. Mary and Anita have purses. Marys purse is black. Anitas purse is brown.

8. Marys in class today. Anitas at home.

9. Whose books are these? This book is mine. Thats yours.

10. Whats wrong? Whats happening? Whos that man? Wheres he going?

11. Im looking at a book. Its a grammar book. Its cover is red. Its on my desk. Its

     open. Its title is *Basic English Grammar.*

12. Theres a bird in the tree. Its black and red. Its chest is red. Its wings, tail, and back

     are black. Its sitting on a branch.

13. People admire the tiger for its beauty and strength. Its a magnificent animal.

     Unfortunately, its survival as a species is in doubt. Its an endangered species.

     Therere very few tigers in the world today.

8-12 摘要：名詞的用法

(a) 名詞 |__**Birds**__|__fly.__| 　主詞　　動詞	名詞可做為： • 句子的主詞，如 (a)。
(b) 　　　　　名詞 |__Ken__|__opened__|__*the **door.***__| 　主詞　　動詞　　受詞	• 動詞的受詞，如 (b)。
(c) 　　　　　　　名詞 |__Birds__|__fly__|__in__|__*the **sky**.*__| 　主詞　動詞　介詞　介詞的受詞	• 介詞的受詞，如 (c)。
(d) 　　　　名詞 |__Yoko__|__is__|__*a **student.***__| 　主詞　be動詞　名詞補語	• *be* 動詞後的名詞補語*，如 (d)。
(e) 　　　　名詞　+　名詞 I don't like **winter** weather.	• 其他名詞的修飾詞，如 (e)。
(f) 　　名詞　+　名詞 I like **Jim's** hat.	• 所有格，如 (f)。

*補語即使句子或想法完整的字。

■ **練習 6**：寫出符合各題文法型式的句子，並將名詞圈出來。

        a. A kangaroo is an animal.
        b. My wallet is in my pocket.

1.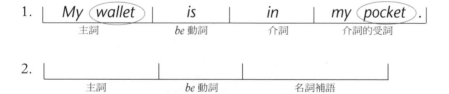
           主詞　　　　　be動詞　　　　介詞　　　介詞的受詞

2. \|_____\|_____\|_____\|
         主詞　　　　　be動詞　　　　名詞補語

        c. Jason works in an office.
        d. Karen held the baby in her arms.
        e. Restaurants serve food.

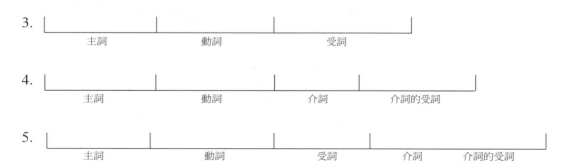

3. \|_____\|_____\|_____\|
       主詞　　　　　動詞　　　　　受詞

4. \|_____\|_____\|_____\|_____\|
       主詞　　　　　動詞　　　　　介詞　　　介詞的受詞

5. \|_____\|_____\|_____\|_____\|_____\|
       主詞　　　　　動詞　　　　受詞　　　　介詞　　介詞的受詞

f. Korea is in Asia.
g. Korea is a peninsula.

6.
主詞	*be* 動詞	介詞	介詞的受詞

7.
主詞	*be* 動詞	名詞補語

h. Children play with toys.
i. Monkeys eat fruit.
j. Jack tied a string around the package.

8.
主詞	動詞	受詞

9.
主詞	動詞	介詞	介詞的受詞

10.
主詞	動詞	受詞	介詞	介詞的受詞

(a)	名詞 + AND + 名詞 |**Birds** *and* **airplanes**| fly. 　　主詞　　　　動詞	*and* 可以連接兩個或兩個以上的名詞。 (a) 句中：主詞 = 兩個名詞 (b) 句中：受詞 = 兩個名詞 (c) 句中：受詞 = 三個名詞 三個（或三個以上）的名詞，要用逗號分開，如 (c)。兩個名詞，如 (a) 和 (b)，不用逗號分開。
(b)	名詞 + AND + 名詞 |Ken| opened |*the* **door** *and* *the* **window.**| 主詞　　動詞　　　　　受詞	
(c)	名詞 + 名詞 + AND + 名詞 |I| have |*a* **book**, *a* **pen**, *and*　*a* **pencil.**| 主詞 動詞　　　　　受詞	
(d)	名詞 + OR + 名詞 I'd like *some coffee* **or**　*some tea.*	*or* 也可以連接兩個名詞，如 (d)。

■ **練習 35**：找出連結的名詞，並討論其作用。

1. You bought apples and bananas.
   → *apples and bananas* = 連結兩個名詞，當動詞（bought）的受詞。

2. I bought apples, bananas, and oranges.

3. Jack and Olga bought bananas.

4. Julia wants apples or bananas.

5. Julia is at the market with Jack and Olga.

6. Tennis and golf are popular sports.

7. Tokyo has excellent museums and libraries.

8. A tree has a trunk, branches, leaves, and roots.

9. Automobiles, trains, and trucks are kinds of vehicles.

10. I'll have some soup or a sandwich for lunch.

1. Ants bees and mosquitoes are insects.
   → *Ants*, *bees*, *and mosquitoes are insects.*★

2. Ants and bees are insects.（不須修改）

3. Bears tigers and elephants are animals.

4. Bears and tigers are animals.

5. I bought some rice fruit and vegetables at the market.

6. I bought some rice and fruit at the market.

7. The three countries in North America are Canada the United States and Mexico.

8. I read a lot of newspapers and magazines.

9. I had some soup and a sandwich for lunch.

10. Shelley had some soup a salad and a sandwich for lunch.

11. My favorite things in life are sunny days music good friends and books.

12. What do birds butterflies and airplanes have in common?

■ **練習 37**：找出名詞，並討論其作用。

1. A turtle is a reptile.
   → *turtle* = 名詞，作句子的主詞。
   → *reptile* = 名詞，作 be 動詞的補語。

2. A turtle has a hard shell.

3. A turtle pulls its head, legs, and tail into its shell.

4. Some turtles spend almost all of their lives in water.

5. Some turtles live on land for their entire lives.

6. Turtles don't have teeth, but they have powerful jaws.

★一連串的連結名詞中，*and* 前面的逗號可有可無。
也可寫成：*Ants, bees and mosquitoes are insects.*

7. Turtles bury their eggs in sand or mud.

8. Baby turtles face many dangers.

9. Birds and fish eat baby turtles.

10. Some green sea turtles live for 100 years.

11. Turtles face many dangers from people.

12. People destroy turtles' natural homes.

13. People replace beaches, forests, and other natural areas with towns and farms.

14. People poison natural areas with pollution.

15. Many species of turtles face extinction.

（a）	I bought some	形容詞　　　＋　　名詞 *beautiful*　　　*flowers*.	形容詞描述名詞，提供名詞的資料。常用的形容詞，請參閱表 4-2。 形容可置於名詞前面，如 (a)。
（b）	The flowers	BE 動詞 ＋ 形容詞 *were*　　　*beautiful*.	形容詞可置於 *be* 動詞後面，如 (b)，用來描述句子的主詞。參閱表 1-6。
（c） （d） （e） （f） （g）	The flowers The flowers I Candy That book	連綴動詞　　　＋　形容詞 *looked*　　　*beautiful*. *smelled*　　　*good*. *feel*　　　*good*. *tastes*　　　*sweet*. *sounds*　　　*interesting*.	形容詞可置於一些其他動詞的後面。這些動詞叫連綴動詞 *linking verbs*。 常用的連綴動詞有： 　　*looks, smell, feel, taste* 和 *sound*。

■ **練習 38**：找出各句的形容詞，並討論其用途。

1. The sun is bright today.
   → *bright* = 形容詞，置於be動詞後，用來描述句子的主詞（sun）。

2. I drank some cold water.

3. My dog's nose is cold.

4. Ice feels cold.

5. This exercise looks easy.

6. Our teacher gives easy tests.

7. English grammar is easy.

8. Lemons taste sour.

9. What's the matter? You look unhappy.

10. I'm sad.

11. Who is your favorite author?

12. What's the matter? You sound angry.

13. Ummm. These flowers smell wonderful!

14. That chair looks soft and comfortable.

15. Mr. White is a good history teacher.

■ **練習 39 — 口語練習：**練習使用連綴動詞。

第一部份：用 feel + 形容詞描述你今天的感覺？

1. good	5. sleepy	9. happy
2. fine	6. tired	10. calm
3. terrible	7. lazy	11. sick
4. terrific	8. nervous	12. old

第二部份：什麼物品帶給你下列的感覺？

13. taste good	17. taste sour
14. taste terrible	18. smell good
15. taste delicious	19. smell bad
16. taste sweet	20. smell wonderful

第三部份：用 look + 形容詞描述教室內的物品。

21. clean	25. expensive
22. dirty	26. comfortable
23. new	27. messy
24. old	28. familiar

■ **練習 40 — 口語練習：**描述同學的樣子。

學生A：選擇以下的一種情緒，並透過臉上表情及動作來表現該情緒。
學生B：用連綴動詞 look 加形容詞，描述學生 A 的樣子。

1. angry	5. busy
2. sad / unhappy	6. comfortable
3. happy	7. surprised
4. tired / sleepy	8. nervous

■ **練習 41：**完成下列句子使用框內的詞或自己的話。

easy	*good / terrific / wonderful / great*	*interesting*
hard / difficult	*terrible / awful*	*tired / sleepy*

1. Rosa told me about a new book. I want to read it. It sounds ___*interesting /*___
   ___*good / terrific*___ .

2. Karen learned how to make paper flowers. She told me how to do it. It sounds
   _____.

3. There's a new play at the community theater. I read a review of it in the newspaper. I'd like to see it. It sounds _____.

4. Professor Wilson is going to lecture on the problems of overpopulation tomorrow evening. I think I'll go. It sounds _____.

5. Chris explained how to fix a flat tire. I think I can do it. It sounds _____.

6. Shelley didn't finish her dinner because it didn't taste _____.

7. What's for dinner? Something smells _____. Ummm! What is it?

8. Amy didn't get any sleep last night because she studied all night for a test. Today she looks _____.

9. Ymmmm! This dessert tastes _____. What is it?

10. A: What's the matter? Do you feel okay?

    B: No. I feel _____. I think I'm getting a cold.

11. A: Do you like my new dress, darling?

    B: You look _____, honey.

12. A: Pyew!★ Something smells _____! Do you smell it too?
    B: I sure do. It's the garbage in the alley.

■ **練習 42**：兩人或小組式練習。在一定時間內（例如：十五秒、三十秒、一分鐘），列出所有可用來修飾以下名詞的形容詞或名詞。

例：car
答：big, little, fast, slow, comfortable, small, large, old, new, used, noisy, quiet, foreign, electric, antique, police, etc.。

1. weather   5. country
2. animal   6. person
3. food   7. river
4. movie   8. student

────────────

★*Pyew*有時說成 "*p.u.*"。*Pyew* 和 *p.u.* 兩者皆用來表示某個東西很難聞。

	主格代名詞	受格代名詞	所有格代名詞	所有格形容詞
單 數	*I* *you* *she* *he* *it*	*me* *you* *her* *him* *it*	*mine* *yours* *hers* *his* *its*	*my* name(s) *your* name(s) *her* name(s) *his* name(s) *its* name(s)
複 數	*we* *you* *they*	*us* *you* *them*	*ours* *yours* *theirs*	*our* name(s) *your* name(s) *their* name(s)

(a) **We** saw an accident. (b) Anna saw **it** too. (c) I have my pen. Sue has **hers**. (d) **Her** pen is blue.	人稱代名詞可做為： • 主詞，如 (a)； • 受詞，如 (b)； • 或表示所有格，如 (c) 和 (d)。
(e) I have a <u>book</u>. **It** is on my desk. (f) I have some <u>books</u>. **They** are on my desk.	用單數代名詞指稱單數名詞。(e) 句中：book 和 it 都是單數。 用複數代名詞指稱複數名詞。(f) 句中：books 和 they 都是複數。

■ **練習 43**：代名詞的複習。找出下列句子中代名詞用法的錯誤，並更正之。

Dear Heidi,

(1) Everything is going fine. I like ~~mine~~ *my* new apartment very much. Its large and

(2) comfortable. I like me roommate too. Him name is Alberto. You will meet them when

(3) your visit I next month. His from Colombia. His studying English too. Were classmates.

(4) We were classmates last semester too.

(5) We share the rent and the utility bills, but us don't share the telephone bill.

(6) He pays for his's calls and my pay for my. He's telephone bill is very high because

(7) he has a girlfriend in Colombia. He calls she often. Sometimes her calls he.

(8) Them talk on the phone a lot.

(9) Ours neighbors are Mr. and Mrs. Black. Their very nice. We talk to it often.

(10) Ours apartment is next to their. Theirs have a three-year-old* daughter.

(11) Shes really cute. Hers name is Joy. Them also have a cat. Its black and white. Its eyes

---

*注意：人的年齡位於名詞前面作形容詞用時，year 一字是單數（而非複數），而且要使用連字號（-）：*a three-year-old daughter*。

　　誤：*They have a three years old daughter.*

　　正：*They have a three-year-old daughter.* 或：*Their daughter is three years old.*

(12)   are yellow. Its name is Whiskers.   Its a friendly cat. Sometimes they're cat leaves

(13)   a dead mouse outside ours door.

(14)   I'am looking forward to you're visit.

Love, Carl

8-16　間接受詞

（a）I wrote ｜ *a letter* ｜ **to Alex.** ｜ 　　　　　　直接受詞　　　間接受詞 （b）I wrote ｜ **Alex** ｜ a letter. ｜ 　　　　　　間接受詞　　　直接受詞 （c）誤：*I wrote to Alex a letter.*	有些動詞後面有兩個受詞：一個直接受詞和一個間接受詞。 (a) 句和 (b) 句同義。 間接受詞在前，直接受詞在後時，不要用介系詞 *to*。
（d）直接受詞 　　　What did you write?　→　A letter.	直接受詞回答 *what* 引導的問題。
（e）間接受詞 　　　Who(m) did you write a letter to?　→　Alex. （f）—Did you write these letters to Alex? 　　—Yes, I did. I wrote **them to him**. （g）誤：*I wrote him them.*	間接受詞回答 *who(m)* 引導的問題。 直接受詞是代名詞（例如：*them*）時，必須置於間接受詞之前，如 (f)。
以下動詞後面接以 TO 引導的間接受詞 　*give*　　　*send* 　*hand*　　*show* 　*lend*　　　*tell* 　*pass*　　　*write*	

■ **練習 44**：用提示的字完成下列的文法句型。

    1.　my pen \ Heidi \ I gave

      a. ｜ *I gave* ｜ *my pen* ｜ *to Heidi.* ｜
         主詞　　動詞　　　直接受詞　　　　間接受詞

      b. ｜ *I gave* ｜ *Heidi* ｜ *my pen.* ｜
         主詞　　動詞　　　間接受詞　　　　直接受詞

    2.　I wrote \ Kim \ a letter

      a. ｜　　　　｜　　　　｜　　　　｜
         主詞　　動詞　　　直接受詞　　　　間接受詞

      b. ｜　　　　｜　　　　｜　　　　｜
         主詞　　動詞　　　間接受詞　　　　直接受詞

3. Jack handed \ a book \ Hiroki

a.

主詞	動詞	直接受詞	間接受詞

b.

主詞	動詞	間接受詞	直接受詞

4. Stacy \ I passed \ the salt

a.

主詞	動詞	直接受詞	間接受詞

b.

主詞	動詞	間接受詞	直接受詞

5. I lent \ my car \ Tom

a.

主詞	動詞	直接受詞	間接受詞

b.

主詞	動詞	間接受詞	直接受詞

6. Alice \ a postcard \ I sent

a.

主詞	動詞	直接受詞	間接受詞

b.

主詞	動詞	間接受詞	直接受詞

7. Ann told \ a story \ us

a.

主詞	動詞	直接受詞	間接受詞

b.

主詞	動詞	間接受詞	直接受詞

8. us \ a picture \ Jack showed

a.

主詞	動詞	直接受詞	間接受詞

b.

主詞	動詞	間接受詞	直接受詞

■ **練習 45 ── 口語練習**：改變下列句子間接受詞的位置。記得要省略 to。

1. I gave my pen to Alex.
   → *I gave Alex my pen.*
2. Please hand that book to me.
3. Rosa wrote a letter to her brother.
4. I gave a birthday present to Ahmed.
5. Please tell a story to us.
6. Did you send a package to your parents?
7. Mr. Hong showed a photograph of his wife to me.
8. Would you lend your camera to me?

■ **練習 46 ── 口語練習（闔上書本）**：改變間接受詞的位置。

例：You gave your book to (. . .). What did you do?
答：I gave (. . .) my book.

1. You gave your pen to (. . .).
2. You wrote a letter to (. . .).
3. You sent a package to (. . .).
4. You told a funny story to (. . .).
5. You showed a photograph to (. . .).
6. You sent a check to the telephone company.
7. You passed your dictionary to (. . .).
8. You handed your notebook to (. . .).
9. You lent （一筆錢） to (. . .).

■ **練習 47 ── 口語練習**：用提示完成下列句子。

1. *a letter, my sister*　　　　　　I wrote . . . yesterday.
   → *I wrote a letter to my sister yesterday.*
   → *I wrote my sister a letter yesterday.*

2. *my parents, a telegram*　　　　I sent . . . two days ago.
3. *some candy, her children*　　　Mrs. Kelly gave . . . after dinner.
4. *her car, me*　　　　　　　　　Sue is going to lend . . . tomorrow.
5. *the class, a joke*　　　　　　　Sam told . . . yesterday.
6. *a letter, the newspaper*　　　　I'm going to write . . . .
7. *the scissors, John*　　　　　　Did you hand . . . ?
8. *me, the soy sauce*　　　　　　Could you please pass . . . ?
9. *Liz, a picture*　　　　　　　　Mr. Schwartz showed . . . of his baby daughter.
10. *the students, some good advice*　Yesterday the teacher gave . . . .

例：Give your book to (. . .). What did you do?
答：I gave my book to (. . .). 或： I gave (. . .) my book.

1. Pass your dictionary to (. . .).
2. Please hand me your pen / pencil.
3. Lend (. . .) some money.
4. Tell (. . .) your name.
5. Please pass my pen to (. . .).
6. Give (. . .) some good advice.
7. Show (. . .) a picture.
8. Write (. . .) a note and pass it to him / her.
9. Give (. . .) a gift.
10. Please hand that piece of chalk to me.

8-17　間接受詞：FOR 的用法

(a)　Bob opened ┃ *the door* ┃ *for Mary.* ┃ 　　　　　　　　　　直接受詞　　間接受詞 (b)　Sue answered ┃ *a question* ┃ *for me.* ┃ 　　　　　　　　　　　直接受詞　　間接受詞 (c)　誤：*Sue answered me a question.* (d)　誤：*Ken opened Anita the door.*	有些動詞其間接受詞前會用 *for*，這些動詞的間接受詞位於直接受詞後面。*for* 不可省略，間接受詞的位置也不可改變。
後面接 FOR + 間接受詞的動詞 *answer*　　　He *answered* a question **for me**. *cash*　　　　The teller *cashed* a check **for me**. *fix*　　　　　Can you *fix* my car **for me**? *open*　　　　Mr. Smith *opened* the door **for his wife**. *pronounce*　I *pronounced* the word **for the students**. *translate*　　I *translated* a letter **for my brother**.	注意例句：所有句子皆表示某人正在幫助另一個人。

1. The teacher answered a question _____ me.

2. I opened the door _____ my mother.

3. My roommate translated a newspaper story _____ me.

4. Fred gave some candy _____ his girlfriend.

5. The teller cashed a check _____ me.

6. The mechanic fixed my car _____ me.

7. Mrs. Baker handed the baby _____ her husband.

8. The teacher pronounced "bat" and "but" _____ the students.

9. Our landlord fixed the air conditioner _____ us.

10. Could you please answer a question _____ me?

11. My hands are wet. Could you please open this jar of pickles _____ me?

■ **練習 50 ─ 口語練習（閤上書本）**：問答練習。
　　　　學生A：用 Could you please...for me? 提出問題。
　　　　學生B：回答問題。

　　例：　　open the window
　　學生A：Could you please open the window for me?
　　學生B：Certainly. / I'd be happy to. / Sure.

1. answer a question
2. translate a word
3. pronounce a word
4. cash a check
5. fix（某物）
6. open the door

■ 練習 51 — 口語練習（閤上書本）：問答練習。
　　　學生A：用 Could you please...? 提出問題，且在問題中使用me, to me 或 for me。
　　　學生B：回答問題。

　　　例：　　pass the butter
　　　學生A：Could you please pass me the butter/pass the butter to me?
　　　學生B：Certainly. / I'd be happy to. / Sure.

　　1. pass the salt　　　　　　　　6. pronounce this word
　　2. hand a napkin　　　　　　　　7. open the door
　　3. pass the salt and pepper　　　8. lend your dictionary
　　4. answer a question　　　　　　9. give（教室內的物品）
　　5. translate this paragraph　　10. fix（某物）

8-18　BUY, GET, MAKE 和間接受詞的用法

（a）　Tina **bought** a gift **for us**. （b）　Tina **bought us** a gift. （c）　I **got** a new toy **for my son**. （d）　I **got my son** a new toy. （e）　Tom **made** lunch **for his wife**. （f）　Tom **made his wife** lunch.	間接受詞和 buy, get 以及 make 等動詞連用，有兩種可能的句型： • 用 for 引導間接受詞，或 • 間接受詞置於直接受詞前面。

■ 練習 52 — 口語練習：用括弧內的字完成下列句子。

　　1. I bought . . . *(Jim, a new hat)*
　　　→　*I bought a new hat for Jim.*
　　　→　*I bought Jim a new hat.*

　　2. Jack got . . . *(a stuffed animal, his daughter)*

　　3. I bought . . . *(some gloves, Robert)*

　　4. I made . . . *(Mike, a cake)*

　　5. Carmen got . . . *(a new television set, her parents)*

　　6. Eric bought . . . *(a necklace, his mother)*

　　7. Oscar made . . . *(his guests, dinner)*

　　8. Heidi bought . . . *(a nice birthday gift, her brother)*

　　9. Could you please get . . . *(a glass of water, me)*

(a) The teacher **explained** the grammar **to us**. (b) Anna **introduced** her sister **to me**. (c) 誤：*She explained us the grammar.* (d) 誤：*Anna introduced me her sister.*	間接受詞和動詞 *explain* 與 *introduce* 連用時，須注意： • 用 *to* 加間接受詞。 • 將間接受詞置於直接受詞後面。

■ **練習 53 —— 口語練習**：用括弧內的字完成下列句子。

1. Elizabeth explained . . . *(me, the problem)*
   → *Elizabeth explained the problem to me.*

2. The professor explained . . . *(the students, the chemistry formula)*

3. Tina introduced . . . *(her son, me)*

4. Mr. Schwartz explained . . . *(the doctor, his problem)*

5. Could you please translate . . . *(me, this sentence)*

6. Could you please explain . . . *(me, this sentence)*

7. Fred told . . . *(me, his ideas)*

8. I explained . . . *(my husband, Fred's ideas)*

■ **練習 54**：將括弧內的字加到句子裡；必要時，再加上 to 或 for。

1. *(Bob)* I wrote a letter.
   → *I wrote Bob a letter.* 或：*I wrote a letter to Bob.*★

2. *(my cousin)* I sent a postcard.

3. *(me)* The teacher answered a question.

4. *(his girlfriend)* Jim opened the car door.

5. *(the bride and groom)* Ann Miller gave a nice wedding present.

6. *(the class)* The teacher pronounced the new vocabulary words.

7. *(us)* The teacher explained the meaning of the word.

8. *(my roommate)* I translated the title of a book.

9. *(me)* My friend answered the phone because my hands were full.

10. *(the University of Texas)* I sent an application.

★*I wrote a letter for Bob* 的寫法是有可能的，但具有特殊的含意：即表達我幫 Bob 代筆之意。（例如：Bob 的手骨折了，不能寫字。但他想寫一封信，因此我幫他寫這封信。）

11. *(his wife)* Ron fixed the sewing machine.

12. *(us)* Don told a funny joke at the party.

13. *(me)* Jane explained her problems.

14. *(me)* My father wrote a letter.

15. *(the teacher)* Samir showed a picture of his family.

16. *(my friend)* I bought a gift.

■ **練習 55 — 口語練習（閣上書本）：**用完整的句子回答問題。

例： It's (. . .)'s birthday next week. What are you going to give her / him?
    再問：What is (學生 A) going to do?
學生A： A box of candy.
教　師： What is (學生 A) going to do?
學生B： She / He's going to give (. . .) a box of candy for her / his birthday. 或
        She / He's going to give a box of candy to (. . .) for her / his birthday.

1. (. . .) is getting married next month. What are you going to give her / him?
   [Followup: What is (學生 A) going to do?]

2. Take something out of your pocket or purse and hand it to (. . .).
   [What did (學生 A) do?]

3. Please explain the location of your country to (. . .).
   [What did (學生 A) explain?]

4. (. . .), ask (. . .) a question.   (. . .), answer the question for her / him.
   [What did (學生 A) do and (Student B) do?]

5. (. . .) needs some money desperately to pay her / his rent so she won't get kicked out
   of her / his apartment. How much money will you lend her / him?
   [What is (學生 A) going to do?]

6. Hide a small item in your hand. Show it to (. . .), but don't show it to (. . .).
   [What did (學生 A) do?]

7. Say a word in your native language and then translate it into English for (. . .).
   [What did (學生 A) do?]

8. Teach (. . .) how to say a word in your native language. Pronounce it for (. . .)
   several times.   [What did (學生 A) do?]

9. Get a piece of chalk for (. . .). [What did (學生 A) do?]

10. Make a paper airplane for (. . .). [What did (學生 A) do?]

1. I wrote _____ _____ yesterday.

2. I sent _____ _____ last week.

3. Please pass _____ _____.

4. The taxi driver opened _____ _____.

5. (. . .) gave _____ _____.

6. Could you please pronounce _____ _____?

7. Could you please lend _____ _____?

8. (. . .) translated _____ _____.

9. Could you please answer _____ _____?

10. My friend explained _____ _____.

11. I bought _____ _____.

12. Could you please get _____ _____?

■ 練習 57 — 複習：選出正確答案。

1. This newspaper is yours. That newspaper is _____.
   A. our   B. ours   C. our's   D. ours'

2. The teacher gave a test paper to every _____ in the class.
   A. student   B. students   C. of student   D. of students

3. Rosa is a _____ woman.
   A. beautiful Mexican young   C. Mexican beautiful young
   B. beautiful young Mexican   D. young beautiful Mexican

4. _____ the students in our class have dark hair.
   A. All most of   C. Almost
   B. Almost of   D. Almost all of

5. I handed _____.
   A. to the teacher my book   C. my book the teacher
   B. my book to the teacher   D. my book for the teacher

6. I had some _____ soup for lunch.
   A. vegetable good   C. vegetables good
   B. good vegetables   D. good vegetable

7. Jack introduced me to one _____.
       A. friends   B. of his friend   C. of his friends   D. his friends

8. My _____ name is Ernesto.
       A. father   B. fathers   C. fathers'   D. father's

9. Ahmed pronounced _____.
       A. for me his name   C. his name to me
       B. me his name   D. his name for me

10. _____ books are these?
       A. Who's   B. Whose   C. Who   D. Who are

■ 練習 58 — 錯誤分析：找出錯誤並更正。

1. I bought an airplane's ticket. Was expensive.

2. Some of those book's is mine.

3. Hiroki is a japanese businessman.

4. Theres an old big tree in our backyard.

5. Did you give to Jim my message?

6. The cat licked it's paw.

7. Everybody want to be happy.

8. One of the building on Main Street is the post office.

9. Whose that woman?

10. What are those peoples names?

11. Is the bedroom's window open?

12. Mr. and Mrs. Swan like their's apartment. Its large and comfortable.

13. I walk in the park every days.

14. Who's book is this?

15. I'am studying English.

16. Tina her last name Miller.

17. Please explain me this sentence.

18. My roommate desks are always messy.

19. Could you pronounce me this word?

20. I know the name's of almost of the students' in my class.

■ **練習 59 — 複習**：小組遊戲。每人各想一個名詞，並描述該名詞，讓組員猜測你心中所想的名詞。

例：

學生A：I'm thinking of a kind of plant. It's small and colorful. It smells good.
組　員：A flower!

學生B：I'm thinking of a person. She has short black hair. She's wearing a blue
　　　　sweater and a black skirt today.
組　員：That's too easy! Yoko!

學生C：I'm thinking of a very big cat. It's a wild animal.
組　員：A lion!
學生C：No. It's orange and black. It lives in Asia. It has stripes.
組　員：A tiger!

■ **練習 60 — 複習**：小組活動。每個人都各自帶一樣物品到教室，向組員描述並介紹該物品：它是什麼？
　　　　　　　　　　怎麼用？為何特別？回答組員的問題。所有的小組都結束討論後，將所有的物品帶到
　　　　　　　　　　教室中央。

學生A：選一樣物品，詢問有關的問題。找出其所有人及物品的用途。（物品的擁有者不要說
　　　　話，由該擁有者的組員提供學生 A 必要的訊息。）
學生B：選另一樣物品並提問題。
學生C：依此類推。

　　　所有的物品都討論完後，從中選五樣，並針對每一樣物品寫一段短文。內容包括它是什麼？
它看起來是什麼樣子？它是誰的？它有何用途？它為何特別？你為何覺得它有趣？等等。

8-20 更多的不規則動詞

become – became	feed – fed
bend – bent	fight – fought
bite – bit	hide – hid
build – built	hold – held
shake – shook	

■ **練習 61 — 口語練習（閤上書本）**：練習使用上表中的不規則動詞。

1. *become - became*　　When strangers meet, they can become friends. I met (. . .) （一段時間）ago. We became friends. What happened between (. . .) and me?

2. *bend - bent*　　When I drop something, I bend over to pick it up. I just dropped my pen, and then I bent over to pick it up. What did I do?

3. *bite - bit*　　Sometimes dogs bite people. Yesterday my friend's dog bit my hand while we were playing. What happened to my hand?

4. *build - built*　　I have some friends who know how to build houses. They built their own house next to the river. What did my friends do?

5. *feed - fed*　　I have a *(dog, cat, parrot, etc.).* I have to feed it every day. Yesterday I fed it once in the morning and once in the evening. What did I do yesterday?

6. *fight - fought*　　People fight in wars. People fight diseases. They fight for freedom and equality. My country fought a war *(against another country in a time period)*. What happened *(in that time period)*?

7. *hide - hid*　　I have a coin in my hand. Close your eyes while I hide it. Okay, open your eyes. I hid the coin. Where's the coin? Why don't you know?

8. *hold - held*　　When it rains, I hold my umbrella. Yesterday it rained. I held my umbrella. What did I do yesterday?

9. *shake - shook*　　People sometimes shake their finger or their head. Sometimes they shake when they're cold. Right now I'm shaking my finger / my head. What did I just do?

■ **練習 62**：用括弧內的字完成下列句子。

1. I *(hide)* _____ my husband's birthday present in the closet yesterday.

2. A: Ow!
   B: What's the matter?

   A: I *(bite)* _____ my tongue.

3. When I asked Dennis a question, he *(shake)* _____ his head no.

4. A: I've lost touch with some of our childhood friends. What happened to Greg Jones?

B: He *(become)* _____ a doctor.

A: What happened to Sandy Peterson?

B: She *(become)* _____ a lawyer.

5. I offered the child a red lollipop or a green lollipop. He *(choose)* _____ the red one.

6. Doug is a new father. He felt very happy when he *(hold)* _____ his baby for the first time.

7. Nancy and Tom saved money. They didn't buy a bookcase for their new apartment.

They *(build)* _____ one.

8. We saw a strong man at the circus. He *(bend)* _____ an iron bar.

9. A: Why did the children fight?

B: They *(fight)* _____ because both of them wanted the same toy.

10. Diane is a computer programmer.

Yesterday she *(feed)* _____ information into the computer.

■ **練習 63**：用框內動詞的正確形式完成下列句子。

become	*build*	*hide*
bend	*feed*	*hold*
bite	*fight*	✔ *shake*

1. When my dog got out of the lake, it _____*shook*_____ itself. Dogs always

_____*shake*_____ themselves when they're wet.

2. Many countries in the world _____ in World War II.

3. Sometimes snakes _____ people. My cousin Jake died after a

poisonous snake _____ him.

4. My daughter _____ a table in her woodworking class in high school.

5. When Kathy dropped her pen, Sam _____ over and picked it up for her.

6. The baby is sleeping peacefully. She's not hungry. Her mother _____ her before she put her in bed.

7. Mike stole a spoon from the restaurant. He _____ it in his pocket before he walked out of the restaurant.

8. David is a Canadian citizen. Maria was born in Puerto Rico, but when she married David, she _____ a Canadian citizen too.

■ 練習 64 — 口語練習（闔上書本）：以 yes 回答，並練習使用不規則動詞。

例：Did you write a letter yesterday?
答：Yes, I did. I wrote a letter yesterday.

1. Did you fly to （本市）?
2. Did you drink a cup of tea this morning?
3. Did you come to class yesterday?
4. Did you go downtown yesterday?
5. Did you eat breakfast this morning?
6. Did you lend some money to (. . .)?
7. Did you lose your pen yesterday? Did you find it?
8. Did you give your dictionary to (. . .)?
9. Did you throw your book to (. . .)? (. . .), did you catch it?
10. Did someone steal your wallet? Did you get it back?
11. Did you wake up at seven this morning?
12. Did you get up at seven this morning?
13. Did the wind blow yesterday?
14. Did you shut the door?
15. Did class begin at (. . .)?
16. Did you say hello to (. . .)?
17. Did you tell (. . .) to sit down? (. . .), did you sit down?
18. Did you hear my last question?
19. Did you teach your daughter/son to count to ten?
20. Did you bring your books to class today?
21. Did you forget your books?
22. Did you see (. . .) yesterday?
23. Did you meet (. . .)'s wife?
24. Did you leave your sunglasses at the restaurant?
25. Did you read the newspaper this morning?
26. Did you go shopping yesterday?
27. Did you drive your car to school today?
28. Did you ride a horse to school today?

29. Did a barber cut your hair?

30. Did you run to class this morning?

31. Did your pen cost （一筆錢）?

32. Did you understand my question?

33. Did you come to class yesterday?

34. Did you make a mistake?

35. Did you take the bus to school today?

36. Did you write a letter yesterday? Did you send it?

37. Did the telephone ring?

38. Did you break your arm?

39. Did you shake your head?

40. Did you draw a picture?

41. Did you bend your elbow?

42. Did you win a million dollars?

43. Did you feel good yesterday?

44. Did you feed the birds at the park?

45. Did you bite your finger?

46. Did you hurt your finger?

47. Did you hold （ . . .)'s hand?

48. Did you build a bookcase?

49. Did you stand at the bus stop?

50. Did you sing in the shower this morning?

51. Did you grow up in （某鄉村）?

52. Did you become an adult?

53. Did （某球隊） win yesterday?

54. Did you fall down yesterday?

55. Did you think about me yesterday?

56. Did you fight yesterday?

57. Which pen do you want? Did you choose this one?

58. Did you hide your money under your mattress?

59. Did your car hit a telephone pole yesterday?

60. Did you put your books under your desk?

第九章
比較的表示法

9-1 比較：THE SAME (AS), SIMILAR (TO) 和 DIFFERENT (FROM) 的用法

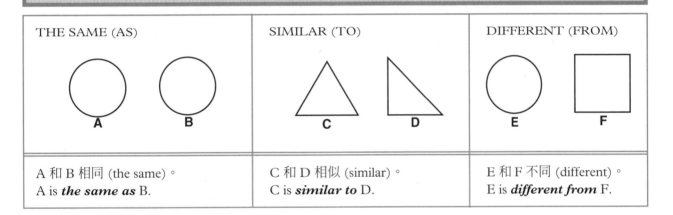

THE SAME (AS)	SIMILAR (TO)	DIFFERENT (FROM)
A 和 B 相同 (the same)。 A is **the same as** B.	C 和 D 相似 (similar)。 C is **similar to** D.	E 和 F 不同 (different)。 E is **different from** F.

■ **練習 1 — 口語練習**：以下圖形何者相同、相似或不同？

 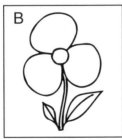 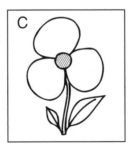 

1. Are Pictures A and B the same?
2. Are Pictures A and C the same?
3. Are Pictures A and C similar?
4. Are Pictures A and C different?
5. Are Pictures C and D similar?
6. Are Pictures C and D different?

■ **練習 2**：用 the same (as), similar (to), 和 different (from) 完成下列句子。

1. A _____*is the same as*_____ F.

2. D and E _____*are similar* 或：*are different**_____.

3. C _____ D.

4. B _____ D.

5. B and D _____.

6. C and D _____.

7. A and F _____.

8. F and G _____.

9. F _____ G.

10. G _____ A and F, but

    _____ C.

■ **練習 3 — 錯誤分析**：找出下列句子的錯誤並更正。

1. A rectangle is similar a square.

2. Pablo and Rita come from same country.

3. Girls and boys are differents. Girls are different to boys.

4. My cousin is the same age with my brother.

5. Dogs are similar with wolves.

6. Jim and I started to speak at same time.

---

*similar 表示兩物在某方面相同（例如：D 和 E 都有四個邊），但又在某方面不同（例如：D 是長方形，而 E 是正方形）。

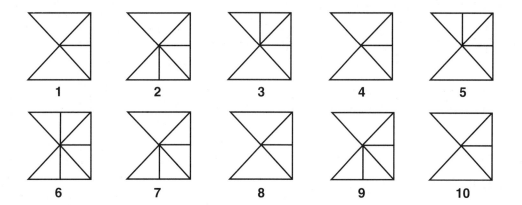

1. Which of the figures are the same?

2. Is there at least one figure that is different from all the rest?

3. How many triangles are there in figure 1? *(answer: Seven.)*

4. How many triangles are there in figure 2?

5. How many triangles are there in figure 6?

■ 練習 **5** 一 口語練習（閣上書本）：練習使用 the same (as), similar (to) 以及 different (from)。

例： Look at (. . .)'s clothes and (. . .)'s clothes. What is different about the clothes they are wearing today?
答： Their shoes are different. Mr. Lopez is wearing running shoes, and Mr. Gow is wearing sandals.

1. Look around the room. Name things that are the same.
2. Look around the room. Name things that are similar but not the same.
3. Find two pens that are the same length. Find two pieces of paper that are the same size. Find two notebooks that are different sizes.
4. Find two people in the class who are wearing (earrings). Are their (earrings) the same, similar, or different?
5. Who in the class has a (notebook, briefcase, bookbag) that is similar to yours? Does anyone have a (notebook, briefcase, bookbag) that is the same as yours?
6. Do any of the people in this room have the same hairstyle? Name two people who have similar hairstyles.
7. Whose shirt is the same color as yours today? Name some things in this room that are the same color. Name things that are similar colors.
8. Do any of the people in this room come from the same country? Who? Name two people who come from different countries.
9. Name an animal that is similar to a tiger. Name a bird that is similar to a duck.
10. Are Egypt and Italy on the same continent? Egypt and Algeria? Thailand and Korea? Mexico and Brazil?

9-2 比較：LIKE 和 ALIKE 的用法

You have a ballpoint pen with blue ink. I have a ballpoint pen with blue ink. (a) Your pen **is like** my pen. (b) Your pen and my pen **are alike**. (c) Our pens **are alike**.	*like = similar to*（與...相似） *alike = similar*（相似） *like* 和 *alike* 同義，但句型不同： *This + be* 動詞 *+ like + that.* *This and that + be* 動詞 *+ alike.*

■ **練習 6**：用 like 和 alike 完成下列句子。

1. You and I have similar books. In other words, your book is _____*like*_____ mine. Our books are _____*alike*_____.

2. Mr. Chang and I have similar coats. In other words, Mr. Chang's coat is _____ mine. Our coats are _____.

3. Ken and Sue have similar cars. In other words, their cars are _____.

4. You and I have similar hats. In other words, your hat is _____ mine.

5. A town is _____ a city in some ways.

6. A foot and a hand are _____ in some ways, but different in other ways.

7. A dormitory and an apartment building are _____ in many ways.

8. A motorcyle is _____ a bicycle in some ways.

■ **練習 7 — 口語練習**：用 like 造句。比較 A 欄和 B 欄的事物，並討論兩物有何相似之處。

例：A pencil is like a pen in some ways. They are both writing instruments.

A 欄	B 欄
an alley	a glass
a bus	a human hand
a bush	a lemon
a cup	a chair
a hill	a mountain
honey	an ocean
a monkey's hand	✔ a pen
an orange	a street
✔ a pencil	sugar
a sea	a suit coat
a sofa	a taxi
a sports jacket	a tree

9-3　比較級：-ER 和 MORE 的用法

Mary is 25 years old. John is 20 years old. (a)　Mary is **older than** John. (b)　Health is **more important than** money. (c)　誤：*Mary is more old than John.* (d)　誤：*Health is importanter than money.*	用形容詞（例如：*old, important*）比較兩人或兩物時，形容詞有其特定形式： (a) 句中：在形容詞字尾加 **-er**，或 (b) 句中：在形容詞前面加上 **more**。 這兩種形式稱為比較級。
	注意例句：*than* 位於比較級之後：　*older **than**, more important **than**.*

	形容詞	比較級	
單音節形容詞	**old** **cheap** **big**	**older** **cheaper** **bigger**	單音節形容詞字尾加 **-er**。
			注意拼法：形容詞字尾是一個母音字母加一個子音字母時，須重複子音字母：　*big–bigger, fat–fatter, thin–thinner, hot–hotter*。
字尾是 -Y 的形容詞	**pretty** **funny**	**prettier** **funnier**	形容詞字尾是 -y，將 -y 改成 *i*，再加 **-er**。
雙音節或 多音節形容詞	**famous** **important** **interesting**	**more famous** **more important** **more interesting**	雙音節或多音節的形容詞（字尾是 -y 的形容詞除外），前面加 **more**。
不規則比較級	**good** **bad** **far**	**better** **worse** **farther | further**	*good, bad* 和 *far* 的比較級是不規則形式。

■　**練習 8**：寫出下列形容詞的比較級。

1. old ___*older than*___

2. small _____

3. big _____

4. important _____

5. easy _____

6. difficult _____

7. long _____

8. heavy _____

9. sweet _____

10. expensive _____

11. hot _____

12. cheap _____

13. good _____

14. bad _____

15. far _____

16. lazy _____

1. *comfortable*   This chair is ____*more comfortable than*____ that chair.

2. *large*   Your apartment is _____ mine.

3. *warm*   It's _____ today _____ yesterday.

4. *dark*   Tom's mustache is _____ Don's.

5. *important*   Love is _____ money.

6. *lazy*   I'm _____ my roommate.

7. *tall*   My brother is _____ I am.★

8. *heavy*   Iron is _____ wood.

9. *difficult*   My physics course is _____ my math course.

10. *good*   Nadia's English is _____ her husband's.

11. *long*   The Nile River is _____ the Mississippi.

12. *intelligent*   A dog is _____ a chicken.

13. *good*   My wife's cooking is _____ mine.

14. *bad*   My cooking is _____ my wife's.

15. *short*   My little finger is _____ my middle finger.

16. *pretty*   This dress is _____ that one.

17. *far*   Your apartment is _____ from school

_____ mine.

18. *strong*   A horse is _____ a person.

19. *curly*   Ken's hair is _____ mine.

20. *beautiful*   A rose is _____ a weed.

★正式的書寫英文：*My brother is taller than I (am).*
非正式的口語英文：*My brother is taller than me.*

1. *good*   The weather today is _____ it was yesterday.

2. *bad*   The weather yesterday was _____ it is today.

3. *funny*   This story is _____ that story.

4. *interesting*   This book is _____ that book.

5. *smart*   Joe is _____ his brother.

6. *famous*   A movie star is _____ I am.

7. *wide*   A highway is _____ an alley.

8. *deep*   The Pacific Ocean is _____ the Mediterranean Sea.

9. *confusing*   This story is _____ that story.

10. *hot*   Thailand is _____ Korea.

11. *thin*   A giraffe's neck is _____ an elephant's neck.

12. *far*   My house is _____ from downtown _____ your house is.

13. *good*   Reading a good book is _____ watching television.

14. *easy*   My English class is _____ my history class.

15. *nervous*   The groom was _____ at the wedding _____ the bride.

例：A mouse is smaller than an elephant.

1. a mouse an elephant *(small)*	5. biology chemistry *(interesting)*	9. this book that one *(good)*
2. my old shoes my new shoes *(comfortable)*	6. I my brother *(thin)*	10. the weather here the weather in my hometown *(bad)*
3. your hair my hair *(dark)*	7. my hair her hair *(curly)*	11. this chapter Chapter 8 *(easy)*
4. my arm your arm *(long)*	8. her hair his hair *(straight)*	12. Japanese grammar English grammar *(difficult)*

■ **練習 12 ─ 口語練習（闔上書本）**：練習比較級。

A. 在教室中央放置數本不同的書。用提示的形容詞將書本互相作比較。

例：big
答：This book is bigger than that book/that one.

1. large	5. difficult	9. expensive
2. interesting	6. easy	10. cheap
3. small	7. good	11. thick
4. heavy	8. bad	12. important

B. 下列形容詞描述的是一位叫 Bob 的人，另一位叫 Jack 的人沒有相同的特質。在黑板上畫出 Bob 和 Jack，並將兩人作比較。

例：tall
答：Bob is taller than Jack.

1. tall	5. young	9. friendly★
2. strong	6. happy	10. responsible
3. lazy	7. kind	11. famous
4. intelligent	8. generous	12. busy

★*friendly* 的比較級有兩種形式：*friendlier than* 或 *more friendly than*。

big	*easy*	*important*
bright	*expensive*	*intelligent*
cheap	*fast*	*large*
cold	*high*	*small*
comfortable	*hot*	*sweet*

1. An elephant is ___*bigger than / larger than*___ a mouse.

2. A lemon is sour. An orange is _____ a lemon.

3. The weather today is _____ it was yesterday.

4. A diamond costs a lot of money. A diamond is _____ a ruby.

5. I can afford a radio, but not a TV set. A radio is _____ a TV set.

6. An airplane moves quickly. An airplane is _____ an automobile.

7. A lake is _____ an ocean.

8. A person can think logically. A person is _____ an animal.

9. Hills are low. Mountains are _____ hills.

10. The sun gives off a lot of light. The sun is _____ the moon.

11. Texas is a large state, but Alaska is

    _____ Texas.

12. Sometimes my feet hurt when I wear high heels. Bedroom slippers are

    _____

    shoes with high heels.

13. Arithmetic isn't difficult. Arithmetic is

    _____ algebra.

14. Good health is _____ money.

■ **練習 14** ─ 口語練習（闔上書本）：比較下列事物。

例：an elephant to a mouse
答：An elephant is bigger than a mouse / more intelligent than a mouse, etc.

1. an orange to a lemon
2. a lake to an ocean
3. good health to money
4. a radio to a TV set
5. an airplane to an automobile
6. (Alaska) to (Texas)
7. a person to an animal
8. the sun to the moon
9. a mountain to a hill
10. arithmetic to algebra
11. a diamond to a ruby
12. bedroom slippers to high heels
13. a child to an adult
14. a horse to a person
15. the Nile River to the Mississippi River
16. your little finger to your ring finger
17. love to money
18. your hair to (. . .)'s hair
19. food in （自己國家） to food in （別的國家）
20. the weather today to the weather yesterday

■ **練習 15** ─ 口語練習（闔上書本）：用下列形容詞的比較級 -er / more 造句。

例：large
答：Canada is larger than Mexico. / My feet are larger than yours. / etc.

1. tall
2. important
3. cold
4. curly
5. expensive
6. long
7. easy
8. comfortable
9. old
10. strong
11. small
12. intelligent
13. big
14. heavy
15. cheap
16. sweet
17. high
18. interesting
19. good
20. bad

■ **練習 16**：用練習 15 中的一個形容詞比較級寫一個句子，然後將句子撕成數張上面僅有一個字或片語的紙片，再將紙片交給一位同學重組。用不同的形容詞寫新的句子，重複做此練習。

9-4 AS...AS 和 LESS 的用法

	注意句型： AS + 形容詞 + AS
John is 21 years old. Mary is 21 years old. (a) John **is as old as** Mary.	(a) 句中：他們的年齡相同。
(b) This watch **is as expensive as** that watch.	(b) 句中：兩隻手錶價格相同。
Fred is 20 years old. Jean is 21 years old. (c) Fred **isn't as old as** Jean. (d) Fred **is younger than** Jean.	(c) 句和 (d) 句同義。
(e) This book **isn't as expensive as** that book. (f) This book **is cheaper than** that book.	(e) 句和 (f) 句同義。
(g) This book **isn't as expensive as** that book. (h) This book **is less expensive than** that book.	(g) 句和 (h) 句同義。*less* 是 *more* 的相反詞 *less* 與雙音節或多音節形容詞（字尾是 -y 的形容詞除外）連用。*less* 通常不與單音節或字尾是 -y 的形容詞連用。 誤： *Fred is less old than Jean.* 正： *Fred isn't as old as Jean.* 　　*Fred is younger than Jean.*

■ **練習 17**：用 as...as 加形容詞完成下列句子。

1. *tall*　　　　Mary is _____ *as tall as* _____ her brother.

2. *sweet*　　　A lemon isn't _____ an orange.

3. *big*　　　　A donkey isn't _____ a horse.

4. *friendly*　　People in this city are _____ the people in my hometown.

5. *dark*　　　Paul's hair isn't _____ his brother's.

6. *cold*　　　The weather isn't _____ today _____ yesterday.

7. *pretty*　　This dress is _____ that one.

8. *expensive*　A pencil isn't _____ a pen.

1. This book isn't as expensive as that book.
   → *This book is less expensive than that book.*

2. Bob isn't as old as Jim. →（不須修改）

3. Arithmetic isn't as difficult as algebra.

4. Arithmetic isn't as hard as algebra.

5. This chair isn't as comfortable as that chair.

6. This box isn't as heavy as that box.

7. A hill isn't as high as a mountain.

8. Swimming isn't as dangerous as boxing.

9. I'm not as tall as my brother.

10. This letter isn't as important as that letter.

■ **練習 19**：用 as...as 加括弧內的形容詞造出與下列各題同義的句子。

1. Bob is younger than Sally. *(old)*
   → *Bob isn't as old as Sally.*

2. This book is less expensive than that one. *(expensive)*
   → *This book isn't as expensive as that one.*

3. I'm shorter than my sister. *(tall)*

4. This exercise is more difficult than the last one. *(easy)*

5. My new shoes are less comfortable than my old shoes. *(comfortable)*

6. My little finger is shorter than my index finger. *(long)*

7. A radio is less expensive than a TV set. *(expensive)*

8. This book is worse than that book. *(good)*

9. My apartment is smaller than yours. *(big)*

10. In my opinion, chemistry is less interesting than psychology. *(interesting)*

■ **練習 20**：用 as...as 造出與下列各題同義的句子。

1. This room is smaller than that room.
   → *This room isn't as big as that room.*

2. An animal is less intelligent than a human being.

3. Soda pop is less expensive than fruit juice.

4. The Mississippi River is shorter than the Nile River.

5. Tom's pronunciation is worse than Sue's.

6. Algebra is more difficult than arithmetic.

7. Money is less important than good health.

8. American coffee is weaker than Turkish coffee.

9. A wooden chair is less comfortable than a sofa.

10. A van is smaller than a bus.

學生A：打開書本。
學生B：闔上書本。用完整的句子回答。

例： Name something that is sweeter than an apple.
學生A： What's sweeter than an apple? / Can you name something that is sweeter than an apple? / Name something that is sweeter than an apple.
學生B： Candy is sweeter than an apple.

1. Name a country that is larger than Mexico.
2. Name a planet that is closer to or farther away from the sun than the earth.
3. Name someone in the class who isn't as old as (I am, you are).
4. Name an animal that is more dangerous than a zebra.
5. Name an animal that is as dangerous as a wild tiger.
6. Name a bird that is larger than a chicken.
7. Name something that is more expensive than a diamond ring.
8. Name something that is less expensive than （教室內的一項物品）.
9. Name someone who is more famous than （某位名人）.

角色互換
10. Name something that is more interesting than （某學科）.
11. Name something that is less important than good health.
12. Name a place that is as far away from here as （某地名）.
13. Name an ocean that is smaller than the Pacific Ocean.
14. Name an animal that is stronger than a horse.
15. Name an animal that isn't as strong as a horse.
16. Name a game that is, in your opinion, more exciting than （某項運動）.
17. Name a sport that is less popular internationally than （某項運動）.
18. Name a place that is more beautiful than this city.

■ **練習 22**：用自己的語詞完成下列句子。

1. I'm taller _____

2. I'm not as old _____

3. A monkey isn't as big _____

4. American food isn't as good _____

5. An ocean is deeper and wider _____

6. An apple is less expensive _____

7. It's warmer / colder today _____

8. _____'s hair isn't as curly _____

9. A hill isn't as high _____

10. A dog is less intelligent _____ but more intelligent

    _____

11. _____'s hair is darker _____

12. A hotel room is less comfortable _____

13. Moonlight isn't as bright _____

14. Money is less important _____

15. English grammar isn't as difficult _____

16. Earth is closer to the sun _____

17. Venezuela isn't as far south _____

18. Tokyo isn't as far north _____

19. People in _____ are friendlier _____

20. Children are less powerful _____

9-5　BUT 的用法

(a) John is rich, ***but*** Mary is poor.	*but* 表示「此物和彼物相反」的含意。
(b) The weather was cold, ***but*** we were warm inside our house.	*but* 之前通常有逗號。

■ **練習 23**：用形容詞完成下列句子。

1. An orange is sweet, but a lemon is _____*sour.*_____

2. The weather is hot today, but it was _____ yesterday.

3. These dishes are clean, but those dishes are _____

4. This suitcase is heavy, but that suitcase is _____

5. My hair is light, but my brother's hair is _____

6. These shoes are uncomfortable, but those shoes are _____

7. Linda is tall, but her sister is _____

8. This street is narrow, but that street is _____

9. This exercise is easy, but that exercise is _____

10. My old apartment is big, but my new apartment is _____

11. This food is good, but that food is _____

12. A chicken is stupid, but a human being is _____

13. Smoke is visible, but clean air is _____

14. This answer is right, but that answer is _____

15. This towel is dry, but that towel is _____

16. This cup is full, but that cup is _____

17. This street is noisy, but that street is _____

18. This picture is ugly, but that picture is _____

19. This sentence is confusing, but that sentence is _____

20. This car is safe, but that car is _____

21. A kitten is weak, but a horse is _____

22. This watch is expensive, but that watch is _____

23. Tom is hard-working, but his brother is _____

24. My apartment is messy, but Bob's apartment is always _____

25. A pillow is soft, but a rock is _____

9-6 BUT 之後接動詞的用法

	肯定動詞	+ BUT +	否定動詞	
(a)	John *is* rich,	*but*	Mary *isn't*.	*but* 後面的動詞語詞經常會用縮短的形式，如例句。
(b)	Balls *are* round,	*but*	boxes *aren't*.	
(c)	I *was* in class,	*but*	Po *wasn't*.	
(d)	Sue *studies* hard,	*but*	Sam *doesn't*.	
(e)	We *like* movies,	*but*	they *don't*.	
(f)	Alex *came*,	*but*	Maria *didn't*.	
(g)	People *can* talk,	*but*	animals *can't*.	
(h)	Olga *will* be there,	*but*	Ivan *won't*.	
	否定動詞	+ BUT +	肯定動詞	
(i)	Mary *isn't* rich,	*but*	John *is*.	
(j)	Boxes *aren't* round,	*but*	balls *are*.	
(k)	Po *wasn't* in class,	*but*	I *was*.	
(l)	Sam *doesn't* study,	*but*	Sue *does*.	
(m)	They *don't like* cats,	*but*	we *do*.	
(n)	Maria *didn't come*,	*but*	Alex *did*.	
(o)	Animals *can't* talk,	*but*	people *can*.	
(p)	Ivan *won't* be there,	*but*	Olga *will*.	

■ **練習 24**：用適當的肯定或否定動詞完成下列句子。

1. Sara is at home, but her husband ____*isn't*____.

2. Hiroki isn't at home, but his wife _____.

3. Beds are comfortable, but park benches _____.

4. I wasn't at home last night, but my roommate _____.

5. Kim was in class yesterday, but Anna and Linda _____.

6. Jack wants to go to the zoo, but Barbara _____.

7. I don't want to go to the movie, but my friends _____.

8. Pablo went to the party, but Steve _____.

9. Ahmed can speak French, but I _____.

10. Amanda will be at the meeting, but Helen _____.

11. I was at home yesterday, but my roommate _____.

12. This shirt is clean, but that one _____.

13. These shoes aren't comfortable, but those shoes _____.

14. I like strong coffee, but Karen _____.

15. Mike doesn't write clearly, but Ted _____.

16. I ate breakfast this morning, but my roommate _____.

17. Carol has a car, but Jerry _____.

18. Jerry doesn't have a car, but Carol _____.

19. Ron was at the party, but his wife _____.

20. Ron went to the party, but his wife _____.

21. Ellen can speak Spanish, but her husband _____.

22. Boris can't speak Spanish, but his wife _____.

23. I won't be at home tonight, but Sue _____.

24. Ken will be in class tomorrow, but Chris _____.

25. Amy won't be here tomorrow, but Alice _____.

■ **練習 25 — 口語練習（闔上書本）**：練習使用 but...。

例： Who in the class was at home last night? Who wasn't at home last night?
教 師：Who was at home last night?
學生A：I was.
教 師：Who wasn't at home last night?
學生B：I wasn't at home last night.
教 師：Summarize, using *but*.
學生C：(Ali) was at home last night, but (Kim) wasn't.

1. Who wears glasses? Who doesn't wear glasses?
2. Who is married? Who isn't married?
3. Who didn't watch TV last night? Who watched TV last night?
4. Who will be in class tomorrow? Who won't be in class tomorrow?
5. Who has a car? Who doesn't have a car?
6. Who studied last night? Who didn't study last night?
7. Who can play（某項樂器）? Who can't play（該項樂器）?
8. Who is hungry right now? Who isn't hungry right now?
9. Who lives in an apartment? Who lives in a house or in a dorm?
10. Who doesn't drink coffee? Who drinks coffee?
11. Who won't be at home tonight? Who will be at home tonight?
12. Who was in class yesterday? Who wasn't in class yesterday?
13. Who can't speak（某語言）? Who can speak（某語言）?
14. Who didn't stay home last night? Who stayed home last night?
15. Who has（鬍子）? Who doesn't have（鬍子）?

圖 A   圖 B

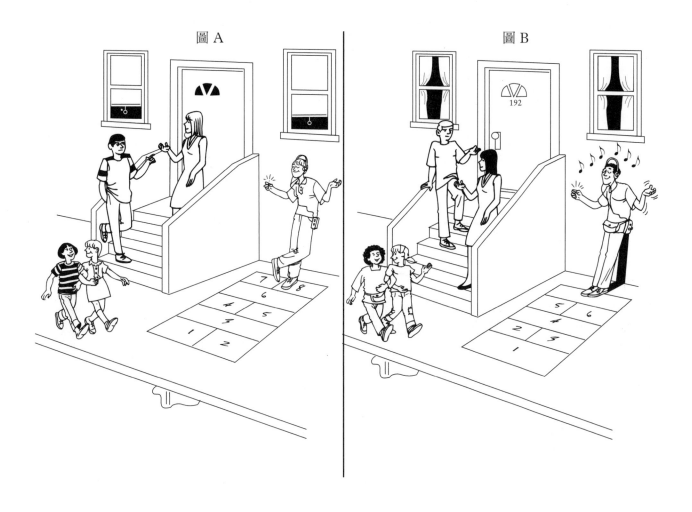

■ **練習 27 — 錯誤分析**：找出下列句子的錯誤，並作更正。

1. My cousin is the same tall as my brother.

2. A blue whale is more large from an elephant.

3. A dog is less small as a wolf.

4. Your handwriting is more better than mine.

5. Robert and Maria aren't same age. Robert is more young than Maria.

6. A lake isn't as deep than an ocean.

■ **練習 28 — 書寫練習**：用以下的一個或多個主題作書寫練習。

1. Write about this city. Compare it to your hometown.
2. Write about your present residence. Compare it to a past residence. For example, compare your new apartment to your old apartment.
3. Write about two members of your family. Compare them.
4. Write about two animals. Compare them.
5. Write about two countries. Compare them.

比較級的用字

the same (as)	*like*	*-er / more*
similar (to)	*alike*	*less*
different (from)		*as . . . as*
		but

9-7 最高級：-EST 和 MOST 的用法

（a） 比較級： My thumb is ***shorter than*** my index finger. （b） 最高級： My hand has five fingers. My thumb is ***the shortest*** (finger) of all.	比較級 *(-er / more)* 比較兩個事物或人。 最高級 *(-est / most)* 比較三個或三個以上的事物或人。

	形容詞	比較級	最高級
單音節形容詞	***old*** ***big***	***older*** *(than)* ***bigger*** *(than)*	***the oldest*** *(of all)* ***the biggest*** *(of all)*
字尾是 -Y 的形容詞	***pretty*** ***easy***	***prettier*** *(than)* ***easier*** *(than)*	***the prettiest*** *(of all)* ***the easiest*** *(of all)*
雙音節或 多音節形容詞	***expensive*** ***important***	***more expensive*** *(than)* ***more important*** *(than)*	***the most expensive*** *(of all)* ***the most important*** *(of all)*
不規則形式	***good*** ***bad*** ***far***	***better*** *(than)* ***worse*** *(than)* ***farther / further*** *(than)*	***the best*** *(of all)* ***the worst*** *(of all)* ***the farthest / furthest*** *(of all)*

■ **練習 29**：寫出下列形容詞的比較級和最高級。

	比較級	最高級
1. long	*longer (than)*	*the longest (of all)*
2. small	_____	_____
3. heavy	_____	_____
4. comfortable	_____	_____
5. hard	_____	_____
6. difficult	_____	_____
7. easy	_____	_____
8. hot★	_____	_____
9. cheap	_____	_____
10. interesting	_____	_____
11. pretty	_____	_____
12. strong	_____	_____
13. good	_____	_____
14. bad	_____	_____
15. far	_____	_____

■ **練習 30**：用形容詞的正確形式完成下列句子。

1. *large*   _____ *The largest* _____ city in Canada is Toronto.

2. *long*   The Nile is _____ river in the world.

3. *interesting*   I'm taking four classes. My history class is _____

           _____ of all.

4. *high*   Mt. McKinley in Alaska is _____
           mountain in North America.

5. *tall*   The Sears Tower is _____ building in
           Chicago.

★注意拼法：形容詞字尾是一個母音字母加一個子音字母時，重複子音字母再改成最高級：
big-biggest, fat-fattest, thin-thinnest, hot-hottest。

6. *big*   Lake Superior is _____ lake in North America.

7. *short*   February is _____ month of the year.

8. *far*   Pluto is _____ planet from the sun.

9. *beautiful*   In my opinion, Seattle is _____ city in the United States.

10. *bad*   In my opinion, Harry's Steak House is _____ restaurant in the city.

11. *good*   In my opinion, the Doghouse Cafe has _____ food in the city.

12. *comfortable* Ken is sitting in _____ chair in the room.

13. *fast*   _____ way to travel is by airplane.

14. *good*   When you feel depressed, laughter is _____ medicine.

15. *large*   Asia is _____ continent in the world.

16. *small*   Australia is _____ continent in the world.

17. *expensive*   Sally ordered _____ food on the menu for dinner last night.

18. *easy*   Taking a taxi is _____ way to get to the airport.

19. *important*   I think good health is _____ thing in life.

20. *famous*   The Gateway Arch is _____ landmark in St. Louis, Missouri.

■ **練習 31**：比較每組的圖片。

A. 比較三個球的大小。

1. The golf ball is _____*smaller than*_____ the baseball.

2. The soccer ball is _____ the baseball.

3. The soccer ball is _____ of all.

4. The baseball isn't _____ as the soccer ball.

B. 比較三個小孩的年齡。

TOMMY　　　HELEN　　　ANN
(3 years old)　(6 years old)　(8 years old)

5. Ann is _____ Helen.

6. Tommy is _____ Helen and Ann.

7. Ann is _____ of all.

8. Helen isn't _____ as Ann.

C. 比較三位女士的身高。

LINDA   KAREN   ALICE

9. _____ is the tallest

10. _____ is the shortest.

11. _____ is taller than _____ but

    shorter than _____.

12. _____ isn't as tall as _____.

D. 比較三位男士的力氣。

MIKE   JOE   DON

13. _____

14. _____

15. _____

16. _____

E. 比較這三種交通工具的價格。

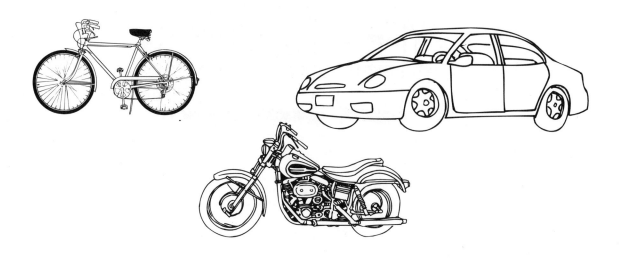

17. _____

18. _____

19. _____

20. _____

F. 比較三張考卷的優劣。

21. _____

22. _____

23. _____

24. _____

G. 比較三本書（對你）的吸引力。

25. _____

26. _____

27. _____

28. _____

■ **練習 32**：用形容詞的正確形式（比較級或最高級），完成下列句子。

1. *long*   The Yangtze River is _____ the Mississippi River.

2. *long*   The Nile is _____ river in the world.

3. *large*   The Caribbean Sea is _____ the Mediterranean Sea.

4. *large*   The Caribbean Sea is _____ sea in the world.

5. *high*   Mt. Everest is _____ mountain in the world.

6. *high*   Mt. Everest is _____ Mt. McKinley.

7. *big*   Africa is _____ North America.

8. *small*   Europe is _____ South America.

9. *large*   Asia is _____ continent in the world.

10. *big*   Canada is _____ the United States in area.

11. *large*   Indonesia is _____ Japan in population.

12. *good*   Fruit is _____ for your health

_____ candy.

13. *good*   The student cafeteria has _____ roast
beef sandwiches in the city.

14. *comfortable*   I have a pair of boots, a pair of sandals, and a pair of running

shoes. The sandals are _____

the boots, but the running shoes are _____

_____ of all.

15. *easy*   This exercise is _____ that one. This is

one of _____ exercises in the book.

16. *bad*   There are over 800 million people in the world who don't get to

eat. With few exceptions, poverty and hunger are _____
in rural areas than in cities and towns.

9-8 ONE OF + 最高級 + 複數名詞的用法

（a）The Amazon is **one of the longest rivers** in the world.	最高級經常位於 *one of* 之後。 注意句型：
（b）A Rolls Royce is **one of the most expensive cars** in the world.	*one of* + 最高級 + 複數名詞
（c）Alice is **one of the most intelligent people** in our class.	有關 *one of* 的資料，請參閱表 8-5。

■ **練習 33**：用 one of ＋ 最高級 ＋ 複數名詞造下列句子。

1. a high mountain in the world
   → *Mt. McKinley is one of the highest mountains in the world.*

2. a pretty park in（本市）
   → *Forest Park is one of the prettiest parks in St. Louis.*

3. a tall person in our class
   → *Talal is one of the tallest people* in our class.*

4. a big city in the world

5. a beautiful place in the world

6. a nice person in our class

7. a long river in the world

_____
*people 通常用來代替 *person* 的複數 *(persons)*。

8. a good restaurant in （本市）

9. a famous landmark in the world

10. an important event in the history of the world

■ **練習 34 — 書寫練習**：用 one of ＋ 最高級 ＋ 複數名詞造句。

例：a big city in Canada
答：Montreal is one of the biggest cities in Canada.

1. a big city in Asia

2. a large state in the U.S.

3. a beautiful city in the world

4. a friendly person in our class

5. a good place to visit in the world

6. a famous person in the world

7. an important thing in life

8. a bad restaurant in （本市）

9. a famous landmark in （某國）

10. a tall building in （本市）

11. a dangerous sport in the world

12. a serious problem in the world

■ **練習 35 — 口語練習**：討論下列問題。

1. How many brothers and sisters do you have? Are you the oldest?
2. Who is one of the most famous movie stars in the world?
3. In your opinion, what is the most exciting sport?
4. What is one of the most interesting experiences in your life?
5. In your opinion, what is the most beautiful place in the world?
6. What is one of the most important inventions in the modern world?
7. What is one of the worst experiences of your life?
8. What are the best things in life?
9. What was the happiest day of your life — or one of the happiest days of your life?
10. Who are the most important people in your life today?

隨堂測驗。若不知答案，就用猜的。測驗完後，全班分成小組討論答案。參閱 410 頁的統計表，找出答案。

第一部份

1. What is the longest river in the world?
   A. the Yangtze
   B. the Amazon
   C. the Nile
   D. the Mississippi

2. Is the Amazon River longer than the Mississippi River?
   A. yes
   B. no

3. Is the Yangtze River longer than the Mississippi River?
   A. yes
   B. no

4. Is the Yangtze River as long as the Nile River?
   A. yes
   B. no

5. Which two rivers are almost the same length?
   A. the Nile and the Amazon
   B. the Amazon and the Yangtze
   C. the Nile and the Mississippi
   D. the Mississippi and the Amazon

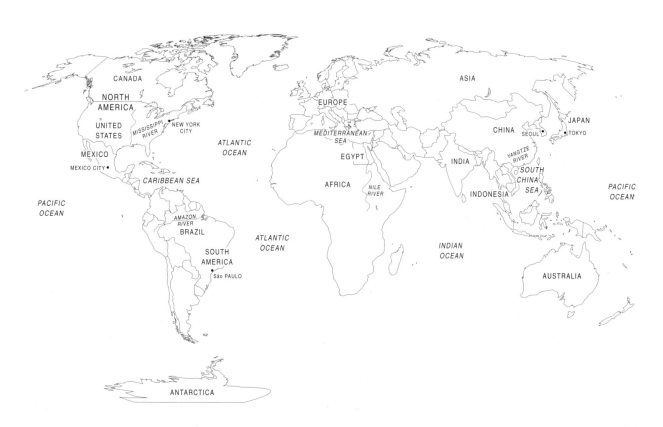

6. What is the largest sea in the world?
   A. the Mediterranean Sea
   B. the South China Sea
   C. the Caribbean Sea

7. Is the South China Sea the smallest of the three seas listed above?
   A. yes
   B. no

第三部份

8. What is the deepest ocean in the world?
   A. the Atlantic Ocean
   B. the Indian Ocean
   C. the Pacific Ocean

9. Is the Indian Ocean larger than the Atlantic Ocean?
   A. yes
   B. no

第四部份

10. Below is a list of the continents in the world. List them in order according to size, from the largest to the smallest.

    Africa   *Europe*
    ✔ *Antarctica*   *North America*
    Asia   *South America*
    Australia

    (1) _____ (the largest)

    (2) _____

    (3) _____

    (4) _____

    (5) ___*Antarctica*_____

    (6) _____

    (7) _____ (the smallest)

11. Which of the following cities is the largest in population in the world?
    A. New York City, U.S.A.
    B. Seoul, Korea
    C. Mexico City, Mexico
    D. Tokyo, Japan

12. Is the population of Sao Paulo, Brazil, larger than the population of New York City, U.S.A.?
    A. yes
    B. no

13. Is the population of Sao Paulo, Brazil, larger than the population of Seoul, Korea?
    A. yes
    B. no

14. What is the largest city in North America?
    A. Mexico City
    B. New York City

第六部份

15. Which of the following countries is the largest in area in the world?
    A. Canada
    B. China
    C. the United States
    D. Brazil

16. Which of the following two countries is larger in area?
    A. Canada
    B. Brazil

17. Which of the following countries is the largest in population in the world?
    A. India
    B. China
    C. the United States
    D. Indonesia

18. Which of the following two countries is larger in population?
    A. India
    B. Indonesia

19. Which of the following two countries is larger in population?
    A. the United States
    B. Brazil

20. Which of the following two countries is smaller in population?
    A. Egypt
    B. Japan

統　計　表

第一部份

河流	長度
the Amazon River	3,915 miles
the Mississippi River	2,348 miles
the Nile River	4,145 miles
the Yangtze River	3,900 miles

第二部份

海	面積
the Caribbean Sea	970,000 square miles
the Mediterranean Sea	969,000 square miles
the South China Sea	895,000 square miles

第三部份

洋	面積	平均深度
Atlantic Ocean	33,420,000 square feet	11,730 feet
Indian Ocean	28,350,500 square feet	12,598 feet
Pacific Ocean	64,186,300 square feet	12,925 feet

第四部份

洲	面積
Africa	11,707,000 square miles
Antarctica	5,500,000 square miles
Asia	17,129,000 square miles
Australia	2,942,000 square miles
Europe	4,057,000 square miles
North America	9,363,000 square miles
South America	6,886,000 square miles

第五部份

城市	人口★
Mexico City, Mexico	28 million
New York, U.S.A.	15 million
Sao Paulo, Brazil	25 million
Seoul, Korea	22 million
Tokyo, Japan	30 million

第六部份

國家	面積	人口★
Brazil	3,286,470 sq mi	180 million
Canada	3,851,809 sq mi	29 million
China	3,691,000 sq mi	1,250 million ★★
Egypt	386,650 sq mi	65 million
India	1,269,339 sq mi	960 million
Indonesia	788,430 sq mi	205 million
Japan	145,740 sq mi	128 million
the United States	3,615,123 sq mi	268 million

★　表中人口數乃西元 2000 年的估計數字。

★★　1,250 *million*（十二億五千萬）唸作 *"one billion, two hundred and fifty million."*。（舊式英文中也唸做 *"one thousand, two hundred and fifty million"*。）

(A) Ann is a **careful** driver. 形容詞 (b) Ann drives **carefully**. 副詞	形容詞 **careful** **slow** **quick** **easy**	副詞 **carefully** **slowly** **quickly** **easily**	形容詞修飾名詞。 (a) 中：careful 修飾 driver。 副詞修飾動詞的動作。 (b) 中：carefully 修飾 drives。 多數副詞是由形容詞加 -ly 所構成。
(c) John is a **fast** driver. 形容詞 (d) John drives **fast**. 副詞	**fast** **hard** **early** **late**	**fast** **hard** **early** **late**	fast, hard, early, late 等字的形容詞和副詞形式相同。
(e) Linda is a **good** writer. 形容詞 (f) Linda writes **well**. 副詞	**good**	**well**	well 是 good 的副詞形式。★

★well 也可作形容詞用，意為「身體無恙」。例如：Paul was sick last week, but now he's well.

■ **練習 37**：用斜體字的形容詞或副詞完成下列句子。

1. quiet, quietly — My hometown is small and ___quiet___.
2. quiet, quietly — Mr. Wilson whispered. He spoke ___quietly___.
3. clear, clearly — Anna pronounces every word _____.
4. clear, clearly — We like to go boating in _____ weather.
5. careless, carelessly — Boris makes a lot of mistakes when he writes. He's a _____ writer.
6. careless, carelessly — Boris writes _____.
7. easy, easily — The teacher asked an _____ question.
8. easy, easily — I answered the teacher's question _____.
9. good, well — You speak English very _____.
10. good, well — Your English is very _____.

1. *careful*   Do you drive _____?

2. *correct*   Carmen gave the _____ answer to the question.

3. *correct*   She answered the question _____.

4. *fast*   Mike is a _____ reader.

5. *quick*   Mike reads _____.

6. *fast*   Mike reads _____.

7. *neat*   Barbara has _____ handwriting. It is easy to read what she writes.

8. *neat*   Barbara writes _____.

9. *hard*   I study _____.

10. *hard*   The students took a _____ test.

11. *honest*   Roberto answered the question _____.

12. *slow*   Karen and Fumiko walked through the park _____.

13. *careless*   I made some _____ mistakes in my last ___ composition.

14. *quick*   We were in a hurry, so we ate lunch _____.

15. *early*   Last night we had dinner _____ because we had to leave for the theater at 6:00.

16. *early*   We had an _____ dinner last night.

17. *good, well*   Jake has poor eyesight. He can't see

_____ without his glasses.

18. *good, well*   David is kind, generous, and thoughtful. He is a

_____ person.

19. *loud*   I speak _____ when I talk to my grandfather because he has trouble hearing.

20. *slow, clear*   Kim speaks English _____ and _____.

■ **練習 39：** 用的正確的形式（形容詞或副詞）完成下列句子。

1. *good*   Did you sleep _____ last night?

2. *fast*   Anita is a _____ learner.

3. *quick*   She learns everything _____.

4. *fast*   Ahmed walks too _____. I can't keep up with him.

5. *soft*   Please speak _____. The children are asleep.

6. *easy*   This is an _____ exercise.

7. *hard*   It rained _____ yesterday.

8. *clear*   Our teacher explains everything _____.

9. *late*   Spiro came to class _____ yesterday.

10. *safe*   The plane arrived at the airport _____.

11. *hard*   Ms. Chan is a _____ worker.

12. *hard*   She works _____.

13. *late*   I paid my telephone bill _____.

14. *easy*   Ron lifted the heavy box _____. He's very strong.

15. *quiet*   Olga entered the classroom _____ because she was late for class.

16. *fast*   Mike talks too _____. I can't understand him.

17. *honest* Shelley is an _____ person. I trust her completely.

18. *honest* She speaks _____.

19. *good*   I didn't understand the teacher's explanation very _____.

20. *good*   We had a _____ time at the party last night.

21. *good*   Linda speaks _____, but she doesn't write

_____.

22. *fluent*   Nadia speaks French _____.

9-10 副詞的比較

	比較級	最高級	
(a) Kim speaks **more fluently than** Ali (does). (b) Anna speaks **the most fluently of all**.	**more fluently** **more slowly** **more quickly**	**the most fluently** **the most slowly** **the most quickly**	字尾是 *-ly* 的副詞用 *more* 和 *most*。★
(c) Mike worked **harder than** Sam (did). (d) Sue worked **the hardest of all**.	**harder** **faster** **earlier** **later**	**the hardest** **the fastest** **the earliest** **the latest**	不規則副詞 *(hard, fast, early, late)* 用 *-er* 和 *-est*。
(e) Rosa writes **better than** I do. (f) Kim writes **the best of all**.	**better**	**the best**	副詞 *well* 的形式是 *better* 和 *best*。

★例外：*early–earlier–earliest*.

■ **練習 40**：用副詞的正確形式（比較級或最高級）完成下列句子。

1. *late*   Karen got home _____*later than*_____ Alice (did).

2. *quickly*   I finished my work _____ Tom (did).

3. *beautifully*   Gina sings _____ Susan (does).

4. *beautifully*   Ann sings _____ of all.

5. *hard*   My sister works _____ I (do).

6. *hard*   My brother works _____ of all.

7. *carefully*   My husband drives _____ I (do).

8. *early*   We arrived at the party _____ the Smiths (did).

9. *early*   The Wilsons arrived at the party _____ of all.

10. *well*　　　You can write _____ I (can).

11. *well*　　　Ken can write _____ of all.

12. *clearly*　　Anita pronounces her words _____ Tina (does).

13. *fast*　　　I work _____ Jim (does).

14. *fast*　　　Toshi finished his work _____ of all.

15. *loudly*　　Ali speaks _____ Yoko (does).

16. *fluently*　Sue speaks Spanish _____ I (do).

17. *fluently*　Ted speaks Spanish _____ of all.

18. *slowly*　　A snail moves _____ a crab (does).

■ **練習 41**：用正確的形式（形容詞或副詞，比較級或最高級）完成下列句子。

1. *careful*　　Karen drives ___*more carefully than*___ her brother does.

2. *beautiful*　A tiger is _____ a goat.

3. *neat*　　　Paul's apartment is _____ mine.

4. *neat*　　　Peter's apartment is _____ of all.

5. *neat*　　　You write _____ I do.

6. *neat*　　　Ann writes _____ of all.

7. *heavy*　　This suitcase is _____ that one.

8. *clear*　　　This author explains her ideas _____ that author.

9. *good*   I like rock music _____ classical music.

10. *good*   My husband can sing _____ I can.

11. *good*   My daughter can sing _____ of all.

12. *hard*   Sue studies _____ Fred.

13. *hard*   Jean studies _____ of all.

14. *long*   Almost universally, wives work _____ hours than their husbands because women take primary responsibility for household chores and child-rearing.

15. *late*   Robert usually goes to bed _____ his roommate.

16. *clear*   Anna pronounces her words _____ of all the students in the class.

17. *sharp*   A razor is usually _____ a kitchen knife.

18. *artistic*   My son is _____ my daughter.

19. *slow*   I eat _____ my husband does.

20. *dangerous* A motorcycle is _____ a bicycle.

9-11　AS...AS 和副詞的連用

	注意句型： *as* ＋副詞 ＋ *as*
（a）　Bob doesn't study ***as hard as*** his brother (does). （b）　I didn't finish my work ***as quickly as*** Sue (did). （c）　Yoko can speak English ***as well as*** Tony (can).	
（d）　I'm working ***as fast as I can***. （e）　I'm working ***as fast as possible***. （f）　Alex came ***as quickly as he could***. （g）　Alex came ***as quickly as possible***.	注意句型： *as* ＋ 副詞 ＋ *as* 後面經常接主詞 ＋ *can /* *could* 或 *possible*。

■ **練習 42**：把 John 和自己或同學作比較，完成下列句子。

1. John is lazy. He doesn't work as hard ____*as Yoko (does). / as I (do).*____

2. John is a reckless driver. He doesn't drive as carefully _____

3. I can't read John's handwriting. He doesn't write as neatly _____

4. John goes to bed late. He doesn't go to bed as early _____

5. John was the last person to finish the test. He didn't finish it as quickly

   _____

6. John speaks softly. He doesn't speak as loudly _____

7. John is never in a hurry. He takes his time. He doesn't walk as fast _____

8. John is an insomniac. He doesn't sleep as well _____

9. John rarely studies. He doesn't study as hard _____

■ 練習 **43** — 口語練習：用 as...as + possible 或 can / could 更改下列句子。

例：Please come early.
答：Please come as early as possible. / Please come as early as you can.

例：(. . .) walked fast.
答：Surasuk walked as fast as possible. / Surasuk walked as fast as he could.

1. Please come quickly.
2. (. . .) came quickly.
3. Please write neatly.
4. I opened the door quietly.
5. Please come soon.
6. (. . .) came soon.
7. Pronounce each word clearly.
8. Do you study hard?
9. When (. . .) saw a mean dog, he/she ran home fast.
10. I write to my parents often.
11. (. . .) is working fast.
12. Please give me your homework soon.
13. I'll get home early.
14. (. . .) answered the question well.
15. I'll call you soon.
16. (. . .) goes swimming often.
17. Please finish the test soon.
18. I'll pay my telephone bill soon.

■ 練習 **44** — 複習：選出正確答案。

1. A lion is _____ a tiger.
   A. similar   B. similar with   C. similar from   D. similar to

2. Lions and tigers are _____.
   A. the same   B. similar   C. similar to   D. the same as

3. Good health is one of _____ in a person's life.
   A. best thing   C. the best things
   B. the best thing   D. best things

4. There were many chairs in the room. I sat in _____ chair.
   A. the comfortablest   C. most comfortable
   B. the most comfortable   D. more comfortable

5. Jane's story was _____ Jack's story.
   A. funnier than
   C. more funnier than
   B. funny than
   D. more funny

6. My last name is _____ my cousin's.
   A. same   B. same from   C. same as   D. the same as

7. I live _____ away from school than you do.
   A. far   B. farther   C. more far   D. farthest

8. Ali speaks _____ than Hamid.
   A. more clearly
   C. more clear
   B. clearlier
   D. more clearer

9. The weather in Canada _____ the weather in Mexico.
   A. is less hot than
   C. is hotter
   B. isn't as hot as
   D. isn't hot

10. Robert works hard every day, but his brother _____.
    A. is   B. isn't   C. does   D. doesn't

■ 練習 45 — 錯誤分析：找出下列句子的錯誤，並作更正。

1. Your pen is alike mine.

2. Kim's coat is similar with mine.

3. Jack's coat is same mine.

4. Soccer balls are different with basketballs.

5. Soccer is one of most popular sports in the world.

6. Green sea turtles live more long from elephants.

7. My grade on the test was worst from yours. You got a more better grade.

8. A monkey is intelligenter than a turtle.

9. Africa isn't as large than Asia.

10. Pedro speaks English more fluent than Ernesto.

11. The exploding human population is the most great threat to all forms of life on earth.

12. The Mongol Empire was the bigger land empire in the entire history of the world.

學生A：打開書本。
學生B：閤上書本，用完整句子回答。

1. What's the longest river in the world?
2. What's the biggest continent? What's the second biggest continent?
3. What country has the largest population?
4. Is a square the same as a rectangle?
5. Name a country that is farther south than Mexico.
6. Name an animal that is similar to a horse.
7. Name a place that is noisier than a library.
8. Is a dormitory like an apartment building? How are they different? How are they similar?
9. Is (. . .)'s grammar book different from yours?
10. What is one of the most famous landmarks in the world?

角色互換

11. Is the population of Seoul, Korea, larger or smaller than the population of Sao Paulo, Brazil?
12. Is the Atlantic Ocean deeper than the Indian Ocean?
13. What's the smallest continent in the world?
14. Name two students in this class who speak the same native language. Do they come from the same country?
15. Look at (. . .) and (. . .). How are they different?
16. Is a lake like a river? How are they different? How are they similar?
17. Name an insect that is smaller than a bee.
18. Name a city that is farther north than Rome, Italy.
19. What is the most popular sport in your country?
20. What is one of the most important inventions in the modern world? Why is it more important than （他項發明）.

■ 練習 47 ― 複習：用書寫或口語方式，比較教室內的人和物。

■ 練習 48 ― 複習：針對以下的一個或數個主題做書寫練習。

1. Write about your family. Compare the members of your family. Include yourself in the comparisons. (Who is younger than you? Who is the youngest of all? Etc.)
2. Write about your childhood friends when you were ten years old. Compare them. Include yourself in the comparisons. (Who could run faster than you? Who could run the fastest of all? Etc.)
3. What are your three favorite places in the world? Why? Compare them.
4. What are the roles of health, money, and love in your life? Compare them.

第十章
動詞的特定用法及其表達方式

10-1　SHOULD 的用法

(a)　My clothes are dirty. I *should wash* them. (b)　Tom is sleepy. He *should go* to bed. (c)　You're sick. You *should see* a doctor.	*should* 表示「這是個好主意，這建議很好。」
(d)　$\left.\begin{array}{l} I \\ You \\ She \\ He \\ It \\ We \\ They \end{array}\right\}$ ***should go***.	*should* 後面用原形動詞。 誤：　*He should goes.* 誤：　*He should to go.*
(e)　You ***should not leave*** your grammar book at home. You need it in class. (f)　You ***shouldn't leave*** your grammar book at home.	否定式：　*should not* 縮寫式：　*should + not = shouldn't*

■　**練習 1**：用 You should... 加框內或自己的語詞完成下列句子。

> *buy a new pair of shoes*　　　　✔ *go to the post office*
> *call the landlady*　　　　　　　　*go to bed and take a nap*
> *go to the bank*　　　　　　　　　*see a dentist*
> *go to the immigration office*　　　*study harder*

1.　A:　I want to mail a package.

　　B:　*You should go to the post office.*

2. A: I'm sleepy.

   B: _____

3. A: I need to cash a check.

   B: _____

4. A: I have a toothache.

   B: _____

5. A: I'm flunking all of my courses at school.

   B: _____

6. A: The plumbing in my apartment doesn't work.

   B: _____

7. A: I need to renew my visa.

   B: _____

8. A: My shoes have holes in the bottom.

   B: _____

■ 練習 2：用 should 或 shouldn't 完成下列句子。

1. Students _____*should*_____ come to class every day.

2. Students _____*shouldn't*_____ cut class.

3. We _____ waste our money on things we don't need.

4. It's raining. You _____ take your umbrella when you leave.

5. Jimmy, you _____ pull the cat's tail!

6. People _____ be cruel to animals.

7. Your plane leaves at 8:00. You _____ get to the airport by 7:00.

8. Life is short. We _____ waste it.

9. You _____ smoke in a public place because the smoke bothers other people.

10. We _____ cross a street at an intersection. We

_____ jaywalk.

11. When you go to New York City, you _____ see a play on Broadway.

12. You _____ walk alone on city streets after midnight. It's dangerous.

13. When you go to Bangkok, you _____ visit the Floating Market.

14. When you go to a football game, you _____ throw things on the field.

■ 練習 3 — 口語練習：四人一組，輪流用 should 和 shouldn't 提供建議。

   1. 學生A： English is not my native language. What advice can you give me about good ways to learn English?
   2. 學生B： I am a teenager. What advice can you give me about being a good person and living a happy life?
   3. 學生AC： I am a newcomer. What advice can you give me about going to this school and living in this city?
   4. 學生D： I have a job interview tomorrow. What advice can you give me about going to a job interview?

■ 練習 4 — 書寫練習：用一張紙，參考以下問題，寫一篇描寫自己故鄉的作文。

I'm a tourist. I'm going to visit your hometown. Is your hometown a good place for a tourist to visit? Why? What should I do when I'm there? Where should I go? What should I see? What shouldn't I do? Are there places I shouldn't visit? Will I enjoy my visit? Write a composition in which you tell me (a tourist) about your hometown.

(a)	Bob: What should we do tonight? Ann: ***Let's go to a movie***. Bob: Okay.	*Let's (do something)* = 我提議你、我一起做某事。 *(let's = let us)* (a) 中： *Let's go to a movie.* = 我認爲我們該去看場電影。你想去嗎？
(b)	Sue: I'm tired. Don: I'm tired, too. ***Let's take a break***. Sue: That's a good idea!	

■ **練習 5**：用 let's 加框內或自己的語詞完成下列對話。

> eat　　　　　　　　　　go to a seafood restaurant
> get a cup of coffee　　 go to the zoo
> go dancing　　　　　 ✔ leave at six-thirty
> go to Florida　　　　　walk
> go to a movie

1. A: What time should we leave for the airport?

   B: _____*Let's leave at six-thirty.*_____
   A: Okay.

2. A: Where should we go for our vacation?

   B: _____
   A: That's a good idea.

3. A: Where do you want to go for dinner tonight?

   B: _____

4. A: The weather is beautiful today. _____
   B: Okay. Great!

5. A: I'm bored. _____
   B: I can't. I have to study.

6. A: Should we take the bus downtown or walk downtown?

   B: It's a nice day. _____

7. A: Dinner's ready! The food's on the table!

   B: Great! _____ I'm starving!

8. A: Where should we go Saturday night?

   B: _____

   A: Good idea!

9. A: We have an hour between classes. _____
   B: Okay. That sounds like a good idea.

■ **練習 6 — 口語練習**：兩人一組，用 let's 做練習。
   學生A：書本打開，唸出書中的句子。
   學生B：書本闔上，用 let's 提出建議。
   學生C：附和學生 B 的建議

   例：   It's a beautiful day today. What should we do?
   學生A：It's a beautiful day today. What should we do?
   學生B：Let's go to Woodland Park Zoo.
   學生A：Great! What a good idea! Let's go!

1. What time should we go out to dinner tonight?
2. When should we go to（某處）?
3. What should we do this evening?
4. I want to do something fun tomorrow.

角色互換

5. What should we do tomorrow? It's a holiday, and we don't have to go to class.
6. I'm bored. Think of something we can do.
7. My plane leaves at six. What time should we leave for the airport?
8. It's（某同學）'s birthday tomorrow. Should we do something special for him/her?

10-3　HAVE + 不定詞 (HAS TO / HAVE TO) 的用法

(a) People **need to eat** food. (b) People **have to eat** food. (c) Jack **needs to study** for his test. (d) Jack **has to study** for his test.	(a) 句和 (b) 句同義。 (c) 句和 (d) 句同義。 *have* + 不定詞表示必須 *(need)* 之意。
(e) I **had to study** last night.	過去形式：*had* + 不定詞
(f) **Do** you **have to** leave now? (g) What time **does** Jim **have to** leave? (h) Why **did** they **have to** leave yesterday?	疑問句形式：*have to* 的疑問句，要用 *do, does* 或 *did* 表示。
(i) I **don't have to** study tonight. (j) The concert was free. We **didn't have to** buy tickets.	否定形式：*have to* 的否定句，要用 *do, does* 或 *did* 表示。

1. What do you want to do today?
2. What do you have to do today?
3. What do you want to do tomorrow?
4. What do you have to do tomorrow?
5. What does a student need to do or have to do?
6. Who has to go shopping? Why?
7. Who has to go to the post office? Why?
8. Who has to go to the bank? Why?
9. Where do you have to go today? Why?
10. Where do you want to go tomorrow? Why?
11. What did you have to do yesterday? Why?
12. Did you have responsibilities at home when you were a child? What did you have to do?
11. If you're driving a car and the traffic light turns red, what do you have to do?
12. What do you have to do before you cross a busy street?
13. Do you have to learn English? Why?
14. Who has a job? What are some of the things you have to do when you're at work?
15. What kind of job did you have in the past? What did you have to do when you had that job?

■ 練習 **8** — 口語練習（閤上書本）：用 have to / has to 及 because 造句。

例：　go downtown / buy some new shoes
學生A：I have to go downtown because I have to buy some new shoes.
教　師：Why does (學生A) have to go downtown?
學生B：(學生A) has to go downtown because he / she has to buy some new shoes.

1. go to the drugstore / buy some toothpaste
2. go to the grocery store / get some milk
3. go shopping / get a new coat
4. go to the post office / mail a package
5. stay home tonight / study grammar
6. go to the hospital / visit a friend
7. go to the bank / cash a check
8. go downtown / go to the immigration office
9. go to the bookstore / buy a notebook
10. go to（某商店）/ buy（店內某物品）

1. A: Jack can't join us for dinner tonight.
   B: Why not?

   A: *(he, work)* ___*He has to work*___ .

   B: *(he, work)* ___*Does he have to work*___ tomorrow night too? If he doesn't, maybe we should postpone the dinner until then.

2. A: Why *(you, go)* _____ to the library later tonight?

   B: *(I, find)* _____ some information for my research paper.

3. A: It's almost four-thirty. What time *(Sue, leave for)* _____ the airport?

   B: Around five. *(she, be)* _____ at the airport at six-fifteen.

4. A: Why did you go to the bookstore after class yesterday?

   B: *(I, buy)* _____ some colored pencils.

   A: Oh? Why *(you, buy)* _____ colored pencils?
   B: I need them for some drawings I plan to do for my botany class.

5. A: *(I, go)* _____ to the store.
   B: Why?

   A: Because *(I, get)* _____ some rice and fresh fruit.

6. A: Kate didn't come to the movie with us last night.
   B: Why?

   A: Because *(she, study)* _____ for a test.

7. A: What time *(you, be)* _____ at the dentist's office?
   B: Three. I have a three o'clock appointment.

8. A: *(Tom, find)* _____ a new apartment?
   B: Yes, he does. He can't stay in his present apartment.

9. A: *(Yoko, not, take)* _____ another English course. Her English is very good.

   B: *(you, take)* _____ another English course?
   A: Yes, I do. I need to study more English.

10. A: Was Steve at home yesterday evening?

B: No. *(he, stay)* _____ late at the office.

B: Why?

A: *(he, finish)* _____ a report for his boss.

10-4 MUST 的用法

(a) People need food. People **have to eat** food. (b) People need food. People **must eat** food.	(a) 句和 (b) 句同義： *must eat = have to eat*
(c) $\left.\begin{array}{l}I\\You\\She\\He\\It\\We\\They\end{array}\right\}$ **must work**.	*must* 後面要接原形動詞。 誤：*He must works.* 誤：*He must to work.*
(d) You **must not be** late for work if you want to keep your job.	**must not** = 不可這麼做！沒有選擇的餘地。
(e) You **don't have to go** to the movie with us if you don't want to.	**don't have to** = 沒必要，但有選擇的餘地。

比較下列例句。注意 **should** 和 **must** 之間的不同。

MUST 表示非常重要且必須做的事，沒有選擇的餘地。	**SHOULD** 表示某事是個好主意，但有選擇的餘地。
(f) I **must study** tonight. I'm going to take a very important test tomorrow.	(g) I **should study** tonight. I have some homework to do, but I'm tired. I'll study tomorrow night. I'm going to go to bed now.
(h) You **must take** an English course. You cannot graduate without it.	(i) You **should take** an English course. It will help you.
(j) Johnny, this is your mother speaking. You **must eat** your vegetables. You can't leave the table until you eat your vegetables.	(k) Johnny, you **should eat** your vegetables. They're good for you. You'll grow up to be

close the door behind you	*pay an income tax*
go to medical school	*read English newspapers and magazines*
✔ *have a driver's license*	*speak English outside of class every day*
have a library card	*stop*
have a passport	*study harder*
listen to English on the radio and TV	*talk to myself in English*
make new friends who speak English	*take one pill every six hours*

1. According to the law,★ a driver _____ *must have a driver's license.* _____

2. If a traffic light is red, a car _____

3. If you want to check a book out of the library, you _____

   _____

4. Nancy has a job in Chicago. She earns a good salary. According to the law, she

   _____

5. I failed the last two tests in my biology class. According to my professor, I

   _____

6. I want to travel abroad. According to the law, I _____

   _____

7. If you want to become a doctor, you _____

8. John's doctor gave him a prescription. According to

   the directions on the bottle, John _____

   _____

9. Jimmy ! It's cold outside. When you come inside, you

   _____

MIDTOWN PHARMACY
305 MAIN ST.
321-5277
No. 94122-38
Dr. Hansen
Take one tablet
every six hours.
John Smith
Penicillin 500 mg.

10. I want to improve my English. According to my teacher, I _____

   _____

_____

★*according to the law* = 法律規定。

1. When must you have a passport?
2. If you live in an apartment, what is one thing you must do and one thing you must not do?
3. Name one thing a driver must do and one thing a driver must not do.
4. If you are on an airplane, what is one thing you must do and one thing you must not do?
5. Name something you must have a ticket for. Name something you don't have to have a ticket for.

■ 練習 12：選擇正確答案。

1. If you want to keep your job, you _____ be late for work. It is necessary for you to be on time.
   A. must not   B. don't have to   C. doesn't have to

2. My office is close enough to my apartment for me to walk to work. I _____ take a bus. I only take a bus in bad weather.
   A. must not   B. don't have to   C. doesn't have to

3. Some schools require schoolchildren to wear uniforms to school, but my children's school doesn't require uniforms. My children _____ wear uniforms to school.
   A. must not   B. don't have to   C. doesn't have to

4. Jimmy, it is very important to be careful with matches! You _____ play with matches.
   A. must not   B. don't have to   C. doesn't have to

5. Jack is twenty-four, but he still lives with his parents. That saves him a lot of money.

   For example, he _____ pay rent or buy his own food.
       A. must not   B. don't have to   C. doesn't have to

6. The water in that river is badly polluted. You _____ drink it.
       A. must not   B. don't have to   C. doesn't have to _____

7. If you have a credit card, you _____ pay for a purchase in cash. You can charge it.
       A. must not   B. don't have to   C. doesn't have to

8. When an airplane is taking off, you have to be in your seat with your seat belt on.

   You _____ stand up and walk around when an airplane is taking off.
       A. must not   B. don't have to   C. doesn't have to

10-5　語態助動詞

(a)	Anita	*can* *couldn't* *may* *might* *must* *should* *will*	go to class.

語態助動詞是助動詞的一種，後面接主要動詞的原形。以下助動詞稱為語態助動詞 (*modal auxiliaries*): *can, could, may, might, must, should, will, would*。
它們後面要接原形動詞（不加 *to*）

(b)	Anita	*is able to* *is going to* *has to*	go to class.

和語態助動詞相似的用語有：*be able to, be going to, have to*。

■ **練習 13**：在必要的空格內填上 to，如不須要，就寫 "X"。

1. My sister can _____X_____ play the guitar very well.

2. We have _____to_____ pay our rent on the first of the month.

3. Could you please _____ open the window? Thanks.

4. I wasn't able _____ visit my friends yesterday because I was busy.

5. You shouldn't _____ drink twenty cups of coffee a day.

6. Will you _____ be at the meeting tomorrow?

7. Does everyone have _____ be at the meeting?

8. You must not _____ miss the meeting. It's important.

9. Jennifer might not _____ be there tomorrow.

10. May I _____ use your telephone?

11. We couldn't _____ go to the concert last night because we didn't have tickets.

12. Can you _____ play a musical instrument?

13. What time are you going _____ arrive?

14. It may _____ be too cold for us to go swimming tomorrow.

10-6 摘要整理表：語態助動詞和相似用語

語態助動詞★	意義	例句
(A) *can*	表示能力	I *can* sing.
	禮貌性問句	*Can* you please help me?
(b) *could*	表示過去的能力	I *couldn't* go to class yesterday.
	禮貌性問句	*Could* you please help me?
(c) *may*	表示可能性	It *may* rain tomorrow.
	禮貌性問句	*May* I help you?
(d) *might*	表示可能性	It *might* rain tomorrow.
(e) *must*	表示必要性	You *must* have a passport.
(f) *should*	表示建議	You *should* see a doctor.
(g) *will*	表示未來將發生之事	My sister *will* meet us at the airport.
(h) *would*	禮貌性問句	*Would* you please open the door?
(i) *be able to*	表示能力	I *wasn't able to* attend the meeting.
(j) *be going to*	表示未來將發生之事	Tina *is going to* meet us at the airport.
(k) *has / have to*	表示必要性	I *have to* study tonight.
(l) *had to*	表示過去的必要性	I *had to* study last night too.

★相關資料請參閱以下表格：can 見表 7-1 和 7-2；could 見表 7-4；may 和 might 見表 6-10；must 見表 10-4；should 見表 10-1；will，見表 6-5, 6-6 和 6-10；would 見表 7-14；be able to 見表 7-12；be going to 見表 6-1；has / have / had to 見表 10-3。

例：Name something you *had to* do yesterday.
學生A：I had to go to class.
學生B：I had to go to the post office to buy some stamps.
學生C：I had to study for a test.
學生D：依此類推。

1. Name something you *can* do.
2. Name something you *couldn't* do yesterday.
3. Name something you *may* do tomorrow,
4. Name something you *might* do tomorrow.
5. Name something you *must* do this week.
6. Name something you *have to* do today.
7. Name something you *don't have to* do today.
8. Name something you *should* do this evening.
9. Name something you *will* do this evening.
10. Name something you *are going to* do this week.
11. Name something you *weren't able to* do when you were a child.
12. Name something you *had to* do when you were a child.
13. You want to borrow something from a classmate. Ask a polite question with **could**.
14. You want a classmate to do something for you. Ask a polite question with **would**.
15. A classmate has something that you want. Ask a polite question with **may**.
16. Name something that *may* happen in the world in the next ten years.
17. Name something that (probably) *won't* happen in the world in the next ten years.
18. Name some things that this school *should* do or *shouldn't* do to make the school a better place for students.

■ 練習 **15** — 錯誤分析：找出下列句子的錯誤並作更正。

1. Would you please to help me?

2. I will can go to the meeting tomorrow.

3. Ken should writes us a letter.

4. I have to went to the store yesterday.

5. Susie! You must not to play with matches!

6. May you please hand me that book?

7. Ann couldn't answered my question.

8. Shelley can't goes to the concert tomorrow.

9. Let's to go to a movie tonight.

■ **練習 26 — 動詞的複習**：選擇正確答案。

1. Tom _____ every day.
   A. shaves   B. is shaving   C. has to shaves

2. _____ go to class every day?
   A. Are you   B. Do you have   C. Do you

3. Yoko _____ to be here tomorrow.
   A. will   B. may   C. is going

4. Jack _____ be in class yesterday.
   A. didn't   B. can't   C. couldn't

5. Fatima _____ to her sister on the phone yesterday.
   A. spoke   B. can speak   C. speaks

6. I _____ my rent last month.
   A. might pay   B. will pay   C. paid

7. Shh. Ken _____ on the phone right now.
   A. talks   B. can talk   C. is talking

8. I want to go to a movie tonight, but I _____ home and study.
   A. should stay   B. stayed   C. stay

9. We _____ to the zoo tomorrow.
   A. will going   B. might go   C. will can go

10. I _____ in class right now.
    A. sit   B. am sitting   C. sitting

現在進行式（表示此刻） （a） It's 10:00 now. Boris *is sitting* in class.	現在進行式描述說話當時正在進行的活動。參閱表 3-1。 (a) 中：現在是 10：00。Boris 十點前開始坐下來，而且十點時還坐著。
過去進行式（表示昨天正在進行） （b） It was 10:00. Boris *was sitting* in class.	過去進行式描述過去某一特定時間正在進行的活動。 (b) 中：Boris 昨天十點前開始坐下來；十點時，坐在教室的動作還在進行。

現在進行式句型： **am, is, are + -ing**
（c） It's 10:00.   I   *am sitting*   in class.
                Boris *is sitting*   in class.
                We   *are sitting*   in class.
	現在進行式和過去進行式的句型都含有 *be* 動詞 + -ing。
	現在進行式用 *be* 動詞的現在式：
	am, is 和 *are* + -ing。

過去進行式句型： **was, were + -ing** （d） It was 10:00. Boris *was sitting* in class. We *were sitting* in class.	過去進行式用 *be* 動詞的過去式：*was* 和 *were* + -ing。

Boris *is sitting* in class right now at ten o'clock.

Boris *was sitting* in class yesterday at ten o'clock.

1. I _____ *am sitting* _____ in class right now.

2. I _____ *was sitting* _____ in class yesterday too.

3. You _____ in class right now.

4. You _____ in class yesterday too.

5. Tony _____ in class right now.

6. He _____ in class yesterday too.

7. We _____ in class today.

8. We _____ in class yesterday too.

9. Rita _____ in class now.

10. She _____ in class yesterday too.

11. Rita and Tony _____ in class today.

12. They _____ in class yesterday too.

■ 練習 18：用括弧內的提示完成下列句子。

1. Paul started to eat dinner at 7:00. At 7:05, Mary came. Paul *(eat)* _____

_____ when Mary *(come)* _____ at 7:05.

2. Bobby was at home yesterday evening. His favorite program was on television last

night. It started at 8:00. It ended at 9:00. At 8:30, his friend Kristin called. When

Kristin *(call)* _____ at 8:30, Bobby *(watch)* _____

_____ TV.

3. Rosa played her guitar for an hour yesterday morning. She started to play her guitar

at 9:30. She stopped at 10:30. Mike arrived at her apartment at 10:00. At 10:00,

Rosa *(play)* _____ her guitar.

Mr. and Mrs. Gold invited several friends to their house for the weekend. A thief stole Mrs. Gold's jewelry at midnight on Saturday. What were the guests doing at midnight?

10-8 WHILE 和過去進行式的用法

(a) The phone rang **while** *I was sleeping.* 或： (b) **While** *I was sleeping*, the phone rang.	*while* + 主詞 + 動詞 = 時間子句 *While I was sleeping* 是一個時間子句。 *while* -子句用來描述當另一個活動發生的同時，正在進行的活動。 *while* -子句裡的動詞經常用過去進行式（例如： *was sleeping* ）。

■ **練習 20 — 口語練習**：用 while 連結下列句子。

1. I was studying last night.
   Rita called.
   → *While I was studying last night, Rita called.*
   → *Rita called while I was studying last night.*

2. Someone knocked on my apartment door.
   I was eating breakfast yesterday morning.

3. I was cooking dinner yesterday evening.
   I burned my hand.

4. I was studying last night.
   A mouse suddenly appeared on
   my desk.

5. Yoko raised her hand.
   The teacher was talking.

6. A tree fell on my car.
   I was driving home yesterday.

10-9 過去時間子句中 WHILE 和 WHEN 的比較

(a) The mouse appeared *while* **I was studying**. 或： (b) *While* **I was studying**, the mouse appeared. (c) *When the mouse* **appeared**, I was studying. 或： (d) I was studying *when the mouse* **appeared**.	*while*-子句裡的動詞經常用過去進行式，如 (a) 和 (b) 。 *when*-子句裡的動詞經常用過去簡單式，如 (c) 和 (d) 。

■ **練習 21**：完成下列句子。while-子句用過去進行式，when-子句用過去簡單式。

1. While I *(wash)* _____ **was washing** _____ dishes last night, I *(get)*

   _____ **got** _____ a phone call from my best friend.

2. When my best friend *(call)* _____ last night, I *(wash)*

   _____ dishes.

3. My friend Jessica *(come)* _____ while I *(eat)*

   _____ dinner last night.

4. I *(eat)* _____ dinner when my friend Jessica *(come)*

   _____ last night.

5. Jason *(wear)* _____ a suit and tie when I *(see)*

   _____ him yesterday.

6. My roommate came home late last night. I *(sleep)* _____

   when she *(get)* _____ home.

7. When Gina *(call)* _____ last night, I *(take)*

   _____ a bubble bath.

8. While I *(watch)* _____ TV last night and *(relax)*

   _____ after a long day, my new puppy *(take)*

   _____ my wallet from my bedside table.

學生A：做出動作，然後用現在進行式描述正在做的動作，並繼續做此動作。
學生B：做出動作，然後停止不做。
學生A：學生 B 停止後，你也停止動作。

例： A: erase the board
　　 B: open the door

教　師：（學生 A），what are you doing?
學生A：I'm erasing the board right now.
教　師：（學生 B），would you please open the door?
學生B：（學生 B 打開門。）
教　師：Thank you. You may both sit down again. （學生 C），will you please describe the two actions we saw?
學生C：While （學生 A） was erasing the board, （學生 B） opened the door. 或：
　　　 （學生A） was erasing the board when （學生 B） opened the door.

1. A: Write on the board.
   B: Drop a book on the floor.
2. A: Walk around the room.
   B: Say hello to (Student A).
3. A: Look out the window.
   B: Take (Student A)'s grammar book.
4. A: Draw a picture on the board.
   B: Ask (Student A) a question.

10-10　過去簡單式和過去進行式的比較

(a) Jane **called** me yesterday. (b) I **talked** to Jane for an hour last night. (c) We **went** to Jack's house last Friday. (d) What time **did** you **get up** this morning?	過去簡單式描述過去某一特定時間（例如：*yesterday, last night*）發生且結束的活動或情況。
(e) I **was studying** when Jane called me yesterday. (f) While I **was studying** last night, Jane called.	過去進行式描述當另一個動作發生時，正在進行的活動。 (e) 和 (f) 中：Jane 打電話來時，讀書的動作正在進行中。
(g) I **opened** my umbrella when it **began** to rain.	*when*- 子句和主要子句都是過去簡單式時，表示 *when*-子句的動作發生在前，主要子句的動作發生在後。 (g) 中：先下雨，然後我打開傘。
比較 (h) When the phone **rang**, I **answered** it. (i) When the phone **rang**, I **was studying**.	(h) 中：電話先響，然後我才接聽。 (i) 中：讀書的動作在進行中，然後電話響了。

1. I *(have)* _____ a busy day yesterday. I *(go)* _____ to class in the morning. I *(eat)* _____ lunch with my brother after class. In the afternoon, I *(drive)* _____ to the airport to pick up my cousin. I *(take)* _____ her to a restaurant for dinner. After dinner, we *(go)* _____ back to my apartment and *(watch)* _____ a movie on TV. After the movie, we *(talk)* _____ for a couple of hours before we *(go)* _____ to bed.

2. While I *(walk)* _____ to class yesterday morning, I *(see)* _____ Abdullah. We *(say)* _____ hello and *(walk)* _____ the rest of the way to school together.

3. I *(eat)* _____ lunch with my brother when I suddenly *(remember)* _____ my promise to pick my cousin up at the airport.

4. While I *(drive)* _____ to the airport, I *(see)* _____ an accident.

5. While my cousin and I *(have)* _____ dinner at the restaurant last night, we *(see)* _____ a friend of mine. I *(introduce)* _____ her to my cousin.

6. When I *(hear)* _____ a knock at the door last night, I *(walk)* _____ to the door and *(open)* _____ it.

7. When I *(open)* _____ the door, I *(see)* _____ my brother. I *(greet)* _____ him and *(ask)* _____ him to come in.

8. My cousin and I *(watch)* _____ a movie on TV last night when my brother *(come)* _____. He *(watch)* _____ the end of the movie with us.

1. Mrs. Reed *(turn)* _____ on the radio in her car while she *(drive)*

   _____ home yesterday. She *(listen)* _____

   to some music when she suddenly *(hear)* _____ a siren.

When she *(look)* _____ in her rearview mirror, she *(see)* _____

an ambulance behind her. She immediately *(pull)* _____ her car

to the side of the road and *(wait)* _____ for the ambulance to pass.

2. I *(have)* _____ a strange experience yesterday. I *(read)*

   _____ my book on the bus when a man *(sit)*

   _____ down next to me and *(hand)* _____ me

   some money. I *(want, not)* _____ his money. I *(be)*

   _____ very confused. I *(stand)* _____ up and

   (walk) _____ toward the door of the bus. While I *(wait)*

   _____ for the door to open, the man *(offer)*

   _____ me some money again. When the door *(open)*

   _____, I *(get)* _____ off the bus quickly. I still

   don't know why he was trying to give me money.

3. A: I *(be)* _____ at my friends' house last night. While we *(eat)*

_____ dinner, their cat *(jump)* _____

on the table. My friends *(seem, not)* _____

_____ to care, but I lost my appetite.

B: What *(you, say)* _____?
A: Nothing.

B: Why *(you, ask, not)* _____ your friends to get their cat off the table?

A: I *(want, not)* _____ to be impolite.
B: I think your friends were impolite to let their cat sit on the table during dinner.

■ 練習 25 — 複習：選擇正確的答案。

1. I was watching TV. I heard a knock on the door. When I heard the knock on the

door, I _____ it.
    A. open   C. opened
    B. am opening   D. was opening

2. "When _____ you talk to Jane?"
"Yesterday."
    A. do   B. should   C. did   D. were

3. I _____ TV when Gina called last night. We talked for an hour.
    A. watch   C. was watching
    B. watched   D. am watching

4. Mike is in his bedroom right now. He _____, so we need to be quiet.
   - A. is sleeping
   - B. sleeps
   - C. slept
   - D. was sleeping

5. Kate _____ tell us the truth yesterday. She lied to us.
   - A. don't
   - B. doesn't
   - C. didn't
   - D. wasn't

6. I saw a fish while I _____ in the ocean yesterday.
   - A. swim
   - B. was swimming
   - C. were swimming
   - D. was swimming

7. When I heard the phone ring, I _____ it.
   - A. answer
   - B. am answering
   - C. answered
   - D. was answering

8. "_____ you go to concerts often?"
   "Yes. I go at least once a month."
   - A. Do
   - B. Did
   - C. Was
   - D. Were

9. While I _____ dinner last night, I burned my finger.
   - A. cooking
   - B. cook
   - C. was cooking
   - D. was cook

10. "Where _____ after work yesterday?"
   - A. you went
   - B. you did go
   - C. did you went
   - D. did you go

10-11 HAVE BEEN（現在完成式）的用法

狀況：我於二月一日來到本市，現在是四月一日， 　　　我仍在此地。 （a）I **have been** here **since** *February 1st*. （b）I **have been** here **for** *two months*. 狀況：Kim一月一日來到本市，現在是四月一日， 　　　Kim還在此地。 （c）Kim **has been** here **since** *January*. （d）Kim **has been** here **for** *three months*.	*have been* 表示某狀況發生於過去，而現在仍然存在。*have been* 和 *since* 或 *for* 連用，表示狀況存在的時間長度。(a) 句和 (b) 句同義。 第三人稱單數形式 = *has been*，如 (c) 和 (d)。
狀況：我 9 點到達教室，現在是 9 點半了， 　　　我還在教室內。 （e）I *have been* here **since nine o'clock**. （f）I *have been* here **for 30 minutes**. 狀況：Ann 住在另一個城市，她星期一早上來拜訪 　　　我，現在是星期五早上，她還在這裡。 （g）Ann *has been* here **since Monday**. （h）Ann *has been* here **for four days**.	*since* 後面接特定時間： 　　　*since February*（特定月份） 　　　*since nine o'clock*（特定鐘點） 　　　*since 1995*（特定年份） *for* 後面接時間長度： 　　　*for two months*（月數） 　　　*for 30 minutes*（鐘表時間長度） 　　　*for four days*（天數） 　　　*for three years*（年數）

1. I came to this city six months ago. I am still here. I have been in this city

   _____*for*_____ six months.

2. Kim has been in this city ____*since*____ January.

3. It's now two o'clock. Carmen has been in class _____ one o'clock.

4. Carmen has been in class _____ an hour.

5. Erica has been a teacher _____ 1994.

6. Mr. Gow has been a plumber _____ 20 years.

7. My parents are visiting me this week. They have been here _____ five days.

8. They have been here _____ last Saturday.

9. India has been an independent nation _____ 1947.

10. I have been awake _____ six o'clock this morning.

11. My friend is very ill. She has been in the hospital _____ four days.

12. I hope the weather gets warmer soon. It's been cold and rainy _____ two weeks.

■ 練習 **27**：用自己的語詞完成下列句子。

例：

a. Today is ____*Monday, March 4*____.

b. I came to this city ____*in January* 或：*two months ago*____.

c. I have been in this city since ____*January*____.

d. I have been in this city for ____*two months*____.

例：

a. Today is ____*Monday, March 4*____.

b. I came to this city ____*on Friday, March 1* 或：*three days ago*____.

c. I have been in this city since ____*Friday* 或：*March 1*____.

d. I have been in this city for ____*three days*____.

1. a. Today is _____.

   b. I came to this city _____.

   c. I have been in this city since _____.

   d. I have been in this city for _____.

2. a. Today is _____.

   b. _____(同學名)_____ came to this city _____.

   c. _____ has been in this city since _____.

   d. _____ has been in this city for _____.

3. a. I am in the classroom. The time right now is _____.

   b. The time I entered the classroom today was _____.

   c. I have been in this room since _____.

   d. I have been in this room for _____.

4. a. Our teacher taught her / his first class in her / his life _____.

   b. She / He has been a teacher since _____.

   c. She / He has been a teacher for _____.

5. a. I started to go to school in (year) _____. I am still a student.

   b. I have been a student since _____.

   c. I have been a student for _____.

10-12 SINCE-子句的用法

(a)	主詞 動詞	since 後面可接主詞和動詞。(a) 中：since I was a child = 一個since-子句。★
	I've been afraid of dogs **since I was a child.**	
	主要子句　　　　　　since-子句	注意例句：主要子句的動詞是現在完成式，since-子句的動詞是過去簡單式。

(b) Mr. Lo has been a teacher **since** *he graduated from college.*

(c) Sue and I have been friends **since** *we were children.*

★*since*-子句是時間子句。有關時間子句的資料，請參閱表 5-18 和 5-19。

1. Maria got some bad news last week. She *(be)* ___*has been*___ sad since she *(get)* ___*got*___ the bad news.

2. I started school when I was five years old. I *(be)* _____ in school since I *(be)* _____ five years old.

3. Ann's brother arrived a few days ago to visit her. She loves her brother and is happy to be with him. She *(be)* _____ happy since her brother *(come)* _____.

4. Jack moved to Hong Kong after he graduated from the university. Jim *(be)* _____ in Hong Kong since he *(graduate)* _____ from the university.

5. The weather was hot and dry for many weeks. Two days ago it rained. The weather *(be)* _____ cool and wet since it *(rain)* _____ two days ago.

6. Jack broke his leg five days ago. He's in the hospital. He *(be)* _____ in the hospital since he *(break)* _____ his leg.

原形	過去簡單式	過去分詞	現在完成式的形式：

原形	過去簡單式	過去分詞
be	*was, were*	**been**
know	*knew*	**known**
have	*had*	**had**
see	*saw*	**seen**
live	*lived*	**lived**
own	*owned*	**owned**
work	*worked*	**worked**
touch	*touched*	**touched**

現在完成式的形式：
　　have / *has* + 過去分詞
不規則動詞有不規則的過去分詞。（其他的不規則動詞見表 10-18 和附錄 5。）

規則動詞的過去分詞和過去簡單式相同：
　　動詞 + *-ed*

(a) I **have known** Tom for five years.
(b) Sue **has had** a bad cold for three days.
(c) They **have lived** here since 1994.
(d) We **have owned** our own home since 1989.

注意例句：
現在完成式的結構為
have / *has* + 過去分詞

(e) I've
　　We've
　　You've
　　They've ⎬ been here for two months.
　　She's
　　He's
　　It's

如例句所示，*have* 和 *has* 可以和主格代名詞縮寫。

比較
(f) **She's** been here for two months.
(g) **She's** in my class.

(f) 中： *she's = she has*
(g) 中： *she's = she is*

■ **練習 29**：用提示的動詞及現在完成式完成下列句子。

1. *teach*　　Mr. Jackson is a teacher.　He **'s taught**＿＿＿＿ biology for twenty years.

2. *know*　　I ＿＿＿＿＿＿＿＿＿＿ Mary Adams since I was a child.

3. *be*　　She ＿＿＿＿＿＿＿＿＿ a good friend for a long time.

4. *live*　　My parents live in a suburb of Mexico City.　They ＿＿＿＿＿＿＿

＿＿＿＿＿＿ in the same apartment for twenty-five years.

5. *have*　　Janet and Sam ＿＿＿＿＿＿＿＿＿ their dog Fido for three years.

6. *work*　　My uncle ＿＿＿＿＿＿＿＿＿ at the automobile factory for

seventeen years.

7. *be*　　We ＿＿＿＿＿＿＿＿＿ in class since nine o'clock this morning.

8. *own*   Ken is a businessman. He sells car parts. He _____ his own business since 1994.

9. *have*   Mr. Cook's hair started to turn gray when he was forty. He _____

_____ gray hair since he was forty years old.

10. *see*   I _____ several movies since I came to this city.

■ 練習 30 — 口語練習：用提示的動詞以現在完成式完成下列句子。

例：   know   I . . . （某人）for . . . .
→ *I've known Li Ming for three months.*
→ *My best friend is Maria Alvarez. I've known her for fifteen years.*

1. *be*   I . . . in this classroom today since . . . .
2. *live*   Right now I am living（公寓、宿舍等）. I . . . there since . . . .
3. *have*   I have （某擁有物）. I . . . it / them for . . . .
4. *be*   I . . . in （某處）since . . . .
5. *know*   I . . . （某同學）since . . . .
6. *work*   （某位熟人) works at （某處）. He / She . . .
            there for . . . .
7. *be*   I . . . awake since . . . .
8. *teach*   Our teacher . . . English since . . . .
9. *live*   My （某位家人）. . . （某處）for . . . .
10. *be*   I . . . afraid of . . . since . . . .

10-14 NEVER 和現在完成式的用法

（a） *I've **never** touched an elephant.* （b） Anna *has **never** seen* the Pacific Ocean.	*never* 經常用於現在完成式。 (a) 中：說者意指，「從出生到現在，我從未摸過象。」

■ 練習 31 — 口語練習：練習使用 never 以及現在完成式。

例：   Name some places you have never lived.
學生A：I've never lived in a small town.
學生B：I've never lived in a dormitory.
學生C：I've never lived in South America.
學生D：依此類推。

1. countries you've never been in
2. cities you've never lived in
3. pets you've never had
4. animals you've never touched
5. things you've never seen
6. things you've never owned

(a)　**Have** you **lived** here for a long time? (b)　**Has** Ken **been** in this class since the beginning of the term?	現在完成式的疑問句形式： 　　*have / has* ＋ 主詞 ＋ 過去分詞
(c)　I **have not (haven't) lived** here for a long time. (d)　Ken **has not (hasn't) been** in the class since the beginning of the term.	現在完成式的否定式： 　　*have / has* ＋ *not* ＋ 過去分詞 否定式的縮寫： 　　*have not = haven't* 　　*has not = hasn't*

■ **練習 32：**用現在完成式完成下列句子。

1. (*Mr. Jackson, teach*) _____Has Mr. Jackson taught_____ biology for a long time?

2. Ms. Smith is a new teacher. She (*teach, not*) _____hasn't taught_____ biology for a long time.

3. (*you, know*) _____ Mary Adams since you were a child?

4. I met Mary Adams only two months ago. I (*know, not*) _____

    _____ her for a long time. I've known her for only a short time.

5. (*she, be*) _____ a good friend of yours for a long time?

6. She (*be, not*) _____ a friend of mine for a long time.

7. (*your parents, live*) _____ near Mexico City for a long time?

8. I came here only a couple of months ago. I (*live, not*) _____ here for a long time.

9. (*Janet and Sam, have*) _____ their dog Fido for a long time?

10. Pedro got his new bicycle a few months ago. He (*have, not*) _____

    _____ his bicycle for a long time.

11. (*your uncle, work*) _____ at the automobile factory for a long time?

12. My aunt has a new job at a candy factory. She (*work, not*) _____ there for a long time.

(a)	*Have* you **ever** *been* in Hawaii?	(a) 中：ever 意為「生平，從出生到現在。」
(b)	*Has* Pedro **ever** *had* a job (in his lifetime)?	和 ever 連用的疑問句經常用現在完成式。

(c)	A: Have you ever been in London? B: Yes, I **have**. (I have been in London.)	現在完成式的 yes / no 問句，簡答用助動詞（have 或 has）。
(d)	A: Has Tom ever lived in Chicago? B: Yes, he **has**. (He has lived in Chicago.)	(c) 中：說者 B 表示他生平某個時間曾到過 London。
(e)	A: Have you ever been in Korea? B: No, I **haven't**. (I haven't ever been in Korea.)	
(f)	A: Has Sue ever lived in Paris? B: No, she **hasn't**. (She hasn't ever lived in Paris.)	

(g)	I **haven't ever been** in Korea.	(g) 句和 (h) 句同義。
(h)	I**'ve never been** in Korea.	*haven't ever been = have never been*
(i)	She **hasn't ever lived** in Paris.	(i) 句和 (j) 句同義。
(j)	She**'s never lived** in Paris.	*hasn't ever lived = has never lived*

■ **練習 33**：用簡答回答下列問題。

1. A: *(you, be, ever)* _____*Have you ever been*_____ in Russia?

   B: No, I _____*haven't*_____. I *(be, never)* *'ve never been*_____ in Russia.

2. A: *(you, be, ever)* _____ in Turkey?

   B: Yes, I _____. I *(be)* _____ in Turkey several times.

3. A: *(you, visit, ever)* _____ the
   Metropolitan Museum of Art in New York City?

   B: No, I _____. I *(visit, never)* _____
   that museum.

4. A: *(Sam, be, ever)* _____ in Argentina?

   B: No, he _____. He *(be, never)* _____
   in Argentina.

5. A: *(Carmen, be, ever)* _____ in Canada?

   B: Yes, she _____. She *(be)* _____ there many times.

6. A: *(you, have, ever)* _____ a serious illness?

   B: No, I _____. I *(have, never)* _____
   a serious illness. I've been very lucky.

7. A: *(your brother, live, ever)* _____
   in an apartment by himself?

   B: No, he _____. He still lives with my parents.

8. A: *(you, talk, ever)* _____ to a famous
   person?

   B: No, I _____. I don't know any famous people.

9. A: *(you, see, ever)* _____

   _____ a hummingbird?

   B: Yes, I _____.

■ 練習 3 — 口語練習（閤上書本）：用簡答回答下列問題。

例： Have you ever been in (Africa)?
學生A： No, I haven't.
學生B： No, I haven't.
學生C： Yes, I have.

1. Have you ever been in (Egypt)? (Italy)?
2. Have you ever been to (Indonesia)? (Venezuela)?★
3. Have you ever been in (Washington, D.C.)? (Tokyo)?
4. Have you ever been to (Toronto)? (Istanbul)?
5. Have you ever had a pet?
6. Have you ever had a bicycle?
7. Have you ever had a（某種車）?
8. Have you ever had a purple umbrella?
9. Have you ever lived in an apartment? a dormitory?
10. Have you ever lived in a one-room apartment?
11. Have you ever lived in（某市、某國）?
12. Have you ever touched an elephant? a snake? a cow?
13. Have you ever called (. . .) on the phone?
14. Have you ever stayed in a hotel in this city?
15. Have you ever watched（某電視節目） on TV?
16. Have you ever been to（某處）?
17. Have you ever seen a whale?

★*Have you ever been **in** Indonesia* 和 *Have you ever been **to** Indonesia* 同義。

10-17 現在完成式：HOW LONG 引導的疑問句

(a) A: *How long **have you been** in this city?* 　　B: For five months. (b) A: *How long **has Ali had** a mustache?* 　　B: Since he was twenty-one years old. (c) A: *How long **have you known** Maria?* 　　B: Since the beginning of the school term.	現在完成式的疑問句形式： 　　*have* + 主詞 + 過去分詞

■ **練習 35**：用括弧內的提示完成下列句子。

1. A: How long *(you, be)* _____*have you been*_____ at this school?
　 B: Since the middle of January.

2. A: How long *(you, know)* _____ Shelley?
　 B: For three years.

3. A: How long *(Mr. Lake, be)* _____ a teacher?
　 B: Since he graduated from college in 1990.

4. A: How long *(you, have)* _____ your car?
　 B: For a couple of years.

5. A: How long *(your roommate, be)* _____
　 out of town?
　 B: Since Friday.

■ **練習 36 — 口語練習**：兩人一組練習。

第一部份：
學生A：用 how long 及現在完成式提出問題。
學生B：回答問題。

例：　　have a mustache
學生A：How long have you had a mustache?
學生B：I've had a mustache since I was seventeen years old.

1. be in （本市 / 本國）
2. be in this class
3. know （同學名）
4. be a student at （本校）
5. be in this room today
6. live at your present address
7. have （學生 B 的擁有物）
8. have （學生 B 其他的擁有物）

第二部份：角色互換
學生A：提出問題。如果答案是 Yes，就用 how long 加現在完成式句型詢問更多的相關資料。
假如答案是 No，就再問其他問題，直到學生 B 答 Yes。
學生B：回答問題。

例： Do you have a pet?
學生A：Do you have a pet?
學生B：Yes, I do.
學生A：What kind of pet do you have?
學生B：A dog.
學生A：How long have you had your dog?
學生B：She's six years old. I've had her since she was a puppy. I've had her for six years.

例： Do you have a pet?
學生A：Do you have a pet?
學生B：No.
學生A：Do your parents have a pet?
學生B：No.
學生A：Does anyone you know have a pet?
學生B：Yes. My brother does.
學生A：What kind of pet does he have?
學生B：A cat.
學生A：How long has he had a cat?
學生B：For five or six years.

9. Do you have a pet? (Do your parents? Does anyone you know have a pet?)

10. Are you a student at （本校名）?

11. Do you live in an apartment? (a dormitory? a house?)

12. Do you have a roommate?

13. Do you have a briefcase or a bookbag? (a wallet? a purse?)

14. Do you know （同學名）?

15. Do you have a car? (a bicycle? a personal computer? a calculator?)

16. Are you married? (Is the teacher married? Is anyone in this class married?)

(a) I *have* never ***touched*** an elephant.	規則動詞的過去分詞是在動詞字尾加 *-ed*。
(b) *Has* Jim ever ***stayed*** at a hotel in Bangkok?	例：*touched, stayed.*
(c) Tom *has* never ***eaten*** Thai food.	不規則動詞有不規則的過去分詞形式。
(d) *Have* you ever ***gone*** to a rock concert?	例：*eaten, gone.*

常用的不規則動詞

原形	過去式	過去分詞
be	*was, were*	*been*
eat	*ate*	*eaten*
go	*went*	*gone*
have	*had*	*had*
know	*knew*	*known*
lose	*lost*	*lost*
meet	*met*	*met*
read	*read★*	*read★*
see	*saw*	*seen*
speak	*spoke*	*spoken*
take	*took*	*taken*
tell	*told*	*told*
wear	*wore*	*worn*
write	*wrote*	*written*

★ 動詞 *read* 的過去式與過去分詞的發音皆與 *red* 紅色的發音相同。

■ **練習 37 — 口語練習（闔上書本）**：說出下列動詞的過去分詞。

例：eat, ate, . . .
答：eaten

1. eat, ate, . . .
2. go, went, . . .
3. have, had, . . .
4. know, knew, . . .
5. lose, lost, . . .
6. meet, met, . . .
7. read, read, . . .
8. see, saw, . . .
9. speak, spoke, . . .
10. take, took, . . .
11. tell, told, . . .
12. wear, wore, . . .
13. write, wrote, . . .

第一部份：

go	✔ *take*
lose	*tell*
meet	*write*

1. I've never _____*taken*_____ a physics class.

2. Have you ever _____ Maria's sister?

3. Have you ever _____ the keys to your apartment?

4. I've never _____ to a rock concert in my whole life.

5. Have you ever _____ a lie?

6. Have you ever _____ a poem?

第二部份：

eat	*see*
know	*speak*
read	*wear*

7. How long have you _____ Abdul? Have you been friends for a long time?

8. I've never _____ the movie *Gone with the Wind*.

9. Have you ever _____ the book *Gone with the Wind?*

10. Ann has never _____ raw meat.

11. Mr. Cook never dresses casually. He has never _____ blue jeans in his life.

12. Have you ever _____ to your teacher on the phone?

■ 練習 39 — 口語練習：兩人一組練習。
學生A：打開書本，用 Have you ever...? 提出問題。
學生B：闔上書本，並用簡答方式回答問題。

例： be in （某國名）
學生A：Have you ever been in Malaysia?
學生B：Yes, I have. 或：No, I haven't.

 1. meet （某人）
 2. go to （某處）
 3. lose the keys to your front door
 4. be in （某建築物）
 5. read （某書名）
 6. wear cowboy boots
 7. speak to （某同學） about （某事）
 8. eat fish eggs
 9. write a letter to （某人）
10. tell （某教師） about （某事）
11. see （某部電影）
12. have （某種食物）

角色互換
13. read （書名）
14. eat （某種食物）
15. write a letter to （某人）
16. see （某電視節目）
17. go to （某處）
18. have （某種食物）
19. be in （本校某處）
20. meet （某人）
21. wear （某種衣物）
22. speak to （某教師） about （某事）
23. lose （學生 B 的某物）
24. tell （某同學） about （某事）

■ 練習 40 — 錯誤分析：找出下列句子的錯誤，並作更正。

 1. Let's going to a restaurant for dinner tonight.

 2. I've never see a whale.

 3. The phone rang while I was eat dinner last night.

 4. How long you have been a student at this school?

5. Ken doesn't has to go to work today.

6. I must to study tonight. I can't going to the movie with you.

7. I have been in this city since two months.

8. Why you have to leave now?

9. You shouldn't to speak loudly in a library.

10. I've known Olga since I am a child.

11. You don't must be late for work.

12. Have you ever went to a baseball game?

13. I am in this class since the beginning of January.

■ **練習 41 — 書寫練習**：寫出在本班上課的經驗。

內容提示：
- 上課的第一天
- 教師
- 同學
- 教室
- 自己的學習經驗
- 教科書
- 本班值得紀念的事

附錄 1
英文字母

A	a		N	n
B	b		O	o
C	c		P	p
D	d		Q	q
E	e		R	r
F	f		S	s
G	g		T	t
H	h		U	u
I	i		V	v
J	j		W	w
K	k		X	x
L	l		Y	y
M	m		Z	z

母音 = *a, e, i, o u*
子音 = *b, c, d, f, g, h, j, k, l, m, n, p, q, r, s, t, v, w, x, y, z*

附錄 2
數詞

1	one	1st	first
2	two	2nd	second
3	three	3rd	third
4	four	4th	fourth
5	five	5th	fifth
6	six	6th	sixth
7	seven	7th	seventh
8	eight	8th	eighth
9	nine	9th	ninth
10	ten	10th	tenth
11	eleven	11th	eleventh
12	twelve	12th	twelfth
13	thirteen	13th	thirteenth
14	fourteen	14th	fourteenth
15	fifteen	15th	fifteenth
16	sixteen	16th	sixteenth
17	seventeen	17th	seventeenth
18	eighteen	18th	eighteenth
19	nineteen	19th	nineteenth
20	twenty	20th	twentieth
21	twenty-one	21th	twenty-first
22	twenty-two	22nd	twenty-second
23	twenty-three	23rd	twenty-third
24	twenty-four	24th	twenty-fourth
25	twenty-five	25th	twenty-fifth
26	twenty-six	26th	twenty-sixth
27	twenty-seven	27th	twenty-seventh
28	twenty-eight	28th	twenty-eighth
29	twenty-nine	29th	twenty-ninth
30	thirty	30th	thirtieth
40	forty	40th	fortieth
50	fifty	50th	fiftieth
60	sixty	60th	sixtieth
70	seventy	70th	seventieth
80	eighty	80th	eightieth
90	ninety	90th	ninetieth
100	one hundred	100th	one hundredth
200	two hundred	200th	two hundredth
1,000	one thousand		
10,000	ten thousand		
100,000	one hundred thousand		
1,000,000	one million		

附錄 3
星期及月份

星期

星期一	Monday	(Mon.)
星期二	Tuesday	(Tues.)
星期三	Wednesday	(Wed.)
星期四	Thursday	(Thurs.)
星期五	Friday	(Fri.)
星期六	Saturday	(Sat.)
星期日	Sunday	(Sun.)

月份

一月	January	(Jan.)
二月	February	(Feb.)
三月	March	(Mar.)
四月	April	(Apr.)
五月	May	(May)
六月	June	(June)
七月	July	(July)
八月	August	(Aug.)
九月	September	(Sept.)
十月	October	(Oct.)
十一月	November	(Nov.)
十二月	December	(Dec.)

用數詞寫日期：

月/日/年
10/31/41 = October 31, 1941（1941年10月31日）
4/15/92 = April 15, 1992（1992年4月15日）

日期的說法：

一般書寫形式	一般口語形式
January 1	January first/the first of January
March 2	March second/the second of March
May 3	May third/the third of May
June 4	June fourth/the fourth of June
August 5	August fifth/the fifth of August
October 10	October tenth/the tenth of October
November 27	November twenty-seventh/the twenty-seventh of November

9:00	It's nine o'clock.
	It's nine.
9:05	It's nine-oh-five.
	It's five (minutes) after nine.
	It's five (minutes) past nine.
9:10	It's nine-ten.
	It's ten (minutes) after nine.
	It's ten (minutes) past nine.
9:15	It's nine-fifteen.
	It's a quarter after nine.
	It's a quarter past nine.
9:30	It's nine-thirty.
	It's half past nine.
9:45	It's nine-forty-five.
	It's a quarter to ten.
	It's a quarter of ten.
9:50	It's nine-fifty.
	It's ten (minutes) to ten.
	It's ten (minutes) of ten.
12:00	It's noon.
	It's midnight.

A.M. = morning（早上）　It's nine A.M.
P.M. = afternoon / evening / night（下午/傍晚/晚上）　It's nine P.M.

附録 5
不規則動詞

原形	過去式	過去分詞	原形	過去式	過去分詞
be	was, were	been	keep	kept	kept
become	became	become	know	knew	known
begin	began	begun	lend	lent	lent
bend	bent	bent	leave	left	left
bite	bit	bitten	lose	lost	lost
blow	blew	blown	make	made	made
break	broke	broken	meet	met	met
bring	brought	brought	pay	paid	paid
build	built	built	put	put	put
buy	bought	bought	read	read	read
catch	caught	caught	ride	rode	ridden
choose	chose	chosen	ring	rang	rung
come	came	come	run	ran	run
cost	cost	cost	say	said	said
cut	cut	cut	see	saw	seen
do	did	done	sell	sold	sold
draw	drew	drawn	send	sent	sent
drink	drank	drunk	shake	shook	shaken
drive	drove	driven	shut	shut	shut
eat	ate	eaten	sing	sang	sung
fall	fell	fallen	sit	sat	sat
feed	fed	fed	sleep	slept	slept
feel	felt	felt	speak	spoke	spoken
fight	fought	fought	spend	spent	spent
find	found	found	stand	stood	stood
fly	flew	flown	steal	stole	stolen
forget	forgot	forgotten	swim	swam	swum
get	got	gotten/got	take	took	taken
give	gave	given	teach	taught	taught
go	went	gone	tear	tore	torn
grow	grew	grown	tell	told	told
hang	hung	hung	think	thought	thought
have	had	had	throw	threw	thrown
hear	heard	heard	understand	understood	understood
hide	hid	hidden	wake up	woke up	woken up
hit	hit	hit	wear	wore	worn
hold	held	held	win	won	won
hurt	hurt	hurt	write	wrote	written

索引

subject (e.g., *I, they*), 6–7, 131, 171–172, 177, 192, 363

Pronunciation:
-*ed*, 180, 186
-*s/-es*, 49, 51, 54

Punctuation:
apostrophe, 7, 352
colon, 72*fn.*
comma, 216, 357, 358*fn.*, 393
full stop, 57*fn.*
period, 21
question mark, 21

Q

Quantity, expressions of, 334, 336–337
Question mark, 21
Question words, 32
how many/how much, 109
what, 32, 67, 206, 212
what time, 66–67, 203
when, 66–67, 203, 219
where, 24, 64, 67, 89, 203
who, 32, 206, 209
who(m), 209
why, 89, 203

Questions:
with *be*, 21, 24, 61, 89, 173
with *be + going to*, 231, 245-246
with *can*, 282
with *could*, 302, 304
with *did*, 194, 209
with *do/does*, 61, 64, 66-67, 212
information, 64
polite, 302, 304
with *there is/there are*, 107, 109
about time, 203
with *will*, 243, 245-246
yes/no, 64 (see also Question words, Yes/no questions)

S

-*S/-es*:
plural nouns, 4, 6, 134
simple present verbs, 44, 54
spelling and pronunciation, 49, 51, 54

Same, similar, different, 379

See, look at, watch, 97
Short answers, 21, 173, 194, 203, 206, 243fn.
Should, 420, 430–431
vs. *must*, 427
***Similar* (*to*)**, 379
Simple past, 171, 177
irregular verbs, 190, 463
negative, 172, 192
vs. past progressive, 440
questions, 173, 194, 203
summary of forms, 245–246
Simple present, 44, 54
with *be*, 4, 8, 20–21, 24
in *if*-clauses, 260
negative, 57
vs. present progressive, 92
present time words, 239
questions, 61, 64, 66
summary of forms, 245–246
in time clauses, 258
Since, 444, 446
Singular nouns, 134
defined, 2
with pronouns, 6, 44
Some, 141
vs. *a/an*, 144
vs. *any*, 161
Some of, 334
Someone/something, 163
Spelling:
-*ed*, 183, 186
-*ing*, 87, 186
-*s/es*, 49, 51, 54
Subject, defined, 10*fn.*, 20
Subject pronouns, 6–7, 131, 171–172, 177, 192, 363
Subject-verb agreement, 336
Subjects and objects, 127
Superlatives (***-est/most***), 398, 405

T

Tenses:
future, 231, 235, 238–239, 242, 258, 260, 263
past progressive, 434, 438, 440